2/84

£300p

£12

Andrew Linn
Cambridge 1994

D1610451

STUDIES IN THE HISTORY OF
WESTERN LINGUISTICS

STUDIES IN THE HISTORY OF WESTERN LINGUISTICS

IN HONOUR OF R.H. ROBINS

EDITED BY

THEODORA BYNON AND F.R. PALMER

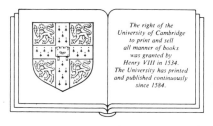

The right of the
University of Cambridge
to print and sell
all manner of books
was granted by
Henry VIII in 1534.
The University has printed
and published continuously
since 1584.

CAMBRIDGE UNIVERSITY PRESS

CAMBRIDGE

LONDON   NEW YORK   NEW ROCHELLE

MELBOURNE   SYDNEY

Published by the Press Syndicate of the University of Cambridge
The Pitt Building, Trumpington Street, Cambridge CB2 1RP
32 East 57th Street, New York, NY 10022, USA
10 Stamford Road, Oakleigh, Melbourne 3166, Australia

© Cambridge University Press 1986

First published 1986

Printed in Great Britain at
University Press, Cambridge

British Library cataloguing in publication data
Studies in the history of Western linguistics:
in honour of R.H. Robins.
1. Linguistics – History
I. Bynon, Theodora   II. Palmer, F.R.
III. Robins, R.H.
410'.9   P121

Library of Congress cataloguing in publication data
Main entry under title:
Studies in the history of Western linguistics.
Includes index.
1. Linguistics – History – Addresses, essays, lectures.
2. Robins, R.H. (Robert Henry) I. Robins, R.H. (Robert Henry)
II. Bynon, Theodora.   III. Palmer, F.R. (Frank Robert)
P61.S78 1986   410'.9   85–26936

ISBN 0 521 26228 3

CONTENTS

THE CONTRIBUTORS

Hans Aarsleff, Department of English, Princeton University

Herbert E. Brekle, Institut für Allgemeine und Indogermanische Sprachwissenschaft, Universität Regensburg

Theodora Bynon, Department of Phonetics and Linguistics, School of Oriental and African Studies, University of London

N.E. Collinge, Department of General Linguistics, University of Manchester

Michael A. Covington, Advanced Computational Methods Center, University of Georgia

Regna Darnell, Department of Anthropology, University of Alberta

Helmut Gipper, Institut für Allgemeine Sprachwissenschaft, Westfälische Wilhelms-Universität Münster

Henry M. Hoenigswald, Department of Linguistics, University of Pennsylvania

Dell Hymes, Graduate School of Education, University of Pennsylvania

Vivien Law, Department of Linguistics, University of Cambridge

Giulio Lepschy, Department of Italian Studies, University of Reading

P.H. Matthews, Department of Linguistics, University of Cambridge

Anna Morpurgo Davies, Somerville College, University of Oxford

F.R. Palmer, Department of Linguistic Science, University of Reading

W. Keith Percival, Department of Linguistics, University of Kansas

Vivian Salmon, Keble College, University of Oxford

FOREWORD

F.R. PALMER

The most difficult, though most important, task faced by most editors of a volume published in honour of a distinguished scholar is that of deciding upon a theme that will truly characterize the individual contribution that he has made to his subject. The task of the editors of this volume has, by contrast, been very simple. R.H. Robins has established himself as the first and foremost authority of our age on the history of linguistics and, in particular, of Western linguistics, and the appropriateness of some such title as *Studies in the history of Western linguistics* was immediately obvious.

Robins' interest in the subject began early in his professional career when a series of lectures was published as *Ancient and mediaeval grammatical theory in Europe* in 1951, though, undoubtedly, it was his classical training that had led him to see that this was an exciting field of study. A more definitive work was his *A short history of linguistics*, published in 1967, which, as several contributors have noted, made many original observations and was responsible for establishing the importance of times and places that had long been (often deliberately) neglected. Robins' place within the subject was recognized, a few years ago, when he was deservedly elected the first president of the newly founded Henry Sweet Society. This volume can do no more than underline the importance of the contribution he has made.

Yet it must not be forgotten that Robins' major work was his *General linguistics: an introductory survey*, first published in 1964, and later revised and expanded. In this he shows his wide and perspicuous understanding of linguistic theories, ideas and attitudes. It is important in the evaluation of his contribution to linguistics not only for its own sake, but because it provides a linguistic framework for the understanding of that work, and partly because the scholarship it involved over the years undoubtedly helped Robins himself to clarify his own ideas when dealing with the history of the subject.

If a few personal remarks may be forgiven, I should like to say that it is particularly gratifying for me to act as one of the editors and to write this short foreword, for our careers have been closely associated since our student days. It was at Robins' suggestion that I joined him as a member of the Department of Phonetics and Linguistics in the School of Oriental and African Studies, which was then very much 'Firth's Department', and we are both ending our careers as members of the quite small group of Professors of Linguistics in the United Kingdom. Moreover, my first contact with a publisher was when I undertook to see *Ancient and mediaeval grammatical theory in Europe* through the press while Robins was on study leave in the USA. I regret that I failed to notice a quite serious printing error: but retribution was on its way – one of the reviewers thought he detected another error in Robins' note of thanks to me and wrote 'For "F.R. Palmer" read "L.R. Palmer"'!

Part of the aim of this volume was to provide a fairly wide coverage of the history of Western linguistics from Classical times to the present day. Contributors were asked to deal in depth with a topic, period or personality, but it was inevitable that if there was to be a reasonable spread, the editors should approach individual scholars with fairly specific suggestions. Almost all those who were approached agreed to contribute, but it is naturally a matter of regret that it was simply not possible to invite all those who might have liked to honour Robins in this way.

The shape of the final collection of papers is very close to what was planned. It begins with a general, introductory, paper on the history of linguistics and its rationale by Brekle. Collinge has a paper on the Classical tradition which looks particularly at dualism. Within the Middle Ages Covington is concerned with Speculative (universal) grammar and Law with the often underestimated originality of the period. Percival relates the linguistic ideas of the Renaissance to the general cultural history of the period. For the seventeenth century Salmon illustrates the contribution of the many unknown scholars on whose efforts the work of the great pioneers was founded. There are five papers about the nineteenth century. Hoenigswald deals with the period's view of itself, while Bynon and Morpurgo Davies are concerned with Schleicher and Brugmann respectively. Aarsleff provides a detailed account of an early, but very influential, scholar, while Gipper considers a specific problem with which Humboldt wrestled.

Each of the three papers dealing with the twentieth century has its own special relevance. The contribution of Darnell and Hymes discusses an aspect of Sapir's work on the languages of North America which recalls Robins' early and continuing interest in these languages. Lepschy's article on the European tradition makes clear de Saussure's great contribution to modern linguistics. In my view de Saussure's work is a link, or a kind of watershed, between the old and the new; it discusses almost all the fundamental, theoretical issues of linguistics and answers both 'Where have we got to?' and 'Where are we going?' Matthews' paper brings us even more up-to-date in a detailed discussion of the most relevant issue separating (or linking?) American structuralism and Chomsky.

It is hoped that this volume will form a fitting companion to *A short history of linguistics* and that it will both please and honour the scholar to whom it is dedicated. One last personal point may, I trust, be permitted. 'Bobby' Robins (and the editors) will have one regret – that his devoted and charming wife, Sheila, is not with us to see this honour done.

1

WHAT IS THE HISTORY OF LINGUISTICS AND TO WHAT END IS IT STUDIED? A DIDACTIC APPROACH

HERBERT E. BREKLE

Taking as a starting point the famous title of Schiller's inaugural lecture 'Was heisst und zu welchem Ende studiert man Universalgeschichte?' held at the University of Jena on the twenty-sixth of May, 1789, the aim of this paper is to discuss various factors and aspects which might be relevant to, or included in, the history of linguistics, from both a substantive and a methodological point of view.

On a relatively elementary level this can be done by applying the age-old forensic question schema *quis, quid, ubi, quibus auxiliis, cur, quomodo, quando*. It is advisable to differentiate these questions so that the subject of historiographical endeavours under their respective historical conditions (which is what is meant by linguistics here) is taken into account – but also so that the characteristics of the historiographical process and its products are clarified by this battery of questions.

The first question to be discussed is *Quid*, the WHAT. What is the subject of the history of linguistics? What is the historiography of linguistics about? The first trivial answer would be: the subject-matter of a history of linguistics includes all the traditions that are scientifically related to one or several aspects of that which can be called language and/or linguistic communication. But how broadly or narrowly shall the concept of linguistics be defined? Should it start from a modern understanding of what is called linguistics today, or would it be better to try to understand the subject-matter in a historically relativizing way, so that all questions which have to do with language in its more special sense, the various functions of the use of language, the construction of grammars of particular languages, the ontogenetic as well as the phylogenetic development of languages, and so on, are included?

A decision in favour of the first alternative would mean limiting to a great extent the domain of linguistics in its historical dimension, so that only 'precursors' of present-day conceptions and theories would be looked for in such a history; this would certainly amount to an unhistorical approach. If, on the other hand, the full range of the history of the discipline is taken into account, at least in principle, then only the second alternative is left. In this case the concept of linguistics from a methodological point of view would not be taken in too narrow a sense; one should not start out from present-day epistemological criteria, but as far as possible try to take into consideration the motivations for dealing with linguistic questions which existed under the respective historical situations and spheres of interest, and to reconstruct step by step a model of the respective linguistic–theoretical approach. In this connection it is inevitable (in principle) that attempts at reconstructions of this type will always be based on the state of knowledge and the interests of the respective historiographer of linguistics. In other words, there can never be an interpretation or reconstruction of earlier linguistic conceptions which is valid once and for all. Every generation of linguists will, in so far as there is a necessity for historiographical research at all, write its own history. It is, however, to be expected that there will be phenomena which will not vary from generation to generation in central areas of the history of linguistics: 'There can be as many histories of linguistics . . . as reasons for interest in the history, and should be. Still, chaos is not the inevitable outcome, and history is not illimitably plastic' (Hymes 1974a: 23).

Next to be considered is the *Quid*-question both with respect to history and to writing about history. A history of a science does not consist, as might sometimes seem to be the case, in an 'unrelieved chain of successes and advances' (Hymes 1974a: 21); as Hymes again correctly states 'the nature of the history of linguistics clearly is not continuous and cumulative'. So historiography is then not a 'monumentalische Betrachtung des Vergangenen' by which 'ganze, grosse Teile desselben . . . vergessen, verachtet werden und fortfliessen wie eine graue ununterbrochene Flut, und nur einzelne geschmueckte Facta heben sich als Inseln heraus': . . . 'the monumental vision of the past' . . . when 'very great portions of the past are forgotten and despised, and flow away like a grey uninterrupted flood, and only single embellished facts stand out as islands' (Nietzsche 1972: 258= 1980: 17).

If we then try to take all questions which have ever been asked about language or about particular languages into the overall domain of linguistic historiography, this would mean that the historian of linguistics would have to take into account all sources which can be interpreted with respect to reflection upon language. In order not to set an artificial and arbitrary limit on the preconditions for the philosophical and (in a narrow sense) scientific study of linguistic phenomena and questions, one would have to take into consideration such apparently heterogeneous things as mythological traditions relating to the problem of the origin of language, popular beliefs about the difference of languages and similar things (in other words the broad range of that which today is called folk-linguistics) as falling within the area of research of the history of linguistics; in addition, implicit reflection upon linguistic phenomena, for example the invention and development of systems of writing, and early language philosophy and first approaches towards grammatical statements should be taken into account. In order to get as complete a picture of the history of linguistics as possible, it would seem to be sensible and desirable to include the prehistory of linguistics and the naive opinions and ideas of peoples and individuals who did not have a scientific interest in language in the modern sense.

Thus it could be held that in such a history every possible type of historical reflection upon language and linguistic phenomena should be described. It is in principle irrelevant whether we have to do with archaic traces of linguistic reflection or, to take things to the extreme, some linguistic underground paper from yesterday evening. The historiographer of today must also take into account in his descriptions the statements of earlier or contemporary historians of linguistics and this is often the only way to gain access to primary data (compare for example the tradition of Stoic writings). In this sense then the task of the historiographer is of an accumulative and conservatory nature; in an ideal sense nothing that has been said about language is lost.

In connection with the question of the *Quid* of the history of linguistics there is also the question whether texts that have been handed down and which contain reflections about language are to be our sole or only our main concern. That is, whether the interest of the historiographer of linguistics in a broader sense should concentrate on reconstructing the linguistic contents of such texts, for example in the sense of the literary New Criticism, or whether he should also take into account the conditions for the genesis of such texts with respect to biographical and social details and the whole of the history of ideas and civilization, and traditions as well. Canguilhem (1979a: 27) complains that this question seems generally to be considered solved merely because it is not asked at all. In fact in the most recent methodological discussions about the WHAT and HOW of linguistic historiography several people have made proposals to this effect. Canguilhem (1979) made suggestions about the relative importance of internalistically versus externalistically orientated historiographical approaches. In his article which appeared in the mid-sixties on the subject-matter of the history of science (Canguilhem 1979a) he characterizes the externalistic direction in the historiography of science thus: 'The historiography of science tries to explain a series of events which is traditionally considered to be part of science on the basis of critical analysis by referring to economical and social interests, to technical necessities and practices and to religious and political ideologies' (my translation). He harshly criticizes the externalistic approach as 'a diluted and impoverished Marxism such as is common in the Western societies'. This judgement on externalistic questions cannot be maintained so one-sidedly; there are certainly relationships between religiously motivated or theological positions and semiotic and linguistic theoretical statements (compare for example the well-known controversy about the origin of language between Herder and Suessmilch around the middle of the eighteenth century).

Furthermore, aspects such as the affiliation of an author and his texts to institutions such as schools, universities and so on, the influence of individual interests on linguistic productions, social and economic conditions of such productions and similar matters can be seen in their full relationships to the linguistic content of these texts in a way which is historically and epistemologically profitable.

Within the framework of the controversy between externalism and internalism the question of the *Quis*, the role of the producer of historiographically relevant traditions can be answered straightforwardly. For the internalists, questions about the authorship and conditions under which the work was produced, about the social status of the author and so on are almost irrelevant. For them, the question of influences upon one author by another or by something like a climate of opinion is relevant only in so far as information of a biographical or general historical nature about identities, and similarities among authors established purely by comparison, can be used as a basis for historically relevant statements about dependencies and influences of one author on another.

Representatives of the externalistic view on the other hand consider it very important to elaborate upon the dimension of the *Quis* by means of detailed biographies of the authors or scientists in question, including their intellectual orientation. In this case one is bound to admit that the interpretations of the works of these authors sometimes do not go beyond pure summaries. Basically, the difference is that between epistemologically reflected text-immanent historiography (a historiography which reconstructs the theoretical substance of works considered relevant in the history of science) and the presentation of biographical details of an author together with his intellectual and cultural setting. It is important to emphasize that results of this kind of historiography can, as a marginal effect, sometimes be enlightening for historiographical analyses in the strict sense.

The question WHY (*Cur*) in connection with the texts to be treated historiographically or with respect to their communicative intentions, demands answers in which the reasons (interests, motivations of the author) for the production of these texts are made plain. By showing the *causae efficientes* we may also find information about possible *causae finales*, the aims which an author pursues through his work; in other words we are also dealing with the *Cui bono* question (for whom is the work useful?). Questions of this nature have in principle to do with external aspects of the history of linguistics in so far as we can try to reconstruct the linguistic substance of a text, the genuine subject-matter of linguistic historiography, in its theoretical nucleus, without having recourse to external motivations and aims. Of course, different types of texts (for example school grammar versus speculative theoretical tract) can influence the conceptual inventory of a reconstruction, but in both cases there are text-internal indicators which, besides their relevance for the reconstruction of a model of the linguistic substance of a text, can also provide information about the causes and aims of a text. Answers to the WHY-question from an externalistic point of view can be gained from biographical circumstances (that is the social standing, the economic necessities, etc.) of an author.

The WHY-question aimed at the activity of the historiographer himself demands information about the reasons for this very activity; in other words we are concerned with possible interests and motivations of the historiographer or, from an abstract point of view, with justifications for linguistic historiography. One reason for the historiographical activity, as has just been said, could be its orientation towards certain aims. In this sense it is simply a case of systematically applying and extending the principle of reading and criticizing the results of research of others who are seeking knowledge in the same area. Canguilhem understands the history of a science 'as the essence of reading in a specialized library'; it is an 'archive and store of knowledge which has been produced and extended from the tablet and the papyrus through parchment and incunables to the magnetic tape'.

In this sense the reason for a historiography of science is simply the attempt to keep available the knowledge which has once been accumulated, to communicate to later generations of linguists what earlier generations have thought about linguistic problems in the broadest sense, or what attempts at solutions they have made. From this aspect the possible usefulness of the history of a specific subject may in fact reflect particular interests. A possible example for this is Chomsky's *Cartesian Linguistics* (1966); many critics have reproached Chomsky with only wanting to find precursors for his own rationalist view on language and grammar, in other words with wanting to set up for himself a noble line of ancestors.

Another reason for the historiography of linguistics, which has to do with the discipline's search for identity, is described by Robins, one of the fathers of modern linguistic historiography, thus: 'The current interest shown by linguists in past developments and the earlier history of their subject is in itself a sign of the maturity of linguistics as an academic discipline, quite apart from any practical applications of linguistic science' (Robins 1967: V). This point of view can be criticized on the one hand for postulating a certain automatism for the development of a science (only a 'mature' science is seriously interested in its own history – is this then a reliable indicator for its maturity, whatever that may mean?) and on the other for lacking historical facticity.

Thirdly, the historiography of linguistics can be regarded as part of general historiography. If it is looked at from this aspect, further reasons can be adduced. Presumably the universal human need, the curiosity about what existed previously, belongs here. Embedded in general historiography, the historiography of linguistics could be regarded as a part of the description of the history of human activities and search for knowledge, and of the results handed down to later generations.

Finally, one could look for philosophical reasons for the interest in what has happened in history. I shall limit myself, thus making clear my preference in respect of possible philosophical reasons, to Ernst Bloch's ideas of the 'surfeit of historical positions and knowledge', 'das Unabgegoltene'. In his introduction to *Avicenna und die aristotelische Linke*, Bloch gives the following evaluation of the relativity of historical knowledge:

Everything sensible may have already been thought seven times. But when it was thought again in another time and position, it was no longer the same. Not only the thinking but above all that which was thought about has changed in the meantime. Sensible ideas will have both to prove that they are new and to prove that, being new, they can be upheld. (Bloch 1952: 3, my translation)

The historiographer of linguistics should not shut himself off from this view of earlier findings; he should not discard earlier findings as being simply outdated or as not fitting into his descriptive framework, nor should he simply claim certain particular directions and tendencies as precursors for a theory of grammar and language which he happens to prefer. He would do better, in constructing his descriptive framework, his terminology, to take into account the findings of research in the domain of the history of ideas and the history of sciences in such a way that he will arrive at an appropriate and adequate interpretation of data and texts of his historical subject-matter.

Numerous recent studies on linguistic historiography are concerned with methodological problems, that is with the *Quomodo*, the HOW, and the conditions of the possibility of linguistic historiography. This ongoing discussion cannot and need not be given in detail here; its results are not yet such that one could speak of a solid conceptual framework for a methodology of present-day – or even of a future – historiography of linguistics. Canguilhem (1979) was right when he said of the relationships between epistemology and the history of science that 'we have at the present time in this field more manifestoes and programmes than examples for their realization'; this applies in an even stronger measure to the history of linguistics. Disregarding the relatively unclarified epistemological and methodological situation in linguistic historiography, we can nevertheless discuss several aspects.

(1) The historistic and positivistic attitude of the nineteenth century, often connected with an absolute belief in progress concerning the development of the science in question – as in Benfey (1869), a book which is nevertheless today very readable – can no longer be accepted today. This applies not only to the historiography of science but also to general historiography. Danto (1965: 33) stresses the inevitable subjective interests of an historian. He adduces long chains of arguments in favour of his conclusion '. . . that our entire knowledge of organizing the past is causally involved with our own local interests, whatever they may be'. Yet on the other hand he compares critically the respective activities of historians and scientists: both stand in an indirect relationship to their respective subject-matter: '. . . what scientists can directly observe may stand in no more intimate a relationship to their subject-matter than what historians can observe – medals and manuscripts and potsherds – stands to theirs' (1965: 95). Both, the scientist and the historian, need to have recourse to theoretical prerequisites in order to 'read the marks on photographic plates or the tracks in cloud chambers or oscilloscopes' or to read documents or interpret artifacts. 'There are plain and obvious differences between history and the sciences, but they do not lie here' (1965: 95–6); not, that is to say, in the methodological aspect at issue here. Consequently Danto harshly criticizes Charles Beard, a representative of the historiography of the thirties: 'What Beard fails to understand is that even if we could witness the whole of the past, any account we could give of it would involve selection, emphasis, elimination, and would presuppose some criteria of relevance, so that our account could not, unless it wished to fail through succeeding, include everything.' History-as-actuality cannot be duplicated, not even imitated; instead it is the task of the historian to aim at a principled interpretation of data which he, again according to certain criteria, considers to be relevant.

(2) In connection with the presentation, with the choice of what the historiographer considers to be worthwhile writing about and the HOW of historiographical work, Nietzsche's well-known trichotomy about historiography is still valid. In his famous treatise 'Vom Nutzen und Nachtheil der Historie für das Leben' ('On the advantage and disadvantage of history for life') he distinguishes a monumentalist, an antiquarian and a critical type of historiography. As we have already seen, monumentalistic historiography only deals with those segments of the historical process which are regarded as important by the respective historiographer; as can be seen in the history of historiography, this type of historiography is particularly prone to being influenced by ideologies. Monumentalistic historiography is necessarily incomplete. This applies basically also to the large handbooks on the history of linguistics. The historiography of linguistics should also deal with the

results of linguistic reflection, of scientific endeavours in language and languages which have up to now had no effect, neither in their own time nor later on. Grotsch (1982: 266f) states quite correctly: 'It is not completely useless to get to know the horizons of possibilities of history, as the possibilities which are not realized are just as characteristic for a given state of a science as those possibilities which have been realized.' Nietzsche recognizes, on the one hand, the usefulness of antiquarian historiography if it is a question of gaining as many relevant facts and data as possible for a particular topic of historiography and of integrating them in a systematic reconstruction of a certain segment of history. But, 'antiquarian historiography degenerates the moment that the fresh life of the present no longer animates and inspires it' (1980: 21). Nietzsche then makes his acid and polemic comments about such historiographers (the following passage is quoted first in German because of its typically Nietzschean stylistic qualities):

Jetzt dorrt die Pietät ab, die gelehrtenhafte Gewöhnung besteht ohne sie fort und dreht sich egoistisch-selbstgefällig um ihren eigenen Mittelpunkt. Dann erblickt man wohl das widrige Schauspiel einer blinden Sammelwut, eines rastlosen Zusammenscharrens alles einmal Dagewesenen. Der Mensch hüllt sich in Moderduft . . .; oftmals sinkt er so tief, dass er zuletzt mit jeder Kost zufrieden ist und mit Lust selbst den Staub bibliographischer Quisquilien frisst.

Now piety withers away, scholarly habit endures without it and, egoistically complacent, revolves around its own centre. Then you may well witness the repugnant spectacle of a blind lust for collecting, of a restless raking together of all that once has been. Man envelops himself in an odour of decay; . . . often he sinks so low as finally to be satisfied with any fare and devours with pleasure even the dust of bibliographical quisquilia. (Nietzsche 1972: 264=1980: 21)

For his third type of historiography, the critical type, Nietzsche postulates that it should serve the interests of life. In the case of linguistic historiography this can only mean that the linguistic historiographer has to interpret and reconstruct earlier statements about language in such a way that contemporary linguists and others who are interested in language can make use of the linguistic content of earlier texts about language or languages. Nietzsche's idea of critical historiography sounds very grand but, one might ask, which minimal methodological preconditions ought to be met so that this idea can be realized even approximately? In preparation for this, hermeneutics, the doctrine of the understanding and interpretation of texts, can bring us a little further along the way. By forming hypotheses about possible text meanings and continually correcting these we may arrive at the conditions for a reconstitution of a text understood as the result of human activities.

Today we know that human activities are basically rule-governed; it is necessary to find out these rules. Thus the linguistic historiographer must reconstruct the theme and its exposition as it is given in a text including the premises, chain of arguments which the author uses and his strategies for convincing his audience. With this work, which includes both analysis as well as synthesis, the historiographer may try to answer the questions about the *Quid* and the *Quomodo* of the text he examines.

The terminology chosen for the reconstruction of the theoretical content of a text should allow the historiographer to represent the subject-matter of a text as completely as possible; furthermore, it is desirable that the chosen terminology can be situated within a consistent linguistic framework so that eclectic interpretations can be avoided. From a metatheoretical point of view, the historiographer should give explicit information about his methodological position, about his chosen methods with which he hopes to arrive at results, and about the aims he is following with his attempt at reconstruction.

Which auxiliary devices (*Quibus auxiliis*) can and should the linguistic historiographer use in order to arrive at adequate interpretations or reconstructions of the linguistic substance of earlier texts and at the large scale diachronic systematic connections of just these reconstructions?

Which auxiliary devices can be made available to the historiographer by hermeneutics? From the century-old specifically German tradition of hermeneutics and exegetics, numerous approaches for present-day investigations on the history of science, specifically as to the HOW and the WHEREWITH of rational reconstruction of the meaning of texts, can fruitfully be used. Mention may be made of just one example which is straightforwardly compatible with present-day approaches for the understanding and analysis of texts. 'The understanding and explication of a work is actually a reproducing of that which has already been produced' (Ast 1807, §80). In actual fact Ast's dictum says that the production of a text, which is in several ways rule-governed, can be re-experienced by finding and applying the rules which constitute just this text. This should not be an exact graphemic, or even only a morphological-syntactic, replica of the text, but it should be a question of finding and applying above all the semantic and text-constitutional rules which determine the possible meaning or meanings of a text. This would explain the text in so far as, for example, in a given argumentative text, the axioms and the theorems following from these by means of derivational rules, and thus the theory contained in the text, are extracted and also *a fortiori* understood. The actual reconstructive achievement of the historiographer thus consists in an explanation of this type.

REFERENCES

Ast, D.F. 1807. *Grundriss einer Geschichte der Philosophie*. Landshut: J. Thomann.
Benfey, Th. 1869. *Geschichte der Sprachwissenschaft und orientalischen Philologie in Deutschland, seit dem Anfange des 19. Jahrhunderts mit einem Rückblick auf frühere Zeiten* (Geschichte der Wissenschaften in Deutschland; Neuere Zeit, 8) Munich: Cotta.
Bloch, E. 1952. *Avicenna und die aristotelische Linke*. Berlin: Bütten & Loening.
Canguilhem, G. 1979. *Wissenschaftsgeschichte und Epistemologie. Gesammelte Aufsätze*. Ed. by W. Lepenies. Frankfurt on Main: Suhrkamp.
    1979a. Der Gegenstand der Wissenschaftsgeschichte. In Canguilhem 1979: 22–37.
Chomsky, N. 1966. *Cartesian Linguistics: A Chapter in the History of Rationalist Thought*. New York & London: Harper & Row.
Danto, A.C. 1965. *Analytical philosophy of history*. Cambridge: Cambridge University Press.
Grotsch, K. 1982. *Sprachwissenschaftsgeschichtsschreibung. Ein Beitrag zur Kritik und zur historischen und methodologischen Selbstvergewisserung der Disziplin*. (Göppinger Arbeiten zur Germanistik, 352) Göppingen.
Hymes, D. (ed.) 1974. *Studies in the history of linguistics*. Bloomington: Indiana University Press.
    1974a. Introduction: traditions and paradigms. In Hymes 1974: 1–38.
Nietzsche, F. [1874] 1972. *Unzeitgemässe Betrachtungen. Zweites Stück. Vom Nutzen und Nachtheil der Historie für das Leben*. In *Werke*, ed. by G. Colli & M. Montinari, part 3, vol. 1: 239–330. Berlin & New York: de Gruyter; *On the advantage and disadvantage of history for life*, translated by Peter Reuss. Indianapolis & Cambridge: Hackett 1980.
Robins, R.H. 1967. *A short history of linguistics*. London: Longman.

2

GREEK (AND SOME ROMAN) PREFERENCES IN LANGUAGE CATEGORIES

N.E. COLLINGE

Hellenic linguistic analysis is conveniently divisible into three epochs. The first is that of the pre-Socratic philosophers and Plato and Aristotle; one might say it was characterized by its relating of grammatical categories and structure to entities and existence – and, towards its end, to truth values. This is the 'early philosophic' epoch; its successor, the 'later philosophic', is that of the Stoics. They were a fairly close-knit school who operated in a more or less homogeneous way over several centuries; and they concentrated on the propositional and dialectic aspects of grammar. The third period combines the Hellenistic-Alexandrian and Byzantine after-glow, taxonomic in outlook and regularist in inclination. The respective findings of these epochs are quite various (more fundamentally so than is allowed to appear by the cumulative and corrective nature of the Greek tradition); the differences may be worth relating to the variety, and that in a virtually arithmetical sense, of the underlying impulse of thought in each epoch.

The basic such impulse for the Greeks was obviously binarist. There is the regular antithetical pairing of words, phrases, clauses and sentences in discourse (commonly marked by the particles *mèn . . . dè. . . .*); there are the often implicit antitheta occasioning surface opacities like Thucydides' use of the adverb *mâllon* (so at Thuc. 2.70.1, where the Spartan incursions into Attica, which 'were not deflecting the Athenians *any the more'*, are quite implicitly, but thus unmistakably, related in their effect to diplomatic approaches not here mentioned at all and occurring many months earlier); there is, again, the startlingly otiose inclusion by Andocides (*de myst.* 39) of an informer's likely avoidance of naming those he did *not* want to frame (after supposing that his report of suspicious loiterers was a device to proscribe those he did) – and all these are unmistakable pointers to compulsive mental dualism. It even becomes a stylistic convention: Heracles' odd evocation of a friend to help him not only from near at hand but also from afar (at Euripides, *Heracles* 1106) prompted an erudite and famous note by Wilamowitz on this pervasive aspect of Hellenic mentality; it is a sense of parallelism which is exploited also in many matched *antilogíai*, or paired legalistic arguments, in both tragedies and comedies. In linguistic theory the more obvious (and less interesting) traces of it were two notorious controversies. The first was over the natural versus the conventional status of categories (the role of *phýsis* versus *nómos* or *thésis*); the second was over the location of pattern-spoiling phenomena of grammar, whether in performance (so that the language itself shows *analogía*, which its speakers do not always observe) or in competence (so that *anōmalía* is already intrinsic in the forms of the language itself). More central is Plato's division of the sentence into *ónoma* and *rhêma*, 'performer' and 'action' (for so they are really glossed at *Sophistes* 262a–263d). This dichotomy prefigures, with more or less directness, not so much Noun and Verb as any or all of such later pairs as Subject and Predicate, or Topic and Comment, or an entity and its linkage with truth in a possible world. Another pervasive dualism is that of *lógos* and *léxis*. Curiously, for Aristotle these seem respectively to mean 'sentence' and 'grammar including phonology' (cf. Pinborg 1975: 72); for the Stoics they convey 'meaningful sound-sequence' and 'merely possible sound-sequence' (cf. DL 7.57); while among the analysts of the third epoch they denote simply 'sentence' and 'word' (cf. Dion §11=GG 1.1.22.4f).

Yet a subtler aspect of linguistic dualist theory (the sort of balancing act which so affronted J.R. Firth) was the predilection for handling phenomena by a pairing of sub-units, the unmarked (or basic) and the marked (or derivative). The conception is of base plus variant, and the variants might be several. This thinking produces the term *ptôsis*, a falling, a declension from the pristine, so to speak. Despite its Aristotelian width of application (eight uses, according to Koller 1958: 34f), and despite commentators' despair in seeking to pin it down in later Greek thought (on which see Pinborg 1975: 8off), the inherent concept of an 'upright' lexemic shape with warped paradigmatic or derivational reshapings is always clear. Hence the epithets *orthós* (or *euthýs*) – the nominative being called 'upright' or 'straight-up' – versus *plágios* (for oblique case in the Noun), while *hýptios*, 'supine', is used for non-active voice in the Verb. (Sittig's old 'fall of the dice' derivation for *ptôsis* is to be discarded: cf. Pinborg 1975:76. That it means a realization of thought in speech – the *ektýpōsis* of Plato, *Theaetetus* 206d, according to Koller 1958: 39 – seems equally incredible.) Our term 'case' preserves as a calque, and so obscures, the original image. Again, if a lexeme has meaning (that is, it can *sēmaínein*), then its subsequently adhering morphosyntactic properties – which is what *parepómena* seem to convey – allow it to vary its basic meaning in marked ways (that is, it is able to *prossēmaínein*). This latter is a term of interest to the mediaeval thinkers, and it is somewhat akin even to Grice's recent use of the label 'non-natural meaning'. More immediately to the point, it adds alternation to a base.

The binarism is undeniable (even if in Koller 1958 it is observed in so widespread a fashion as to strain credulity). Still, in two ways it suffered a shift, at least in the direction of tripartition. For one thing, if you work with a minimum of categories you soon find in natural languages things which will not fit in. Either their characteristics qualify them for both of an existing pair of categories, or they suit neither. The early Greeks occasionally admitted the second possibility: so with terms like *oudéteron*, 'neither' – whether for neuter gender (neither masculine nor feminine) or for intransitive verb (neither active nor passive). More often they grasped at the former solution; understandably enough, but with some straining. In effect, they saw the dually qualified as constituting a sort of middle ground. After all, Euripides (*Helen* 1137) could write of 'god, non-god, or some median status' (*hóti theòs è mè theòs è tò méson*); and Aeschylus assumed that middle ground even between man and woman (*Septem* 197: *anḗr gynḗ te khóti tôn metaíkhmion* – as to which one should recall that *metaíkhmion* normally means 'no-man's-land' or literally 'the space between the spears', an alarming thought). From this arises the widespread use of 'middle' as a technical term in phonology, accentology, gender, verbal 'diathesis', and even for adverbial status (see Collinge 1963; fn. 5 there notes a possible Pythagorean basis for the underlying binarism).

Secondly, if in two systems each of two terms intersect, then either the result is a 2×2 matrix *or* (if one opposition is essentially privative and only its positive alternative really intersects with the second system) a conditioned choice is enforced of which the 'flow chart' is

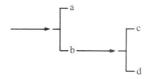

with output a,c,d. It may be the first of these paths which led to Aristotle's new class of *sýndesmos* (*Rhet.* 3.5, 12); this, in spite of its typifying title, is illustrated so widely as to include really anything that is not entity and predicate, or simply Noun or Verb (even pronouns). Aristotle offers here an enforced 'rag bag' term. (In passing, one must strongly reiterate suspicions about the twentieth chapter of the *Poetics*, as being doubtfully genuine and as combining categories in a way too bizarre for words.) There is no fourth term for Aristotle. Varro, however, achieved a quadrant (noun, verb, participle, the rest) by a subsequent 'rubbish-bin' exercise. But the second path is already Plato's. As Robins notes (1979: 23, citing *Cratylus* 424a, *Theaetetus* 203b), Plato's phonology handled the stop/continuant difference in consonants as itself subordinate to the more basic vowel/consonant distinction. This two-step analytic technique was later recognized as *hypodiaíresis* (DL 7.61). That is how two terms become three.

These inescapable consequences of a really dualist approach mean that by the immediate post-Aristotelian phase the Greeks were sometimes only crypto-binarists, or (if you like) were already pseudo-triadists. (A real triadism is claimed for Plato by Householder, 1981: 8; but what he quotes seems really to be a matter of binary relations within a series involving *four* levels of language: letter, word, sentence, and discourse.)

Reasonably, then, the first period of Greek grammar may be judged basically binarist in strategy. Even Protagoras' worries over gender were of a binary (sexist) kind; but he did leave binarism in discussing sentence types (DL 9.53–4). The widening had begun. Some sort of case can, however, be made for triadism as the *dominant* inclination of the second epoch. It is, after all, a widespread trait among intellectuals, yet its base is popular. That famous rhetorical trope, the tricolon, with its common controlled incremental or diminishing movement – 'Friends, Romans, Countrymen', and so forth – exploits a deep-seated human instinct for triple rhythmic sequencing: Wilkinson (1963: 175ff) well describes and wittily exemplifies the trend. Studies abound called 'Language, thought and reality' or 'Language: truth and logic' and the like. These echo the juvenile cry 'ready . . . steady . . . go' or the commercial slogan 'sicher . . . schnell . . . bequem' – but they show a naturally tripartite 'editing' of a subject. (Possibly the trait is characteristic of the philosophic mind: at least, in the 1970s, books appeared – to quote those in English alone – such as 'Language, belief and metaphysics', 'Mind, language and reality', 'Truth, probability and paradox', 'Meaning, reference and necessity'.) Now, for the Indian grammarians the syntactic acceptability of words rested upon a triplet of prerequisites: conformity to pattern (*ākāṅkṣā*), semantic compatibility (*yogyatā*), and textual proximity (*saṁnidhi*). In the same place the mediaeval *modistae* offered their trio of tests: grammatical co-occurrence, morphological appropriateness, and semantic collocability (all well noted by Robins 1979: 145 and 82). At the close of the purely Greek tradition, in the late thirteenth century A D, Maximus Planudes combined (probably at second hand) this triple idiom of thought with a three-fold physical localism. He related the spatial notions 'whence–where–whither' of the adverbials both to the noun's surface case-range of genitive–dative–accusative and to the verb's tense-range of past–present–future; and he took that cubic matrix to be the mainspring of Greek morphosyntax. What then of the men of the second epoch, the Stoics? Did they pioneer the path which leads finally to Planudes? If they were triadists, were they so in a more essential and less adventitious way than their predecessors?

Well, they still displayed traces of an old binarism. The paradigmatic test forced them to split the class of *sýndesmoi* into *árthra*, which inflected, and the rest, which did not. As philosophers they were sensitive to the critical difference between specific 'singular terms' of direct knowledge (names) and descriptively known entities (common nouns): so out of *onómata* were separated the *prosēgoríai*. On the other hand, *ptôsis* and *katēgórēma* look like mere replacement-terms for the old pair of *ónoma* and *rhêma*. Against these dualist indications, however, it is notable that the Stoics divided all philosophy into three parts (DL 7.39); and they did the same for rhetoric (ibid. 42). Their basic philosophic categories are generally counted as four: substance, quality, disposition and relative disposition (see Rist 1971: 40 – with reference to sources; also Lloyd 1971: 62). But Rist's conclusion (55) is that of these categories the last two (termed *pôs ékhōn* and *pròs tí pōs ékhōn* – the accentuation is debated) are merely subdivisions of 'the spatio-temporal situation' of an entity *x* according to whether its situation is free or depends on another entity *y*. So this is really another triad. Again their notion of epistemology via language appears to work with three stages: impression, experience, and speech (*phantasía, hò páskhei, lógos*; see Long 1971: 82; the sources are SE 8.70 and DL 7.49). Stoic phonology is likewise triadic: the segment (*grámma*) is subdivided (in one version) into phonic value (*stoikheîon*), letter-shape (*kharaktêr*), and letter-name (*ónoma*) – the very grouping of *potestas, figura,* and *nomen* which later became a cliché (DL 7.56: but see Robins 1957: 85). And they were alive to the three-step difference between (1) mere speech sounds and their successions, (2) phonologically possible sequences in a language, and (3) actual and meaningful sequences in that language (DL 7.57; their respective terms are *phōnḗ, léxis, lógos*). It would be pleasant to think that this triad presaged the cline /brik/, */blik/, **/bnik/, ranged by decreasing realizability in English, as noted by recent generativists; cf. Robins 1979: 24. But the **/bnik/ type is sadly hard to spot in the sources: Lloyd (1971: 60) goes as far as is possible on this point.

Harder to defend, but equally suggestive, is the Stoic classifying of sentences (DL 7.66) into (1) the (truth-conditional) propositional, (2) the interrogative as to truth, and (3) the interrogative as to fact (*axíōma, erôtēma, pýsma*). It is a pity that the stock third party in this simple illocutionary grouping has subsequently been the jussive (giving the trio of declarations, questions and orders). In either case, the latter two modes have in common the incapacity to be judged true or false *per se*. It looks as if this may just be another example of successive binarisms; and that tactic was undoubtedly available to the Stoics as *hypodiaíresis* (DL 7.61).

These numerous triplets may seem unremarkable or adventitious or (in one case) suspect. Yet it has been noted that the Stoic view of surface negation was also firmly triadic. Negation might be expressed and given its scope (1) by sentential particle, as with *ou* (the type labelled *apophatikón*), or (2) by negated pronoun or adverb, as with *oudeís, oudamôs* etc. (this labelled *arnētikón*), or (3) by privative prefix, as with *aphilánthrōpos* (this labelled *sterētikón*). As revealing is the Stoic three-step calculus of propositional specificity: there is a grading of noun phrases from the unspecific and distant (*tis* or, oddly, *ekeînos*), via the specific and localized but unidentified (*hoûtos*), to the specific and identified (*Díōn*). (The respective terms are *aóriston, katagoreutikón, katēgorikón*.) On these matters, one may note DL 7.69 and 70; Pinborg 1975: 94.

Thus there is a clear shift in the arithmetical underpinning of grammatical theory. The facts seem undeniable if possibly trite. But in two other sectors Stoic analysis needs some attention precisely from this point of view. The first of these sectors is the set of terms for handling meaning, where the opposed pair *sēmaînon* and *sēmainómenon* is famous if only as a prefiguring of the Saussurean two-faced linguistic sign, at once *signifiant* and *signifié*. Now in fact a third Stoic term is present, *tynkhánon* (SVF 2.48): we thus have 'expression', 'content' – and 'object' (cf. Pinborg 1975: 79). Behind which there seems to loom a more embracing epistemic triad: apprehension of object, means of reference, and semantic act in speech. These phrases are cumbersome translations of the terms *phantasthén, ptôsis, lektón*: cf. Long 1971: 84 and 82, who is deducing from the definitions of the last given in SE 8.70 (but contrast DL 7.63). It is true that of the former trio only *sēmainómenon* represents the abstract or incorporeal (*asómaton*), while conversely of the latter group only *ptôsis* is concrete (and, even so, subject to theoretical diagnosis). The status of *asómaton* is important for the Stoics. But, if we grant that the difference between corporeal *tynkhánonta* (the speech-trigger in one series) and abstract *phantasthénta* (the counterpart in the other) is strictly immaterial for grammar, then the crucial equated abstract category here is of *lektón* (=*sēmainómenon*). For its essentially abstract nature, and the tricky question of its existence, see SE 8.74ff.

The Stoics thus seem to have discovered, via triadism, a device to cure a malaise in semantic analysis which had sorely afflicted the pre-Socratics and their successors. The point is this. Expressions and contents (or names and referents) needed to be handled without allowing a fracture between them; but just such a fracture had occurred in meaningful bits of grammatical sentences, namely between being able to be expressed but not needing – or needing not – to exist in this world. This split – which has affinities with Russell's principle – had caused enormous trouble. It had driven Parmenides virtually to discard language; it had led Heraclitus to see the world as full of existential contradictions; and it had persuaded Plato to create a special world for incorporeal referenda (the 'forms') divorced from instantiation. This world actually moved (in the usual Platonic chronology) ever nearer to the concrete in its membership: the forms drifted from 'the good' to 'the bedmaker', and so on. The Stoics transmuted this debatable interface into a more comfortable semantic dimension. Herein, the speaker says *x* of a thing or event *y*. Then *x* is the *lektón*, and it is (probably) the abode of truth and falsity (SE 8.70). It may then be equated with *axíōma* and lie in the world of propositions and connect with a propositional calculus. Or else it is the fusing of concept and expression (DL 7.63; Long 1971: 97), and so must inhabit some inter-world – but this is not the place to debate the precise sense of the relevant verb *hyphístasthai*. But these 'sub-Platonic' possibilities actually cast doubt on a simplistic triadism. Moreover, their semantic triad also can always be reanalyzed as two successive binarisms. That Saussure omits the object from the make-up of the 'sign' would set the *tynkhánon* apart; alternatively, the abstract status of the *lektón* would isolate the *sēmainómenon*; or again the arbitrary *sēmaînon* (which is cross-linguistically different, as Sen.117.13 neatly shows) empirically distances itself from the other terms – and in any of these cases the remaining pair could then be split. Can it be that the Stoics are apparently perceptive of triads just because of a fundamental grasp of the two-step process of *hypodiaíresis*? With which in mind we must confront the remaining (and the most awkward) area, the Stoic analysis of the tense/aspect dimension in the verb. Pinborg (1975: 92) rather charmingly calls it 'the most effusively discussed section of Stoic linguistic thought'. Robins (1979: 29) thinks it most important. It is certainly dreadfully poor in explicit testimony.

Pinborg (1975: 94) has no doubt of Stoic triadism here. His 3×3 matrix permutates the tense trio of past, present and future with an aspect trio of complete, neutral and incomplete. The former set he believes to be the Stoic point of departure; but no text justifies this assumption, for GG 1.1.53.1 and 1.3.248.13 do not refer to the Stoics. The second set is really a pseudo-trio. Well, the terms *téleios parōikhēkós* (*khrónos*) or *hypersyntelikós* for the pluperfect, and *enestòs syntelikós* for the perfect (GG 1.3.250f) certainly assert that the relevant parameter is that of completion – as opposed to contemporaneous occurrence, *paratatikòs khrónos*. The aorist is also said, less clearly, to be indifferent to that parameter (251). But this cubic matrix contains aorist and future as neutral tenses, where the sources do not so equate them; and the future is the only instantiation of the parameter Future. Barwick (1957: 53) scarcely fares better with a triple base; for him the three 'times' intersect first with sensitivity to the start of an action (where he gives aorist and future a value of minus, present of zero), and then with completion. In the column Future of the second submatrix two entries are made possible only by declaring the so-called 'Attic future' a separate and cardinal realizate. Lohmann (1953: 185) likewise has a 'Stoic' trifurcation with its third prong (Future) realized solely by the future; and his Past is split three ways (whereas the Present is binary) by inclusion of the aorist alongside imperfect and pluperfect – which is in direct defiance of the textual evidence. That leaves Pohlenz (1939: 177), for whom Stoicism still means binarism. If his tree-presentation is re-ordered as a series of binary choices (operating like the flow-charts in systemic grammar) it becomes:

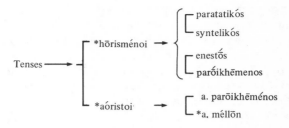

Certainly, the labels are subject to suspicion. The asterisks (not his) mark
unjustified terms: for (a) GG 1.3.249.1 adduces *hōrisménos* without making it
a Stoic usage, (b) the plural *aóristoi* is indefensible, and (c) *aóristos méllōn* is not
a Stoic name (as GG 1.3.251.21f shows). Yet the strategy *could* have been
Stoic. With amended labels it fits their poorly attested nomenclature
perfectly well; and it *is* binary. So here is a clear hint that a Hellenic dualism
survived powerfully in that philosophy. The best defence of triadism here is
the suggestion (GG 1.3.251.18f, 21–25) that the aorist and future lie outside
the quadrant of 'presentive' tense/aspect values for independent reasons,
the aorist by positive indifference or deliberate contradistinction (*pròs
antidiastolēn*) and the future because it simply lacks all relevant temporal
information (*oudèn tétheitai*). But this sounds like desperation; can it be the
truth?

Different cultures have strangely incompatible concepts of time; that fact
is the foundation of Whorfism. On this particular point Kuryłowicz (1973:
77) makes a case for an Indo-European opposition of 'reality' and
'eventuality' (so, in effect, does Langacker (1978: 861), as a virtual
universal). The present and past share the former feature and refer to
verifiable events, presumably by autopsy and memory respectively; the
future is a guess. But other analysts have a different picture: 'the differences
of past and future are blurred' and time 'falls . . . into two spheres: a bright
sphere, illumined by the light of the present and another dark sphere'
(Cassirer 1955: 215–26). It can be argued that of these it is the second
revelation which has spread into all (or most) modern Indian languages
from a non Indo-European source (so Bhardwaj 1984, whose is the apt
quotation of Cassirer). Yet this was already a philosophic commonplace for
the Greeks: cf. GG 1.3.248.16f, 20. It even led to an absolute converse denial
of the existence of a 'present' in a really temporal sense (*oúk estin ára enestós*).
It may be that the Stoics realized that in some way the three 'times'
represented successive dichotomies; but they simply could not be clear
whether existential reality first isolated the future or the present. (The latter
was in Greek a tense relative to some pivot; if that pivot was another verbal
action itself past, it induced the imperfect. The present also acted together
with the presentive perfect.) Then the Stoics would have had a reason, from

this very dilemma, to see a tripartition. They could also have characterized the future as the more independent: it is *not* called 'aóristos méllōn', as we saw; and its partial morphological affinity with the aorist, noted at GG 1.3.25of, forces not the Stoics but others into desperate remarks about these two tenses being akin (in that each fails to define a precise occasion). Quite differently, the aorist may have seemed more fundamental or unmarked or undefined. These glosses fit a lexical item, *aóristos*, applied as an epithet to land, to passions, to propositions and to categories – see the Liddell–Scott–Jones lexicon, s.v.; it could even denote a 'nonterm' if one considers the meaning of *hóros* as 'term' in logic (cf. also DL 7.60, GG 1.1.39). It is indeed the aorist which continues to focus the explanatory ingenuity of analysts: most recently we find it linked with the feature of 'countability', by Armstrong (1981). So there may be a tripartition, after all. Nevertheless, that the Stoics glimpsed semantic time by way of the triad of 'speaker–reference–event', which modern scholars have accepted from Reichenbach (1947), is not to be thought.

Whatever the orchestration of Stoic grammar, the third Greek epoch appears to be rather easier to describe. Clearly, it was inherently motivated by the sort of thinking which informs, shall we say, New Comedy and the novelists. The local and pragmatic dominate. The theoretical scale dwindles, and (despite the conservative opposition to Dionysius Thrax's appeal to *empeiría*) the empirical and procedural aspects blossom. Further, the issues become parochial but awfully complicated; and the heat is occasioned by acrimonious problems of classing and of establishing identity and precedence. And so there is a natural pluralism in categories. In the *Tékhnē* attributed to Dionysius Thrax the neuter gender (*oudéteron*) is no longer the sign of a part-binarist, part-triadist, vision; the genders are now happily extended to five, with *koinón* and *epíkoinon* added (respectively for the types *ho/hē híppos*, for a horse or a mare, and *hē alṓpēx*, whether 'fox' or 'vixen', for example: Dion. §12, see GG 1.1.24f). In effect, the patterns of surface concord have overcome the diagnosis of deep semantic features, as Robins (1957: 99) so well observes. In general, the tally of terms in a system is determined by the simple strategy of freely extending the membership as long as any doubtful assignment (of item to category) suggests it. So the parts of speech become eight (one may contrast Robins 1957: 95 and Pinborg 1975: 107 as to Aristarchus' influence there), the noun's cases are five and its categories five, while the verbal categories number eight (and, within them, the types of *énklisis* 'mood' at least six). Apollonius Dyscolus illustrates the trend. Having discussed words as *phōnaí*, he moves to 'syntax'. In fact, this means first a book specifically on the article and the relative, another on the pronoun, then (after an interlude on grammatical, as opposed to referential, deviance) a third on the verb – with much mental wrestling, for instance, over the true classing of the impersonal verbs *deî* and *khrê* (Ap. *Syntax* 3.67–72) – and then a last book on the preposition (or is it the adverb?). Three other works of his concentrate exclusively on pronouns, adverbs, and conjunctions. The intense preoccupation is with getting all the items in the right classes, and their instances into defensible syntactic slots – defensible by class, that is; so Householder (1981: 9) acutely observes. It is all very practical and utilitarian. Apollonius was not alone but typical in 'becoming a prescriptive grammarian, feeling his duty to lie in the field of speech pathology' (Jones 1967: 72); and, however various the members of this epoch were (cf. Pinborg 1975: 106, citing di Benedetto), with every one of them arithmetical economy and logical control vanish beneath the crushing onset of epiphenomenal taxonomy.

Of this odyssey, through categorial economy and expansion, the Romans knew little. Not nothing, for Varro's Stoic-based statement of Latin tense and aspect (V 9.96–10.48) – however blind to the dual nature of the formal perfect in Latin (Robins 1979: 51f) – is a 2×3 matrix; his 'parts of speech' derive from a 2×2 matrix; and *declinatio* (morphological reshaping) was for him, rightly enough, of two kinds only – inflexional and derivational or natural and facultative. But Priscian codifies at last the purely inherited, and thoroughly pluralist, late Hellenic machinery of grammar (as do the Greek glosses in the African Charisius); by the fifth century A D the early Greek – or Roman – approaches are forgotten. Before Latin had ceased to be only the language of a controlling metropolis the truer Roman preferences, for surface organization and practical application, had been shown to be like those of the later Greeks. They were instanced by Varro's insistence on the need of Latin speakers to mark morphologically the sex distinctions in those animals which farmers use (V 9.56), and by Remmius Palaemon's staff-work in the organizing of Latin declensions and conjugations according to the suffixal difference (for nouns) in the genitive singular or (for verbs) in the second person singular present active indicative forms (so GL 5, 533ff, 543; the *Ars* may be apocryphal, but the ascription seems acceptable). The disagreement between Quintilian and Priscian, whose principles were inconsistent, over the right of the instrumental to be counted as a seventh case in Latin (on which debate, see Robins 1979: 53 and 59f) nicely typifies the preoccupation of late classical grammatical scholarship. If the early Greeks were Ockhamists, for whom 'entia non sunt multiplicanda praeter necessitatem', practically all ancient grammarians after the Stoics, Greek and Roman, became Kantians, believing rather 'entium varietates non temeré esse minuendas'.

REFERENCES

Armstrong, D. 1981. The ancient Greek aorist as the aspect of countable action. In P. Tedeschi & A. Zaenen (eds.) *Syntax and Semantics* 14: 1–12. New York: Academic Press.
Barwick, K. 1957. *Probleme der stoischen Sprachlehre und Rhetorik.* Abhandlungen der Sächsischen Akademie der Wissenschaften, Leipzig (Philosophisch-Historische Klasse 49. 3). Berlin.
Bhardwaj, M.R. 1984. Aspect and temporal reference in the Punjabi verb system. Unpubl. paper; Southall.
Cassirer, E. 1955. *The philosophy of symbolic forms* 1. New Haven: Yale University Press.
Collinge, N.E. 1963. The Greek use of the term 'middle' in linguistic analysis. *Word* 19: 232–41.
Householder, F.W. Jr. 1981. *The syntax of Apollonius Dyscolus.* Amsterdam: Benjamins. (Amsterdam Studies in the theory and history of linguistic science, ser. 3, no. 23)
Jones, G.S. 1967. *Studies in the grammatical theory of Apollonius Dyscolus.* Dissertation, University of Durham.
Koller, H. 1958. Die Anfänge der griechischen Grammatik. *Glotta* 37: 5–40.
Kuryłowicz, J. 1973. Internal reconstruction. In T.A. Sebeok (ed.) *Current Trends in Linguistics* 11: *Diachronic, areal, and typological linguistics,* 63–92. The Hague: Mouton.
Langacker, R.W. 1978. The form and meaning of the English auxiliary. *Language* 54: 853–82.
Lloyd, A.C. 1971. Grammar and metaphysics in the Stoa. In Long 1971: 58–74.
Lohmann, J. 1953. Gemeinitalisch und Uritalisch. *Lexis* 3: 169–217.
Long, A.A. 1971. *Problems in Stoicism.* London: Athlone Press. (Also, therein, Language and thought in Stoicism, 75–113.)
Pinborg, J. 1975. Classical antiquity: Greece. In T.A. Sebeok (ed.) *Current trends in linguistics* 13: *Historiography of linguistics,* 69–126. The Hague: Mouton.
Pohlenz, M. 1939. *Die Begründung der abendländischen Sprachlehre durch die Stoa.* Nachrichten der Gesellschaft der Wissenschaften zu Göttingen, Philosophisch-Historische Klasse n.f.3. 6. 151–98.
Reichenbach, H. 1947. *Elements of symbolic logic.* London: Macmillan. Repr. 1966, New York: The Free Press.
Rist, J.M. 1971. Categories and their uses. In Long 1971: 38–57.
Robins, R.H. 1951. *Ancient and mediaeval grammatical theory in Europe.* London: Bell.
  1957. Dionysius Thrax and the western grammatical tradition. *Transactions of the Philological Society* 1957: 67–106.
  1979. *A short history of linguistics* (2nd edn., 1st edn. 1967). London: Longman.
Wilkinson, L.P. 1963. *Golden Latin artistry.* Cambridge: Cambridge University Press.

SOURCES

Ap.   Apollonius Dyscolus (2nd cent. AD). In GG 2. 1–3.

DL   Diogenes Laertius (3rd cent. AD). *Vitae et placita clarorum philosophorum*. (1964; H.S. Long, ed.) Oxf. class. texts. Oxford: Oxford University Press.

Dion   [Dionysius Thrax] (2nd cent. BC). *Tékhnē grammatikḗ*. In GG 1.1. On authenticity, see Pinborg 1975: 153ff.

GL   Grammatici Latini 5 (1868; H. Keil, ed.) Leipzig: Teubner. Repr. 1961; Hildesheim: Olms.

GG   Grammatici Graeci 1.1. (1883; G. Uhlig, ed.); 1. 3. (1901; A. Hilgard, ed.); 2. 1–3. (1878–1910; R. Schneider & G. Uhlig, eds.) Leipzig: Teubner. Repr. 1965; Hildesheim: Olms.

SE   Sextus Empiricus (c. AD 200). *Adversus mathematicos* 1 (1954; in *Opera*, vol. 3, H. Mutschmann, ed.; rev. J. Mau & K. Janáček). Leipzig: Teubner.

Sen.   L. Annaeus Seneca (ob. AD 65). *Epistulae morales* (1965; L.D. Reynolds, ed.) Oxf. class. texts. Oxford: Oxford University Press.

SVF   *Stoicorum veterum fragmenta* 4 vols. (1–3, 1903–1905; 4, 1924; J. von Arnim, ed.) Leipzig: Teubner.

V   M. Terentius Varro. *De lingua Latina* (1910: G. Goetz & F. Schoell, eds.) Leipzig: Teubner.

3

GRAMMATICAL THEORY IN THE MIDDLE AGES

MICHAEL A. COVINGTON

It was R.H. Robins who, in his 1951 monograph on *Ancient and mediaeval grammatical theory in Europe*, first established a place for medieval speculative grammar in present-day linguistic historiography. There was a time when accounts of the history of linguistics mentioned the medievals, if at all, only for their benightedness,[1] but during the past few decades, as linguistics has turned from data-collection to the formulation of abstract theories, linguists have found medieval speculative grammar increasingly interesting.

The following is an outline of the development of medieval speculative grammar, with special emphasis on concepts of enduring interest.[2] For more extensive treatment of most of the material covered here, and more detailed references to the literature, see Covington (1984); readers new to the field should also see Pinborg (1967) and Rosier (1983).

The career of medieval speculative grammar is conveniently divided into three periods: a gradual rise during which grammar came to be viewed as a theoretical science, a middle period during which one theory (that of *modi significandi*) was dominant, and a sudden, sharp decline resulting from the rise of nominalism.

Early speculative grammar 1125–1250

The trend toward theory-orientation

The rise of speculative grammar was, to use terms introduced by Robins (1974), a shift from data-orientation to theory-orientation. The medievals had inherited thorough, if superficial, descriptions of Latin from antiquity; the concise *Ars grammatica* of Donatus (c. 350) and the compendious *Institutiones grammaticae* of Priscian (c. 500) were their standard handbooks (and remained in use long after the period with which we are concerned). By the tenth or eleventh century, Latin morphology and syntax were, or at least were thought to be, frozen in the Priscianic mould; the observable form of the language was believed to be fixed beyond question.

Curiosity about the deeper nature of language came from a different source – logic. In the tenth and eleventh centuries, scholars such as Gerbert of Aurillac (938?–1003), Garlandus Compotista (fl. c. 1040), and Anselm of Canterbury (1033–1109) began studying Boethius' translations of the logical treatises of Aristotle and Porphyry, which had been available, though neglected, throughout the early Middle Ages.

The approach to logic that arose was linguistically oriented; it was usual to begin, as Aristotle did,[3] by dividing the sentence into subject and predicate and exploring the role of predication in various types of sentences. Medieval logicians always used natural language and almost always assumed that syntactic and semantic structure were isomorphic. As a result grammar and logic began to interact much as they had done in Stoic times. The two fields remained distinct, of course – it was normal for logicians to ignore all the parts of speech except the noun and the verb – but the theoretical nature of the one stimulated a more theoretical approach in the other. Because of space limitations, in what follows I shall concentrate on grammar; medieval logic, though equally interesting, was a separate field in its own time, and a detailed knowledge of it is not required for understanding medieval grammar.

William of Conches and Petrus Helias

Two focal figures in the early development of speculative grammar were William of Conches (c. 1080–c. 1154) and his pupil Petrus Helias (fl. c. 1140). Petrus was considerably the more famous of the two; he was quoted extensively by later writers, and has been referred to as the founder of speculative grammar (Copleston 1972: 270), though in fact his main achievement was in large part a synthesis of the work of his contemporaries.

William of Conches summarized the tone of twelfth-century grammatical thought in the famous plaint at the end of his De philosophia mundi: 'Priscian . . . gives obscure definitions without exposition and in fact leaves out the functional explanations of the various parts of speech and their respective attributes.'[4] The call for clearer definitions is just what one would expect, since Priscian's definitions of his terms are none too rigorous, but the quest for functional explanations (causae inventionis) was a new development first attested in eleventh-century sources (Hunt 1943). The idea behind it was that language resulted from two conscious activities on the part of prehistoric people: the assignment of words to signify particular meanings (impositio), and the devising of linguistic structure (inventio). Everything in the structure of language had been put there to serve a particular communicative function, its causa inventionis. For instance, according to William, the causa inventionis of the family name was that it enabled people to identify themselves as being from the same family as a well-known relative.[5]

William and Petrus were especially interested in the relation between words and real-world objects, and Petrus formulated a concept of referential dependency that was to play a large role in modistic grammar later on. Traditional grammarians had posited that the words in a sentence were held together by a relation called government (*regimen*), and Petrus was trying to define *regimen* in theoretical terms.

The traditional definition was that one word governs another when it requires it to have a particular inflectional feature; for example, the verb governs its subject and object by requiring them to be in the nominative and the accusative case respectively. However, this definition could not be extended to relations between uninflected words, and grammarians set out to define *regimen* in terms of meaning, only to face confusion as to whether it was the governing or the governed word that modified the meaning of the other.

Petrus' contribution was to note that some of the words in the sentence – ordinarily the nouns – refer to the real-world entities while others – verbs, adjectives, prepositions – do not. But the sentence as a whole makes an assertion about real-world entities; hence the words that do not refer directly to entities have to be linked to them somehow. Petrus proposed that this link was *regimen*. In his view, the verb governs the subject and object because it depends on them for its reference to entities in the real world. Similarly, the preposition governs its object, not because it requires its object to be in a particular case, but because it depends on its object to connect it to a real-world entity. In a two-noun construction such as *filius Socratis* 'the son of Socrates', *filius* governs *Socratis* because, rather than standing for an entity directly, it stands for a relation ('son of') that depends on *Socratis* for its real-world reference.[6]

Grammar as an Aristotelian science

The next major development, the reclassification of grammar from a practical art (albeit with increasing interest in its theoretical underpinnings) to a fully-fledged theoretical science, was motivated by Aristotle's *Posterior analytics* and Alfarabi's *Liber de scientiis*, both of which became available in Europe in the mid-1100s.

Because it contained the first clear definition of scientific knowledge, the *Posterior analytics* caused a methodological revolution, not just in grammar, but in medieval science generally. According to Aristotle, scientific knowledge is necessary and general; it consists of facts that apply to all of its subject matter (or to exhaustive subclassifications of it) and could not be otherwise. This corresponds closely to both medieval and modern thinkers' intuitions; present-day scientists agree with Aristotle in holding, for instance, that the science of botany is properly concerned with the principles that determine what plants will grow in what environments, but not with the arbitrary arrangement of plants in a particular garden.

Medieval grammarians reasoned that, by the same criteria, the scientific study of language would have to state principles applicable to all possible languages, not just the ones under study. A hint as to how this might be done came from Alfarabi, who divided the knowledge of language into lexical knowledge, comprising arbitrary details, and rule-knowledge, comprising generalizations (*Liber de scientiis*, p. 121). His mid-twelfth-century commentator Dominicus Gundissalinus went further: he identified rule-knowledge with syntax[7] and stated that, unlike vocabulary, rule-knowledge was practically the same for all peoples.

It was then only a short step from *scientia* to *scientia speculativa*. Aristotle had classified knowledge as practical or theoretical (*praktikế/theōrētikế*, Latin *practica/speculativa*) depending on whether its aim was action or simply truth for its own sake (*Metaphysics* 993 b 21–22), and the new approach to grammar obviously belonged on the theoretical side. Hence it was termed *grammatica speculativa*, 'theoretical grammar'.

The Modistae

Principal modistic authors

Speculative grammar reached the height of its development among a group of grammarians who flourished between 1260 and 1320 and who were afterward called Modistae because of their emphasis on *modi significandi* 'modes of signifying' – their term for all the attributes of a word that are neither phonological nor, in the strict sense, semantic.

During an initial 'premodistic' period, up to about 1260, the concept of *modus significandi* was used to define the parts of speech but not to explain syntactic phenomena. Important premodistic authors include Roger Bacon (c. 1240), Robert Kilwardby and Pseudo-Kilwardby (both c. 1250), and the Simon Dacus who wrote the *Domus grammaticae* (c. 1260).

The first generation of Modistae proper begins with Martin of Dacia (Denmark), who was the first to develop a modistic theory of syntax and whose *Modi significandi* (c. 1270) immediately became a standard textbook. Other important authors from the first generation are Boethius Dacus (c. 1270), Johannes Dacus (1280), and Michael of Marbais (c. 1285).

The beginning of a second generation of Modistae, around 1285, is marked by the appearance of commentaries on the works of earlier Modistae, especially Martin of Dacia. The modistic Simon Dacus belongs to this period (see Covington 1984). The most sophisticated modistic grammarians were a group active at Paris around 1300 and centred around Radulphus Brito, a wide-ranging thinker whose works, only recently rediscovered, will probably prove important for other branches of medieval philosophy as well. Two of Radulphus' contemporaries (and, presumably, colleagues) were Siger de Courtrai and Thomas of Erfurt; Thomas's *Novi modi significandi*, written around 1300, quickly replaced Martin's treatise as the standard handbook of modistic theory.

Modes of signifying

The modes of signifying are not part of the meaning of a word; they are parameters that specify how the word carries its meaning. For example, the verb *currere* 'run' and the noun *cursus* 'a run' signify the same thing – running – but signify it in different ways; that is, they have different modes of signifying, which is why they are different parts of speech.[8] Since the pronunciations of words are arbitrary and the study of meaning involves extralinguistic knowledge, it was obvious to the Modistae that the modes of signifying were the proper concern of the grammatical theorist.

The concept of *modus significandi* was developed to explain the role of grammatical categories, such as part of speech, case, and tense, in the sign–meaning relationship that links words to real-world objects. Priscian had said that every noun signifies an entity (*substantia*) with its particular identity or 'which-ness' (*qualitas*).[9] In the twelfth century, William of Conches had struggled to make it clear that in so doing, the noun does not signify two things, but only one (Fredborg 1981: 31). The modistic solution to William's problem is to hold that a noun, such as *Socrates*, does not signify entity and which-ness per se; it 'consignifies' them. That is, entity and particularity, as properties of the real-world object to which the noun refers, are represented not in the meaning of the noun, but in its modes of signifying.

Figure 1 shows the system in its mature form as laid out by Thomas of

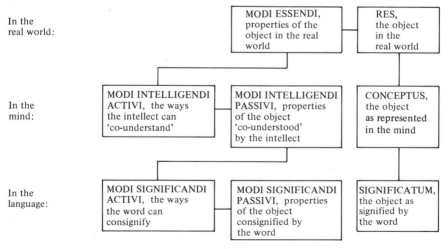

Figure 1. Ontology of the modes of signifying (Thomas of Erfurt)

Erfurt. A real-world object (*res*) gives rise to a concept (*conceptus*) in the human mind, which is represented by a meaning (*significatum*) in language. Simultaneously, various properties (*modi essendi*) of the real-world object are 'co-conceptualized' (*cointelliguntur*) along with the object itself; that is, they are acted upon by the mind's 'modes of understanding' (*modi intelligendi activi*) to give rise to 'modes of being understood' (*modi intelligendi passivi*). These in turn lead, through 'modes of signifying' (*modi significandi activi*) on the part of the word as a linguistic element, to 'modes of being signified' (*modi significandi passivi*) in the word as actually uttered.[10]

It is then the modes of signifying, rather than the meanings of words themselves, that define the parts of speech; the same object can be conceived of and signified either as an action or as an entity, which is why there can be both a verb and a noun meaning 'run'. Modes of signifying also explain inflectional meaning: verb tense, as a mode of signifying, consignifies time, a property of action in the real world. Moreover, modes of signifying explain how words function in syntactic structure, since the variable, voluntary nature of *modi intelligendi* enables dissimilar real-world objects to be conceptualized, and hence signified, in ways that admit of being joined together.

Word class theory

In practice, the Modistae compiled their lists of modes of signifying by converting into modistic terms all the attributes of parts of speech that had been catalogued by Donatus and Priscian. In so doing they were forced to distinguish between essential modes, which are the same in all languages of equal expressive power, and accidental modes, which are arbitrary. The ability to signify predication, for instance, is essential since one cannot imagine communication without it; verb tense is accidental, since, as Boethius Dacus points out (Q. 84), its significative function could easily be taken over by something else, such as temporal adverbs.

A traditional modistic treatise, such as that of Martin of Dacia or Thomas of Erfurt, consists of a brief preamble defining basic terms, followed by a lengthy inventory of the modes of signifying of all the parts of speech (known as *Etymologia*), and then, usually, a treatment of syntax (*Diasynthetica* or *Diasyntactica*). As a sample of what the *Etymologia* was like, the following is a summary of Martin of Dacia's discussion of the modes of signifying of the noun (*Modi significandi*, pp. 10–45); other Modistae treat the same topic quite similarly.

The most essential and general mode of signifying of the noun, the mode that defines it, is the fact that it signifies something conceived of as in a steady state (*per modum habitus et quietus*) and definitely identified (*per modum determinatae apprehensionis*). (The verb signifies things as in action or in process; the pronoun signifies them as in a steady state, but without definite identification.) The highest-order distinction is that between the proper noun, which can have only one referent, and the common noun, which can have many.

Common nouns are then divided into adjectives and substantives (in ancient and medieval usage, the term *nomen* 'noun' comprised both). As evidence that this distinction is indeed based on modes of signifying rather than meanings, Martin points out that an attribute, whiteness, can be signified by either the adjective *albus* or the substantive *albedo* (p. 25). He goes on to divide adjectives into thirteen classes, including positive, comparative, superlative, denominative, patronymic, possessive, and the like, with a mode of signifying for each. Unlike the higher-level modes, these are proposed without argumentation and show little logical structure; they reflect little more than a determination to capture, within the modistic framework, all the distinctions drawn by the ancients. Substantives, on the other hand, are divided into only two classes, those signifying a genus (such as *animal*) and those signifying a species (such as *homo* 'man').

Proper nouns are divided into four classes based on the Latin words *nomen* 'name', *praenomen* 'name given at birth', *cognomen* 'family name', and *agnomen* 'honorific name given later in life'. Seeking broad philosophical definitions, Martin identifies these respectively as naming something per se, naming it to distinguish it from others, naming it for its origins, and naming it as a result of an event. These are substantives; Martin mentions proper adjectives, such as *petrinus*, but does not discuss them.

These are the essential modes of the noun, those that are derived directly from its communicative function. Nouns in any particular human language also have accidental modes of signifying not strictly required for the expression of meaning. According to Martin, the accidental modes of the Latin noun are species (whether or not the word is derived from another), *figura* (whether the word is morphologically simple or compound), gender, number, case, and person.

Syntax

Martin of Dacia was the first to try to explain all syntactic phenomena in terms of modes of signifying, but modistic syntactic theory did not reach mature form until the time of Radulphus Brito and Thomas of Erfurt. It is therefore Thomas's theory that will be summarized here; other modistic theories of syntax included many of the same ideas, though not with the same degree of elaborateness or sophistication.

Thomas views syntax as a process with three stages. *Constructio* is the formation of syntactic linkages from one word to another; *congruitas* imposes well-formedness conditions on individual constructions; and *perfectio* verifies the completeness of the entire sentence.

The linkages formed at the stage of *constructio* are themselves called *constructiones*, and each connects a word to another word, never to a phrase or a constituent. Figure 2 shows the constructions in Thomas's example sentence 'White Socrates runs well.' ('White' was Aristotle's stock example of an adjective; the Modistae applied it to everything. *Socrates*, often abbreviated *Sor*, was their stock noun.)

Socrates albus currit bene.

'White Socrates runs well.'

Figure 2. A sentence resolved into constructions

As shown in figure 3, Thomas classifies each construction as transitive or intransitive depending on whether the two words apply to distinct real-world objects. For example, 'Socrates runs' and 'white Socrates' are intransitive, since in each case only Socrates is being described; 'hit Socrates' and 'similar to Socrates' are transitive, since the person doing the hitting and the person displaying the similarity are distinct from Socrates himself. The underlying concept of *transitio personarum* 'change of referent' goes back to Priscian (*Institutiones* XIII.23, XIV.14).

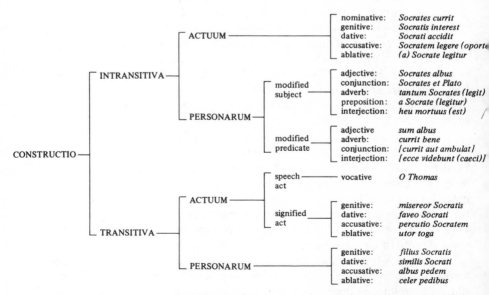

Figure 3. Classification of constructions (Thomas of Erfurt). Parenthesized words are not part of the construction in question but are included to provide context. Examples are Thomas's except for those in square brackets, which I have supplied

Transitive constructions are further classified as to whether the *transitio personarum* includes a *transitio actuum* – that is, whether the change of referent is accompanied by a transfer of action from one referent to another, signified by a verb. For example, 'hits Socrates' is a *constructio transitiva actuum*, since the action of hitting 'goes across' from subject to object; 'similar to Socrates' is termed a *constructio transitiva personarum* because it has *transitio personarum* without *transitio actuum*. Analogously, intransitive constructions are divided into *intransitiva actuum* and *intransitiva personarum* depending on whether they involve the verb.

This transitive–intransitive distinction is accounted for by postulating two superimposed directional relations across each *constructio*. One of them, called the relation of *dependens* to *terminans*, turns out to be equivalent to Petrus Helias' referential dependency, though this is not obvious from medieval discussions of it, which say only that one of the words supplies something required by the other.[11] Figure 4 gives some examples from Thomas of Erfurt.

The other, the relation of *primum* to *secundum*, is similar to the basic relation posited by modern dependency grammar, in that the *secundum* presupposes the presence of the *primum*. Although none of the medievals explicitly does so, it is instructive to construct a sentence by adding constituents one by one in *primum–secundum* order. Figure 5 illustrates this with the type of diagrams used by present-day dependency grammar (the *primum* is the higher end of each sloping line segment). First comes the

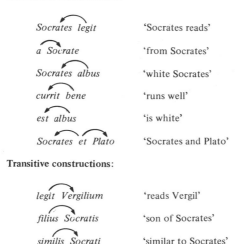

Intransitive constructions:

Socrates legit   'Socrates reads'

a Socrate   'from Socrates'

Socrates albus   'white Socrates'

currit bene   'runs well'

est albus   'is white'

Socrates et Plato   'Socrates and Plato'

Transitive constructions:

legit Vergilium   'reads Vergil'

filius Socratis   'son of Socrates'

similis Socrati   'similar to Socrates'

Figure 4. Arrows point from *dependens* to *terminans*, i.e. toward the element on which the reference depends

32   MICHAEL A. COVINGTON

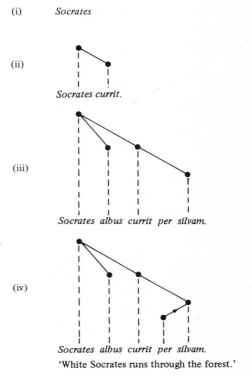

Figure 5. Constructing a sentence in *primum–secundum* order

subject (i), since, in Aristotelian ontology, substance is prior to predication; then the main verb (ii), then modifiers (iii), and finally the preposition, which is attached to the noun like a case marker (iv).

If we add referential dependency arrows like those in figure 4, we find that they point uphill in intransitive constructions and downhill in transitive constructions (figure 6). That is, an intransitive construction is one in which

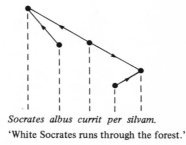

Figure 6. Arrows point from *dependens* to *terminans*

the *primum* is *terminans*, and a transitive construction is one in which the *primum* is *dependens*. The arrows converge on words that refer to real-world entities directly.

Such is *constructio*. The next stage of syntax, *congruitas*, is a set of well-formedness conditions applying to individual constructions. Each requirement is expressed by saying that a particular mode of signifying in the *dependens* requires a particular mode of signifying on the part of the *terminans* (just as the *dependens* itself requires the *terminans* in order to have real-world reference). The correspondence may be simple matching (*similitudo*) or some other relation (*proportio*). Figure 7 shows how this works for *Socrates albus*. It seems awkward to say that the variable gender of the adjective exerts a requirement on the fixed gender of the noun, but the medievals insisted that all of the requirements in each construction were exerted by the *dependens*.

The final stage, *perfectio*, verifies that the sentence as a whole is complete. Thomas of Erfurt lists three criteria that it must fulfil (*Grammatica speculativa*, pp. 286, 314):

(1) There must be a subject and a predicate, linked in a *constructio intransitiva actuum* (subject–verb construction).
(2) There must be *congruitas* throughout.
(3) There must be no un-terminated dependencies. For example, *si Socrates currit*, 'if Socrates runs', is not a complete sentence because the 'if' implies a dependency on something in another clause.

Radulphus Brito adds a fourth: the predicate has to be a finite verb, not an infinitive, since *Socratem currere*, 'for Socrates to run', is not a sentence (I.75, p. 343).

Behind all these criteria lies the idea that the completeness of the sentence is defined by its communicative function. Thomas makes it quite clear that the function of the sentence is to express a concept that is composite

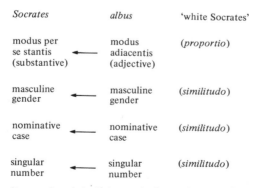

Figure 7. Corresponding modes of signifying as the basis of grammaticality

secundum distantiam, 'with respect to distance' – one in which two simple concepts are joined with the maximum amount of conceptual or semantic distance between them. He explains that *homo albus* 'white man' expresses a concept that is composite, since it combines 'white' with 'man', but not composite *secundum distantiam*, since 'white' and 'man' are grouped together so as to leave the speaker expecting another predicate (as in *homo albus currit bene*, 'a white man runs well'). The fact that a complete sentence needs both a subject and a predicate is, for the Modistae, a consequence of the nature of human cognition, not just an arbitrary formation rule like Chomsky's S → NP VP.

The nominalistic aftermath

The debate over modes of signifying

In its time, modistic grammar was hardly a static body of doctrine; much as with present-day grammatical theory, controversies over the analysis of particular phenomena were numerous (for examples, see Pinborg 1980 and Covington 1984: 83–119). But early in the fourteenth century, the Modistae were forced to turn their attention from these internal controversies to a more basic problem: whether the concept of mode of signifying itself was ill-founded. The resulting debate brought the development of modistic theory to a halt.

The fundamental claim of modism is that the structure of language mirrors the structure of cognition and of reality. This presupposes, of course, that the real world has a definite structure – a presupposition accepted without question by the realist philosophers of the thirteenth century, but vigorously challenged shortly after 1300, largely because of the rise of nominalism. The nominalist position was that words were purely arbitrary representations for thoughts, and hence that language could not have the ontological and cognitive basis that the Modistae claimed for it.

Our first record of the debate is a transcript of a disputation held at Erfurt in October of 1333 or possibly 1332 (see Pinborg 1967: 167–212). The presiding *magister*, one Johannes Aurifaber, argued as follows:[12]

(1) Everything that exists is either a substance (entity) or an attribute of some substance. Modes of signifying are obviously not a substance; if they are attributes, what are they attributes of? Apparently the word, or meaning-bearing sound (*vox significativa*). But *vox significativa* itself is a conventional relationship between sound and meaning, and hence an attribute rather than a substance; *vox* and *significatio* by themselves, though they may be substances, do not have modes of signifying. Hence modes of signifying do not exist.

(2) Modes of signifying are not needed to explain why sentences are

grammatical; Donatus and Priscian got along well enough without them.

(3) If linguistic signs are arbitrary, so are modes of signifying – hence they are not proper objects for scientific study.

(4) There is no empirical evidence for modes of signifying; they have no visible effect on the words in which they are supposed to inhere.

(5) Modes of signifying are not needed to distinguish the parts of speech; logicians distinguish parts of speech on the basis of meaning alone.

(6) Whereas words are arbitrary signs of concepts, concepts are natural signs of real-world objects (in other words, the form of the concept is determined by the form of the object). It is not possible to conceptualize one object under a variety of *modi intelligendi* as modistic theory requires.

Aurifaber's position was that spoken language was fundamentally different from the language of thought, and that only the latter was of philosophical interest. Ten years earlier (1323), William of Ockham had argued the same point in his immensely influential *Summa logicae*: mental language apparently does not contain participles, pronouns, grammatical gender, or morphological structure, since any conceivable proposition can be conceived of without them (I.3). When, late in the fourteenth century, Pierre d'Ailly pursued the same idea in his *Destructiones modorum significandi*,[13] the modistic movement had for all practical purposes long since ended; as far as is known, modistic theory underwent no substantial development after 1300, though it had substantial numbers of adherents for some time afterward.

Modism among the nominalists

It is not hard to see that even if the ontology of *modi essendi* and *intelligendi* is knocked away, many of the insights of modistic theory are still tenable. One does not have to be a realist, for instance, to say that the parts of speech are distinguished, not by their meanings per se, but by how they convey them. Even Ockham said that the term 'mode of signifying' could be used legitimately if one took care to note that 'modes of signifying are not something extra added to the words, but merely a metaphorical way of saying that different words carry their meanings in different ways'.[14]

Though little is known about them, some nominalists did pursue a form of speculative grammar that retained the concept of *modus significandi* in an attenuated form. An example is the anonymous *Expositio Donati nominalis* printed at Rouen by Robert Mace in 1500 (see Covington 1984: 128–32). The author quotes modistic definitions of the parts of speech, but instead of saying that essential modes make a part of speech what it is, he says that they play a criterial role in its definition – a subtle but important shift, since definitions are constructs of the human mind. Again, when he discusses case, he makes a careful distinction between spoken and mental language and argues that the concept of case applies to both. Most strikingly, he has wholly abandoned modistic syntactic theory and gone back to the eleventh-century theory of *regimen*.

Prospects for future research

Our present understanding of medieval grammar is far from complete. The types of work needed to increase it include the following:

(1) Study of relatively unstudied manuscripts. An immense number of medieval grammatical manuscripts are known (see Bursill-Hall 1981 and Pinborg 1967); most of them have not been read in modern times. At present we can hardly even say who the most important medieval authors were; the discovery of the importance of Radulphus Brito, for instance, came almost as a complete surprise. In fact, many grammatical texts remain unrecognized, especially in minor libraries; grammatical works may be classified as logic or some other subject (especially if the treatise takes its title from an example sentence), and even the marginalia in copies of Priscian may provide important information.

(2) Editions of works known to be important. At present, for instance, the only available editions of Thomas of Erfurt use a corrupt text; Michael of Marbais is accessible in print only through the quotations in Thurot (1868). Critical editions of these and other authors would be most welcome. It is of course important for the scholar undertaking such a project to contact other scholars (often identifiable through the libraries that house the manuscripts) to avoid duplication of effort.

(3) Exegesis of modistic doctrines (examples are Bursill-Hall 1971, Rosier 1983, and Covington 1984). The goal of this type of study is to make the content of the medieval theory intelligible to modern readers; its development and external context are given less attention.

(4) Study of medieval grammarians other than the Modistae. Examples are the eleventh- and twelfth-century *regimen* theorists, the postmodistic nominalists, and logicians at various stages. Although the Modistae produced the most sophisticated of the medieval treatises on language, there were many subtle thinkers elsewhere. In addition, one medieval theory often throws light on another.

(5) Historical studies of the development of medieval grammar (for example Pinborg 1967). This type of study traces the transmission of ideas from one thinker to another, with attention to external events and influences. This is the most difficult type of work, since it depends on the results of all of the other types mentioned above.

Anyone doing research on the Modistae should certainly be in contact with the *Institut for Graesk og Latinsk Middelalderfilologi* of the University of

Copenhagen. Largely under the leadership of the late Jan Pinborg, the *Institut* has become an important centre for work on medieval grammar and logic; it houses a substantial microfilm collection and publishes editions and studies in a series titled *Cahiers de l'Institut du Moyen Age Grec et Latin*.

NOTES

1 An example: 'The medieval and Early Modern eras witnessed a tremendous increase in the amount of [available] information about language. Significantly, however, the methods of analysis and interpretation were still those of the ancients. A scientific approach had to wait until the nineteenth century . . .' (Waterman 1963: 13). See also Bloomfield (1933: chapter 1).

2 This paper is based on work supported by (US) National Science Foundation Grant Number BNS–81–05359. All conclusions and opinions expressed here are of course my own.

3 *De interpretatione* I, 16 a 1–19.

4 'Priscianus . . . obscuras dat expositiones nec exponit, causas vero inventionis diversarum partium et diversorum accidentium in unaquaque praetermittit' (Jeauneau 1960: 218).

5 'Cum diversi ab una honesta persona principium generationis haberent ut se de eius familia notarent, nomen illius nomini suo adiungebant et dicebatur cognomen', William of Conches, comm. on Priscian II.24, first edition (c. 1125), quoted by Fredborg (1973: 14).

6 Petrus Helias, ed. Tolson, pp. 153–8. For exposition see Covington 1984: 16–18.

7 'Scientia ordinandi singulas dictiones in oratione ad significandum conceptiones animae', *De divisione scientiarum*, p. 45.

8 This example is from Pseudo-Albertus Magnus, Q.7.

9 'Proprium est nominis substantiam et qualitatem significare', II.18.

10 Siger de Courtrai (*Sophismata*, p. 42) points out explicitly that the terms *activus* and *passivus* are used to make up for the fact that Latin does not distinguish between active and passive gerunds.

11 'Terminum dat vel concedit', Thomas of Erfurt, ed. Bursill-Hall, p. 282, but adopting the reading of Cambridge University Library Ms. Dd.XII.46. The received text, with 'tantum dat vel concedit', is even more cryptic.

12 Aurifaber was himself not a nominalist, but a Latin Averroist following John of Jandun. In all relevant respects, however, his position is very close to nominalism.

13 The attribution to Pierre d'Ailly is not quite certain.

14 'Modi significandi non sunt aliquae res additae ipsis dictionibus, advenientes eis, sed est metaphorica locutio, dicendo quod . . . diversae dictiones diversimode significant illa quae significant' (*Summa logicae*, III.4.10).

ANNOTATED REFERENCES

Primary sources

Albertus Magnus, pseudo- (c. 1285). *Quaestiones Alberti de modis significandi*, ed. and trans. L.G. Kelly. (Amsterdam Studies in the Theory and History of Linguistic Science, III: Studies in the History of Linguistics, 15.) Amsterdam: John Benjamins, 1977. [Author and date unknown; extant only as an early printed book. The doctrinal content of most of the treatise represents the state of modism around 1285, but some of the material appears to be derived from Radulphus Brito, c. 1300. Includes a parallel English translation.]

Alexander de Villa Dei (Alexandre de Villedieu) (1199?). *Doctrinale*. Critical edition with introduction by Dietrich Reichling. (Monumenta Germaniae paedagogica, 12.) Berlin: A. Hofmann, 1893. Reprint, New York: Burt Franklin, 1971. [A mnemonic poem on grammar, widely used as a schoolbook during the Middle Ages. Has nothing to do with speculative grammar per se, but there are many theory-oriented commentaries on it.]

Alfarabi (870–950). *Catálogo de las ciencias* [*Liber de scientiis*], ed. and trans. Ángel González Palencia. (Publicaciones de la Facultad de Filosofía y Letras, Universidad de Madrid, 2.) Madrid: Estanislao Maestre, 1932.

Anonymous (before 1500). *Expositio Donati nominalis* [or] *Praeclara Donati expositio secundum viam Nominalium enucleans de partibus orationis quaestiones*. Rouen: Laurentius Hostingue & Jametus Louys for Robert Mace, 1500.

Aristotle (384–322 BC) *The categories; On interpretation* [*De interpretatione*], ed. and trans. Harold P. Cook. (Loeb Classical Library.) London: Heinemann; Cambridge, Massachusetts: Harvard University Press, 1938.

Metaphysics, ed. and trans. Hugh Tredennick. 2 vols. (Loeb Classical Library.) London: Heinemann; Cambridge, Massachusetts: Harvard University Press, 1933, 1935.

Posterior analytics, ed. and trans. Hugh Tredennick. (Loeb Classical Library.) London: Heinemann; Cambridge, Massachusetts: Harvard University Press, 1938.

Bacon, Roger (c. 1240). *Summa grammatica*, ed. Robert Steele. (*Opera hactenus inedita Rogeri Baconi*, 15.) Oxford: Clarendon Press, 1940. [A speculative grammatical treatise from the period immediately preceding the Modistae; modistic ideas can be seen emerging.]

Boethius, Anicius Manlius Severinus (480–525 AD). *Commentarii in librum Aristotelis 'Peri hermeneias'*, ed. Carolus Meiser. 2 vols. Leipzig: Teubner, 1876, 1880. [Latin translation of the *De interpretatione*, with two commentaries (*editio prima* and *editio secunda*). Very influential in the Middle Ages.]

Boethius Dacus (Boetius Dacus, Boethius of Dacia) (c. 1270). *Modi significandi, sive Quaestiones super Priscianum maiorem*, ed. Jan Pinborg & Heinrich Roos. (Corpus philosophorum Danicorum medii aevi, IV.) Copenhagen: G.E.C. Gad, 1969. [An in-depth treatment of modistic metatheory and the parts of speech; does not cover syntax. Edition includes a contemporary abridgement by Godfrey of Fontaine.]

Donatus, Aelius (c. 350). *Ars grammatica* (including *Ars minor*), ed. Henricus Keil.

(Grammatici Latini, ed. Henricus Keil, vol. 4, 353–402.) Leipzig: Teubner, 1864. Reprint, Hildesheim: Georg Olms Verlag, 1961.

Godfrey of Fontaine (Godefridus de Fontibus) (c. 1270). *Godfrey of Fontaine's abridgement of Boethius of Dacia's 'Modi significandi, sive Quaestiones super Priscianum minorem'*, ed. and trans. A. Charlene Senape McDermott. (Amsterdam Studies in the Theory and History of Linguistic Science, III: Studies in the History of Linguistics, 22.) Amsterdam: John Benjamins, 1980. [The fact that this is an abridgement does not detract much from its completeness; the material omitted consists mostly of answers to counter-arguments. The translation is literal but never misleading. A useful source for scholars who do not read Latin.]

Grosseteste, Robertus de (pseudo-) (c. 1250). *'Tractatus de grammatica': eine fälschlich Robert Grosseteste zugeschriebene spekulative Grammatik*, edited with a commentary by Karl Reichl. (Veröffentlichungen des Grabmann-Institutes, neue Folge, 28.) Munich: Ferdinand Schöningh. [Outside the mainstream of the speculative movement, this treatise could almost be entitled 'A medieval physicist looks at grammar', hence its attribution to Grosseteste. The author's interests tend towards phonetics, co-occurrence relations, and models from physical science; there is little on logic or semantics.]

Gundissalinus, Dominicus (Domingo Gundisalvo) (c. 1150). *De divisione philosophiae*, ed. Ludwig Baur. (Beiträge zur Geschichte der Philosophie des Mittelalters, vol. 4, parts 2–3.) Münster: Aschendorff, 1903.

Johannes Dacus (John of Dacia) (1280). *Opera*, ed. Alfred Otto. 2 vols. (Corpus philosophorum Danicorum medii aevi, I.1–2.) Copenhagen: G.E.C. Gad, 1955. [A very detailed treatise, which the author never finished; discusses only metatheory and the *etymologia* of the noun.]

Jordanus (c. 1230/50). *Notulae super Priscianum minorem magistri Jordani*, partial edition and introduction by Mary Sirridge. (University of Copenhagen, *Cahiers de l'Institut du Moyen Age Grec et Latin* 36.) Copenhagen, 1980.

Kilwardby, Robert (pseudo-) (c. 1250). *The commentary on 'Priscianus maior' ascribed to Robert Kilwardby*, ed. K.M. Fredborg, N.J. Green-Pedersen, Lauge Nielsen, & Jan Pinborg, with introductory matter by Jan Pinborg & Osmund Lewry OP (University of Copenhagen, *Cahiers de l'Institut du Moyen Age Grec et Latin* 15.) Copenhagen, 1975. [A sample of the philosophical climate of which modistic grammar was the later product.]

Martin of Dacia (Martinus de Dacia, c. 1250). *Modi significandi*. In his *Opera*, ed. H. Roos, pp. 1–118. (Corpus philosophorum Danicorum medii aevi, 2.) Copenhagen: G.E.C. Gad, 1961.

Ockham (Occam), William of (1323?). *Summa logicae*, ed. Philotheus Boehner OFM, Gedeon Gál OFM, & Stephanus Brown. (Guillielmi de Ockham opera philosophica, 1.) St Bonaventure, New York: Franciscan Institute Publications, 1974.

Petrus Helias (c. 1140). *The Summa of Petrus Helias on Priscianus minor*, ed. James E. Tolson, with introduction by Margaret Gibson. 2 vols. (University of Copenhagen, *Cahiers de l'Institut du Moyen Age Grec et Latin* 27–8.) Copenhagen, 1978. [Petrus' commentary on the syntactic books of Priscian. According to the preface, Petrus' entire commentary (on all of Priscian) is being edited by L. Reilly of the Pontifical Institute of Medieval Studies, Toronto.]

Pierre d'Ailly (Petrus de Alliaco) (1350–1420). *Destructiones modorum significandi secundum viam Nominalium; Conceptus.* In Ludger Kaczmarek (ed.) *Modi significandi und ihre Destruktionen.* (Materialien zur Geschichte der Sprachwissenschaft und der Semiotik, 1.) Münster: Münsteraner Arbeitskreis für Semiotik, 1980.

Priscianus Caesariensis (c. 500 AD). *Institutionum grammaticarum libri XVIII*, ed. Martinus Hertz. 2 vols. (Grammatici Latini, ed. Henricus Keil, 2–3.) Leipzig: Teubner, 1855, 1859. Reprint, Hildesheim: Georg Olms Verlag, 1961. [In the Middle Ages this was divided into 'Priscianus maior', on the parts of speech (Books I–XVI), and 'Priscianus minor', on syntax (XVII–XVIII).]

Radulphus Brito (Raoul le Breton, Rodolphe le Breton, c. 1300). *Quaestiones super Priscianum minorem*, ed. Jan Pinborg & Heinz W. Enders. 2 vols. (Grammatica speculativa, 3.) Stuttgart–Bad Cannstatt: Frommann-Holzboog, 1980. [Perhaps the single most valuable source of information on modistic grammar; the most sophisticated known treatise from the most sophisticated period. A well-prepared edition; for one textual emendation see Covington 1984: 111–12.]

Siger de Courtrai (Sigerus de Cortraco, c. 1320). *Summa modorum significandi; Sophismata*, ed. Jan Pinborg. (Amsterdam Studies in the Theory and History of Linguistic Science, III: Studies in the History of Linguistics, 14.) Amsterdam: John Benjamins, 1977. [From the same period as Thomas of Erfurt and Radulphus Brito, but slightly less sophisticated and noticeably closer to premodistic school grammar.]

Simon Dacus. *Opera*, ed. Alfred Otto. (Corpus philosophorum Danicorum medii aevi, 3.) Copenhagen: G.E.C. Gad, 1963. [Contains two works, now thought to be by different authors: the *Domus grammaticae* (pp. 1–88), a premodistic treatise apparently written around 1250, and the *Quaestiones super secundum minoris voluminis Prisciani* (pp. 89–178), a modistic treatise on syntax dating from about 1285. I have elsewhere dubbed the two authors Simon Dacus Domifex and Simon Dacus Modista.]

Thomas of Erfurt (Thomasius de Erfordia, c. 1300). *Grammatica speculativa [= Novi modi significandi]*, ed. G.L. Bursill-Hall. London: Longman, 1972. [Contains a close English translation and a brief commentary. This work was the standard handbook of modistic grammar during the last years of the movement; the theory is much the same as Radulphus Brito's, but the presentation is much more concise. The text is from printed editions of Duns Scotus (to whom the work was long attributed); for a few emendations see Pinborg (1974).]

William of Sherwood (Shirwood, Shyreswoode) (c. 1260). Die *Introductiones in logicam* des Wilhelm von Shyreswood, by Martin Grabmann. *Sitzungsberichte der Bayerischen Akademie der Wissenschaften, Philosophisch–historische Abteilung*, 1937, part 10. [An important source for the theory of *suppositio* (reference) and the terminist logic that was popular before and after, but not during, the height of modism.]

Secondary sources

Bloomfield, Leonard. 1933. *Language*. New York: Holt, Rinehart, Winston.
Bursill-Hall, G.L. 1971. *Speculative grammars of the Middle Ages: the doctrine of 'partes orationis' of the Modistae*. The Hague: Mouton.

1981. *A census of medieval Latin grammatical manuscripts.* (Grammatica speculativa, 4.) Stuttgart–Bad Cannstatt: Frommann-Holzboog. [Indispensable for anyone undertaking manuscript work.]

Copleston, F.C. 1972. *A history of medieval philosophy.* London: Methuen.

Covington, Michael A. 1984. *Syntactic theory in the High Middle Ages: modistic models of sentence structure.* (Cambridge Studies in Linguistics, 39.) Cambridge University Press.

Fredborg, Karin Margareta. 1973. The dependence of Petrus Helias' *Summa super Priscianum* on William of Conches' *Glose super Priscianum.* University of Copenhagen, *Cahiers de l'Institut du Moyen Age Grec et Latin* 11: 1–57.

1981. Some notes on the grammar of William of Conches. University of Copenhagen, *Cahiers de l'Institut du Moyen Age Grec et Latin* 37: 21–41.

Hunt, R.W. 1943. Studies on Priscian in the eleventh and twelfth centuries, I: Petrus Helias and his predecessors. *Mediaeval and Renaissance Studies* 1.2: 194–231. Reprinted in his *The history of grammar in the Middle Ages: collected papers.* (Amsterdam Studies in the Theory and History of Linguistic Science, III: Studies in the History of Linguistics, 5.) Amsterdam: John Benjamins, 1980.

Jeauneau, Edouard. 1960. Deux rédactions des gloses de Guillaume de Conches sur Priscien. *Recherches de théologie ancienne et médiévale* 27: 212–47. Reprinted in his *Lectio philosophorum: recherches sur l'école de Chartres.* Amsterdam: Hakkert, 1973.

Koerner, E.F Konrad; Niederehe, Hans-J.; & Robins, R.H. (eds.) 1980. *Studies in medieval linguistic thought dedicated to Geoffrey L. Bursill-Hall.* Amsterdam: John Benjamins. (Also published as *Historiographia Linguistica* 7: 1–321.)

Kretzmann, Norman; Kenny, Anthony; & Pinborg, Jan (eds.) 1982. *The Cambridge history of later medieval philosophy.* Cambridge University Press. [A fundamental reference work; articles by specialists on many subfields. Most histories of medieval philosophy are slanted toward theology; this one inclines toward logic and the natural sciences.]

Pinborg, Jan. 1967. *Die Entwicklung der Sprachtheorie im Mittelalter.* (Beiträge zur Geschichte der Philosophie und Theologie des Mittelalters, vol. 42, part 2.) Münster: Aschendorff; Copenhagen: Arne Frost-Hansen. [The standard work on the modistic movement; includes an extensive list of manuscripts.]

1972. *Logik und Semantik im Mittelalter.* (Problemata, 10.) Stuttgart–Bad Cannstatt: Frommann-Holzboog.

1974. Review of Bursill-Hall's edition of Thomas of Erfurt (1972). *Lingua* 34: 369–73.

1980. Can constructions be construed? A problem in medieval syntactical theory. *Historiographia linguistica* 7: 201–10. (Also in Koerner, Niederehe & Robins 1980.)

Robins, R.H. 1951. *Ancient and mediaeval grammatical theory in Europe, with particular reference to modern linguistic doctrine.* London: G. Bell.

1974. Theory-orientation versus data-orientation: a recurrent theme in linguistics. *Historiographia linguistica* 1: 11–26.

Rosier, Irene. 1983. *La grammaire spéculative des Modistes.* Lille: Presses Universitaires de Lille. [A readable overview of modistic theory.]

Thurot, Charles. 1868. *Notices et extraits de divers manuscrits latins pour servir à l'histoire des doctrines grammaticales au moyen âge.* (Notices et extraits des manuscrits de la Bibliothèque Impériale, vol. 22, part 2.) Paris: Imprimerie Impériale. Reprint, Frankfurt: Minerva, 1964. [A gold mine of transcriptions from manuscripts.

Some attributions are incorrect (for instance, Siger de Courtrai is mistaken for Siger de Brabant), but much of the material is not available elsewhere.]

Waterman, John T. 1963. *Perspectives in linguistics*. Chicago: University of Chicago Press.

4

ORIGINALITY IN THE
MEDIEVAL NORMATIVE TRADITION

VIVIEN LAW

Originality is an elusive quality in any age, and the difficulty of recognizing it is intensified when we seek it in the works of a past epoch. The narcissistic trap of hailing something as original and significant because it foreshadows our own interests lies dangerously close. In linguistic historiography this poses a particular problem precisely because of the invigorating pace of present-day linguistics: scholars who have consciously discarded old ideas and attitudes for new ones understandably have little interest in the background to the concepts they have rejected. Significantly, the two areas in the history of linguistics which have attracted most attention in the last twenty years are precisely those which seem to have most in common with the transformational-generative approach – thirteenth-century Speculative grammar and the *grammaire raisonnée* of the Port-Royal school. But surely few linguists are so self-centred that they are incapable of appreciating original ideas, even those of a very different nature from those currently in favour. We would all like to believe that we are capable of recognizing originality; yet it is a curious feature of current linguistic historiography that while some periods seem to be bursting with new ideas about language, others seem quite barren. Thus, the brief period between approximately 1250 and 1300 is hailed as a particularly fruitful one in the development of linguistic thought, whereas the preceding seven centuries are dismissed as slavishly dependent upon the none-too-original textbooks of ancient Rome.[1] A priori it is unlikely that a period which had its share of distinguished men – Bede, Charlemagne, St Boniface, Godescalc, to name only a few – should have contributed nothing to the study of language. Yet it is repeatedly stated that the earlier Middle Ages, like the later medieval normative tradition, produced no new grammatical doctrine of its own. What if our perception of originality is at fault? The current bias is toward theoretical originality. But overt statements of linguistic theory are not the only area in which originality might be sought. Linguistic theories cannot be evolved without a corpus, an organized body of data which provides the source-material and testing-ground for new theories. The existence of a codified body of data at

any period is in itself significant, quite apart from the subliminal effect
which its structure may have had on the theories developed by the scholars
who worked with it. Why was it compiled? How was it organized? What use
was made of it? The answers to these questions may well provide not only
background information to the development of new theories, but also an
insight into a quieter kind of originality.

The best guide in the search for 'alternative' originality in the Middle Ages
will be the medieval grammarians themselves. What do they have to say
about originality?

One eighth-century grammarian, better known for his activities as a
missionary, St Boniface, left a detailed account of his procedure and
intentions in the dedicatory letter which prefaces his grammar (Löfstedt
1980: 9–12). The *Epistola ad Sigeberhtum* is a remarkable document: in its
explicit description of a grammarian's *modus operandi* it is without parallel
until the Renaissance. The grammar it accompanies, on the other hand, is
almost unrivalled for verbal dependence on classical sources: only five
sentences in the entire work are not based on earlier writers. The paradox of
medieval normative grammar is thus encapsulated in this single work. In
the *Epistola ad Sigeberhtum* Boniface approaches the problem of originality
from an unexpected angle; in the elaborate language characteristic of
English Latinity at the start of the eighth century he says:

. . . should anyone, infected with the foul leaven of venomous envy or with
ignorance, the mother of all error, and driven on by the compelling audacity of his
own cleverness, desire to lacerate these recommendations of the art of grammar with
viper's fangs and bloody jaws, he should be aware that it is the flanks of Priscian and
Donatus, Probus and Audax, Velius Longus and Romanus, Flavianus and Eutyches,
Victorinus and Phocas, Asporius and Pompeius, that he rends. Nor is it a
contemporary rustic at whom he directs his hostile darts; no, he takes aim at the dust
and ashes of defunct rhetors. For not a single twig of a rule will be found grafted into
this little book which is not firmly rooted in one of their works.

Charges of unoriginality were apparently the least of Boniface's worries.
On the contrary, it is by sheltering behind the classical grammarians that he
defends himself against attack. The nature of the criticism he anticipates is
unclear, but it seems to hinge on his own lack of authority as a teacher of
Latin grammar. This was an acute problem in the eyes of the grammarians of
early medieval Europe: for the majority of them Latin was a foreign
language, learnt from books. Their pronouncements lacked authority.
Consequently, they referred constantly to their sources, the works of the
grammatici of Antiquity, and by these references acquired authority at
secondhand. But let us not be deceived into taking their protestations of
unoriginality at face value. If their works were quite indistinguishable from
those of the ancient grammarians, why did they go to the trouble of

compiling them? Not for the glory, certainly; most are anonymous. It is if anything more common in this period to find an original composition being passed off as the work of a Church Father – to give it spurious authority – than to catch an early medieval writer claiming the authorship of an ancient text.

Yet originality there is in many a superficially humble beginners' text. The elementary Latin grammars which appeared during the seventh and eighth centuries arguably reflect as significant a development as anything else that took place in medieval linguistics: the transition from the language-centred grammars of Antiquity to the Latin-centred grammars of the Middle Ages. In the ancient world, the principal concern of most grammarians was to expound the characteristics of language in general – the number and nature of word classes, the properties of each class, the 'virtues' and 'vices' of speech – and this underlying aim, derived from the original philosophical context of linguistic speculation, assisted the easy transferral to the Latin language of the categories arrived at by the Greeks. But linguistic descriptions couched in such general terms that their substance can be applied as readily to one language as to another are of little use when it comes to learning any language *ab initio*. A foreigner whose native tongue was a Celtic or Germanic language would need an exhaustive description of Latin accidence if he was to master the language; but the Roman Empire provided no such help. In the Greek world, the Theodosian *Canones*, a voluminous collection of noun and verb paradigms, entered circulation at an early date, and provided non-Greeks with the foundation they so badly needed. Paradoxically, it may be precisely because the widely-circulating grammar attributed to Dionysius Thrax contained no paradigms at all that the *Canones* were compiled; in the West, the handful contained in Donatus's *Ars minor* rendered the problem less pressing, so delaying any systematic attempt to confront it. It was only upon the conversion of the non-Latin-speaking peoples of northern and western Europe to Christianity that the grammars inherited from ancient Rome were perceived as inadequate. Yet there was no question of discarding them; Boniface's reverent attitude toward the works of his Roman predecessors is typical. Instead, the inherited textbooks were modified – supplemented at different points in the text or with appendices (Law 1982: 53–80). These alterations, haphazard as they may appear, are a clear sign of the nature of the dissatisfaction which seventh- and eighth-century grammarians felt, and an index of the radical shift taking place in the way in which the structure of a language was perceived. Whereas grammarians of the fourth and fifth centuries, like their Hellenistic predecessors, had been concerned with the features of language in general, exemplified through the writer's mother tongue, early medieval grammarians in non-Romance-speaking areas were urgently concerned with the forms of Latin. The nature of an utterance (*vox*), the workings of Roman proper names, the twenty-seven *species* of common noun – all these were of scant interest to people who had still to learn the first declension. But the grammars of the Roman Empire were not form-orientated: they take the forms for granted. Donatus's famous so-called 'beginners'' grammar, the *Ars minor*, is a prime example: its five paradigms are chosen to exemplify the five genders, not the five declensions, and in fact two declensions, the fourth and fifth, are left unrepresented. Only one verb, *legere*, is conjugated in full. The paradigm of *legere* is a perfectly adequate sample of Latin verb accidence, in that it provides a complete range of forms to which such labels as 'indicative mood', 'pluperfect tense', 'passive voice', 'singular number' or 'third person' could be attached; but a foreigner could not begin to solve such problems as '*lego* is to *legunt* as *amo* is to ?' using the *Ars minor* alone. Although the concept of distinct formal classes, declensions and conjugations, was present, it was little used, and is rarely the informing principle behind a Late Latin discussion of noun or verb morphology.[2] Only when non-Latin-speaking peoples embarked upon the task of learning Latin from books – direct contact with Romance speakers was for most early medieval Irishmen or Anglo-Saxons out of the question – did the emphasis change. The textbooks seventh- and eighth-century Insular scholars wrote manifest a shift from the ancient focus on language to focus on form – the morphology of one particular language, Latin. For this there was no Western precedent: the very different methodology and conceptual framework required in providing a simultaneously concise and comprehensive description of a language were developed by the grammarians of the early Middle Ages with minimal help from their predecessors. We are dealing here not with doctrinal novelty – the textbooks of the seventh and eighth centuries tell us nothing about Classical Latin which is not to be found in the works of the later Roman Empire – nor with fresh insights into the nature of language; the contribution of these teachers lies in their ability to perceive the features which characterize one particular language, and to set out a description of these features in an orderly and economical fashion. The solution they arrived at, which was ultimately absorbed into the *Ars minor*, formed the basis of the elementary grammars of the Middle Ages (Law 1984, 1985 and forthcoming), and arguably has descendants at the present day.

The subsequent history of this genre need not occupy us further, nor that of the other grammatical genres which emerged during the Middle Ages. Surprisingly, the Latin grammars of the normative tradition are not alone in the neglect they have suffered for their apparent want of originality: many of the extant vernacular grammars have met with the same treatment. Just because a few among them depart strikingly from the Latin model, they have tended to monopolize linguists' attention: the Old Norse First

Grammatical Treatise (Benediktsson 1972; Haugen 1972; Albano Leoni 1975; Ulvestad 1976) and the various works from the bardic schools of medieval Ireland (Ó Cuív 1965 and 1973; Adams 1970; Ahlqvist 1979–80) have benefited most. But what of the rest – Ælfric's grammar of Latin in Old English, remembered only for the novelty of being written in a vernacular; or the Second, Third and Fourth Grammatical Treatises in Old Norse, by no means devoid of interesting features (although the latter two take traditional Latin doctrine as their starting-point);[3] or the renderings of the *Ars minor* into English, French, Italian, German, Icelandic and the Slavonic languages, which appear in such profusion from the beginning of the fifteenth century; or handbooks of rhetoric and poetics focusing on the vernacular, such as Snorri's *Edda* or the Provençal *Leys d'Amors*? Let us take one group of texts which have so far escaped the notice of linguists – although they are well known to medievalists – and see what contribution they make to the totality of medieval linguistic scholarship.

The period from roughly 1200 to 1350 was a remarkably fertile one, in terms of vernacular grammatical output, in Provence. To cater for the increasing demand among amateurs (particularly those whose mother tongue was not Provençal but Catalan or some form of Italian) for guidance in the complicated forms of verse composition characteristic of troubadour poetry, a number of handbooks of poetics and grammar were compiled. Chief among these are the *Razos de trobar*, composed by the Catalan Raimon de Vidal between 1190 and 1213 (and several other works were based on it: see Marshall 1972); the *Donatz Proensals*, written by an otherwise unknown figure, Uc Faidit, for two Italians in the second quarter of the thirteenth century (Marshall 1969: 63); and the *Leys d'Amors*, composed under Guillaume Molinier at Toulouse and published in 1356 (Gatien-Arnoult 1841). Whilst the *Razos de trobar* contains a brief and patchy account of Provençal grammar interspersed with material relating more directly to poetics, and the *Donatz Proensals* comprises a more systematic, if still uneven, Latin-based description of Provençal grammar, the grammar included in the lengthy third book of the *Leys d'Amors* is a remarkable document fully deserving of linguists' attention. Inevitably, the conceptual framework is taken over from Latin; but it is applied to Provençal in a remarkably intelligent and independent way. A representative problem will show how these various scholars applied inherited theory to a vernacular.

One of the principal points of difficulty encountered by medieval grammarians of Romance vernaculars was the Latin case system: how was it to be applied to a language in which it had been reduced to a rectus/oblique opposition or lost altogether? Countless attempts in more recent times to apply the Latin case system to languages for which it was not intended, for example Quechua (Markham 1864) and Italian (Baumann c. 1978),[4] have drawn scorn upon the whole race of normative grammarians; however, given that this was the only model available in thirteenth-century Provence, the important question is not whether it was applied to the vernacular but how it was applied.

The problem of case presented the medieval grammarian of Provençal with a severe test on two levels, the first practical, the second theoretical. On the practical plane, he had to decide how to frame his description of the vestigial case system of medieval Provençal; and on the theoretical plane, he had to clarify the term 'case' and explain to his audience how the concept could apply to Provençal.

Medieval Provençal is now regarded as having a two-case system (Anglade 1921: 211) marked by the presence or absence of final *s*. The patterns which result are as follows:[5]

Singular
Subject	roza	naus	cavals	emperaire
Oblique	roza	nau	caval	emperador

Plural
Subject	rozas	naus	caval	emperador
Oblique	rozas	naus	cavals	emperadors

Rudimentary though it is, the declension system of medieval Provençal was likely to be a stumbling-block to foreign learners: it clearly required description in any grammar which claimed to be a complete account of the language. Medieval solutions to this problem varied. Raimon Vidal, the earliest of the Provençal grammarians, adopted an essentially latinate approach. He described the endings (Marshall 1972: 10) in terms of 'lengthening' (adding -*s*) and 'shortening' (dropping -*s*):

> Hueimais deves saber qe toutas las paraulas del mon masculinas . . . s'alongan en .vj. cas, so es a saber, el nominatiu (et el vocatiu) singular, el genitiu et el datiu et en l'acusatiu et en l'ablatiu plural; et s'abreuion en .vj. cas, so es a saber, el genitiu et el datiu et el acusatiu et el ablatiu singlar et el nominatiu et el vocatiu plural.

> And you should know that all masculine words . . . lengthen in six cases, that is, nominative (and vocative) singular and genitive, dative, accusative and ablative plural, and shorten in six cases, that is, the genitive, dative, accusative and ablative singular and the nominative and vocative plural.

The model for description in these terms is found in the brief texts on the prosody of noun endings which proliferated from the time of Servius's *De finalibus (De ultimis syllabis)* on. A specimen paragraph from a text of this kind which was in circulation from the ninth century[6] runs as follows:

> Omnis nominatiuus accusatiuus et uocatiuus singularis quartae declinationis breues sunt, genitiuus et datiuus et ablatiuus longi fiunt. Nominatiuus accusatiuus et uocatiuus pluralis producuntur, genitiuus et datiuus et ablatiuus corripiuntur.

Although the information imparted is not strictly comparable, the method and terminology are very similar. Vidal thus seems to borrow a technique of description from traditional Latin grammars for the framework of his own account of Provençal noun morphology. Can he be given any credit for originality? In his defence, it may be said that the Latin scheme was devised with a different purpose in mind – that of setting out the quantity of Latin noun endings, and not that of detailing the endings themselves. Vidal (or an unknown predecessor) had the intelligence to adapt this to the very different end of describing the inflectional system of Provençal; that he did so with reasonable success is the second point in his favour. His description would have been more economical had he departed from the Latin model to the extent of using a single term to refer to his two effective cases, nominative–vocative and genitive–dative–accusative–ablative. This improvement was in fact carried out in later reworkings of his grammar. One version of the *Razos de trobar* introduces the term *oblig* for the genitive, dative, accusative and ablative cases, while using *nominatius* for both nominative and vocative.[7] The *Doctrina d'Acort*, a versified reworking of the *Razos de trobar* based on this version (Marshall 1972: xxviii), goes one step further, speaking of *retz (rectus)* as well as *oblics*,[8] but notwithstanding this greater economy in its versified rules, its author actually writes out complete paradigms, through six cases, for several nouns. A further version by Jofre de Foixà, and Uc Faidit's *Donatz Proensals*, agree in contrasting the nominative (and vocative) with *tuit li altre cas*, while the *Leys d'Amors* returns to *nominatius et vocatius singulars* and *oblics singulars*. Thus, although superficially still tied to the Latin system of six cases, the Provençal grammarians rapidly learnt to turn already existing concepts to their own advantage.

Given that Provençal grammarians after Vidal arrived at what was effectively a two-case system (which they applied to Provençal noun morphology with varying degrees of adroitness), one might well ask why they bothered with the six cases of Latin grammar at all. Did these not remain simply a cumbersome superstructure without practical value outside the theoretical domain of *gramatica*? This might legitimately be argued of Vidal and Uc Faidit. In the *Leys d'Amors*, on the other hand, there is clear evidence of an understanding of the difference between the two senses of 'case', one denoting a syntactic/local relation, and the other denoting the word or word-form which marks that relation. The two very similar definitions of *cas* offered make it clear that case is not equated with *declinatio* (Gatien-Arnoult 1842: 102f):

cas es variamens de dictios cazuals per habitutz o per votz o per la maniera del significar. . . . Cas es variamens o mudamens de dictios – de nom, de pronom o de particip – lequals variamens se fay per habitutz o per votz o per la maniera del significar.

Case is a variation or change in words – noun, pronoun or participle – carried out by means of articles, the form of the words themselves, or the *modus significandi*.

Thus, case is viewed as a change, an alteration (*variamens o mudamens*) which need not necessarily affect the form of the word, the *dictio cazuals*, itself. The change may be effected by an article (with or without a preposition); thus, *dona* may become *la dona*, *de la dona*, or *a la dona*. Alternatively, the word itself may change, as in *le doctors*, *li doctor*, where, as the writer points out, case is shown not only by the article, but also by the ending. However, there are words, such as *bres*, *pers* and *cas* itself, which are invariable and so, when used without the article, give no sign of their case. In such words, it is only the *modus significandi* which can establish the case, in default of formal markers.

This explanation of *cas* demonstrates that 'case' in the sense of inflectional endings was not what our author understood by the term. Inflection, to him, is but one of the three ways of showing 'case'. He goes on to state categorically:

segon romans nos no havem declinatio en lo nom ni en lo pronom ni en lo particip ni en lo verb, quar declinar es lo comensamen tener e la fi variar; e quar tug li cas no varian la fi ni teno lo comensamen, ans lo varian tug que mays, per so no havem declinatio.

In *romans* we have no declension in the noun, pronoun, participle or verb, since 'declining' means to retain the beginning and change the ending. Since none of the cases change the end or retain the beginning, but for the most part change it, for that reason we have no declension. (Gatien-Arnoult 1842: 110)

The author then explains away the vestigial remnants of a case-system, as in *le reys* : *li rey*, as inconsistent, sporadic, and in any case numerically far outweighed by nouns like *dona* and *lutz*, which do not change their ending for case. He gives as a second reason for not identifying declension in *romans* the fact that *la diversitatz de las declinatios* is recognized in Latin by the endings of the genitive and dative singular; but since in *romans* genitive and dative are identical, declension (in the sense of distinct inflectional patterns) cannot be assigned. An interesting third objection is that it could be claimed that since case is indicated at the beginning of the word through the article, declension could be assigned to nouns in *romans* – an argument reminiscent of recent observations that spoken French depends on initial inflection for its plural formation, e.g. [lãfã] – [lezãfã]. The author rejects this idea on the grounds that although it might indeed be possible to identify *one* declension on this basis, more than one such pattern could not be found – confusing the two senses of *declinatio*.[9]

The term *cas* is thus clearly not being used in the formal sense in the *Leys d'Amors*; the fact that *cas* can be shown in three different ways – by articles, by changes in the form of a word or by the *modi significandi* – indicates that it is the semantic or functional value which our author regards as its essential content. This is especially apparent in the section on the individual cases (Gatien-Arnoult 1842: 108f). This discussion is based ultimately (probably via an expanded edition, perhaps in the form of lecture-notes) on Priscian's *Institutiones grammaticae* (II 185,11–186,3). Nevertheless, unless it is a slavish translation of an as yet unidentified source, it is of considerable interest for the independent way in which the cases are treated. Rather than retaining the Latin system in every detail, the author takes what he perceives as the principal functions of each case and gives examples of their realization in *romans*. Thus, under the genitive he uses the example *aquest libres es de Peyre* ('this book is Peter's'), and for the dative *digas aysso ad Esclarmonda* ('tell that to Esclarmonda'), regardless of the fact that in Latin the preposition *de* is construed with the ablative and *ad* with the accusative. The ablative, the most difficult case for vernacular grammarians to adapt owing to its multiplicity of uses, was similarly handled, with interesting results: an example of its comparative function, *Peyres es plus fortz de Guilhem* ('Peter is stronger than William'), elicits the remark *jaciaysso que daquesta locutio gayre no uzam en romans* ('although we make almost no use of this construction in *romans*') and an alternative version with *que*. It is clear from these examples that *cas*, for the Provençal author, denotes not form but function, of which word-form is one realization, but not the only one possible.

This point, the non-equivalence of form and function, is made even more explicitly in the discussion of the *genera verborum* (Gatien-Arnoult 1842: 232ff). In Latin, the *genera* or 'voices' were traditionally set at five: active, passive, neuter (=intransitive), common (verbs having passive form but both active and passive signification, like *osculor* 'I kiss' and 'I am kissed'), and deponent. The author recognizes active, passive, and neuter in *romans*, but says *be vezetz que comu ni deponen no havem* ('note well that we have neither common nor deponent'), and continues:

. . . quar le comus es ditz segon la votz del lati e la maniera del significar. Quar una votz coma *largior* ha doas manieras de significar, so es *yeu doni* e *soy donatz*. E quar en romans no havem una votz passiva que haia doas manieras de significar, so es activamen e passivamen, per so no havem verb comu, quar en romans diversas votz son e diversas manieras de significar.

. . . because the common is so designated on the basis of its Latin form and its *modus significandi*. For a word like *largior* has two *modi significandi*, 'I give' and 'I am given'. And since in *romans* we do not have a passive form to have two *modi significandi*, active and passive, for that reason we do not have a common voice. For in *romans* forms are different from *modi significandi*.

As one might expect of a grammarian aware of Modistic ideas, a clear and consistent distinction is made here, and throughout the work, between *votz*, the form of the word, and its *modus significandi*. [10] There is no question of a wholesale application of the Latin *genera* to the Provençal verb.

Other aspects of the doctrine of the *Leys d'Amors* could equally readily claim our attention. The author shows throughout a remarkable sensitivity to different levels of language: striking examples are his comments on the special status of grammatical metalanguage and of the language used to address trees and animals. He appeals frequently to usage, and insists that it is only the usage of *romans* which can be definitive for *romans*. The usage of other languages, including the ever-controversial Gascon, is irrelevant; and he underlines the independence of *romans* vis-à-vis Latin. His work often bears the appearance of a comparative grammar of two equal languages, *romans* and Latin. Although the author's attempts to make sense of the traditional system of grammar which was his starting point were not always completely successful, they are invariably intelligent and thoughtful, and would merit detailed study.

The *Leys d'Amors* is one example, but by no means the only one, of a medieval author coming to terms with the inherited system of grammar in a way which certainly merits the epithet 'original'. But originality is a delicate quality, and not, as a rule, one which comes with a label attached to alert us to its presence. The use of traditional terminology and concepts often obscures the essential nature of the author's achievement. That type of originality which results in a major upheaval in the status quo can hardly go unnoticed; but just as there are revolutions within revolutions, so too there are subtler kinds of originality. The utter novelty of modistic grammar, importing concepts foreign to grammar as it had developed over almost a millennium, has tended to eclipse movements within the grammatical mainstream. Were it not for the Modistae, it may be that the development of medieval normative grammar would have received more of its due share of attention in the past few decades. Modistic grammar, after all, was a shortlived movement, limited, in its active phase, to two generations. By the beginning of the fourteenth century it was being roundly condemned as a blind alley (Pinborg 1967). Other developments in the Middle Ages, although less noticeable, were far more significant in their long-term effects: the early medieval restructuring of the traditional Roman teaching grammar from a taxonomic account of language in general with reference to Latin, to a detailed account of Latin accidence designed for the foreign learner, resulted in a new genre, the foreign-language grammar, which has remained productive to the present day. In the case of vernacular adaptations of the traditional Latin system, it is more difficult to trace a lasting influence, partly because the history of most vernacular grammatical traditions has yet to be charted. Nonetheless, it is not inconceivable that the increased linguistic awareness brought about by this comparative exercise – and where it was well done, as in the case of the *Leys d'Amors*, contrastive points leap to the eye – contributed to the new initiatives taken by Renaissance scholars and their immediate predecessors.

Much work remains to be done in the historiography of medieval linguistic science. Robins' *Ancient and Mediaeval Grammatical Theory in Europe*, like the relevant chapters of his *Short History of Linguistics*, remains a most valuable outline of the subject, and one of the very few to take into account the earlier part of the Middle Ages. And yet, were anyone to sit down to write a new work covering the same time-span, he would find that many of the areas touched upon over thirty years ago by Robins have attracted so little attention in the intervening period that he would be hard pressed to say anything more about them. Partly due to the more topical appeal of Speculative grammar and partly to the inherent difficulty of working with unedited material in a variety of languages, we have allowed numerous authors to languish unread, thereby depriving ourselves of what might turn out to be an engrossing chapter in Western intellectual history. These authors should be given a chance to speak in their own defence: until we have heard what they have to say, how can we condemn them for unoriginality?

NOTES

1 Bursill-Hall (1975: 181) decided to restrict his discussion of medieval linguistic thought to the period between the eleventh and mid-fourteenth centuries, 'largely because little work of any originality has emerged (if indeed it ever existed), and, although the study of grammar was continued during this period, it would seem that the grammarians of the time were content to repeat the arguments of the great Roman grammarians Donatus and Priscian'. From the source-hunter's point of view this last statement is basically correct (although it overlooks one of the distinguishing characteristics of the early medieval period: the use of many sources besides Donatus; and Priscian's *Institutiones grammaticae* was little used before the Carolingian Renaissance); but it is not the source of the facts that matters so much as how these facts were used.

2 Significantly, only the grammars of Priscian, Phocas and Eutyches, all Greeks or working in a Greek-speaking environment, take form as their starting-point; equally significantly, it is precisely these grammarians who came to the fore during the ninth century. Although the later ninth-century Carolingians rejected the Insular style of elementary grammar, they too required a form-based account of Latin grammar and so turned to these, the only ancient works to provide it.

3 The Second Treatise contains a novel classification of the sounds of Old Norse; the Third consists of an expanded paraphrase of the traditional account of the *littera*, including an interesting discussion of Norse runes; and the Fourth is distinguished for its remarkably apt selection of passages from skaldic verse to replace the traditional Latin examples of the figures of speech.

4 P. 30: 'Das Italienische kennt 5 Fälle, also einen mehr als das Deutsche.'

5 Adapted from Anglade 1921: 227f.

6 And possibly earlier. It is preserved in, for example, Paris, Bibliothèque nationale MS lat. 13025, f.45v–f.46v; Amiens, Bibliothèque municipale MS 426, f.lrv. Similar texts are often found associated with Donatus's *Ars minor*, as in Paris BN lat. 7492 (s. xii), f.108v, and Paris BN lat. 16670 (s. xiv), f.2v.

7 Marshall 1972: 149. This version (preserved in MSS CL) makes the consistent grouping of nominative and vocative *vis-à-vis* the genitive, dative, accusative and ablative clearer than in Vidal's original text: 'lo nominatius e·l vocatius singular, qe se resemblon, et el genitiu, datiu, acusatiu et ablatiu, qi se resemblon eissamen; et aqist qatre cas son apellat oblig'.

8 *Rectus* and *obliquus* are terms of frequent occurrence in Priscian's *Institutiones grammaticae*.

9 Interestingly, the ambiguity inherent in the term *declinatio* was perceived and effectively dealt with in the eighth century by Boniface. His solution was to use the term *ordo* (taken from Charisius) to refer to the five inflectional categories of nouns, reserving *declinatio* to denote the property of inflection (of both nouns and verbs). Unfortunately his grammar did not achieve wide dissemination, so that this terminological clarification failed to gain currency.

10 Well before the middle of the fourteenth century, when the *Leys d'Amors* was written, the basic concepts of Speculative grammar had filtered into general usage.

REFERENCES

Adams, G.B. 1970. Grammatical analysis and terminology in the Irish bardic schools. *Folia Linguistica* 4: 157–66.
Ahlqvist, A. 1979–80. The three parts of speech of bardic grammar. *Studia Celtica* 14–15: 12–17.
Albano Leoni, F. 1975. *Il primo trattato grammaticale islandese*. Bologna: Il Mulino.
Anglade, J. 1921. *Grammaire de l'ancien provençal*. Paris: Klincksieck.
Baumann, M. c. 1978. *Italienisch in 30 Tagen*. Munich: Humboldt-Taschenbuchverlag.
Benediktsson, H. 1972. *The first grammatical treatise*. Reykjavík: University of Iceland Publications in Linguistics 1.
Bursill-Hall, G.L. 1975. The Middle Ages. In T.A. Sebeok (ed.) *Current Trends in Linguistics* 13:1. The Hague: Mouton.
Donatus: see Keil 1857–80 IV 355–402; Holtz 1981.
Gatien-Arnoult, 1841–3. *Monumens de la littérature romane*. 3 vols. (I 1841, II 1842, III 1843). Toulouse: J.B. Paya.
Haugen, E. 1972. *First grammatical treatise: the earliest Germanic phonology*. London: Longman.
Holtz, L. 1981. *Donat et la tradition de l'enseignement grammatical*. Paris: CNRS.
Keil, H. 1857–80. *Grammatici Latini*. 8 vols. Leipzig: Teubner.
Law, V. 1982. *The Insular Latin grammarians*. Woodbridge: The Boydell Press.
   1984. The first foreign-language grammars. *The Incorporated Linguist* 23: 211–16.
   1985. Linguistics in the earlier Middle Ages: the Insular and Carolingian grammarians. *Transactions of the Philological Society* 1985: 171–93.

Forthcoming. *La grammatica normativa*. To appear in the proceedings of the Convegno di studi 'Aspetti della letteratura latina nel secolo XIII'.

Löfstedt, B. 1980. *Bonifatii (Vynfreth) Ars grammatica*. Turnhout: Brepols.

Markham, C.R. 1864. *Contributions towards a grammar and dictionary of Quichua, the language of the Yncas of Peru*. Reprinted Osnabrück: Biblio Verlag (1972).

Marshall, J.H. 1969. *The 'Donatz Proensals' of Uc Faidit*. London: Oxford University Press.

1972. *The 'Razos de trobar' of Raimon Vidal and associated texts*. London: Oxford University Press.

Ó Cuív, B. 1965. Linguistic terminology in the mediaeval Irish bardic tracts. *Transactions of the Philological Society*: 141–64.

1973. The linguistic training of the mediaeval Irish poet. *Celtica* 10: 114–40.

Pinborg, J. 1967. *Die Entwicklung der Sprachtheorie im Mittelalter* (= *Beiträge zur Geschichte der Philosophie und Theologie des Mittelalters* 42.2). Münster: Aschendorff; Copenhagen: Frost-Hansen.

Priscian: see Keil 1857–80 II and III.

Servius, *De ultimis syllabis*: see Keil 1857 IV: 449–55.

Ulvestad, B. 1976. Grein sú er máli skiptir: tools and tradition in the First Grammatical Treatise. *Historiographia Linguistica* 3: 203–23.

5

RENAISSANCE LINGUISTICS:
THE OLD AND THE NEW

W. KEITH PERCIVAL

Most intellectual historians nowadays are receptive to the notion that ideas have no independent reality but exist in relation to particular cultural contexts, which in part determine their character. As Robins has emphasized (1979: 4), scientists and scholars are men of their own age and country, and participate in the culture within which they live and work. This perspective has the virtue of forcing the historian of ideas to consider the general historiographical problems posed by the period he is interested in, and indeed Robins's own work, in its many-sided aspects, has unequivocally oriented historians of linguistics in this direction.

The Renaissance is perhaps an especially interesting case in point here. To a large degree, many of the less tractable problems in the history of Renaissance linguistics reflect broader problems which affect the general history of the period. We should not forget that ever since the appearance in 1860 of Jacob Burckhardt's seminal monograph *Die Cultur der Renaissance in Italien* the Renaissance has posed a host of recalcitrant problems for general historians, many of which are even now far from completely satisfactory solution.[1] In the first place, are we justified in positing the existence of such a period at all? Secondly, what are the relations between the Renaissance, however delimited and defined, and the immediately preceding and following periods? Thirdly, what place does the movement known as humanism occupy in the period? Should it be considered coterminous with the Renaissance or regarded as merely one ingredient in it? Further, was humanism a philosophical movement or an educational programme, or was it to some degree both of these? Was humanism a reaction to scholasticism, and did it lead to or at least contribute to the demise of scholasticism? Perhaps without being fully aware of it, historians of linguistics who deal with this period inherit many of these dilemmas and like their colleagues in other branches of historiography are still grappling with them.

As a point of departure, one might provisionally adopt the Oxford English Dictionary's thumbnail definition of the Renaissance as 'the great revival of art and letters, under the influence of classical models, which began in Italy in the 14th century and continued during the 15th and 16th', and hence also by a familiar semantic extension 'the period during which this movement was in progress'. Not surprisingly, however, such a definition, although it embodies many aspects of the layman's picture of the Renaissance, is open to a variety of objections. To begin with, the word 'revival' implies an antecedent state of decline or neglect, and no general historian writing today would portray the period immediately preceding the Renaissance – the High Middle Ages – as inferior to the Renaissance either in the fine arts or in literature. In this regard, the history of Renaissance grammar is especially illustrative in that one can hardly speak of a restoration of the discipline after a period of inactivity or decline; the Middle Ages can hold their own in comparison with any other period in the area of grammar.

In yet another respect, the history of grammar challenges traditional conceptions of the Renaissance in that the peculiarity of Renaissance grammar does not consist in a return to classical models, for medieval grammar was tied to the very same models. To cite a specific case, the Latin grammar of Priscian (composed c. 500 AD) played a much more central role in medieval grammar than it did during the Renaissance (or indeed in any subsequent period). It was surely a sign of the times when the influential Italian humanist Lorenzo Valla (1407–57) censured Priscian on a number of important points and wryly compared him to the sun, a heavenly body which sometimes suffers eclipse![2] Another indication of the self-confidence Renaissance grammarians felt *vis-à-vis* the grammarians of antiquity is the curious fact that the Viennese humanist Bernard Perger in one of the prefaces to his edition of Niccolò Perotti's *Rudimenta grammatices*, which he adapted for use in German-speaking schools, suggests that the work was so comprehensive that 'we shall no longer have need of Priscian's rules'.[3] One might almost say, therefore, that Renaissance grammarians aimed at superseding the ancients.

On the other hand, the framers of the definition in the Oxford English Dictionary were perhaps on firmer ground in viewing the Renaissance as a movement which started in the *fourteenth* century – a hundred years or more before the advent of printing and the fall of Constantinople to the Turks (1453), and at least a century and a half before the departure of Columbus for the New World. But this poses a problem for the history of linguistics, in that, as August Buck once pointed out (1952: 61), the early humanists gave every appearance of being reasonably satisfied with the dictionaries and grammatical textbooks current at the time. For instance, Petrarch (1304–74) included two medieval lexica, the *Papias* (mid-eleventh century) and the *Catholicon* of John of Genoa (1286), in a list of his favourite books (see Ullman 1955). The first clear indication of discontent comes from Petrarch's protégé Coluccio Salutati (1331–1406), who took offence at the barbarous Latin of his contemporaries – the nonclassical syntax and lexical coinages, and the use of

Latin words in impermissible meanings and combinations (Novati 1905: 216–22).

In the area of grammar in the broadest possible sense, the first piece of professional literature produced by a Renaissance humanist was a short treatise on the metres of Seneca by Lovato Lovati (1246–1309), which introduced such hitherto unknown metrical forms as the iambic senarius.[4] In the narrower area of grammatical textbooks, on the other hand, a distinctively humanistic style was set in motion by Guarino Veronese, who was born in the year of Petrarch's death (1374) and wrote his popular *Regulae grammaticales* some time before 1420.[5]

Whether it is worthwhile arguing about when the Renaissance came to an end is likewise a moot point. It is perhaps sufficient to observe that by the end of the sixteenth century the movement, in both its literary and artistic forms, had spread to much of Europe, but the classical models mentioned in our capsule definition have continued to exert their influence to varying degrees right up to the present time. It would be reasonable to argue, therefore, that the Renaissance has never truly come to an end, but equally reasonable to suggest that humanistic scholarship has a history which overlaps the Renaissance at both ends, for what the Renaissance humanists in essence attempted to do was to assimilate the *whole* of the ancient heritage, not merely those parts of it which had been familiar in previous centuries (Virgil, Ovid, Lucan, large portions of the Aristotelian writings, and so on). In this sense, the humanists may be said to have continued a process already begun in the High Middle Ages.

In line with this, one may profitably break down the study of language during the Renaissance into two main categories. On the one hand, the discipline which since antiquity had been called *grammatica*, devoted to the acquisition of Latin, continued to be actively cultivated. This was a consequence of the sociocultural fact that Latin was the second language of all intellectuals in the Renaissance to no less a degree than it had been in the Middle Ages; a thorough knowledge of that language continued to be a prerequisite for advanced study, especially in the money-making professions of law and medicine. On the other hand, the cultural and linguistic horizon of Latin-speaking western Europe unquestionably assumed a radically different complexion after the discovery, beginning in the middle of the fifteenth century, of new trade routes to the Orient and a whole new continent to the west. As a consequence of this, grammatical manuals dealing with the languages of the newly discovered parts of the world became a practical necessity, and scholars familiar with this new literature were in a position for the first time to pose general questions about the significance of linguistic diversity. To this extent, Renaissance grammarians may be said to have broken new ground, or at least to have faced new challenges.

At the same time, however, the conceptual content of Latin grammar did not undergo quite so radical a transformation as some of the grammarians of the period were accustomed to claim. The revolutionary rhetoric of Renaissance writers obscures the fact that there was no sudden sharp break between the grammatical doctrine of the medieval scholastics and that of the Renaissance humanists.[6]

On the credit side of the balance sheet, as it were, the study of nonexotic languages also received a powerful impetus during the Renaissance, especially in the sixteenth century, when a number of the European vernacular languages received serious grammatical treatment for the first time, and new national grammatical traditions developed in several countries. This is especially true of Italian, Spanish, and French – the Germanic languages followed suit more slowly.

Here again, a number of reservations are in order. First, it is far from being the case that study of the vernacular languages had been completely neglected during the Middle Ages. For instance, the dominant position of the 'Franks' in the Crusades had caused many people to study French (see Bischoff 1967: 229). Moreover, the fact that a variety of Norman French was spoken by the ruling classes in England for about three centuries after the Norman Conquest gave rise to a demand there for instruction in 'good' French (see Lambley's 1920 monograph). Grammatical treatments of a number of other languages (Icelandic, Irish, Provençal) were also attempted. But in most cases these works responded to a need to provide manuals of poetic composition (see Marshall 1969). Secondly, we should not forget that when vernacular grammars came to be composed during the Renaissance this occurred as part and parcel of complex political and social developments. In the case of English, for example, the patriotic zeal concomitant on the long struggle against France may have been an important factor disposing the royal chancery to switch from French to English in the early fifteenth century (see Fisher 1977: 879, 898).

The first major departure from the linguistic traditions of the Middle Ages, however, was the gradual introduction of Greek into the school curriculum. This began in the last decade of the fourteenth century, when Manuel Chrysoloras was invited by the city of Florence to teach Greek in that city. A number of Italian humanists then travelled to Constantinople and learned to speak the language by immersion. One of these budding scholars was Guarino Veronese, who after his return to Italy in 1408 taught Greek alongside of Latin in a number of cities. As the fifteenth century wore on, emigrants from the militarily threatened Byzantine Empire arrived in Italy and taught Greek. The translation of major works of Greek literature into Latin (authors such as Homer, Aesop, Xenophon) was also undertaken in that century. On the debit side, however, the impact of this broadening of linguistic and literary horizons was not immediate. Until the sixteenth century, the familiarity of most Western scholars with Greek language and literature was slight. In general, the primacy of Latin was not significantly shaken by the introduction of the study of Greek. Hence, Renaissance humanism should not be equated, as it sometimes still is, with the discovery of Greek language and literature.

A second major step was taken when scholars in western Europe began to take an interest in the study of what were termed at that time oriental languages, namely Hebrew and Arabic. In the case of both these languages the obstacles to be overcome were formidable. Given the religious attitudes of the time, it was a hazardous undertaking for a Christian scholar to take Hebrew instruction from a rabbi, or even from a convert from Judaism. To learn Arabic, many westerners actually travelled to a Muslim country, which was if anything an even more dangerous undertaking than consorting with a Jewish scholar. But it is easy for us nowadays to forget that the main purpose behind the study of these languages in the West was to gain converts for Christianity and to propagandize against Judaism and Islam; the linguistic benefits, though real, were incidental.

Returning now to the history of grammar, the main point to be borne in mind is that since the study of the so-called humanities developed in northern Italy it was quite naturally the grammatical framework current in that area which furnished the starting point for the Renaissance humanists. Not surprisingly, modistic grammar, which had flourished above all in Germany and France, tended to be viewed with disdain by the early humanist grammarians. This negative attitude may also have been a consequence of the fact that most humanists were educators, not academic philosophers. Modistic grammar, one should recall, had been associated with a particular philosophical milieu, namely the followers of Duns Scotus. In circles where a different philosophical orientation prevailed it tended to be neglected or viewed with suspicion. Thus, the followers of William Ockham in the fourteenth century argued against the view that modes of meaning should be recognized (see Pinborg 1967: 215–304). The hostility to the treatises on the modes of meaning was already widespread by the time the humanists came to the fore, and it is possible that some of them were aware of the philosophical literature directed against modistic grammar.

The continuity between medieval and humanistic grammar is striking if one compares any of the Latin grammars popular in Italy about 1400 with, say, the *Regulae grammaticales* of Guarino Veronese, which may be regarded as the archetypical humanistic grammar. To begin with, there is the same assemblage of rather short treatises on a wide variety of topics. Such works presupposed a knowledge of the rudiments of the language, obtainable from an introductory manual such as the *Ars minor* of Donatus.

Indeed the terminology utilized to refer to sentence constituents underwent surprisingly little change. Thus, the basic terms we encounter in, say, Guarino's *Regulae grammaticales* are virtually the same ones used in the grammars popular in the immediately preceding period. Thus, in an active sentence such as *ego amo Petrum* 'I love Peter', Guarino calls *ego* the agent (*persona agens*) and *Petrum* the patient (*persona patiens*). Accordingly, he has the verb *amo* govern a nominative agent on the left (*ante se*) and an accusative patient on the right (*post se*). In a passive sentence such as *ego amor a Petro* 'I am loved by Peter', the verb *amor* 'am loved' is said to govern a nominative patient on the left and an agent in the ablative case (preceded by the preposition *a*) on the right. In the grammar of Francesco da Buti (1324–1406), the only notable difference is that the agent and patient are termed *res agens* and *res patiens* (see Sabbadini 1902; 1906: 114–15).

Another noticeable feature of Guarino's grammar is the absence of any terminology to refer to sentence parts like the terms *subject* and *predicate*, which logicians had used since antiquity. For this purpose, medieval grammarians had created the pair of terms *suppositum* and *appositum*, the former being defined as all words to the left of the main verb except for verbal modifiers. Thus, Petrus de Insulellis in the mid-thirteenth century offers the following definitions: 'Suppositum est quicquid praecedit principale verbum vel intelligitur praecedere, nisi sit ibi adverbium vel adverbialis determinatio quaelibet quod determinet ipsum verbum, ut *Socrates bene legit* – *Socrates* est suppositum, *bene legit* est appositum' (Fierville 1886: 57).

In the fourteenth century, many Italian grammarians of Latin redefine the term *appositum* to mean the predicate minus the verb, in other words, the verbal complement. This is true, for instance, of the grammars of Giovanni da Soncino and Folchino dei Borfoni. This slight terminological adjustment appears to have continued to be influential since it is found here and there in the humanistic grammars of the fifteenth century. But another trend begins to make itself felt, namely the complete avoidance of the terms *suppositum* and *appositum*. In the grammar of Francesco da Buti, which must be regarded as unaffected by humanism, the term *appositum* is absent, and in most of the rules dealing with verbal government no use is made of the subject concept either. However, the word *suppositum* makes an occasional appearance in some of the general rules.

When we come to Guarino's *Regulae grammaticales*, we again note the extensive use of the notions agent and patient and a very occasional appearance of the term *suppositum*. But it is clear that the tripartite analysis of sentences into the subject, verb, and object was still considered the standard one in the fifteenth century. Thus, in one of his textbooks the Siennese rhetorician Agostino Dati states unequivocally that according to grammarians a complete sentence consists of three parts, subject, verb, and predicate *in that order*, but that writers who aim at stylistic adornment rearrange these parts in the order object, subject, verb.[7]

What characterizes much of the grammatical discussion after Lorenzo Valla is an increasing dissatisfaction with traditional terms. This becomes especially marked by the middle of the sixteenth century in a work such as the *De causis linguae Latinae* by Julius Caesar Scaliger, which contains an at times vitriolic critique of all the inherited grammatical terminology. Later in the sixteenth century Franciscus Sanctius Brocensis even polemicized against the technical term *persona* on the grounds that it is verbs not nouns which exhibit person, but it is curious to note that in the same passage Sanctius advocates the continued use of the (medieval) terms *suppositum* and *appositum* in the sense 'subject' and 'object': 'Cum enim dicimus "Petrus videt parietem", *Petrus* aut *paries* non sunt personae, sed *videt* est persona, id est facies, cuius suppositum est *Petrus*, appositum *paries*' (1587: D4r–v). This blend of the old and the new is not uncommon in Renaissance grammars of Latin.

On the impact of the study of exotic languages on linguistic thought in the sixteenth century we are so far poorly informed. The missionaries who worked on the American Indian languages of Mexico and the Andean highlands produced their grammars for local consumption. Most of them, therefore, were printed in the New World and were probably not widely available in Europe, but one or two works of this kind did appear in Europe; for instance, the Quechua grammar by Domingo de Santo Tomás, which was published in Valladolid (see Porras Barrenechea 1951). However, the production of these grammars was by no means a haphazard affair: the Church organized centres for the training of clerics in the study of the indigenous languages, and many of the grammatical treatments which resulted are remarkable for their comprehensive coverage of the facts. In his *Mithridates* (1555), Conrad Gesner relays a story to the effect that when ten natives of the island of Hispaniola were brought back to Spain it was discovered that their language could be written down in Latin script without difficulty.[8] It would seem, then, that Gesner agreed with his mentor Theodor Bibliander in the belief that no human language existed which could not be reduced to writing and described grammatically.[9]

This new insight may in large measure be attributed to the newly instituted study of Hebrew. What Christian scholars like Bibliander discovered was that Hebrew had already received detailed treatment by Jewish grammarians. To a great extent, therefore, all that the Europeans needed to do was to transmit this indigenous grammatical doctrine to their readers. Moreover, Semitic grammatical theory differed markedly from anything the scholars of western Europe had been familiar with hitherto. The two novel features of, for instance, the Hebrew grammar of Johannes Reuchlin (1506) were the classification of speech sounds by point of articulation and the analysis of words into roots and affixes, both of these being analytic devices which had long been current in the Hebrew grammatical tradition. Bibliander then went so far as to recommend that all languages be described grammatically in the Hebrew fashion and suggested that the resulting grammars, being in conformity with nature, could then be meaningfully compared (1548: 4, 169).

The study of Hebrew had another effect on the general study of language in the sixteenth century and that was to stimulate an interest in the notion of genetic relationship. The indigenous Semitic grammarians had long been convinced that Hebrew, Aramaic, and Arabic were related, and once again all the Western scholars did was to pick up this idea and develop it in their own way. The belief that all languages were derived from a single primordial language became entrenched in the sixteenth century, and what more obvious conclusion could one draw from this assumption than the notion that Hebrew had been the first language of mankind? This conception also harmonized well with etymology as practised in the West, which envisaged the bulk of the vocabulary of any language as generated from phonetic distortions and portmanteau combinations based on a core of primeval onomatopoetic words. Moreover, the notion of a kind of familial relationship among languages was a natural inference from the story of the descent of the whole of postdiluvian mankind from the sons of Noah. Thus, as George Metcalf has demonstrated (see his 1974), the germ of the modern idea of genetic relationship was already present in the sixteenth century. Even Goropius Becanus, whose fanciful suggestion that Adam spoke Dutch in the Garden of Eden earned him nothing but obloquy, had the notion that all the modern European languages were descended from a language spoken in Scythia, that is southern Russia (see Metcalf 1974: 239).

Traditional etymology was further strengthened in the sixteenth century when scholars were for the first time exposed to Plato's *Cratylus*. The interpretation placed on that dialogue was, however, bizarre in that it was taken for granted that the naturalistic views which Plato ascribes to the character Cratylus coincided with Plato's own point of view. Traditional etymology (of the kind we see represented, for example, in Isidore of Seville's *Etymologiae*), was of course ultimately based on Stoic linguistic speculation, which in this regard resembled the ideas which Plato puts into Cratylus's mouth in the dialogue of that name. Thus, the assimilation of the *Cratylus* did no more than reinforce an approach which had stymied etymology for over two thousand years.[10]

Furthermore, the same dialogue was used as evidence for the belief that Plato and Aristotle represent diametrically opposed theories regarding the relation between words and their referents. Aristotle's viewpoint was supposedly contained in the opening sentence of the second chapter of the *De interpretatione*, in which the noun is defined as a piece of sound signifying arbitrarily – *vox significativa secundum placitum* in Boethius's translation (see Engels 1963, Minio-Paluello 1965: 6). This was thought to place Aristotle in the same camp as the character Hermogenes in the *Cratylus*, who argues that words signify by agreement. An avowed Aristotelian like Julius Caesar Scaliger, for example, feels called upon to contrast the two points of view and side with Aristotle (1540: 117). The 'Platonic' position, on the other hand, was defended by Sanctius, who makes a strenuous effort to reconcile Aristotle's statements with Plato's (1587: A5^v). Thus, the main result of the discovery of the *Cratylus* was to rekindle the ancient debate concerning nature and convention.

The development of national vernacular grammatical traditions, finally, was a clear step away from the previous linguistic hegemony of Latin. However, we must be careful to guard against the temptation to impose a Whiggish interpretation on this event. It can hardly be claimed that for the majority of Italians the artificial Italian literary language which was imposed on the peninsula by scholars in the sixteenth and subsequent centuries was a vernacular in the true sense of the term. Indeed, the virulence of the scholarly debate which took place in Italy concerning the choice of an appropriate literary vernacular clearly indicates the contrived nature of the eventual solution (see Migliorini 1949). In countries with a centralized government (Spain and France, for instance), there was no need for such a debate, but it cannot be said that literary French was any more natural to the bulk of the citizens of France than literary Italian was to the majority of Italians. Not surprisingly, a great deal of the effort of vernacular grammarians in all countries was directed towards standardization. Such topics as spelling reform, therefore, occupied a prominent place in the discussions of grammarians. In Spain, for instance, the orthographic debate was initiated by Nebrija himself, who had also distinguished himself in the area of Latin orthography (see his 1503) and carried over many of the arguments he had used in that context.[11]

In conclusion, there are undoubted benefits to be gained from constantly relating developments in the study of language to the background sociocultural situation of the period in question, as I have tried to do here. However, I do not believe that many historians of ideas would go so far as to claim that these connections tell the whole story, for to do so would come dangerously close to reducing intellectual history to a purely epiphenomenal status. If the study of the history of grammar reveals anything at all it is that a disciplinary tradition can acquire enough autonomy to insulate it *to some degree* from societal changes. When shifts *do* occur in the way the discipline is conducted they tend to take place slowly and to lag behind the changes occurring in society as a whole. Moreover, yet another factor complicates the picture, namely the degree to which the study of language in the premodern period was spread over three disciplines: grammar, rhetoric, and logic.[12] For a more revealing account of the history of linguistics, at least prior to the dissolution of the trivium, we need to take this third interdisciplinary dimension into consideration. Having granted this, however, who would hazard the assertion that precisely these dimensions jointly exhaust all the possible perspectives on the history of linguistics? Robins has urged us to regard our aims with as much modesty as possible (1979: 7), and as Hegel once expressed it so trenchantly, 'the battle of reason consists in overcoming what the understanding has made rigid'.[13]

NOTES

1 For a discussion of the general problem of the Renaissance, see Ferguson 1948. In addition to the wider issue of the Renaissance, there are also questions relating to the constellation of modern philosophical concepts referred to loosely by the word *humanism*. It is not clear, first of all, whether humanism in any of its many present-day senses can be said to have existed during the Renaissance. To what extent Renaissance humanists represented a unified *philosophical* position is likewise a moot point. As a general rule, historians of philosophy tend to defend the notion that Renaissance humanism marked a philosophical break with scholasticism; see, for example, Apel 1963, Garin 1961, Grassi 1983. On the other hand, the approach of Paul Oskar Kristeller, which has been especially influential among philologists, emphasizes the literary and pedagogical aspects of Renaissance humanism; see, in particular, Kristeller 1979: 85–105. In my view, three main types of modern humanism can be distinguished: an atheistic movement in the United States which has roots in rationalism, a strand in philosophy beginning in the nineteenth century which was mainly concerned with the notion of human emancipation (Feuerbach, Marx, the twentieth-century Existentialists *et al.*), and a brand of aestheticized philology seeing its model in the culture of the Periclean age which has been practised chiefly in twentieth-century Germany by scholars influenced by Werner Jaeger (see Oppermann 1970 for a useful anthology).

2 'Priscianum quidem solem grammaticae, sed aliquando passum esse eclipsim' (Valla 1543: 799[r]).

3 '. . . ita ut Prisciani regulis amplius non indigeamus' (Perger 1501: D3[r]).

4 On early humanism, see Weiss 1947.

5 On Guarino's grammatical writings, see Sabbadini 1902 and 1906; Percival 1972 and 1978.

6 For a discussion of the issue as to whether Renaissance grammarians of Latin consciously opposed medieval grammatical doctrine, see my 1976 article.

7 'Scis plenam orationem tribus constare partibus, quas suppositum (ut ipsorum vocabulis utar), verbum, et appositum vocant. Dicunt igitur grammatici *Scipio Africanus delevit Carthaginem*. Ornatioris vero eloquii homines converso potius utuntur ordine: *Carthaginem Scipio Africanus delevit*' (Dati 1497: 2A2[v]–2A3[r]).

8 'Colonus decem viros ex Hispaniola secum in Hispaniam adduxit, a quibus posse omnium illarum insularum linguam nostris litteris Latinis sine ullo discrimine scribi compertum est' (Gesner 1555: K1[r]).

9 Bibliander's main thesis is clearly though rather circuitously stated at the beginning of his book: 'Proposui hoc commentario scribere methodum et

rationem qua non modo litteratae illae et a praeclaris ingeniis excultae linguae verum etiam rudes et barbarae linguae omnium nationum comprehendi possint totae et apto quidem ordine nec non rectius explicari et percipi facilius et accommodari melius ad omnem usum scribendi et dicendi, qua denique ratione linguae omnes perspici et iudicari exactius queant et conferri mutuum vel totae vel in qualibet parte' (Bibliander 1548: 1).

10 The complete dialogues of Plato did not become widely available in the West until the edition and Latin translation by Marsilio Ficino, which first appeared in Florence in the 1480s. A crucial role in the interpretation of the *Cratylus* was played by Ficino's introduction to that dialogue, which continued to be reprinted in editions of Plato's works until the early nineteenth century. Subsequent scholarship has amply demonstrated that Cratylus's opinions cannot be equated with Plato's philosophy of language.

11 See Percival 1982 for a discussion of Nebrija's contribution to Latin, Greek, and Hebrew orthography.

12 I have examined the relation between rhetoric and grammar in my 1983 article. Clearly, much remains to be done towards integrating our knowledge of the histories of the separate liberal arts in the late Middle Ages and early Renaissance. Concerning logic in fifteenth-century Italy, for instance, much valuable work has recently been done on Valla's *Dialecticae disputationes*; see Vasoli 1957–8; Jardine 1982: 798–9.

13 'Der Kampf der Vernunft besteht darin, dasjenige, was der Verstand fixirt hat, zu überwinden' (Hegel, *Wissenschaft der Logik*, 3rd ed. [1830], paragraph 32, Zusatz).

REFERENCES

Apel, Karl Otto. 1963. *Die Idee der Sprache in der Tradition des Humanismus von Dante bis Vico*. (Archiv für Begriffsgeschichte, 8.) Bonn: H. Bouvier.

Bibliander, Theodor. 1548. *De ratione communi omnium linguarum et literarum commentarius*. Zürich: Christopher Froschauer.

Bischoff, Bernhard. 1967. The study of foreign languages in the Middle Ages. In Bernhard Bischoff, *Mittelalterliche Studien: Ausgewählte Aufsätze zur Schriftkunde und Literaturgeschichte*, vol. II, 227–45. Stuttgart: Anton Hiersemann.

Buck, August. 1952. *Italienische Dichtungslehren vom Mittelalter bis zum Ausgang der Renaissance*. (Beihefte zur Zeitschrift für romanische Philologie, 94.) Tübingen: Max Niemeyer.

Dati, Agostino. 1497. *Artis dicendi et scribendi preceptorium utilissimum*. Leipzig.

Engels, J. 1963. Origine, sens et survie du terme boécien 'secundum placitum'. *Vivarium* 1: 87–114.

Ferguson, Wallace K. 1948. *The Renaissance in historical thought: Five centuries of interpretation*. Boston: Houghton Mifflin.

Fierville, Charles. 1886. *Une grammaire inédite du XIIIe siècle*. Paris: Imprimerie Nationale.

Fisher, John H. 1977. Chancery and the emergence of standard written English in the fifteenth century. *Speculum* 52: 870–99.

Garin, Eugenio. 1961. *La cultura filosofica del Rinascimento italiano: Ricerche e documenti*. Florence: G.C. Sansoni.

Gesner, Conrad. 1555. *Mithridates: De differentiis linguarum tum veterum tum quae hodie apud diversas nationes in toto orbe terrarum in usu sunt . . . Tigurini observationes*. Zürich: Froschauer.

Grassi, Ernesto. 1983. *Heidegger and the question of Renaissance humanism*. (Medieval and Renaissance Texts and Studies, 24.) Binghamton, New York: Center for Medieval and Early Renaissance Studies.

Jardine, Lisa. 1982. Humanism and the teaching of logic. In Norman Kretzmann, Anthony Kenny, & Jan Pinborg (eds.) *The Cambridge history of later medieval philosophy: From the rediscovery of Aristotle to the disintegration of scholasticism, 1100–1600*, 797–807. Cambridge: Cambridge University Press.

Kristeller, Paul Oskar. 1979. *Renaissance thought and its sources*, ed. Michael Mooney. New York: Columbia University Press.

Lambley, Kathleen. 1920. *The teaching and cultivation of the French language in England during Tudor and Stuart times, with an introductory chapter on the preceding period*. Manchester: The University Press.

Marshall, J.H. 1969. *The 'Donatz Proensals' of Uc Faidit*. London: Oxford University Press.

Metcalf, George J. 1974. The Indo-European hypothesis in the sixteenth and seventeenth centuries. In Dell Hymes (ed.) *Studies in the history of linguistics: Traditions and paradigms*, 233–57. (Indiana University Studies in the History and Theory of Linguistics.) Bloomington & London: Indiana University Press.

Migliorini, Bruno. 1949. La questione della lingua. In U. Bosco *et al.* (eds.) *Questioni e correnti di storia letteraria*, 1–75. (Problemi ed orientamenti critici di lingua e di letteratura italiana, 3.) Milan: Carlo Marzorati.

Minio-Paluello, L. (ed.) 1965. *Aristoteles Latinus* II, 1–2: *De interpretatione vel Periermenias. Translatio Boethii, Specimina translationum recentiorum*. Bruges & Paris: Desclée de Brouwer.

Nebrija, Antonio de. 1503. *De vi ac potestate litterarum deque illarum falsa prolatione*. Salamanca.

Novati, Francesco. (ed.) 1905. *Epistolario di Coluccio Salutati*, 4. (Fonti per la storia d'Italia pubb. dall'Istituto storico italiano. Epistolari, secolo XIV–XV, 18.) Rome: Forzani e C. Tipografi del Senato.

Oppermann, Hans. (ed.) 1970. *Humanismus*. (Wege der Forschung, 17.) Darmstadt: Wissenschaftliche Buchgesellschaft.

Percival, W. Keith. 1972. The historical sources of Guarino's Regulae grammaticales: A reconsideration of Sabbadini's evidence. In *Civiltà dell'Umanesimo: Atti del VI, VII, VIII convegno del Centro di studi umanistici 'Angelo Poliziano'*, 263–84. Florence: Leo S. Olschki.

———. 1976. Renaissance grammar: Rebellion or evolution? In *Interrogativi dell'Umanesimo*, ed. Giovanangiola Secchi Tarugi, 73–89. Florence: Leo S. Olschki.

———. 1978. Textual problems in the Latin grammar of Guarino Veronese. *Res Publica Litterarum* 1: 241–54.

———. 1982. Antonio de Nebrija and the dawn of modern phonetics. *Res Publica Litterarum* 5: 221–32.

———. 1983. Grammar and rhetoric in the Renaissance: *Renaissance eloquence*. In James J.

Murphy (ed.) *Studies in the theory and practice of Renaissance rhetoric*, 303–30. Berkeley: University of California Press.

Perger, Bernard. 1501. *Grammatica nova*. Strasburg: Martin Flach Jr.

Pinborg, Jan. 1967. *Die Entwicklung der Sprachtheorie im Mittelalter*. (Beiträge zur Geschichte der Philosophie und Theologie des Mittelalters, 42: 2.) Münster: Aschendorffsche Verlagsbuchhandlung & Copenhagen: Arne Frost-Hansen.

Porras Barrenechea, Raúl. (ed.) 1951. *Grammatica o arte de la lengua general de los Indios de los reynos del Perú por el maestro Fray Domingo de Santo Tomás*. (Universidad Nacional Mayor de San Marcos, Publicaciones del cuarto centenario.) Lima: Edición del Instituto de historia.

Reuchlin, Johannes. 1506. *De rudimentis Hebraicis libri tres*. Pforzheim: Thomas Anselm.

Robins, R.H. 1979. *A short history of linguistics*. 2nd edn. (Longman Linguistics Library, 6.) London & New York: Longman.

Sabbadini, Remigio. 1902. Dei metodi nell'insegnamento della sintassi latina (considerazioni didattiche e storiche). *Rivista di filologia* 30: 304–14.

—— 1906. Elementi nazionali nella teoria grammaticale dei Romani. *Studi italiani di filologia classica* 14: 113–25.

Sanctius Brocensis, Franciscus. 1587. *Minerva: seu de causis linguae Latinae*. Salamanca: Ioannes & Andreas Renaut fratres.

Scaliger, Julius Caesar. 1540. *De causis linguae Latinae libri tredecim*. Lyons: Seb. Gryphius.

Ullman, Berthold L. 1955. Petrarch's favourite books. In *Studies in the Italian Renaissance*, 117–37. (Storia e letteratura, 51.) Rome: Edizioni di Storia e letteratura.

Valla, Lorenzo. 1543. *Opera*. Basle: Henricus Petrus.

Vasoli, C. 1957–8. Le 'Dialecticae disputationes' del Valla e la critica umanistica della logica aristotelica. *Rivista critica di storia della filosofia* 12: 412–34, 13: 27–46.

Weiss, Roberto. 1947. *The dawn of humanism in Italy: An inaugural lecture*. London: H.K. Lewis.

6

EFFORT AND ACHIEVEMENT IN SEVENTEENTH- CENTURY BRITISH LINGUISTICS

VIVIAN SALMON

The reputation of seventeenth-century linguistics is based mainly on a few outstanding achievements, such as the grammars of Wallis and the gentlemen of Port Royal; and admirable surveys of these and other distinguished writings have recently been provided by H.E. Brekle and R.H. Robins. The former intentionally restricts his survey to 'grammar and the theory of language . . . questions of general linguistics and some adjacent areas, like, e.g., language philosophy and semiotics' (1975: 277). R.H. Robins's chapter on 'The Renaissance and after' ranges further afield, and includes accounts of Arabic and Far Eastern linguistics. But as he notes, 'One gets the impression of numbers of scholars in England and on the continent working . . . on various aspects of language improvement' (1979: 113), and these cohorts of schoolmasters, village curates, missionaries, teachers of foreign languages, of shorthand, of the deaf and dumb, with a smaller number of enterprising academics, are far too numerous for most to be afforded more than a footnote in his account.

Nevertheless, on their patient and devoted efforts the achievements of the great pioneers were founded, and this chapter is intended as a tribute to their work – one which will deliberately avoid more than brief reference to the monuments of seventeenth-century linguistic scholarship which have already been fully described. For reasons of space, this account will be restricted mainly to British enterprises, though the first part, devoted to comparative and historical linguistics, will of necessity refer to scholars in other Germanic fields whose interests are closely associated with those of their British counterparts (cf. Bonfante 1953; Metcalf 1974; and Droixhe 1978).

Unlike the era described as 'the Renaissance', the period known as 'the seventeenth century' needs no definition; but to regard the turn of the sixteenth and seventeenth centuries as the beginning of a new age does perhaps need some justification. It may be provided by pointing to the impressive number of innovatory texts which appeared at about that time, some of which exerted a major influence throughout the century. First in chronological order is the publication of the earliest book of instruction suitable for adults on how to read and spell the vernacular. This was Coote's *English schoole-maister*; the first edition appeared in 1596 and the last – the fifty-fourth – in 1737. Only the Bible can have been as well known to the British household, and Coote must have made one of the most important contributions to the notable development of literacy which occurred in the period. Next is John Willis's *The art of stenographie* (1602), the first shorthand to be based on a largely phonetic method; this appeared in fourteen editions up to 1648, when it was superseded by improved versions by other inventors. As foreign visitors noted, shorthand played an important part in British society, whether in church, the law courts, or the theatre; and it is clear from their writings that it evoked a good deal of linguistic awareness in its creators (Lodwick 1972: 61–2). Next is the first English–English dictionary (as an independent work), Robert Cawdrey's *A table alphabeticall* (1604), which was designed to assist the newly literate in understanding the use of Latinate vocabulary. Fourthly, although the relevant text did not appear for a decade, we may include here the work of the Anglo-Irish Jesuit William Bathe, who, having left his native land, was at work in Salamanca on a Latin-teaching course to be published in 1611 as the *Ianua linguarum*, destined to appear in thirty different reprints and editions by the end of the century, and in many different vernaculars (O'Mahony 1981). Finally among contributions to applied linguistics were the efforts of his Puritan rival, John Brinsley, simultaneously engaged in teaching Latin to the children of a country parish by the methods which he set out in his *Ludus literarius* (1612), the first in a series of texts which constituted the earliest comprehensive language-teaching course of modern times (Salmon 1979: 33–46).

In a more academic field, the linguistic views of Francis Bacon cannot be altogether overlooked, although they have been treated fully elsewhere (e.g. Brekle 1975: 281–7). *The advancement of learning* appeared only five years into the century, and exerted the most profound influence, not only on the development of observational methods in scientific enquiry, but also on attitudes to natural language and the creation of a demand for a new, scientific language which would be both universally comprehensible and completely unambiguous. Less well known to linguists are two other works of theoretical interest, by pioneers in historical linguistics. The first was by William Camden, whose *Remaines* (1605) included an account of the origin and history of the languages of Britain together with examples of the Lord's Prayer at various stages from Old English onwards, showing 'how powerable time is in altering tongues' (1605: 15); the other was by the Anglo-Dutch Richard Verstegan (or Rowlands) whose *Restitution of decayed intelligence* (1605) discussed 'the great Antiquitie of our ancient English toung' (sig. †††.4v.) and included an attempt at an etymological dictionary of 'Saxon' names.

Both Camden and Verstegan also examined a topic which, however unsatisfactory their results, should not be left out of this account since, as Wilkins remarked, 'there is scarce any subject that hath been more thoroughly scanned and debated amongst Learned men, than the *Original* of *Languages* and *Letters*' (1668: 2); and it has more recently been argued that the 'establishment of the basic languages and their sub-branches is one of the essential occupations of seventeenth-century philologists' (Allen 1949: 9). The topics chiefly engaging their attention were:

(1) The origin, identity and character of the original language, and the possibility that it had survived, in part or as a whole, somewhere in the world.
(2) The provenance and kinship of the European languages.
(3) The relationship of European and Oriental languages.
(4) Criteria for determining linguistic relationships.
(5) The discovery of Gothic.
(6) The origin and history of English.

Camden and Verstegan were largely instrumental in determining the direction which philological enquiries were to take in seventeenth-century England; as Jones (1951: 270) remarks, 'the Saxon craze . . . began with these two books'. It was also, no doubt, stimulated by the first translation into English of Tacitus's *Germania* (by Greneway, 1598). Even more important was the work of a logician and astronomer, Edward Brerewood (1614), who examined the spread and decline of Greek and Latin, the rise of the Romance languages, and the nature of some Slavonic and Oriental tongues (cf. Trentman 1976). The influence of these three men may be judged by the frequency with which their works were reprinted; Camden's *Remaines* appeared in seven impressions and Brerewood's in five before 1674, and Verstegan's in six by 1673; while Brerewood's was translated into French in 1640, with three further impressions by 1667, and into Latin in 1659 and 1679. Another contribution to comparative philology was published in 1639, but – perhaps because it was in Latin – was not as popular. This was Thomas Hayne's *Linguarum Cognatio*, which, as well as discussing some theoretical aspects of sound change (Droixhe 1978: 71), also contributed to the development of interest in universal language (Salmon 1979: 141, 155). Most of the topics discussed in the later half of the seventeenth century are adumbrated in the publications of these four scholars, and summarized by Wilkins in Chapters I to III of his *Essay* (1668).

The first topic noted above – the identity of the original language – was already a subject of controversy in the sixteenth century, particularly following Becanus's suggestion (1569) that it was Dutch (cf. Katz 1981 and 1982: 43–88). The Bible was surprisingly unhelpful in the matter, the only reference being to 'the language of Canaan' (cf. Brerewood 1614: 55) which was spoken by Abraham (Isaiah 19:18); but it was generally agreed that it was likely to have been one of the 'sacred languages', that is, one of those in which the inscription on the Cross was written (Gill 1972: II, 190). Of these three, Hebrew, Greek and Latin, it was Hebrew which was favoured; as Butler (1633: sig.*2r.) remarked, 'The Hebrew . . . [is] the language of our great Grandfather Adam, which, untill the Confusion, all people of the earth did speake'. On the origin of Hebrew, there were two views; in the earlier seventeenth century, trust was more often placed in the account of Genesis (2: 19–20) which recorded that God paraded all creatures before Adam so that he might name them, and he, 'by seeing into the nature of every creature, could see their names' (Richardson 1657: 13); later, scholars like Wilkins (1668: 2) argued that the original language was 'con-created' with Adam and Eve, who immediately understood 'the voice of God speaking to them in the Garden' of Eden. Whatever the original language, it was generally accepted that it was spoken until Babel, when seventy-two new tongues arose from the 'confusion' (Weigand 1942). But Genesis 10:5 posed another problem. This verse relates how the sons of Noah – S(h)em, Ham and Japhet – divided the 'Isles of the Gentiles' – 'every one after his tongue'. S(h)em, who has given his name to the Semitic languages, and who was the ancestor of Heber, travelled with his family eastwards; Ham, after whom the Hamitic languages are named, moved into Africa; and Japhet, after whom the European languages have sometimes been called 'Japhetic', moved west towards Europe. (This account is given in, inter alia, Verstegan 1605: 7–8.) The Old Testament therefore suggests that the sons of Noah dispersed after the Flood, and this reading enabled some scholars to postulate that the original language had survived somewhere on earth. John Webb (1669) proposed that it was to be found in China, one reason being that Chinese was thought to consist only of monosyllabic words. Such a lexicon, as Camden had remarked long before (1605: 21), was 'most fit for expressing briefly the first conceipts of the minde, or Intentionalia', and therefore most appropriate for the original, 'natural', language. Belief in the monogenesis of language was, however, called into question when missionaries and merchants discovered so many exotic languages in the course of the century, and the idea of polygenesis was strengthened by the publication of Isaac de la Peyrère's Men before Adam (1656) which argued that non-European languages arose from a second Creation (Lodwick 1972: 83).

The second major topic of discussion was that of the provenance and kinship of the European languages. Of their provenance, the seventeenth century came to believe that they originated in Asia Minor or north of the Black Sea. The Cimmeri, a tribe mentioned by Homer, and historically living near the sea of Azov, were suggested as one source, unfortunately becoming confused by seventeenth-century scholars with the Cimbri, the Germanic tribe living in the Cimbric peninsula (Jutland); they in turn became confused with the Celts solely on the grounds of the similarity of their names in the vernacular (cf. *Gazophylacium Anglicanum*, 1689: sig.cc2r.). Indeed, a pioneering commentator on Tacitus's *Germania*, Philip Clüver (1616), concluded that the Germani were Celts. Another possible origin was found in a nomadic tribe, the Scythians, recorded by Herodotus. Moving west from the Eurasian steppes, they eventually arrived in Hungary, where they were absorbed into another lost tribe, the Sarmatians. The Scythian hypothesis too was liable to confusion, because of the similarity of the name to that of the Scots; at least one distinguished linguist, John Wallis, argued (1972: 105) that the Scots were descended from the Scythians. The idea was treated with respect by various other English scholars, including John Wilkins, who cites Boxhorn's opinion (1668: 4) that Scythian was the common ancestor of Greek, Latin, German and Persian. The common origin of the European languages was, however, disputed by J.J. Scaliger (1610) who argued that there were eleven 'matrix' languages in Europe, unrelated to one another. The four major ones, Latin, Greek, German and Slavonic, were each associated with several 'daughter' languages, assigned to a matrix group, in part, by the name for 'God' in each. There were also seven 'minor' matrix languages. Brerewood, while accepting these eleven groups, added four of his own; these were Arabic, which was still spoken in Spain until the seventeenth century; a dialect, 'Illyrian', spoken on the island of Veggia in what was formerly Dalmatia; another spoken in Hungary by the descendants of the Sarmatian people; and 'Cauchian' in East Frisia (1614: 21). Brerewood was an intelligent and original scholar, and in addition to these unusual observations he also postulated theories of linguistic change which would now be known as the 'substratum' and 'superstratum' theories (Rea 1976: 259). Many other English scholars discussed the origin of European languages, for example, James Howell the grammarian who, writing in 1630 to a friend, gave a brief account of 'the original Mother-Tongues of the Countries of *Europe*' (1890: 459–78). By the end of the century, a Swede, Andreas Jäger, was able to propose a theory of the origin and kinship of European languages which in many respects would be quite acceptable today (Metcalf 1974: 233).

Wilkins's reference to 'Persian' as a daughter language of Scythian is not as surprising as it might appear; its possible relationship to European vernaculars had been noted by the learned printer François Raphelengius, who communicated his discovery to the Flemish scholar Bonaventura de Smet; he included it in a volume he edited in 1597 in which were discussed (*inter alia*) relationships between Gothic, Old High German, Old English and Persian. In spite of Scaliger's hesitation and doubts expressed by

Verstegan (1605: 27–8), the evidence from cognates proved persuasive; and it was reinforced in the publications of English scholars like John Greaves, whose Persian grammar appeared in 1649, Thomas Hyde, who edited a Persian manuscript of the Old Testament for Brian Walton's *Polyglot Bible* (1657–69) and Edward Bernard (1689) who also noticed the probable kinship of Russian in the glossary he added to Hickes's Old English *Grammar*. Unfortunately, the learned merchant Filippo Sassetti, who noticed the relationship between Sanskrit and Italian when he was living in Goa (1583–8), put his ideas on record only in private letters to two friends, so that they remained otherwise unknown until the nineteenth century.

In determining criteria for discovering linguistic relationships, seventeenth-century scholars were seriously hampered by fundamental difficulties such as their ignorance of whether a given language was a parent or a descendant of another; for example, some scholars held that Latin was a 'daughter' language of German; and so little were language groupings understood, that James Howell was able to propose the not untypical thesis that the 'pedigree' of English is to be derived 'of the *Saxon*, the *Saxon* of the *Dutch*, the *Dutch* of the *Slavonick*, the *Slavonick* of the *Persian*, the *Persian* of the *Caldaic*, and the *Caldaic* of the *Hebrew*' (1660: sig. *2v.). When printing made exotic languages and alphabets easily available, linguists began to draw up lists of postulated cognates, some fantastic but some (in the case of known European languages) as accurate as those proposed by Gill (1972: II, 85). What was more difficult was to discover any regularity in relationships. One suggestion was that sounds changed in accordance with certain figures of rhetoric, for example prosthesis, apharaesis, epenthesis and syncope (Minsheu 1617: sig.A3r). By mid-century, this view was under attack, as de Laet commented: 'If you are willing to change letters, to transpose syllables, to add and subtract, you will nowhere find something that cannot be forced into this or that similarity' (Metcalf 1974: 247). Skinner (1671: sig.D3r.) cautiously retains the classification of sound change with reference to the rhetorical figures, but he also specifies the actual correspondences possible: 'Cognatae maximè sunt B & V consona, B & F, F & V consona, V consona & W, D & T' etc., since by 1671 such correspondences were well known. Henry Rose, however, following his French source (Besnier 1674), is more perceptive: 'all the astonishing and surprizing depravations and Corruptions that are met withall in the words that one Language borrows from another . . . have their basis in nature . . . Vowels . . . admitt of easie changes among themselves . . . [but not] Consonants, where we must not admitt indifferently all sorts of changes; the sole affinity of the Organs is that which must regulate almost all their varieties: the Labiall letters easily supplant one another but the Dentall or Linguall with more difficulty succeed them' (1675: 46–8).

For scholars speaking Germanic vernaculars, one of the most interesting topics of discussion in the second half of the century was the publication of a Gothic text. The Codex Argenteus was found in 1563 at the Abbey of Werden, in Westphalia, and the news of the discovery was passed on to Gesner, author of a treatise on languages, *Mithridates* (1555), and to Becanus. The latter included the first piece of Gothic to appear in print in his *Origines Antwerpianae* (1569), and Gothic was one of the languages discussed by de Smet (1597). The existence, although not the location, of the Codex was known to Brerewood (1614: 191); it found its way to Queen Christina's library in Stockholm as a result of the Thirty Years' War, and was removed from there by her librarian, Isaac Vossius, following a dispute with his employer. Vossius was a kinsman of the Dutch scholar Franciscus Junius, who had lived in England for some thirty years as librarian to Sir Thomas Howard. Having returned temporarily to Amsterdam, he took up the study of Gothic in 1654 and, deriving great benefit from William Somner's pioneering Old English *Dictionarium* of 1659, produced first a glossary of Gothic (1664) and then an edition of Ulfilas's Bible, both being published as a single volume in 1665. The availability of a Gothic text created enormous scholarly interest; it was used in England by Skinner (1671) and Hickes (1689); in Sweden by Stiernhjelm (1671), and in Germany by Kirchmaier (1693).

Finally, a topic of paramount importance to English scholars was the history of their own vernacular after Japhet had moved westward with his family (cf. Jones 1953 and Metcalf 1980). Following the suggestions of Becanus (1569), Verstegan explained that Japhet's grandson Ascena (Clüver's *Ashkenaz*), with his son Gomer, had travelled to Europe where Gomer's son Tuisco had given his name to the Germans (*Tuytsch*) and to Teutonic (1605: 11). The Saxons, named after the weapons (*seaxe*) which they bore, were a branch of the German stock (1605: 21) who eventually found a new home in England. Butler (1633: sig.*2v.) was probably the first to explain clearly that English was a 'dialect' of Teutonic, the language of 'the Germans, of whom our Fathers [the Saxons, Juites, and Angles] are a part' and who have 'spred themselves and their Teutonick tongue . . . in divers dialects, which time hath caused'. Similar descriptions of the origin of Anglo-Saxon appear later in the century, for example, in the tract *On languages* by Sir Thomas Browne, who dealt at some length with what he called Saxon (1928); he also recorded the opinions of another scholar whose work has recently been highly praised (Eros 1976), Meric Casaubon, whose belief in the close relationship between English and Greek led him to suggest that 'a Dialogue might be composed in Saxon onely of such words as are derivable from the Greek' (Browne 1928: 78). Such a relationship was seen by Camden as something 'to brag of' (1605: 24), but he himself was more interested in the recorded history of the language. For this reason, and to demonstrate the inevitability of linguistic change, he printed the Lord's

Prayer as it was in Old English and at various later periods of the language (1605: 15–17). Camden's initiative in printing Old English was soon followed by lawyers and theologians such as William L'Isle (1623) who were looking for legal or doctrinal precedents in early England. A concern for Old English literature was shown by Junius's edition of the Caedmon manuscript (1655), and for Old English studies in general by the publication of the first dictionary (except for brief word-lists) of Old English, a remarkable achievement (Somner 1659: and cf. Schäfer 1982) and the first grammar of the language, by George Hickes (1689). This volume also contained a reprint of the earliest Icelandic grammar, first published by Runolf Jonsson in 1681, and a polyglot vocabulary by Edward Bernard.

English scholars were not interested solely in the language of the Germanic past; some took an active interest in the study of Oriental, Celtic and Amerindian languages as well, to a large extent for religious reasons. Protestant ministers were equally involved with the Jesuits in the cause of conversion, and were strongly supported by the English government. When the Virginia Company received its charter one of the conditions was that it should convert the natives after establishing its first settlement in 1607. A number of tentative efforts were made to learn the native languages, and to teach English in return, but the first printed account did not appear until 1643, when Roger Williams published his *Key into the language of America*. This was not a grammar, but a colloquial phrase book of Eastern Algonkian as spoken by the Narragansett Indians; the first grammar was produced by John Eliot, who settled near Boston in 1632 and, after years of study, published a description of Natick in 1666 (Miner 1974). Nearer home, Irish was studied by English Protestant clergy anxious to convert the Catholic population, both for the sake of their souls and in the hope of integrating them within an English state. The brilliant English linguist, William Bedell, who was Provost of Trinity College, Dublin, from 1627 to 1629, organized teaching in Irish for students in training for the ministry and assisted, very actively, in the translation of the Old Testament into Irish (Salmon 1986b). A different approach to conversion was adopted by John Brinsley – that of teaching the English language to potential converts. For this purpose he wrote a handbook of instruction, designed to teach 'all those of the inferiour sort, and all ruder countries and places; namely, for Ireland, Wales, Virginia . . . and for their more speedie attaining of our English tongue . . . that all may speake one and the same Language' (1622, title-page).

Other exotic languages, particularly of the Near and Far East, were also of interest to British scholars. William Bedwell, one of the translators involved in the highly professional production of the Authorised Version of the Bible in 1611 (Allen 1970), was an outstanding Arabist whose grammar was eventually published as part of a larger work (Castell 1669). In 1633 a Chair of Arabic was endowed at Cambridge, and occupied by Abraham Wheloc, who also held a lectureship in Anglo-Saxon from about 1640; the first Chair of Arabic at Oxford was established in 1636 and occupied by another distinguished Arabist, Edward Pocock. Hebrew grammars were published by William Robertson (1654) and John Davis (1656), while Chinese attracted both universal language projectors like Francis Lodwick (who owned some manuscripts in the character) and John Wilkins, to whom he lent them, in the expectation that Chinese might prove a useful model for a universal language. The expectation was defeated, as Wilkins explains in the *Essay* (Wilkins 1668: 450–1). Finally, it may be noted that a grammar of Russian (a language which particularly interested many German and Scandinavian scholars) was published in Oxford in 1696. The author was the German scholar Heinrich Ludolf, who had spent some years in England as secretary to the Danish envoy, while at the same time cementing many academic friendships; it was an Oxford scholar, Edward Bernard, who arranged for the printing of his grammar, pointing out to the Oxford delegates that it would be a useful book 'to our Russian merchants', but also no doubt recognizing that originality which has earned praise at the present day (Ludolf 1959). The work of the brilliant Celtic scholar Edward Lhuyd – like Bernard in Oxford in the 1690s – belongs mainly to the next century, though it should not be forgotten that great advances in Celtic studies had been made earlier in the century, for example by John Davies in his grammar of Welsh (1621) and dictionary of English and Welsh, published in 1632; Celtic had first been recognized as related to other European languages by Abraham Mylius (Metcalf 1953).

While the more academic linguists were debating problems of language change and language relationships, the mass of the population was engaged on a far more practical task – the teaching and acquisition of literacy. Armed with Coote, Cawdrey and the Authorised Version, many Protestants were able to respond to the exhortations of their Church and study the Bible for themselves, since, as one lexicographer proclaimed, the Word of God was 'a Lanterne to their feete and a light vnto their paths' (Evans 1621: sig. A2v.). It was not surprising that, as another schoolmaster put it in his attractively illustrated text-book, 'the Multitudes . . . which canot read at all . . . cry aloud for our utmost Compassion' (Ellis 1680: To the Reader). The Protestant ethic also encouraged efforts at material improvement and success in business enterprise, so that equally welcome to the newly literate was the ability, learned from their reading-texts, to 'frame all bills obligatorie with iudgement, certainety, and reason' (John Evans 1621: sig.A5r.). The level of literacy attained by many 'ordinary Trades-men' was unfavourably noticed by Hoole (Comenius 1659: sig.A8r.); many of them, he says, 'write such false English, that none but themselves can interpret what they scribble, in their Bills and Shop-Books'. A third reason for acquiring literacy was the improvement of social status; two motives are combined in

Preston's comment (1673: To the Reader) that to *'write well, and yet not to know how to write true* English *must needs be a great disparagement, and to my knowledg, hath rendered many uncapable of business, that would have been much to their advantage'*: while Cocker advised parents (1696: 2) to instruct their children in reading and writing to prevent them from having to gain their subsistence by *'such Slavish Labour as the Ignorant and Illiterate* are *subjected to'*.

Contemporary schoolmasters aimed, like Coote, at inculcating linguistic competence in four respects: first, acceptable spelling (cf. Brengelman 1980); secondly, acceptable pronunciation which would provide the foundation for correct orthography; thirdly, the avoidance of grammatical solecisms; fourthly, the comprehension and use of vocabulary derived from classical sources. The most serious difficulty in acquiring 'correctness' in orthography was, as Butler explained (1633: sig.*4r.), not only that the English alphabet was inadequate to represent unambiguously all the speech-sounds of the language, but also that the sounds it did represent were often those of a past age: 'in many words wee are fallen from the old pronunciation: and therefore some write them according to the new sound, and some, for antiquities sake, doe keepe the old writing'. By the last third of the century there are numerous references to unacceptable orthography, among them one by Holder, who remarks (1669: 107) that 'uncouth Spelling' provokes laughter, and another by Lye (1677: sig.a2v.), who says of all the ill-educated *'Read*, they hope they can; but *spell* they cannot; and therefore to *write* either to Child, Friend, or Servant, they are ashamed.' For autodidacts who had little access to printed material, it was necessary to be acquainted with the spoken standard in order to spell acceptably; if, for example, a student was accustomed to say 'strea' he would not know that it should be spelt 'strawe' (Brinsley 1612: 17). Consequently, Coote and his successors provide lists of dialect pronunciations which must be carefully avoided. Furthermore, there was the particularly English problem of homophones; however 'correct' one's pronunciation, one had to learn by rote how to make orthographical distinctions between the different meanings, so that text-books normally provided lists, with exemplification of usage. A third difficulty was that standard English licensed some remarkable discrepancies between pronunciation and spelling, for example (Coles 1674: 87–9) ‹hapm› for *happen*, ‹neeze› for *sneeze* and ‹medsn› for *medicine*. Although serious attempts at orthographic reform largely foundered with Butler's *English grammar* (1633), later grammarians put forward arguments in its favour, examples being Howell (1645 and 1662) and Ray (1674), while other authors and printers silently adopted reformed spelling (for instance Dury 1651), or explained to their readers why they had done so (as did, for example, the 'Corrector' to the press in John Philly's *Arrainment of Christendom*, 1664).

By the latter half of the period, regional variation in speech was being condemned as 'barbarous' and social variation as 'vulgar' – two terms which were beginning to undergo semantic change in the direction of their current pejorative connotations. Grammatical solecisms, usually regarded as the hobby-horse of eighteenth-century prescriptivists, were beginning to be noted also. A few years before the century began, Paul Greaves mentions the errors perpetrated even by well-educated people (1594: sig.A3v.); these include lack of subject–verb concord, preposition followed by nominative pronoun, and double comparative; while the first (destroyed) version of Ben Jonson's grammar appears to have been aimed at the 'puritie' of English, and at freeing our language from 'Rudenesse' (1947: 207, 465). Although Jonson's exact target is not certain, his close friend James Howell, writing after the second version of Jonson's grammar appeared (1640), points out solecisms which are obviously grammatical, such as double superlatives, the use of *you* where *ye* is required, and what he describes as the typically English custom of asking questions in the negative form (1662: 86–7). By the end of the century, a dedicatory verse to another English grammarian acknowledged that his predecessors '*by degrees the Tongue did rectifie*' but that, nevertheless,

> . . . *still there wanted a more perfect Rule,*
> *An* English Grammar *for the English School.* (Aickin 1693: sig.A2r.)

Finally, from Cawdrey (1604) on, those without a grammar school education could acquaint themselves with 'hard words' in a number of fairly elementary dictionaries (Riddell 1973–4; Hayashi 1978), and could even acquire a polished style by replacing their simple vocabulary with the elegant Latinate synonyms to be found in Cockeram's dictionary (1623). Later in the period, dictionaries began to be prescriptive, calling attention, for example, to a careless failure to distinguish between pairs like *contemptible* and *contemptuous*, *ingenious* and *ingenuous* (Coles 1676: sig.A2v.). It is not surprising, when demands for correctness in speech, orthography and vocabulary were increasing, that moves were made towards the establishment of an English Academy comparable with the Italian *Accademia della Crusca* (whose dictionary was published in 1612), the German *Fruchtbringende Gesellschaft* (set up at Weimar in 1617) and the *Académie française*, founded in 1635, though unable to publish its long-awaited dictionary until 1693. The Royal Society, whose revised charter was granted in 1662, established a committee to investigate the desirability of a similar project; but although the diarist John Evelyn drew up fairly detailed proposals for both a grammar (Evelyn 1984) and a dictionary, nothing came of the enterprise (Emerson 1921–3).

Having acquired basic literacy with the assistance of the parish curate, the more fortunate children went on to grammar school to learn Latin and, possibly, Greek. In 1600, the teaching of the classics depended on a good deal of rote learning of the Latin grammar by Lily and Colet which was prescribed by law in 1540, and whose use was enforced by regular diocesan inspections. This grammar, based on the Priscianic categories, was partly in Latin, and it is not surprising that many of the less well-educated clergy found its 'obscurities' difficult to expound to their pupils, until one of their colleagues, John Brinsley, set out to assist them by devising a complete Latin-teaching course, the first of its kind. It begins with a manual for the teacher, *Ludus literarius* (1612); adds a simple text which guides the schoolmaster to the questions he should ask about Lily; and goes on to provide what Brinsley calls 'grammatical translations' – literal translations of the usual prescribed texts, with marginal notes where idioms prevent literal translation. Brinsley's major contribution to language-teaching was his insistence that children should be taught the vernacular, so that they might 'proceed as well in our English tonge as in the latine' (1612: 106); and his example was followed by many others who produced what were practically contrastive grammars of English and Latin (Enkvist 1975), and aimed *explicitly* at contrast; as Daines notes (1640: sig. A4r.), his planned *Etymology* will give Latin and English together 'the better to demonstrate the difference between both Tongues'. Nearly all these scholars were Protestants, and regarded the enormous amount of time spent in teaching Latin grammar as an appalling waste of effort which could be better devoted to observation of, and enquiry into, the phenomena of the natural world, and who sought all possible means of relieving the boredom of teaching a language which was, they believed, seriously defective because of its innumerable inflections and its complex grammar (Wilkins 1668: 444–50). A further contribution which Brinsley made to linguistic education was to popularize the so-called 'golden rule' of a less well-known predecessor, which taught a consistent method of transposing elements in a Latin sentence into a 'natural' English order (Salmon 1979: 41). Brinsley's promotion of the 'golden rule' must undoubtedly have had some influence on grammarians' increasing awareness of the vital syntactic function of word order in the vernaculars.

Brinsley's method, though apparently successful, was superseded by another, devised by a Recusant teacher, who stressed the importance of 'pattern drills' in learning languages. Joseph Webbe explained his aims in a manifesto entitled *An appeale to truth* (1622) with which he introduced a number of text-books whose contents (fairly simple classical pieces) were printed in parallel Latin–English columns. The texts were divided into phrases and clauses, and arranged on the page in such a way that the Latin and English equivalents were visible at a glance (Salmon 1979: 15–31). Webbe's argument that memorization of these 'pieces' as he called them, would enable a pupil to learn the language was opposed by another schoolmaster, William Brookes, who argued that 'judgement' and 'reason', not mere memory, were the primary requirements for language acquisition (Salmon 1979: 3–14). This debate on the relative merits of the 'direct' and the 'grammar-based' methods was echoed many times in the period after Webbe had made his views public and explicit: 'no reason', he argued (1627: sig. A3v.) 'can giue rule to speech, but vse and custome, from whence all petty rules and reasons are deriued'. Poole, for example, claimed that if Latin were taught by 'discourse' without rules, a pupil 'would bee able to say no more in Latine then he hath beene taught' (1646: sig. B1r.). Walker argued that examples, rather than rules, might mislead through ambiguity: 'Nor is every young Scholar', he pointed out, 'able to guide himself by mere Examples (which often are seemingly alike, but really different)' (1655: sig. A2r.). Smith remarks that 'he who learns a Tongue . . . by rote, will never be able, either to write it, or speak it perfectly' (1674: sig. A2r.); while Rose echoed Brookes's words by claiming that the judging and reflecting faculties are of far greater importance than memory (1675: 74).

A third influential innovation in language-teaching reached Britain from abroad. This was the method expounded in Bathe's *Ianua linguarum*, published in Salamanca in 1611 and first appearing in an English version in 1617. The original Latin preface (abbreviated in English reprints) is an extremely sophisticated discussion of educational linguistics, and deserves to be better known (cf. O'Mahony 1981). The *Ianua* consisted of twelve sections each devoted to some fairly abstract topic, such as 'Justice' or 'Wisdom'. Each section contains one hundred separate sentences, and there are 5,200 vocabulary items overall, none of which (apart from purely grammatical forms) were repeated. The Latin sentences were arranged in parallel with their translation in the students' vernacular, and no separate grammar was provided, since Bathe claimed that 'All precepts which are set out in grammars as rules can also be taught aptly in sentences, so that they impress themselves on the mind with greater facility' (O'Mahony 1981: 160). The surprising popularity of this method is attested by its publication in some thirty different editions and reprints, with the Latin accompanied by a variety of vernaculars, sometimes, as in the first edition, with more than one. Its Jesuit provenance assured its success in the Catholic world; it was soon imitated by the Protestant educational reformer, Jan Comenius, who saw it as a means of 'entry' not only to language, but to an understanding of the observable phenomena of the real world. The English version of his innovatory text begins 'If thou askest, whats to bee learned? haue for answer *To know the differences of things, and to bee able to giue its name vnto euery thing*. Is there nothing more? Truly nothing at all' (Comenius 1631: 1). This *Porta linguarum* incorporated 9,000 words arranged in 1,058 numbered sentences devoted to what were intended as scientific topics such as 'the firmament', directions for growing crops, and lists of herbs, spices and grasses. As a follower of Bacon, Comenius believed in the importance of observation, to be implemented by 'visual aids' in the absence of the object itself; he eventually improved on the *Porta* by producing an illustrated text, the *Orbis sensualium pictus* (1658), where the word-lists show, not merely objects but activities such as a printing-house at work. Illustration, particularly of alphabets, had been used before, but apart perhaps from Olearius's *Deutsche Sprachkunst* (1630; Padley 1985: 118), nothing on a comparable scale had yet appeared as an aid to language-learning. So influential were Comenius's views on the importance of visual aids that we find his admirers using quite bizarre devices to impress even grammatical inflections on their pupils' memories (Salmon 1986a).

Another device used in language-teaching, though not consistently enough promoted to be regarded as an English 'method', was the attempt to discover and describe the principles which were thought to underlie all languages; to teach these principles first by means of the mother-tongue, and only then to teach the 'accidental' differences to be found in the target language. The concept of linguistic universals was no novelty in 1600, being familiar to mediaeval grammarians such as Roger Bacon, who claimed: 'Grammatica una et eadem est secundum substanciam in omnibus linguis, licet accidentaliter varietur'[1] (Michael 1970: 30). Two German scholars, Ratke and Helvig, made use of the concept of underlying principles, as Kaltz (1978) and Padley (1985: 221–3) have explained, while the most disting- uished exponents of this method of language-teaching are the Gentlemen of Port Royal (1660). But a rather similar belief inspired English scholarship at an earlier date, being hinted at by Webbe (Salmon 1979: 27) and stated explicitly by Daines (1640: sig. A3v.) 'The perfection of all Arts (whereto the knowledge of Tongues ought to be reduced) consists as well in the Theory, as the Practice . . . and this Theory [consists] in the . . . knowledge of Universals; wee are, as well in this, as all other Tongues or Languages, to have recourse to Grammar, as the generall fountain.' Bassett Jones (1659), writing an explanatory text on Lily's grammar, notes that 'the Nations, differing in vocality . . . do nevertheless in point of Syntaxe agree as one' (Salmon 1979: 70); and Lewis (1674: 1), acknowledging a debt to Wilkins, but not to Port Royal, argues that 'Though it be natural to Speak, yet it is accidental to use this or that Tongue.' Rose, translating from French, claims (1675: 3) that *'there is a certain accord between the severall Languages'* but accepts that he must 'make choice of one Language as a rule to measure by, and a principle to reduce all the rest too' (1675: 8); but no English scholar until Lane, at the very end of the period, makes much practical use of the idea of underlying grammar in his teaching. Lane, however, divides his text-book into two parts, 'The first containing such Precepts as are common to all Languages' and the second, 'what is more peculiar to the Latin Tongue' (1695: title-page).

Associated with this belief that meaning was a non-verbal concept in the mind was the view (also influential in language-teaching) that some elements in that concept might remain unexpressed in speech, or even actively 'suppressed'. There were two classic sources of this belief, one grammatical, the other rhetorical. Priscian had used the term 'subaudiri' to refer to sentence elements 'understood' but not spoken (cf. Salmon 1979: 76); traditional rhetoric came to terms with this view by distinguishing between two types of syntax, which are familiar to seventeenth-century scholarship; Gill (1972: II, 134) describes 'simple' syntax as that which is normally used in speech and writing, and 'rhetorical' syntax as that which is used 'either out of necessity or for the sake of graceful ornament' and 'illuminates discourse'. The first of the rhetorical 'figures' which he cites is ellipsis, 'the omission of a word or clause' (1972: II, 155). Later in the century, Wilkins expands his description of 'regular' and 'figurative' syntax (1668: 447): the former is realized in normal use, the latter occurs because there are 'some words always either *redundant*, or *deficient*, or *transposed*, or *changed*, from their proper notion'. The English scholar Linacre had adopted the theory of ellipsis as a basis for his grammar (Padley 1976: 54), and had been imitated by Sanctius (Breva-Claramonte 1983); his ideas were in turn enthusiastically adopted by Lancelot in the third edition of his Latin grammar, since he believed that the operation of ellipsis enabled him to discern regularities in certain forms of usage which seemed, on the surface, to be irregular (cf. Lakoff 1969). Not until a quarter of a century later did an English grammarian exploit the concept of ellipsis to any extent: Cooper (1685: 175) actually used Priscianic terminology in pointing out that 'quando nominativus casus subauditur . . . verbo anteponitur it'.[2] His English examples include (1685: 177)

> The man, whom I spake of
> The man I spake of is dead
> The work he was about, is finished
> The work about which he was imployed

Lane provides even more detailed examples of what he terms 'suppression', analyzing 'I write a better hand than thou' into 'I write a hand, which hand is a better hand, than the hand is good which hand thou writest' (1700: 106). But, as Michael notes (1970: 22–3), it was not until the publication of Harris's *Hermes* in 1751 that Sanctius and his concept of ellipsis were 'given the respect which they deserved'.

The grammars discussed above were designed to teach Latin in conjunction with English to native speakers of the vernacular; most grammars dealing with English alone were designed to teach it as a foreign language, or in one case, to assist Englishmen resident abroad for a long period – 'linguam integram . . . praeservare aptum est instrumentum'[3] (Cooper 1685: sig.b5v.). At the beginning of the century, there was little demand for English because it was 'si peu estimee des estrangers . . . qu'il y en a peu qui veulent se pener de l'apprendre . . . si ce ne sont les seruiteurs ou facteurs pour l'vsage des choses vtiles & necessaires à la vie, lesquelles dependent du menu peuple qui ne sçait parler autre langue'[4] (Duret 1613: 876). This contemptuous attitude towards English may, of course, merely have reciprocated the English attitude toward French; as Camden noted (1605: 21), in Wolsey's embassy to France, he 'commanded all his servaunts to vse no French, but meere [pure] English to the French, in all communications whatsoever'. But for cultural, diplomatic and commercial reasons interest in English grew, and the most substantial grammars were written in Latin, as a potentially 'universal' language, by Gill (1619), Wallis (1653, cf. Constantinescu 1974) and Cooper (1685). The most important scholars to write in English were Butler (1633), Jonson (1640), Howell (1662) and Miège (1668); and grammars written in foreign vernaculars became fairly common after the middle of the century. Those composed by English scholars, although mainly based on the Priscianic categories, frequently drew attention to differences and similarities between English and Latin. As Gill remarked, 'So much for the forms of our native verbs, in so far as they are analogous with Latin, but (as with all languages) the English language has its peculiar idioms which cannot readily (if at all) be translated into Latin' (1972: II, 132), and he provides several examples. As Kemp points out, Wallis (1972: 31) is even more explicit about [mainly morphological] contrasts, but does not provide a section specifically devoted to syntax; and this was an aspect of English grammar which was quite clearly problematic. Howell (1662: To the Reder) admitted that it is 'a hard task to make a Grammar of a *Mother* Toung', but like Gill and Jonson, he did at least attempt some independent observations. Although Gill and Jonson depended to a large extent on exemplification from poetry (of an earlier generation), they also quoted a few instances from contemporary usage; and Howell goes so far as to cite certain grammatical errors among his contemporaries against which he warns the Spaniards for whom his grammar is chiefly intended (1662: 86, 87).

Only a few general comments can be made here on seventeenth-century English grammars, which have been fully described elsewhere (Michael 1970; Vorlat 1975 and 1979). First, their authors understood that a grammar should be more than a rehearsal of paradigms, and from Gill on, we find remarks like his opening sentence, 'GRAMMAR consists of the understanding of rules' (1972: II, 92) and Price's comment on the provenance of those rules, 'All Grammars are rules of common speech' (1665: sig.A3v.). Secondly, grammarians become increasingly aware of the nature of clauses and clause subordination. So unfamiliar was the concept of clause that Webbe thought it necessary to explain 'Because we talke so much of clauses, it may bee thou wilt aske vs what we meane by a clause . . . [it is] a perfect member of speech, consisting of one or moe words rightly knit vnto other members. . . . Which being broken off in any other part than in his true ioynt or knitting, breeds a fracture and disorder.' Webbe also advises his readers to 'take notice of two sorts of clauses; the one simple, th'other compounded, inuolued, or intermingled. . . . And these . . . may be . . . called pregnant clauses, as . . . they carry other clauses in their bellies' (1627: sig.A2v.). Mark Lewis (1672: 2) refers to 'depending verbs' and 'principal propositions' and Lane (1700: 91–4) describes in detail 'relative sentences' joined by the 'relative adjectives' *who* and *which*. In view of Webbe's early appreciation of the existence of subordinate clauses it is possible that he, Lewis and Lane were all indebted to traditional logic, but by 1672 it is perhaps more likely that grammarians would be indebted to Port Royal. But traditional logic was certainly responsible for the third development worth noting in a brief survey – the equation of sentence with 'proposition', the 'nominative of the verb' with 'subject', and 'verb' with 'predicate'. Webbe and Brookes had noted the sentence/proposition equation in their debate, but Wilkins, followed by Cooper and Lane, was the first to treat subject and predicate, quite explicitly, as terms in grammar. A different kind of reference to logic occurs in Wallis (1972: 291) who comments on the function of prepositions to 'indicate logical connections . . . or local relationships'. Prepositions belonged to the category known in mediaeval logic as *consignificatae*, which the seventeenth century termed 'particles'. English grammarians found them of increasing interest, to the extent that Walker devoted a whole treatise to them, describing them as 'like the Arteries in the body, running through the whole' (1655: sig.A1v.). A final important aspect of the growing seventeenth-century sophistication in grammatical studies is the attention given to word order (Kohonen 1978). It arose *ad hoc* as a result of the practice of Latin–English translation, but it was reinforced by Latin–English grammars like Poole's (1646: and cf. Enkvist 1975). Wallis notes how order changes for questions and commands (with pronoun subject); Walker (1669) provides rules, and Cooper gives some very detailed and specific examples, such as the difference in adjective order between 'three very wise grave philosophers' and 'A man skil'd in all manner of learning' (1685: 176).

Surprisingly enough in view of the growing interest in the sentence as a whole, there is also a contrary movement towards concentration on 'etymology' in the sense of word-formation. Gill deals with derivatives and compounds in two chapters at the beginning of his *Accidence*, and nearly all later grammarians devote some space to the topic, particularly Miège (1688) and Wallis, who enlarged the scope of the relevant section in each successive edition of his grammar. There are three likely sources of this interest; first, the school grammars of Latin which included treatments of various types of formation to indicate semantic categories like *agent* and *diminutive*; secondly, philosophical grammars like those of Caramuel (1654) and Wilkins (1668) which gave word-formation a central position in creating related names for related concepts; and thirdly, there may have been some influence from Schottel's great German grammar (1663) which Padley (1985: 112) describes as an attempt to erect 'a whole theory of linguistic description on German's exceptional capacity for word-building'.

The grammars of English written in England for the benefit of foreigners were supplemented from about the middle of the century by several grammars published abroad, though French–English grammars were also published in England by Mason (1622, 1633), Festeau (1672) and Miège (1685). English grammars were first published abroad in Holland (1646), Hungary (1664), Germany (1665), Copenhagen (1678) and Uppsala (1686). One problem which faced all these authors working overseas was that of teaching a native accent. Some took refuge in advising conversation practice where possible; others attempted semi-phonetic spelling, like: 'let me hiér haoú you pronouns de Inglich letters' (Mason 1622: 2). Since the author was writing in England this attempted phonetic transcription was hardly necessary, but his interest might have been aroused by a recent (1617) publication by Robert Robinson which attempted to provide a description of, and notation for, speech-sounds in general. In *The art of pronuntiation* Robinson succeeds in describing place and manner of articulation, but fails to perceive the role of voice. By far the most distinguished phonetician of the earlier seventeenth century was Montanus (1635), whose treatise, being written in Dutch, appeared to have little influence outside Holland; but the middle years of the period in England were remarkable for some extraordinarily advanced treatments (cf. Abercrombie 1981) of phonetics. Wallis's *De loquela* (1653), Holder's *Elements of speech* (1669) and Lodwick's contribution to the Royal Society's *Transactions*, in which he attempted to provide an iconic phonetic transcription (1686), are specially praiseworthy; but two authors primarily interested in other topics must also be credited with some important insights. First, Price (1665) produced the first known attempt to illustrate the sounds of English by means of facial drawings; and Wilkins (1668) has been described as the most brilliant of all these early phoneticians, having used quite explicitly and consistently a binary feature system (Subbiondo 1985). Wilkins has also been praised for his insights in characterizing articulatory settings (Laver 1978), but in fairness to his predecessors it should be noted that many of them had been interested in a similar topic, though in an unfortunately amateurish way. Camden, for example (1605: 23), pointed out that some people 'pronounce more fully, some flatly, some broadly, and no few mincingly . . . which is rather to be imputed to the persons and their education, than to the language . . . the Northerne Nations . . . are noted to soupe their words out of the throat with fat and full Spirits'. Among other similar comments, Howell (1890: 463) claims that German is spoken 'as if one had bones in his tongue instead of nerves'. Of these early phoneticians, it has been said: 'The insights of the seventeenth century were not more clearly developed until the nineteenth and early twentieth centuries' (Fromkin and Ladefoged 1981: 7). It was an important motivation for many of these linguists that they were attempting to assist the deaf and dumb to speak, and their efforts have been fully described in recent surveys (Mullett 1971 and Read 1977). Others believed the most useful form of communication for people so handicapped was by gesture, which is discussed by Bulwer (1648) among others (cf. Seigal 1969).

The teaching of English to foreigners was therefore largely responsible for the outstanding development of phonetics which characterized seventeenth-century England. Another necessary teaching aid was dictionaries, and in this respect the seventeenth century merely continued a form of linguistic enterprise which was already flourishing (Collison 1982). Polyglot dictionaries, phrase books and dialogues were particularly popular, a set of colloquies by Noel van Barlement, first published in Antwerp in 1536, appearing in edition after edition throughout the seventeenth century; the first extant version containing an English text was printed in 1576. The earliest genuine polyglot dictionary was published in Germany by Megiser in 1603; the first similar attempt in England was John Minsheu's dictionary (1617), including entries from eight or more languages, together with a comprehensive Spanish–English dictionary. Other lexical aids included James Howell's dictionary of Spanish, French, Italian and English (1659), a French–English dictionary by Guy Miège (1677; cf. Bately 1983) and a Dutch–English one by Henry Hexham in 1648.

Conversely, the English diplomat or merchant abroad needed foreign-language grammars and dictionaries, especially as the English were notoriously inept at communicating in Latin because of their idiosyncratic pronunciation. As Howell remarked, 'They say abroad, that none write better Latin than the *English*, and none pronounce it worse' (1662: 86). By mid-century however, an acquaintance with foreign languages had become fashionable; as 'T.B.' remarks, in a prefatory verse for Daines (1640: sig.B3r.)

> Where can one walke along the streets, but hee
> May Schollers, Courtiers, and good Linguists see?
> But all for Forreigne Tongues. Poore English now
> Is onely left for him that drives the plough.

Most of these treatises were published abroad, but among those printed in England were John Sanford's grammars of French (1604), Italian (1605) and Spanish (1611), grammars of French by Mauger (1653), Mauger and Festeau (1690) and Berault (1688); and a grammar of German by Offelen (1686–7). The last three were 'double grammars', but they were all to some extent contrastive, and therefore of special linguistic interest.[5]

It is possible to mention here only briefly some of the less important concerns of British scholars in the seventeenth century. One is their study of regional and social dialects, which began with occasional comments by Coote (1596), Gill (1619), Webbe (1622) and Daines (1640), and proceeded to extensive investigations by Coles (1676) for his English dictionary, and by Head (1665 and 1673) for dictionaries of 'cant' – low-class and/or criminal language. Scholarly English dialectology may be said to begin with John Ray (1674) the botanist, whose interest in regional variation in plant names was due in part to his assistance with Wilkins's *Essay*. Another – and specifically English – linguistic interest of the period was the invention of shorthand. Willis's innovatory text (1602) has already been noted, and the development of the technique was directed to a more genuinely phonetic transcription of the spoken language, rather than an abbreviated form of the normal orthographical representation. The extent to which interest in shorthand led to genuine linguistic insights is suggested by the attention paid to the subject by universal language inventors, including Lodwick, Dalgarno (1661) and Wilkins (cf. Lodwick 1972: 60–4 and Salmon 1979: 157–75); it was used extensively by linguists like the Orientalist Edmund Castell (Morley 1945); and it was also associated in the seventeenth-century mind with cryptography, an art in great demand during the Civil War. Another matter of practical importance (though linked with a more academic interest in the derivation of the alphabet from a putative Hebrew source) was the design and commissioning of founts for new scripts, and the publication of comparative tables of such scripts.

This chapter began with a list of innovatory texts published at the turn of the sixteenth and seventeenth centuries; the turn of the seventeenth and eighteenth centuries is distinguished by other texts which mark the beginning of a new era, or the end of an old one. First, there is a parallel to Bacon. Just as his call for a physiological study of sounds and a characterization of individual languages (1905: 523–4), may have inspired later phoneticians and grammarians, and his remarks on 'real character' and 'philosophical' grammar (1905: 121–2) the ideas of the language projectors, so Locke's views on language, set out in the *Essay concerning humane understanding* (1690), inspired linguistic philosophers and grammarians of the eighteenth century. A second indication of a new age was Lane's grammar of 1700, which Poldauf (1948: 93) has described as the first grammar to proceed from a philosophical basis to find rules of general validity, though he argues convincingly that Lane was not acquainted with the Port Royal grammar. A third text which represents a new departure was John Kersey's dictionary of 1702, which differed markedly from its predecessors – concerned, as they were, only with 'difficult' or 'technical' words – in including for the first time vocabulary in normal usage, though by 1656 Blount had introduced etymologies and citations. On the other hand, the end of the century also marked the end of the universal language movement, which was praised extravagantly as late as 1692, only to become a target for Swift's satire in the early years of the next century (Salmon 1983b: 27).

The universal language movement, in its social and intellectual contexts, has recently been one of the most frequently discussed developments in seventeenth-century linguistic scholarship, and although this study is devoted primarily to minor figures it must at least draw attention to the numerous books and articles on the subject which have appeared since the first detailed treatment in Lodwick (1972) and Knowlson (1975). Most important of these are two full-length studies by Frank (1979) and Slaughter (1982), and several articles, among them Hamans (1974–5), Subbiondo (1977), Cram (1980 and 1985), Clauss (1982), Salmon (1983a and b) and Dolezal (1984). Related to, though not primarily concerned with the universal language movement, are Formigari (1970), Padley (1976 and 1985), Cohen (1977), Forie (1981) and Bell (1982).

As Padley has noted, 'In the seventeenth century, European linguistic culture is still largely one and unfragmented, and grammars written in the vernacular cannot be considered *in vacuo*' (1985: 361). This view may be confirmed by a glance at the sources of many (even minor) English works such as *Gazophylacium* (1689) which cites Vossius, Salmasius, Bochert and Menage. It is therefore difficult, without the sort of detailed study beyond the scope of this chapter, to make a precise assessment of the contribution of English scholars to the achievements of seventeenth-century linguistics; but they certainly shared in the establishment, if not the actual discovery, of a family of languages which included Persian and European members, the placing of English within the Germanic group, and the inauguration of Old English and Gothic as university disciplines. In the first half of the century, Bathe, Brinsley and Webbe contributed much to both the theory and practice of language-teaching, and soon after the middle of the century, Wallis published the first genuinely 'scientific' grammar of English, and English scholar-missionaries had recorded, for the first time, North American Indian languages. By the third quarter of the century, English phonetics had reached a stage of sophistication not to be rivalled until the mid-nineteenth century, and the universal language movement had produced its finest achievements. Finally, a more modest contribution to linguistic studies, though far-reaching in its effects on society, was the invention of a viable, semi-phonetic form of shorthand which achieved the flattery of imitation in Holland (Lodwick 1972: 248–50), France (Cossard 1651), and Germany (1678; cf. *Dictionary of National Biography*, Ramsay [including Cossard]).

NOTES

1 Grammar in all languages is one and the same in respect of substance: it is varied by accidents.
2 When the nominative case is understood . . . *it* is placed before the verb.
3 It is a useful means of preserving the integrity of the language.
4 . . . so little valued by foreigners . . . that there are few of them who are willing to take the trouble to learn it . . . other than servants and agents for the employment of valuable and necessary things of life which depend on the humble people who cannot speak another language.
5 A fuller account, entitled 'The study of foreign languages in seventeenth-century England', is forthcoming in *Histoire Épistémologie Langage*, 1986.

REFERENCES

I. *Primary sources*
The bibliography of primary sources is limited to those texts cited above which are not included in Alston (1974), except that where recent editions have appeared, full details are given.

Bacon, F. 1905. Of the proficiencie and advancement of learning, divine and humane (1605); De dignitate et augmentis scientiarum (1623). In John M. Robertson (ed.) *The philosophical works*. London: Routledge.
Becanus, G. 1569. *Origines Antwerpianae*. Antwerp.
Browne, T. 1928. Of languages, and particularly of the Saxon tongue. In G. Keynes (ed.) *Works*, III. London: Faber.
Caramuel y Lobkowitz, J. 1654. *Praecursor logicus, complectens Grammaticam audacem*. Frankfurt.
Casaubon, M. 1650. De lingua Anglica vetere. In: *De quatuor linguis commentationis pars prior*. London.
Castell, E. 1669. *Lexicon heptaglotton*. London.
Clüver, P. 1616. *Philippi Cluverii Germaniae antiquae libri tres*. Leyden.
Comenius, J.A. 1631. J. Anchoran (trans.) *Porta linguarum trilinguis reserata. The gate of tongues unlocked*. London.
    1659. C. Hoole (trans.) *Orbis sensualium pictus . . . Commenius's Visible World*. London.
Davies, J. 1621. *Antiquae linguae Britannicae rudimenta*. London.
    1632. *Antiquae linguae Britannicae . . . et linguae Latinae dictionarium duplex*. London.
Davis, J. 1656. *A short introduction to the Hebrew tongue, being a translation of . . . J. Buxtorfius' Epitome*. London.
Duret, C. 1613. *Thresor de l'histoire des langues de cest univers*. Cologne.
Eliot, J. 1666. *The Indian grammar begun; or, an attempt to bring the Indian language into rules*. Cambridge, Mass.
Evelyn, J. 1984. A.B. Cook (ed.), The English grammar. *Leeds Studies in English* n.s. 15: 117–46.

Gesner, K. 1555. *Mithridates*. Zürich.

Gill, A. 1972. B. Danielsson & A. Gabrielson (eds.), with a translation by R.C. Alston, *Alexander Gill's Logonomia Anglica*. 2 vols. Stockholm: Almqvist and Wiksell.

Greaves, J. 1649. *Elementa linguae Persicae*. London.

Hayne, T. 1639. *Linguarum cognatio, seu de linguis in genere et de variarum linguarum harmonia dissertatio*. London.

Hexham, H. 1648. *A copious English and Nether duytche dictionarie composed out of our best English authors*. Rotterdam.

Howell, J. 1890. J. Jacobs (ed.) *The familiar letters. Epistolae Ho-Elianae*. London.

Jonson, B. 1947. The English grammar. In C.H. Herford & P.E. Simpson (eds.) *Works*, vol. 8, 465–553. Oxford: Oxford University Press.

Jonsson, R. 1689. *Recentissima antiquissimae linguae septentrionalis incunabula*. In G. Hickes, *Institutiones grammaticae Anglo-Saxonicae, et Moeso-Gothicae*. Oxford.

Junius, F. 1655. *Caedmonis monachi paraphrasis poetica*. Amsterdam.

1665. *Quatuor D.N.I.C. Evangeliorum versiones perantiquae duae, Gothica scilicet*. Dordrecht.

Kirchmaier, G. 1697. *Parallelismus et convenientia XII linguarum ex matrice Scytto-Celtica*. Wittenberg.

Lewis, M. ?1672. *Plain and short rules for pointing periods and reading sentences grammatically*. London.

Lodwick, F. 1972. V. Salmon (ed.) *The works of Francis Lodwick: a study of his writings in the intellectual context of the seventeenth century*. London: Longman.

Ludolf, H. 1959. B.O. Unbegaun (ed.) *Grammatica Russica*. Oxford: Clarendon Press.

Montanus, P. 1964. W.J.H. Caron (ed.) *De Spreeckonst*. Trivium 5. Groningen: Wolters.

Peyrère, I. de la. 1656. *Men before Adam*. London.

Prasch, J. 1686. *Dissertatio prima de origine germanica linguae latinae*. Regensburg.

Robertson, W. 1654–5. *A gate . . . to the holy tongue*. London.

Robinson, R. 1957. E.J. Dobson (ed.) *The phonetic writings* (Early English Text Society, 238). London: Oxford University Press.

Sanford, J. 1604. *Le guichet françois*. Oxford.

1605. *A grammar or introduction to the Italian tongue*. Oxford.

1611. *An entrance to the Spanish tongue*. London.

Scaliger, J.J. 1610. Diatriba de Europaeorum linguis. In *Opuscula varia ante hac non edita*. Paris.

Schottel, J.G. 1663. *Ausführliche Arbeit von der teutschen Haubt Sprache*. Brunswick.

Smet, B. de 1597. *De literis et linguâ Getarum sive Gothorum*. Leyden.

Stiernhjelm, G. 1671. *D.N. Jesu Christi SS. Evangelia ab Ulfila . . . Gothice translata*. Stockholm.

Tacitus, Cornelius. 1598. R. Greneway (trans.) *The annales*. London.

Wallis, J. 1972. J.A. Kemp (ed.) *Grammatica linguae Anglicanae*. London: Longman.

Walton, B. 1657–69. *Biblia sacra polyglotta*. London.

Webbe, J. 1627. *Lessons and exercises out of Cicero ad Atticum*. London.

Wexionius, M.O. 1650. *Epitome descriptionis Sueciae, Gothiae, Fenningiae*. Åbo.

Williams, R. 1643. *A key into the language of America*. London.

II. Secondary sources

Abercrombie, D. 1981. Extending the Roman alphabet. In R.E. Asher & E.J.A. Henderson (eds.) *Towards a history of phonetics*. Edinburgh: Edinburgh University Press.

Allen, D.C. 1949. Some theories of the growth and origin of language in Milton's age. *Philological Quarterly* 28: 1–16.

Allen, W. 1970. *Translating for King James*. London: Allen Lane.

Alston, R.C. 1974. *A bibliography of the English language from the invention of printing to the year 1800*. A corrected reprint of vols. 1–10. Ilkley: Janus.

Bately, J. 1983. Miège and the development of the English dictionary. In E.G. Stanley & D. Gray (eds.) *Five hundred years of words and sounds. For E.J. Dobson*. Woodbridge: Boydell & Brewer.

Bell, D.L. 1982. Classical thought, egologism and the philosophy of language. *History of European Ideas* 3: 201–21.

Bonfante, G. 1953. Ideas on the kinship of the European languages from 1200 to 1800. *Cahiers d'histoire mondiale* 1: 679–99.

Brekle, H.E. 1975. The seventeenth century. In T.A. Sebeok (ed.) *Current trends in linguistics* 13: *Historiography of linguistics*. The Hague, Paris: Mouton.

Brengelman, F.H. 1980. Orthoepists, printers and the rationalisation of English spelling. *Journal of English and Germanic Philology* 79: 332–54.

Breva-Claramonte, M. 1983. *Sanctius' theory of language*. Amsterdam: Benjamins.

Butler, E.H. 1951. *The story of British shorthand*. London: Pitman.

Clauss, S. 1982. John Wilkins' *Essay Towards a Real Character*: its place in the seventeenth-century episteme. *Journal of the History of Ideas* 43: 531–53.

Cohen, M. 1977. *Sensible words: linguistic practice in England 1640–1785*. Baltimore & London: Johns Hopkins University Press.

Collison, R. 1982. *A history of foreign language dictionaries*. London: Deutsch.

Constantinescu, I. 1974. John Wallis (1616–1703): a reappraisal of his contribution to the study of English. *Historiographia Linguistica* 1: 297–311.

Cram, D. 1980. George Dalgarno on *Ars signorum* and Wilkins' *Essay*. In K. Koerner (ed.) *Progress in linguistic historiography*. Papers from the International Conference on the history of the language sciences (Ottawa, 28–31 August 1978). Amsterdam: Benjamins.

   1985. Language universals and 17th century universal language schemes. In K. Dutz and L. Kaczmarek (eds.) *Rekonstruktion und Interpretation: Problemgeschichtliche Studien zur Sprachtheorie von Ockham bis Humboldt*. Tübingen: Narr.

Davies, W.J.F. 1973. *Teaching reading in early England*. London: Pitman.

Dolezal, F. 1984. The construction of entries in John Wilkins' and William Lloyd's 'Alphabetical dictionary'. *Lexicographia*: Series Major, 1. Tübingen: Niemeyer.

Droixhe, D. 1978. *La linguistique et l'appel à l'histoire*. Geneva: Droz.

Emerson, O.F. 1921–3. John Dryden and a British Academy. *Proceedings of the British Academy* 10: 45–58.

Enkvist, N.E. 1975. English in Latin guise: a note on some Renaissance textbooks. *Historiographia Linguistica* 2: 283–98.

Eros, J.F. 1976. A 17th-century demonstration of language relationships: Meric Casaubon on English and Greek. *Historiographia Linguistica* 3: 1–15.

Forie, J.E. 1981. Secularization, the language of God and the Royal Society at the turn of the seventeenth century. *History of European Ideas* 2: 221–35.

Formigari, L. 1970. *Linguistica ed empirismo nel seicento inglese.* Bari. Laterza.

Frank, T. 1979. *Segno e significato: John Wilkins e la linguistica filosofica.* Naples: Guida Editori.

Fromkin, V. & Ladefoged, P. 1981. Early views on distinctive features. In R.E. Asher & E.J.A. Henderson (eds.) *Towards a history of phonetics.* Edinburgh: Edinburgh University Press.

Hamans, C. 1974–5. 'De gehele aarde was één van taal en één van spraak' (Gen. 11:1). *Spektator* 4: 321–40.

Hayashi, T. 1978. *The theory of English lexicography, 1530–1791.* Amsterdam: Benjamins.

Jones, R.F. 1951. *The seventeenth century.* Stanford: Stanford University Press.

——— 1953. The ancient language. Chapter 7 of *The triumph of the English language.* London: Oxford University Press.

Kaltz, B. 1978. Christoph Helwig, ein vergessener Vertreter der allgemeinen Grammatik in Deutschland. *Historiographia Linguistica* 5: 227–35.

Katz, D.S. 1981. The language of Adam in seventeenth-century England. In H. Lloyd-Jones, V. Pearl & B. Worden (eds.) *History and imagination. Essays in honour of H.R. Trevor-Roper.* London: Duckworth.

——— 1982. *Philosemitism and the readmission of the Jews to England, 1603–1655.* Oxford: Oxford University Press.

Knowlson, J. 1975. *Universal language schemes in England and France, 1600–1800.* Toronto & Buffalo: University of Toronto Press.

Kohonen, V. 1978. On the development of an awareness of English syntax in early (1550–1660) descriptions of word-order by English grammarians, logicians and rhetoricians. *Neuphilologische Mitteilungen* 79: 44–58.

Lakoff, R. 1969. Review of H. Brekle (ed.), C. Lancelot & A. Arnauld, *Grammaire générale ei raisonnée. Language* 45: 343–64.

Laver, J. 1978. The concept of articulatory settings: an historical survey. *Historiographia Linguistica* 5: 1–14.

Metcalf, G.J. 1953. Abraham Mylius on historical linguistics. *Publications of the Modern Language Association* 68: 535–54.

——— 1974. The Indo-European hypothesis in the sixteenth and seventeenth centuries. In D. Hymes (ed.) *Studies in the history of linguistics. Traditions and paradigms.* Bloomington & London: Indiana University Press.

——— 1980. Theodor Bibliander (1504–1564) and the language of Japheth's progeny. *Historiographia Linguistica* 7: 323–33.

Michael, I. 1970. *English grammatical categories and the tradition to 1800.* Cambridge: Cambridge University Press.

Miner, K.L. 1974. John Eliot of Massachusetts and the beginnings of American linguistics. *Historiographia Linguistica* 1: 169–83.

Morley, M. 1945. John Willis: Elizabethan stenographer. *Notes and Queries* 189: 222–7.

Mounin, G. 1967. *Histoire de la linguistique. Des origines au XXᵉ siècle.* Paris: Presses Universitaires de France.

Mullett, C.F. 1971. An arte to make the dumbe to speake, the deafe to heare. *Journal of the History of Medicine* 26: 123–49.

O'Mahony, S.F. 1981. The preface to William Bathe's *Ianua linguarum* (1611). *Historiographia Linguistica* 8: 131–64.

Padley, G.A. 1976. *Grammatical theory in Western Europe, 1500–1700: the Latin tradition.* Cambridge: Cambridge University Press.

1982. L'Importance de Thomas Linacre. *Langues et Linguistique* (Université Laval) 8: 17–56.

1983. La Norme dans la tradition des grammairiens. In E. Bédard and J. Maurais, *La Norme linguistique*. Quebec & Paris: Gouvernement du Québec.

1985. *Grammatical theory in Western Europe: Trends in vernacular grammar*, 1. Cambridge: Cambridge University Press.

Poldauf, I. 1948. On the history of some problems in English grammar before 1800. Prague: Facultas philosophica Universitatis Carolinae Pragensis 55.

Rea, J. 1976. Linguistic speculations of Edward Brerewood. In M.A. Jazayery, E.C. Polomé & W. Winter (eds.) *Linguistic and literary studies in honour of Archibald A. Hill*. Lisse: The de Ridder Press.

Read, M.K. 1977. Linguistic theory and the problem of mutism. *Historiographia Linguistica* 4: 303–18.

Riddell, J.A. 1973–4. The beginning: English dictionaries of the first half of the seventeenth century. *Leeds Studies in English* n.s. 7: 117–53.

Robins, R.H. 1979 (2nd edn.). *A short history of linguistics*. London: Longman.

Salmon, V. 1979. *The study of language in seventeenth-century England*. Amsterdam: Benjamins.

1983a. William Bedell and the universal language movement in seventeenth-century Ireland. *Essays and Studies* 36: 27–39.

1983b. Nathaniel Chamberlain and his *Tractatus de literis et lingua philosophica* (1679). In E.G. Stanley & D. Gray (eds.) *Five hundred years of words and sounds.* Woodbridge: Boydell & Brewer.

1986a. Bathsua Makin: a pioneer linguist and feminist in seventeenth-century England (forthcoming).

1986b. Missionary linguistics in seventeenth-century Ireland. *Historiographia Linguistica* 12.

Schäfer, J. 1982. Alt- und Mittelenglisch in der lexicographischen Tradition des 17. Jahrhunderts. In E. S. Dick & K. R. Jankowsky (eds.) *Festschrift für Karl Schneider.* Amsterdam: Benjamins.

Seigal, J.P. 1969. The Enlightenment and the evolution of a language of signs in France and England. *Journal of the History of Ideas* 30: 96–115.

Slaughter, M. 1982. *Universal languages and scientific taxonomy in the seventeenth century*. Cambridge: Cambridge University Press.

Subbiondo, J.L. 1977. John Wilkins' theory of meaning and the development of a semantic model. *Cahiers linguistiques d'Ottawa*, 5: 41–61.

1978. William Holder's *Elements of speech* (1669): a study of applied English phonetics and speech therapy. *Lingua* 46: 169–84.

1986. John Wilkins' theory of articulatory phonetics (forthcoming).

Trentman, J.A. 1976. The study of logic and language in the early 17th century. *Historiographia Linguistica* 3: 179–201.

Vorlat, E. 1975. *The development of English grammatical theory, 1586–1737*. Leuven: Leuven University Press.

1979. Criteria of grammaticalness in 16th and 17th century English grammar. *Leuvense Bijdragen* 68: 129–40.

Weigand, H.J. 1942. The two and seventy languages of the world. *Germanic Review* 17: 241–60.

7

JOSEPH DE MAISTRE AND VICTORIAN THOUGHT ON THE ORIGIN OF LANGUAGE AND CIVILIZATION

HANS AARSLEFF

The eighteenth century devoted a large part of its intellectual energies to the argument that man had made himself. Placed in the state of nature with the innate faculties that set him apart from all other creatures, he had raised himself to levels which, even at their lowest, showed improvement beyond the initial state. His first advance was the invention of language, and experience showed that no nation of savages was without language and some rudimentary arts. This argument was elaborated into the natural history of man, thought, and society, whose origins and progress were argued and discussed with only minor variations that left the core of the argument intact, in France, Italy, Scotland, England, and Germany. The exception was Rousseau's upsetting claim that man was not naturally a sociable creature, but this view did not gain serious attention until it was later taken up by the reaction. In the deistic atmosphere of the Enlightenment, the philosophy of man and progress did not create conflict with religious belief, but was rather seen to offer a beautiful illustration of the benevolence and wisdom of the creator. The only challenge was philosophical criticism of the argument from design itself, and such criticism was invariably seen to pose a greater threat to religion than the argument it opposed. In the next century Victorian divines also believed in the progress of civilization through the moral and intellectual improvement of man. They even called it evolution, thus setting the stage for the harsh conflicts over Darwinian thought, in which the principle of natural selection took away all hope of finding a design that revealed indications of the creator. But by that time the origins of civilization had for decades been a fiercely debated question. Historical events had brought about the change. If the recent philosophy of the nature of man and society had helped generate the French Revolution, as both its advocates and soon also its opponents claimed, then that philosophy must have contained unsuspected seeds of evil.

Now, since no one on either side of the question doubted that speech and reason were the defining characteristics of man, it was evident that the origin of language was the heart of the matter. Language was the condition for all human institutions and arts; it was both the source and expression of man's moral and intellectual being. Civilization was at point zero before language. The eighteenth century held that nature – that is, the Deity – had made man for language, and on this basis it placed the human invention of language at the centre of the natural history of man. In its context this account of the origin of language became strikingly successful because it confirmed and extended Locke's philosophy, both in regard to epistemology and to what Locke called the 'progress of the mind'. Language was the key to our knowledge of the minds of its speakers, a principle that was in some measure open to empirical confirmation and study in universal grammar and etymology. Contemporaries such as D'Alembert, Turgot, and Monboddo were lavish in their admiration for this achievement. But even the later critics accepted this principle while at the same time rejecting some of the consequences that had been drawn from it. William Whewell admitted that 'this school of metaphysicians rendered a very valuable service to the philosophy of science' by bringing 'into prominent notice the great importance of *words* and *terms* in the formation and progress of knowledge', and by pointing out 'that the office of language is not merely to convey and preserve our thought, but to perform the analysis in which reasoning consists' (Whewell 1840: II.461–2). Joseph de Maistre made it a cardinal principle that 'thought and speech are nothing but two magnificent synonyms' (1884–6: IV, 120). In this respect, Condillac prevailed even with his severest critics.

But barely ten years after the Revolution matters had changed, and a reaction set in. It had long been taken for granted that the languages of savage or primitive nations could be used to throw light on the history of civilization. What they are now, we were once. In the year 1800 Degérando drew up an anthropological programme for a planned expedition to distant parts of the world. By such study, he wrote:

we somehow find ourselves carried to the first epochs of our own history. We can gain certain experimental evidence on the origin and generation of ideas, on the formation and progress of language, on the interrelations that hold between these two modes of operations. The philosophical voyager who sails to the extremities of the earth, in effect traverses the course of ages. (1883: 155)

Entirely based on the eighteenth-century philosophy of man, this programme took for granted that the history of civilization, taken at large, is unidirectional; examples of decline and degeneration are merely local and temporary phenomena. According to this view it would follow that the seeds of the present wisdom and moral stature of modern European man could be found in savages, even when they seemed the total negation of civilized virtues. But if man had made himself, who could say that he was not entitled to make a revolution or become an atheist or, in Victorian

England, even a Benthamite utilitarian? Such relativism was intolerable. But there was an obvious solution: language was not a human invention but in some form a divine gift, and with this gift civilization began. Savages were not on the upward move, but nations who had fallen into abject degeneration from their initial state; their languages illustrated not the rudiments of speech but its ruins. On these grounds the eighteenth-century philosophy of the origin of language and civilization could be rejected. Joseph de Maistre was the most eloquent exponent and advocate of this rejection.

De Maistre (1753–1821) was not French but born at Chambéry in what was then the Duchy of Savoy. He was born into a family deeply committed to the Church, had a Jesuit education, and in his youth came under the influence of the illuminist mystic Louis-Claude de Saint-Martin, whose thought left a lasting impression upon him. De Maistre was ultraconservative, ultramontane, and maintained the infallibility of the pope long before it became doctrine. He railed against science, academies, the metric system and all other innovations that had swept the world since the Renaissance and Protestantism. He believed that reality was spiritual, that only faith and tradition raise man above criminality, and that laws and constitutions cannot be written but exist only in the age-old customs of the people. His defence of absolute monarchy was a justification of despotism. He saw the French Revolution as divine punishment for what he called the 'theophobia' of the eighteenth century. In philosophy the beginning of wisdom was contempt for Locke, whose *Essay* was the preface to the entire philosophy of the eighteenth century, which is all negative and consequently nothing – like the *'mauvais principe'* of Protestantism (1884–6: IV, 380). Equally fatal was Locke's political philosophy, which, 'having been called to life in the steaming filth of Paris, produced the revolutionary monster that has devoured Europe' (1884–6: IV, 372). All this may sound bizarre and even forbidding, but de Maistre combined an incisive mind with great learning and a ravishing style. The importance of his social thought has been acknowledged by many, including Auguste Comte, who have not shared his opinions. His chief work and the one that concerns us here was the unfinished *Soirées de Saint-Pétersbourg*, which consists of eleven fictive conversations that were written around 1809 while he was the King of Sardinia's minister in the Russian capital. It was published in 1821 shortly after his death.[1]

De Maistre denied that language could have been invented either by a single individual or a group, for in neither case would the requisite understanding have been possible (87) – this was an old argument, used by Rousseau among others. The origin of language ('langage') was coterminous with that of innate ideas (90). Languages have a beginning, but 'never *la parole*, and not at all with man. The one necessarily preceded the other; for *la parole* is made possible only by the Word' (99). '*Verbe, parole* et *raison*, c'est la même chose' (119). Thus 'la parole' means the divinely given faculty of speech. Man was never speechless, and it is 'with sublime reason that the Hebrews have called him a "speaking soul"', but every individual language ('langue') is created by means of 'sudden birth and development' (99). Signs, therefore, cannot be arbitrary, for 'each word has its reason (99) . . . An arbitrary sound has never expressed an idea, nor could it ever do so. As thought necessarily exists before words, which are only the physical signs of thought, words in turn exist before each new language, which receives them fully made and modifies them as it sees fit' (101). 'It is perfectly clear', he wrote, that we owe the origin of language to 'the prodigious talent of infant nations for the formation of words'. Philosophers are utterly incapable of doing so, as is shown by their foolish efforts to apply their doctrine of signs to the a priori creation of a perfect philosophical language (90–1).

The divine foundation of language ensures that elements of inspired wisdom can still be found in words, especially in India where the initial illumination has suffered less effacement. The very word *etymology* is proof of this ancient and prodigious talent, 'for it supposes that each word is *true*, which means that it was not imagined arbitrarily' (101). This 'talent *onomaturge*' is invariably lost as we approach the epochs of civilization and science, for 'the formation of the most perfect words, the most meaningful, the most philosophical, in the full force of the term, belongs without exception to the times of ignorance and simplicity' (103). Etymology and what he calls 'the torch of analogy' show that words have never been invented arbitrarily; they have been received by divine instruction. He offers many curious etymologies in support of this doctrine, such as '*caro, data, vermibus*, which make "cadaver", flesh abandoned for worms' (91). These convictions contained a new conception of the state of nature and of the savage nations who had been said to live not far beyond it.

De Maistre's answer was clear: 'If mankind has begun with knowledge, the savage can only be a branch torn away from the tree of society . . . The state of civilization and knowledge in a certain sense, is the natural and primitive state of man. Thus all the oriental traditions begin with a state of perfection and light, even supernatural light.' The golden age was at the beginning of things (80–1). The savage state has been misjudged for two very different reasons, first because the Catholic priesthood that came with Columbus, putting charity before reality, had given much too good an account of it; and secondly because the eighteenth century brought all its bad faith to bear on the question. It is 'moral degradation that has in the end created what we call savages. What Rousseau and his companions call the state of nature is the last stage of brutalization' (81–4). De Maistre presents a long catalogue of savage vices, including this: 'He is a thief, he is cruel, dissolute, but he is so differently from us. When we are criminal, we go beyond our nature, but the savage follows his, he has an appetite for crime, he has no remorse' (85). The proportional mean between man and savage is the barbarian, who is capable of civilization, while the savage has entered upon a course of moral degradation for which there is no remedy.

Now, if the savage does not illustrate the state of primitive man, but 'is nothing but the descendant of man torn from the great tree of civilization by some transgression', then it must also be an error to place the languages of savages at the beginning, for 'they are not and can be nothing but the débris of ancient languages, *ruined* . . . and degraded like their speakers. In fact, every individual or national degradation is at once proclaimed by a rigorously proportional degradation in the language. How could man lose an idea or merely the rectitude of an idea without losing the speech ('parole') or the justness of speech that expresses it' (63). Language is a gauge or barometer of the moral state of its speakers, and de Maistre wished that we, for our moral instruction, had dictionaries of savage languages – in fact he suggests that we would have had them if 'the destructive fanaticism of the eighteenth century' had not for its own protection done away with such knowledge. For he did not doubt that in them we would find evident remnants 'of an earlier language spoken by an enlightened nation. But even if we did not find any, it would merely mean that the degradation had arrived at the point of effacing the last remnants. . . We would probably be more terrified by the words they have than by those they lack. Among the savages of New-Holland there is no word to express the idea of God, but there is a word to express the operation that destroys an infant in the womb of its mother' (106–7).

These were de Maistre's answers to the natural history of man. His history was divine. It began with divine instruction, with language first of all. A certain measure of improvement was possible if under providential guidance, but without it degradation was the inevitable punishment. Civilization was at degree zero before language, but language did not begin at zero. Both wisdom and civilization could be lost, and the savage was the proof and lesson of this loss.

In England Joseph de Maistre found a sympathetic reader in the future archbishop of Dublin, Richard Chenevix Trench. He also was interested in the state of civilization and the moral lessons of words, though he confined this interest chiefly to his own language and nation. Trench is best remembered for the signal service he performed in the late 1850s by formulating the scope and plan of the new English Dictionary, which eventually became the *Oxford English Dictionary*. This act alone surely puts him in the first rank of Victorian notables. But the prelude to this work was two very instructive volumes, *On the Study of Words* (1851) and *English Past and Present* (1855) both of which saw a large number of editions right into the middle of this century both in England and in America.

Trench usually let his etymologies and word histories speak for themselves; grouped under such chapter titles as 'On the Morality of Words', 'Gains of the English Language', and 'Diminutions of the English Language', there could be no doubt about his intention to reveal the admonitory but unregarded wisdom contained in words. But in the opening lectures of the first book, he set forth his thoughts on the nature and origin of language, about its divine beginning, and about its relation to civilization and its origin. Here Trench's debt to de Maistre is evident. We may begin with a passage in the second lecture that states his entire programme:

Seeing then that language contains so faithful a record of the good and of the evil which in time past have been working in the minds and hearts of men, we shall not err, regarding it as a moral barometer, which indicates and permanently marks the rise and fall of a nation's life. To study a people's language will be to study *them*, and to study them at best advantage; there where they present themselves to us under fewest disguises, most nearly as they are. (1952 [1851]: 40)

The barometer metaphor is from an earlier work of de Maistre's than the *Soirées*: 'A true philosopher must never lose sight of language, a true barometer of which the variations infallibly announce *le bon et le mauvais temps*' (1884–6: I, 301).[2] Of course, Trench never made explicit reference to de Maistre, for their religious worlds were not the same, and Trench would on occasion speak severely of Roman doctrine and practice, but the urgency of the common cause transcended such differences. De Maistre became the guide to the right understanding of the rise and fall of language and civilization.

At the very beginning of *On the Study of Words*, Trench explained why his subject was important: 'Not in books only, which all acknowledge, nor yet in connected discourse, but often also in words contemplated singly, there are boundless stores of moral and historic truth, and no less of passion and imagination, laid up – [so] that from these, lessons of infinite worth may be derived, if only our attention is roused to their existence.' To study words as 'living powers' – a Coleridgian phrase – is 'like the dropping of scales from [our] eyes, like the acquiring of another sense, or the introduction into a new world'. Some ten pages later he extended Emerson's characterization of language as 'fossil poetry' to include 'fossil ethics' and 'fossil history', a truth that 'rested on some deep analogy of things natural and things spiritual, bringing those to illustrate and to give an abiding form and body to these'. Also for Trench the spiritual world held the greater truth, and analogy was the key to the recovery of this truth.

There were, Trench explained, two theories on the origin of language. One 'would put language on the same level with the various arts and inventions with which man has gradually adorned and enriched his life', tracing its origin to 'inarticulate cries by which he expressed his natural wants'. This was the eighteenth-century theory, though Trench did not call it that, which he said few would now prefer to 'the truer answer . . . that God gave man language, just as He gave him reason, and just because He gave him reason . . . He gave it to him because he could not be man, that is, a social being, without it' (1952 [1851]: 17). This is the lesson of the first three chapters of Genesis. Adam had imposed the first names by himself, 'however, at the direct suggestion of his Creator'. Here 'we have the clearest intimation of the origin, at once divine and human, of speech; while yet neither is so brought forward as to exclude or obscure the other'. In this sense Trench, like de Maistre, conceded 'a limited amount of right to those who have held a progressive acquisition, on man's part, of the power of embodying thought in words'. Man did not come into the world 'with names, but with the power of naming', a divine capacity that 'could not remain dormant in him, for man could be man only through its exercise. . . . Man makes his own language, but he makes it as the bee makes its cells, as the bird its nest.'

This view involves a rejection of the eighteenth-century distinction between art and nature; art is human nature, as de Maistre maintained. Here is an inexplicable mystery that can be approached only by analogy, 'if we liken it to the growth of a tree springing out of, and unfolding itself from, a root, and according to a necessary law – that root being the divine capacity of language with which man was created' (1952 [1851]: 17–18). These words show the rhetorical power of the organic metaphor: final causes are not within the province of human knowledge, which in Whewell's phrase will merely 'converge to the same invisible point: and this point is the Origin of the Moral and Spiritual, as well as of the natural world' (1840: I, xxxvi; see Aarsleff 1982: 31–41). The rightness of the divine theory and the wrongness of the natural theory were, as in de Maistre, made plain by the degraded state of savage languages.

On this subject Trench borrowed details and examples from de Maistre. The history of civilization is not unidirectional, but a story of both progress and degradation. If the natural theory were true, then language would be 'an accident of human nature', and if so, 'we certainly should somewhere encounter tribes sunken so low as not to possess it', but even 'the most degraded horde of South-African bushmen, or Papuan cannibals . . . employ this means of intercourse with one another' (16). Thus both Genesis and 'every notice of our actual experience' disprove the

'orang-outang' theory . . . according to which the primitive condition of man was the savage one, and the savage himself the seed out of which in due time the civilized man was unfolded; whereas, in fact, so far from being this living seed, he might more justly be considered as a dead withered leaf, torn violently away from the great trunk of humanity. . . . So far from being the child with the latent capacities of manhood, he is himself rather the man prematurely aged, and decrepit, and outworn.

Their language shows 'in every case what they are themselves, the remnant and ruin of a nobler past' (18). Trench cited a missionary account of a tribe that once had a word to designate 'Him that is above', but the word had survived only to mean 'a fabulous ghost, of whom they told the absurdest and most contradictory things' (19). Another account told of a tribe with no word for 'thanks' and thus without any sense of gratitude, 'never saying more than "This will be useful to me", or, "This is what I wanted"'. Here and elsewhere it is clearly implied that the Utilitarians are the new modern savages.

Trench closed his observations on savage languages with these words:

> Nor is it only in what they have forfeited and lost, but also in what they have retained or invented, that these languages proclaim their degradation and debasement, and how deeply they and those that speak them have fallen. Thus I have heard of a tribe in New Holland which has no word to signify God, but has a word to designate a process by which an unborn child may be destroyed in the bosom of its mother. (1952 [1851]: 20)

These are de Maistre's words and example, already quoted. In both authors the argument is the same: progress is divine, degradation is natural.

Trench's anthropology was about his own nation. From a word that meant the threshing sledge used to separate the grain from the chaff, Latin had created the word *tribulation* in the sense of separation, but in Scripture and the Liturgy it means 'affliction, sorrow, anguish'. For Trench, this change of meaning contains a lesson, for Christian writers had made the word the vehicle of a 'higher truth' by 'calling these sorrows and griefs "tribulations", threshings, that is, of the inner spiritual man, without which there could be no fitting him for the heavenly garner'. Adversity and pain are the instruments of divine progress, as shown by the advance of the Latin word beyond the sense of mere separation known to classical and heathen times (12–13). The word *pain* contains the same lesson. Pain 'is the correlative of sin, it is *punishment*; and to this the word "pain", which there can be no reasonable doubt is derived from "poena", bears continual witness'. Thus, again with reference to the Utilitarians, this word gives the lie to 'some modern "false prophets", who . . . tell us that pain is only a subordinate kind of pleasure' (1952 [1851]: 31). In a somewhat different way the word *pastime* tells the same story by showing how the world's 'amusements and pleasures do not really satisfy the mind and fill it with the sense of an abiding and satisfying joy'. This is degradation, through pleasure and indolence. But in drawing this lesson we see even here that God has 'impressed such a seal of truth upon language, that men are continually uttering deeper things than they know, asserting mighty principles, it may be asserting them against themselves, in words that to them may seem nothing more than the current coin of society' (1952 [1851]:

13–14). Like de Maistre, Trench was committed to the crucial principle that 'words are not merely arbitrary signs, but living powers' (1952 [1851]: 23).[3]

De Maistre wished for the lessons to be found in dictionaries of savage languages, but Trench would be satisfied with a work on English

in which all the most remarkable words should be traced through their successive phases of meaning, and in which moreover the causes and occasions of these changes should be explained; such a work would not only abound in entertainment, but would throw more light on the development of the human mind than all the brainspun systems of metaphysics that ever were written. (1952 [1855]: 1)

These words, on the first page of *English Past and Present*, were credited to Julius Charles Hare, Trench's teacher and friend at Trinity College, Cambridge. Trench often acknowledged his debt to Hare, whose *Guesses at Truth* had anticipated Trench's own arguments. In this work Hare had, with full reference, cited a whole page from the *Soirées*, which he called 'one of the most delightful works of recent times, which, though its author is sometimes overfanciful, and not seldom led astray by his Romish prejudices, is full of high and holy thoughts on the loftiest subjects of speculation' (1847–8: I, 337). Hare had a very large library from which his friends were allowed to borrow; it was later given to Trinity College, where one still finds the *Soirées*, in the first edition, heavily marked by pencil in the margins. Hare's fondness for de Maistre was also well known to Whewell.

Trench was certainly aware that he was taking part in the larger Victorian debate going on around him on the civilization and evolution of man. The lectures that became *On the Study of Words* were planned early in 1845 within a year of the publication of Robert Chambers' *Vestiges of the Natural History of Creation*, which had presented the natural history of language in favour of the development doctrine that was the book's thesis. It was no doubt with *Vestiges* in mind that Trench and others talked of the 'orang-outang' theory. But the degradation argument was already powerful before *Vestiges* appeared in 1844, and this is surely the chief reason why the book offended so greatly by placing both the natural and moral evolution of man within the natural history of creation. In the crucial chapter entitled 'Early History of Man', Chambers rejected the universal validity of the degradation doctrine; civilization had certainly suffered local setbacks, 'but there was always a vitality in it, nevertheless, and a tendency to progress, and at length it seems to have attained a strength against which the powers of barbarism can never more prevail'. Chambers did not mention his opponent, but he was clearly referring to Richard Whately's *Introductory Lectures on Political Economy*, delivered at Oxford in 1831 and published the same year, in which Whately had used the evidence of savage nations to prove that civilization could not have been self-originated – 'If this was not the work of a divine instructor, *produce an instance*, if you can, of a nation of savages *who have civilized themselves'* (1847: 114). In the chapter on the 'Early History of Man' Chambers produced this instance.

He found it in the account of the Mandan Indians in George Catlin's *Letters and Notes on the Manners, Customs, and Condition of the North American Indians* (1841). For Catlin the Mandans showed such a high state of civilization that he could explain it only by positing intermixture with a band of Welsh colonizers who had, he believed, entered the mid-continent in pre-Columbian days. But apart from this implausible solution, Catlin in fact gave much evidence that Mandan civilization was self-originated, enough for an English reviewer to write that

their advancement seems sufficiently explained by their more settled mode of life. They have always lived in the presence of the numerous and warlike Sioux, and necessity has compelled them to establish themselves in dwellings more permanent and capable of defence; – thus giving them, what in England we should call 'a stake in the country', and enabling them to cultivate arts which could not flourish in a roving community.[4]

Chambers agreed: 'Fixity of residence and thickening of population are perhaps the prime requisites for civilization.' Both Chambers and the reviewer merely repeated familiar eighteenth-century arguments about the unassisted natural origin of civilization; Adam Ferguson, among others, had been the exponent of this view, which had not raised a quiver of objection until now, two generations later, it appeared in a new context that made it subversive. So Whately could not let the matter rest.

He took the first opportunity he had to get into print on the Mandans. It came with the issue of the seventh edition of his *Elements of Rhetoric* in 1846, to which he, among the appended illustrative texts, added three pages of quotation from the *Introductory Lectures* on savages, civilization, and the necessary role of the divine instructor. These were followed by three new pages of argument against the use to which the Mandans had been put, clearly aimed at *Vestiges*, though of course he did not say so (1853: 286–92). But he did not stop there. When the *Lectures* came in a third edition the next year, Whately added an eight-page appendix which consisted for the most part of quotation of all the new matter on the Mandans which he had recently put into the *Rhetoric*; he in fact made reference to this new appendix at the quotation from *Lectures* given above. But Whately still did not let go. In 1854 he published a thirty-six-page pamphlet *On the Origin of Civilization*, issued with the imprint of the YMCA, for which it was prepared as a lecture he had been unable to deliver.

All this happened during Whately's long years as archbishop of Dublin, a post in which he was succeeded by Trench in 1863. It seems unlikely that any other Victorian divine engaged in such virulent racism, fully as strong as de Maistre's, though I see no obvious reason to believe that Whately had read de Maistre – and there are other possibilities, such as Louis de Bonald. But the virulence is itself a measure, even a barometer of the intensity with which the problem of civilization was moving toward the climax of *The Origin of the Species* and Darwin's evolution. The issue was whether man's moral being and evolution were contained within his natural history, and this explains why little distinction was made between *Vestiges* and Darwin's provoking book. The central issues were the possibility of miracles, the reality of uniformitarianism, and the theophobia of the eighteenth century. These were issues of great public importance, for the stability of society and its foundations were at stake.

On 25 November 1864 Disraeli spoke in the Sheldonian Theatre at Oxford to a large and responsive audience on the occasion of the annual meeting of the Society for the Increasing of Small Livings in the Diocese of Oxford. In the chair was the bishop of Oxford, Samuel Wilberforce, who a few years earlier, also in Oxford, had imprudently put the famous question to Huxley whether it was 'through his grandfather or his grandmother that he claimed descent from a monkey'. That was in June of 1860, and during the following months he must have written the review of *Essays and Reviews*, in which he voiced the opinion that 'the real shame of originating this attack upon the faith' belonged to 'our English deists, who were the true fathers of French atheism and German unbelief'.[5] Disraeli did not forget the bishop and his causes. Referring to *Essays and Reviews*, by implication only, he praised the contributors' knowledge of Hebrew and 'their mastery in the new power of the study of language', but said that in all this they had been preceded by the scholars of the seventeenth and eighteenth centuries, represented by such figures as Jean Astruc and Father Simon. He continued:

The discoveries of these men . . . formed the mind and inspired the labours of the two great bodies of intellectual beings that have existed since the Greek philosophers . . . the freethinkers of England, and the philosophers of France . . . and they produced their effect. There was the greatest revolution, I will not say occasioned by these opinions, but no one will deny that the promulgation of these opinions largely contributed to that great revolution popularly called the French Revolution, which is not yet ended. . . . I cannot, therefore, believe that the views of the new school will succeed.

But the new Biblical criticism was not the only source of unbelief.

Toward the end, more briefly but with greater intensity, Disraeli came to the other great question: 'There is a characteristic of the present day which never existed in preceding ages, and which must be ruinous and destructive to the Church, and to all religious establishments, and that is the progress of science.' He quickly came to the heart of the matter. 'What is the question?' he asked.

It is now placed before society with, I might say, glib assurance which to me is astonishing – the question is, is man an ape or an angel? (A laugh). Now, I am on the side of the angels (Cheers). I repudiate with indignation and abhorrence these new-fangled theories (Cheers). I believe that they are an outrage to the conscience of humanity.

Disraeli did not doubt that the 'scientific teaching of the Church upon the most important of all subjects is, in fact, infinitely superior to anything that has been brought forward by any of these new discoveries'. The concluding words reveal the depth of his concern: 'In fact, society must decide between these and the acceptance of that Divine truth of which the Church is the Guardian, and on which all sound, sensible, coherent legislation depends – the only security of civilization, and the only guarantee of real progress.'[6] Divine truth was a public and political matter. Any weakening of this truth would cause a change in the present and future state of the nation.

Disraeli's analysis is interesting because he joined the two sources of the mid-Victorian crisis into a single threat to the same truth. He found one of these sources in the eighteenth century and he called the French Revolution its manifestation. The other he traced only to recent science, but here also the source was the same, for evolution was the issue that decided the nature of man. The evolution of man had taken form in the eighteenth century and received its strongest support from speculation on the origin and nature of language. These were basic questions. They were questions of Genesis and truth, of Adam and language. Language, Trench said, is 'the great universal conscience of men' (1952 [1851]: 31). There were other monuments in the debate over language, evolution, and civilization: some – those by Max Müller and Charles Lyell – very recent, others – those of John Lubbock and Darwin – to come in the near future. But the greatest and most enduring monument was Trench's plan for a new dictionary that must have all words and meanings in the course of time to reveal their lessons. It was to be the conscience of the nation.

NOTES

1 Page references given in the text refer to volume IV of the new edition (1884–6: IV).
2 De Maistre also used the barometer metaphor with reference to Bacon (see 1884–6: IV, 271–2). For Hare's use of it, see Aarsleff 1983: 241. The last chapter of this book has relevant matters on Trench, Hare, and de Maistre.
3 For Trench on dictionaries, see also his [1851] (1952: 25–6, 84–5).
4 *Edinburgh Review* 74 (January 1842), 424–5.
5 Wilberforce in *Quarterly Review* 109 (January 1861), 294, 288.
6 *The Times*, Saturday 26 November 1864. Disraeli's observations on science and religion agree closely with Wilberforce's 'Darwin's *Origin of Species*', *Quarterly Review* 108 (July 1860), 225–64.

108   HANS AARSLEFF

REFERENCES

Aarsleff, Hans. 1982. *From Locke to Saussure*. London: Athlone Press.
   1983. *The study of language in England 1780–1860*. London: Athlone Press; first
   edition Princeton 1967.
Degérando, Joseph. 1883. Considérations sur les diverses méthodes à suivre dans
   l'observation des peuples sauvages. *Revue d'anthropologie*, 2nd ser., 5. English
   translation in *The observation of savage peoples*, tr. by F.C.T. Moore, with a preface
   by E.E. Evans-Pritchard. Berkeley: University of California Press 1969.
Hare, Julius Charles. 1847–8. *Guesses at truth by two brothers*. 2 vols., 3rd edn. London:
   Taylor & Walton.
Maistre, Joseph de. 1884–6. *Oeuvres complètes*. 14 vols., new edition. Lyons.
   Vols. 4 and 5 contain the *Soirées de St-Pétersbourg* [1821]; vol. 1 the *Essai sur le
   principe générateur des constitutiones politiques* [1814].
Trench, Richard Chenevix. 1952. *On the Study of Words* [1851]; *English Past and Present*
   [1855]. London: Everyman's Library.
Whately, Richard. 1847. *Introductory lectures on political economy*. 3rd edn. London:
   Parker.
   1853. *Elements of rhetoric*. repr. from the 7th edn. New York: Harper.
Whewell, William. 1840. *The philosophy of the inductive sciences*. 2 vols. London:
   Parker.

8

UNDERSTANDING AS A PROCESS OF LINGUISTIC APPROXIMATION: THE DISCUSSION BETWEEN AUGUST WILHELM VON SCHLEGEL, S.A. LANGLOIS, WILHELM VON HUMBOLDT AND G.W.F. HEGEL ON THE TRANSLATION OF THE *BHAGAVADGITA* AND THE CONCEPT OF 'YOGA'

HELMUT GIPPER

The question of the attitude of Wilhelm von Humboldt to the philosophy of his age is one which has engaged me repeatedly in the course of my studies on this great philosopher of language, and I am particularly interested in his view of the critical philosophy of Kant and the idealistic philosophy of Hegel, and in the way his ideas differed from theirs.[1] About Humboldt's relationship to Kant much has already been said (Cassirer 1923, Gipper 1965, Slagle 1974). We know that the young Humboldt especially was strongly attracted by Kant's philosophy and that it had a lasting influence on his thoughts on language philosophy. It is also common knowledge that Humboldt strongly defended Kant's views against misunderstanding in his discussion with French *idéologues* during his time in Paris (1793–4) (Gipper & Schmitter 1979: 99–113). Finally, modern research has shown that Humboldt gained important insights into the nature of language and the characteristic world-view of individual languages fundamentally contrary to Kant (Gipper 1965; Gipper & Schmitter 1979: 99–113).

Far less is known about Humboldt's relationship with Hegel. They met in Berlin, certainly had official dealings with one another, and took up opposing positions in questions of educational policy. They also came into contact with each other in the philosophical field. Their biographers point out that relationships between the two men remained cool (Haym 1965: 580–3, 613–15; Menze 1985). It is suggested that Humboldt's reserved attitude towards Hegel resulted from the latter's opinion on his essay about the Indian didactic poem *Bhagavadgita*. Humboldt praised this Sanskrit epic as being probably the only truly philosophical poem of antiquity; Hegel contested its philosophical and ethical value.

The starting point for the present study was, therefore, my desire to investigate the background to this suggestion, and in this endeavour I found myself addressing the problem of translation which has been with me since my 1950 thesis (Gipper 1966).

It emerged that in the case of the *Bhagavadgita* the problem of translation gave rise to scholarly controversy that involved, directly or indirectly, distinguished scholars from England, France and Germany and both Sanskritists and philosophers. The discussion was sparked off by a review of Schlegel's translation of the *Bhagavadgita* by the French Sanskritist Langlois. Humboldt reacted to this critical review in great detail, whereupon Hegel, in a lengthy treatise, commented in detail on Humboldt's view of the Indian poem, and in particular on the question of whether it was perhaps the only classical poem with genuine philosophical content, as Schlegel and Humboldt had claimed. Schlegel himself also addressed himself to the translation problem.

All the participants in that discussion also referred to English Sanskritists who had studied the *Bhagavadgita*, first to Colebrooke (1824) who had made important statements on the Indian theory of yoga, and then to Wilkins, who had produced the first English translation of the *Bhagavadgita* (1785).

The contents of the Bhagavadgita *(18 cantos)*
(From the Mahabharata tales of the great fight of the Bharatas, the history of a kinship conflict):

Before the battle, the hero Arjuna stands at the head of an army facing his tyrannical relations. He begins to have misgivings about whether he has the moral right to kill his relations in the approaching battle, and turns to his charioteer Krishna for advice. This is no less a person than the god Vishnu in his eighth human incarnation. Krishna urges Arjuna to fight bravely and fulfil his duty. His caste membership forces him to fight. He cannot shrink from killing his relations. For one thing, the battle is justified: the relations have committed many offences. Therefore killing them is no crime. Moreover, people must die anyway, and in any case their souls are immortal. The only difficulty would arise from the consequences: by wiping out the male kinsmen the performance of the necessary religious sacrifices could be endangered. Preservation of the families might necessitate union between the women and members of other castes, and this would destroy the holy order of the castes. But Krishna's advice does not stop at this point. He emphasizes that battles must be fought without regard for success or fame, and explains that the actual road to self-perfection lies elsewhere. There then follow trains of thought which contain the nucleus of Indian philosophy and which gave rise to the dispute between Humboldt, Schlegel, Langlois and Hegel.

The first one considered is the so-called *sānkhya* doctrine. This reveals a road to perfection that is to be reached with the help of reasoning intellect. More important and more correct, however, is a second road, which is based on renunciation and self-concentration achieved through non-intellectual meditation. It is with this doctrine of *yoga* that we shall be concerned here.

Humboldt admired the Bhagavadgita poem and expounded its philosophical content in a lecture to the Berlin Academy of Sciences on 30 June

1825 entitled 'On the episode of the Mahabharata known as Bhagavadgita' (Humboldt [1825] 1906a: 190–232, 325–44). He emphasized the ways of thinking that were peculiar to India and, while drawing attention to apparent contradictions, he acknowledged that he was generally impressed by the 'benevolent tolerance' which was revealed by the work, even though it advocated one specific way to salvation.[2] For his part, Hegel referred to Humboldt's interpretation of the poem, and also to other relevant publications, and commented on the moral and ethical views expressed in the *Bhagavadgita*. He emphasized the contradiction between the call to spill blood on the battlefield and praise of the ascetic doctrine of yoga, and he denied the poem any serious ethical and moral value. He pilloried the Indian caste system as the main barrier to genuine ethical and moral behaviour because it granted exceptional rights to the privileged Brahmin caste and discriminated against members of lower castes in a thoroughly inhumane manner.

In this context, Humboldt's views on the concept of 'yoga' and his assessment of the problem of translation are of particular interest. He did indeed write to Hegel expressing his gratitude for the essay – which, incidentally, is written in a tone of great respect for Humboldt – but nevertheless it is clear that he felt he was under attack from Hegel for being less than competent in philosophical matters (see K. Hegel 1887: II, 234; Freese 1955: 902–3). I shall take Schlegel's Latin translation as my starting point, and then incorporate the criticism by Langlois, the French Sanskritist. Following that I shall consider Hegel's view and finally Schlegel's answer to his critics. All this leads to specific assessments of the problems of comprehension and more particularly of translation. These will be discussed from the present-day point of view and from the point of view of Humboldt's philosophy of language.

August Wilhelm von Schlegel, the first person to hold the chair of Sanskrit at the University of Bonn, translated the *Bhagavadgita* into Latin (1823), considering the Latin language to be particularly suitable for rendering the abundant nuances of Sanskrit. As an alternative he had considered Greek. In his Latin translation Schlegel tried to retain the context-dependent semantic variations of the Sanskrit term *yoga* by using different Latin words. Thus the following variants appear in his translation: *exercitatio, applicatio, destinatio, disciplina activa, devotio, mysterium, facultas mystica,* and *maiestas*.

It would be revealing to know which German terms he was trying to capture with these Latin words, or rather, why he considered these Latin terms suitable. The catalogue of Schlegel's book collection at his death shows that he possessed and therefore almost certainly used Hederich's *Lexicon Manuale Latino–Germanicum* (1766) and Scheller's comprehensive *Lateinisch–deutsches Lexicon* and *Deutsch–lateinisches Wörterbuch* (1804).[3] These dictionaries give a broad spectrum of German equivalents – more than fifty different words – for the Latin words that Schlegel used. The unity of the original term *yoga* seems thus to be seriously endangered. This refractive divergence of *yoga* via Latin into German is shown clearly in table 1.

In the first translation of the *Bhagavadgita* by Wilkins (1785), Schlegel found the English expressions *junction, devotion, bodily or mental application of the mind in spiritual things*. Colebrooke, co-founder of Sanskrit studies, had spoken of *meditation on special topics* with regard to Patanjali's theory of *yoga* in his *Essays on the philosophy of the Hindus* (1824). Humboldt mentioned this passage, as we shall see. Schlegel, however, referred in the sixth canto, which is devoted to the doctrine of *yoga*, only to *devotio*, using *devotus* for the *yogi* devoted to it.

Naturally, the fragmentation of the uniform Sanskrit term into several English, Latin and German expressions is problematic. This would be immediately clear if one were to imagine translating Schlegel's Latin text back into Sanskrit. It seems highly unlikely, in fact impossible, that the different facets would then merge together again into the one term *yoga*.

Langlois' (1824) criticism of Schlegel's Latin translation was severe, and also unjust. His main demand was that for each word in the original language one and the same word should always be used in the target language – that *yoga* should consistently be translated by one given word. He decided on *dévotion* and *dévot*, although the latter word in particular had taken on a pejorative connotation in French.

On 17 June 1825 Humboldt wrote a long letter to Schlegel in which he took up all the points in Langlois' criticism and specifically commented on the question of translation (Humboldt [1826] 1906b: 158–89; Leitzmann 1908: No. 24):

When assessing any translation it must first of all be remembered that translating is in principle an impossible undertaking, since different languages do not constitute synonymies of identically structured concepts. A good translation can be expected only from one who has realized and assimilated this point. No translation can be more than an approximation, not only to the beauty, but also to the sense of the original. For someone who does not know the language, this is all it can be; but for someone who knows the language, it must achieve more. Given a good translation, he must be able to recognize from every word of the translation the corresponding word in the original. Only the best of translations make this possible. I do not think it an exaggeration to praise your translation for achieving this distinction, along with many other qualities, such as simplicity, brevity, emphasis, lightness, elegance, and finally true Latinity. (There are only few exceptions, which, like *dêhin*, discussed above, concern the simpler rather than the more abstruse concepts.) If, as is the case with many philosophical expressions in Sanskrit, words have meanings of such many-sidedness that they cannot be rendered by any one word in the language into which one is translating, then there is no choice but to represent each aspect of the meaning with one word and to use the appropriate one on each occasion (1906b: V, 167f).

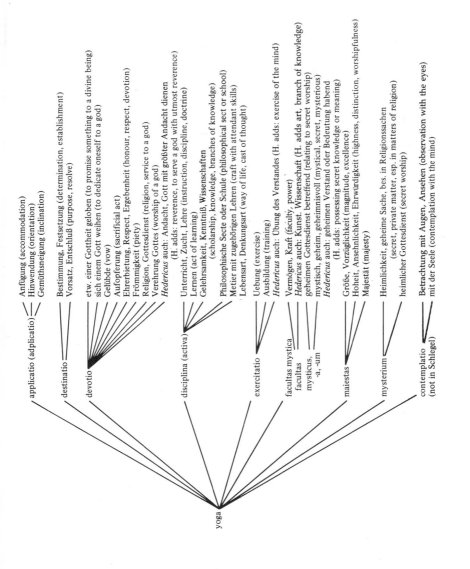

applicatio (adplicatio)
- Anfügung (accommodation)
- Hinwendung (orientation)
- Gemüthsneigung (inclination)

destinatio
- Bestimmung, Festsetzung (determination, establishment)
- Vorsatz, Entschluß (purpose, resolve)

devotio
- etw. einer Gottheit geloben (to promise something to a divine being)
- sich einem Gott weihen (to dedicate oneself to a god)
- Gelübde (vow)
- Aufopferung (sacrificial act)
- Ehrerbietung, Respect, Ergebenheit (honour, respect, devotion)
- Frömmigkeit (piety)
- Religion, Gottesdienst (religion, service to a god)
- Verehrung Gottes (worship of a god)
- *Hedericus* auch: Andacht, Gott mit größter Andacht dienen
  (H. adds: reverence, to serve a god with utmost reverence)

disciplina (activa)
- Unterricht, Zucht, Lehre (instruction, discipline, doctrine)
- Lernen (act of learning)
- Gelehrsamkeit, Kenntniß, Wissenschaften
  (scholarship, knowledge, branches of knowledge)
- Philosophische Secte oder Schule (philosophical sect or school)
- Metier mit zugehörigen Lehren (craft with attendant skills)
- Lebensart, Denkungsart (way of life, cast of thought)

exercitatio
- Uebung (exercise)
- Ausbildung (training)
- *Hedericus* auch: Übung des Verstandes (H. adds: exercise of the mind)

facultas mystica
facultas
mysticus, -a, -um
- Vermögen, Kraft (faculty, power)
- *Hedericus* auch: Kunst. Wissenschaft (H. adds art, branch of knowledge)
- geheimen Gottesdienst betreffend (relating to secret worship)
- mystisch, geheim, geheimnisvoll (mystical, secret, mysterious)
- *Hedericus* auch: geheimen Verstand oder Bedeutung habend
  (H. adds: possessing secret knowledge or meaning)

maiestas
- Größe, Vorzüglichkeit (magnitude, excellence)
- Hoheit, Ansehnlichkeit, Ehrwürdigkeit (highness, distinction, worshipfulness)
- Majestät (majesty)

mysterium
- Heimlichkeit, geheime Sache, bes. in Religionssachen
  (secret, private matter, esp. in matters of religion)
- heimlicher Gottesdienst (secret worship)

contemplatio
(not in Schlegel)
- Betrachtung mit Augen, Ansehen (observation with the eyes)
  mit der Seele (contemplation with the mind)

yoga

Humboldt comments as follows on the term *yoga*:

But since this expression is the key word of the *gita*, I will venture here to go through the various ways you have translated it. It would have been impossible for you to find in any language a single translation suitable for every occurrence of a term which derives from the very depths of the characteristic mental disposition of the originating nation. Consequently, you have had to choose several, and even though objections may be raised against some of these, though it might even be accepted that anybody who knows the Sanskrit word *yoga* only through translations can never grasp its true meaning, it would nevertheless be difficult to suggest better renderings, and impossible to eliminate every blemish. For languages tend to use a word for a sense perception in order to express an intellectual meaning. This intellectual meaning is then philosophically treated, analysed and applied. Everything that accrues to the meaning is then applied to the word itself, but the connection with the original meaning of the word of course remains, since the applied and original meaning are always thought of together. Initially they were no more than compatible, but the original concept did not oblige the mind to adopt the applied one. The translator thus merely has a choice between two methods, only one of which he can adopt successfully. He must either seek in his own language the one word which corresponds to the original concept, or else different words which render appropriately the different uses. If he does the former, he needs to add a commentary in order to be understood, for since the original concept with all its uses was not thought out in his language, it will not occur spontaneously to the reader. If, as a result, the translator is driven to the latter course, he will encounter two further disadvantages, to the detriment of philosophical exactness and depth. First, the common link between the various applied meanings and the one original concept will be lost; moreover, the nuance of each word that originates from the same source will be lost. If you translate *yoga* – entirely impeccably, I repeat – by *exercitatio*, *applicatio*, *destinatio*, *disciplina activa*, *devotio*, *mysterium*, *facultas mystica*, and the same concept in *yukta* by *intentus*, then given all these different expressions the reader will fail to perceive the original general concept of the word, without which individual uses, each with its own special connotation, cannot be fully understood; but I reserve discussion of the general concept for another occasion. Furthermore, the reader will fail to understand the distinctive character of the *facultas mystica* currently under discussion, and will understand even less *devotio* in the sense corresponding to the Sanskrit expression. For it is remarkable that you, Wilkins (p. 140) and Mr. Langlois in a way agree that *devotio* and *dévotion* are the most suitable general expressions for *yoga*; and I too acknowledge that you are right to show that *yoga* is orientated towards the deity; but nevertheless, in my opinion these particular expressions do not adequately denote the essence of *yoga* (1906b: 168–70).

Humboldt's own suggestion for the translation of *yoga* is found in his Academy lecture on the *Bhagavadgita*. In it he writes:

Yoga is a noun formed from the root *yuj* 'to connect, to tie', Latin *jungere*, and expresses the link between one object and another. All the multiple derived meanings of the word can be traced back to it. In the philosophical sense *yoga* is the constant orientation of the mind [*Gemüth*] towards the deity. This constant orientation of the mind, withdrawn from all other objects, even from innermost thoughts, hinders as much as possible any movement and bodily function, sinking itself only and exclusively into the essence of the deity and striving to unite with it. I will express this concept as 'absorption' [*Vertiefung*], and I have already done so in some places translated above (p. 215; VIII, 8–10). For even if an expression arising in one language from a very specific perception cannot adequately be translated by a single word in another language, then internal meditation [*Insichgekehrtheit*] still remains the most striking feature by which the *yogî*, one dedicated to *yoga* and immersed in it, may be recognized. The expression 'absorption' also implies the mystical frame of mind peculiar to the *yogî*, which in places where the word is used absolutely, is related most naturally to the ultimate cause of all things. Through orientation towards the deity the concept changes into that of 'piety' (II, 61; VI, 47; IX, 14); through the exclusive orientation towards one object it changes into that of 'consecration' or 'dedication', and it is suited on the basis of these two aspects to the Latin term *devotio* and terms derived from it in modern languages. But too much of the original concept of 'connecting' disappears with this translation, and the whole meaning of the word even, is probably too narrowly defined. ([1825] 1906a: 221–2).

Hegel commented on Humboldt's academy lecture on the *Bhagavadgita* in the long essay of the same year (1825) mentioned above, 'Wilhelm von Humboldt and the episode of the Mahabharata known as Bhagavadgita' (Hegel [1825] 1970: 131–204). As we have already seen, Hegel was concerned with the philosophical and ethical value of the Sanskrit poem, and had carefully studied all the available sources, expressly assessing Humboldt's essay in detail. He felt compelled as a result to deny morality in its true sense to Indian thinking, because for him there was an absolute contradiction between the demand for action without regard for gain on the one hand and the endeavour to achieve contemplative absorption in the brahma on the other. Hegel himself suggested 'abstractive devotion' (*abstraktive Andacht*) as a translation of *yoga*, and was of the opinion that this led to the complete emptying of the mind and renunciation of thought; but *brahma* itself was not comparable with our idea of God, being, rather, a matter of simple personification. As we have seen, Hegel was outspoken in his criticism of the Indian caste system with its unjust categorization of people and the exceptional privileges it bestowed on the brahmins. For Hegel this alone was sufficient to inhibit the development of ethics and morality; he also criticized the *Bhagavadgita* because of its excess of superstitious ideas and its endless repetitions. His verdict was thus negative. Hegel saw clearly that he was dealing with an unfamiliar way of thought, but nevertheless held that what we believed we understood from it was hardly worthy of our admiration. Although Hegel's great respect for Humboldt is obvious, the latter nevertheless interpreted this essay as adverse criticism directed at him on account of the admiration he had expressed for the Sanskrit poem.

Hegel's comments on the problem of translation and in particular on the translation of the term *yoga* were as follows:

It certainly runs counter to the nature of the matter to demand that an expression in the language of a people possessing a specific mentality and culture different from our own should be rendered by an expression in our own language which corresponds to it with complete exactitude, when such an expression refers not to immediately material objects, such as sun, sea, tree, rose, etc., but to an intellectual content. A word in our language gives us *our* specific conception of such an object and, naturally, not that of other people who possess not only another language but also other conceptions. While mind [*Geist*] is a common possession of all peoples and may be assumed to have developed, variation can only arise in the way a content is identified by its class (*genus*) and the attributes (*species*) of its class. There may be special words in a language for many, but certainly not all, specific variants, and perhaps not for the general class comprising them. On the other hand, the word may be either limited solely to the general class or used to denote a variety of it. Hence while the expression 'time' [*die Zeit*] comprises time gone by as well as time available and the appropriate moment, it often happens that *tempus* has to be translated by 'occasion' [circumstances, *Umstände*] or 'the appropriate moment' [*die rechte Zeit*]. What we find cited in dictionaries as different *meanings* of a word are mostly aspects of one and the same underlying meaning. ([1825] 1970: 149).

Hegel then commented on the suggestions of Humboldt, Langlois, and Schlegel for translating *yoga*:

Herr von Humboldt opposes the translation of the expression *yoga* by the French *dévotion* and the Latin *devotio* (see p. 250), remarking that they fail to denote the particular features of *yoga*. In fact, they do not express the overall concept itself, but only a derivation not contained in the meaning of *yoga*. The German expression *Vertiefung* [absorption] made use of by the eminent author, proves to be both significant and suitable; it expresses the general meaning which *yoga* conveys, and for which *destinatio* and *applicatio* (p. 41) are suitable renderings. But *yoga* has, above all, its specific meaning, which is essential for knowledge of the distinguishing features of the Indian religions. Wilkins (in the notes to his translation, p. 1409) says after mentioning the direct and general meaning of *junction* and *bodily or mental application* that it 'is generally used' in the *Bhagavadgita* 'as a theological term, to express the application of the mind in spiritual things, and the performance of religious ceremonies'. This specific meaning is here shown to predominate in the expression of the general basic meaning. It is impossible for our language to possess a word corresponding to such a meaning, because the concept does not exist in our culture and religion. For this reason, also, the appropriate term *Vertiefung* [absorption] does not go far enough; *yoga* with its specific meaning is neither absorption [*Vertiefung*] in an object, as one may become engrossed in studying a portrait or a scientific phenomenon, nor absorption in oneself, i.e. in one's objective intellect, in its feelings or wishes, etc. *Yoga* is rather absorption in nothingness, relinquishment of all attention to external objects, of activity of the senses, quite as much as it is freedom from all inner emotion, from the stirring of a wish, a hope or a fear, the cessation of all inclinations and passions, as well as the absence of all images, ideas and all specific thoughts. In as far as this elevation is considered only a momentary state we would be able to call it *Andacht* [devotion]; but our devotion stems from an objective intellect and is aimed at a God who has substance [is *inhaltsvoll*]; it is a prayer which has substance, a fulfilled movement of the religious soul. Therefore, *yoga* could only be termed 'abstract devotion' [*abstraktive Andacht*], because it moves upwards to complete fusion of subject and object and in doing so moves towards absence of consciousness. ([1825] 1970: 150–1).

Hegel and Humboldt have similar views about the fundamental difficulties of translation, but Hegel views the difference in conceptualization between the source and target languages only in terms of a logical species–genus relationship, that is, in terms of classical differentiation between *differentia specifica* and *genus proximum*. This is highly problematic, however, and it may well be the case in the concrete-objective domain that a language has, for example, terms for individual kinds of trees but no general term for 'tree'. It is also possible, though improbable, that the broad generic term exists and the terms for the species do not. But this can scarcely be established in the field of abstract concepts, for there are no extra-linguistic classifications and structures here as there are in zoology or botany to oblige us to match them linguistically; but these extra-linguistic classifications and structures might stimulate us to devise and set up corresponding conceptual pyramids. Fields of intellectual concepts can hardly be classified in this way. Moreover, there would still remain the task of first discovering the actual *differentia specifica* which is presumed to be contained in a term for the species. In the case of the different words used to translate *yoga* this would scarcely seem possible. A corresponding logical analysis of its distinguishing features would in any case be hopeless. Hegel's suggestion of rendering yoga as 'abstractive devotion' [*abstraktive Andacht*] is scarcely acceptable in a readable translation, though it could be used in an annotated paraphrase of the original. Nevertheless, we must acknowledge that Hegel made every attempt to grasp the meaning of the Sanskrit term as adequately as possible.

We can now return to Schlegel, who was the source of this discussion. With Humboldt's permission, Schlegel printed Humboldt's comments on his translation in his own periodical *Indische Bibliothek* (1826: 218–58) and went on to express his opinion on the problem of translation in general and on his own work as translator:

The relationship of the translations to their originals, the difficulties and the limits of the art of translating, and the demands which therefore justly have to be made; all these are expressed with utmost clarity in the penultimate paragraph. I endorse all the general points, though the praise of my translation of the *Bhagavadgita* needs some qualification. When I was young, I read in the works of one of my favourite writers (Hemsterhuis, *Oeuvres* vol. 1, p. 51):
'It is absolutely impossible for sublimity of this degree and nature to be translated. In

order to copy something well, not only do I need to do what the first author of the piece did, but I also need to use the same tools and materials as he did. Now, in the arts, where one uses signs and words, the expression of a thought acts upon the reproductive faculty of the soul. Imagine now that the minds of the author and translator turn in exactly the same way, with the latter, however, using totally different tools and materials. To that add that the measure, the fullness of sound, and the flow of a happy succession of consonants and vowels originated together with the original idea and form part of its essence.'

But I did not allow myself to be discouraged by this. I tried translating all sorts of texts: Dante, Shakespeare, Calderón, Ariosto, Petrarch, Camoës, and so on, even some poets of Classical Antiquity. I might now say that as a result of so much effort I have only come to the conclusion that translating is indeed a voluntary yet awkward servitude, an unrewarding skill, a thankless craft; thankless, not only because the best translation is never valued as highly as the original work, but also because the translator must increasingly feel the inevitable imperfection of his work as he gains in insight. I prefer, however, to emphasize the other side. One could praise the genuine translator, who is able not only to convey the contents of a masterpiece, but also to retain its noble form, its characteristic stamp, as being a herald of genius, spreading its renown, distributing its high talents, beyond the narrow barriers imposed by the separation of languages. He is a messenger from nation to nation, an agent of mutual respect and admiration, where otherwise indifference or even aversion prevailed.

I must admit that my efforts in this field have rarely received any public criticism from which I could derive enlightenment. People set themselves up as critics of poetic works, lose their footing in climbing the treacherous heights of metaphysics, not even knowing the basic elements of prosody, let alone how to use them, though this is the first technical requirement of poetry and a thing which can be taught and learnt. I would be inclined to reply to such critics: 'My friend, I got up earlier than you; I have long been aware of what you say in reproach: I have selected from several shortcomings or weaknesses the one that seemed the most acceptable. If you can suggest something better, providing it is metrically feasible, then state it. If not, you might as well have stayed at home.'

It seems to me a reasonable demand that criticism of translations should always be accompanied by a suggestion for improvement. I might perhaps be able to communicate much that is useful from my own experiences about the art of poetic imitation, but not as theory. There are few things I would be able to express profitably in general statements; I would always have to make my opinion clear through examples. But I do not know whether I would succeed, for the powerful impressions which poetry evokes through the choice of words, their connection and arrangement, through metre and euphony in their alternation and recurrence are based on a network of such infinitely fine perceptions that it is difficult to force them into concepts. Everything, even the concept of faithfulness to the original, is determined by the nature of the text in hand and by the relationship of the two languages. Given their languages, and also their taste, social behaviour and education, the nations of Europe, for all their differences, constitute a large family. The same thing applies to a certain extent to classical antiquity; we have inherited its intellectual achievements and built on this foundation. But if we venture across to Asia we shall find ourselves set in a quite different world. In India especially, both the development of the language and the formation of ideas are immeasurably remote from anything we are familiar with.

The translation of a philosophical poem, a translation, moreover, from Sanskrit into Latin, was a tentative experiment on my part. Although reduction into prose was necessary, I did not want to lose the form completely: I aimed to give readers at least an idea of the overwhelming majesty and grandeur of the original text.

Monsieur Langlois' demand that for each expression in the original one and the same word should be used everywhere may be valid for the translation of a geometry textbook. In the translation of philosophical texts it may only be made to the extent that they approach geometry textbooks in content and method. It will suit the works of Plato less than those of Aristotle. A poetic representation of the mind's innermost conceptions of itself and of the infinite and eternal, can by no means be treated like a collection of algebraic signs.

Now add the incommensurability of the two languages. There would be no alternative but either to use the Sanskrit word itself, as Wilkins did in many cases, as also did the Persian translators of the *Upanishad* (this method is very convenient but quite unprofitable), or else to adopt a Latin word to render a range of various meanings: this would be inadmissible arbitrariness. Take, for example, the word *dharma*. It means in continuous progression: *lex, jus, justitia, officium, religio, pietas, sanctitas*; it also means *mos*, even a mere institution of nature, for that relating to human reproduction, for example, is commonly called *mathua-dharma* in the writings of the Buddhists, as in the admonition *abstinete a rebus venereis*. This many-sidedness can be grasped quite well, and justified from the Indian system. But is there any Latin word capable of climbing up and down the scale according to the requirements of the respective context?

The word *yoga* is a true Proteus: its intellectual metamorphoses compel us to use cunning and force to tie it down and make it present itself to us and reveal its secrets. I have searched everywhere and left nothing untried. I even hit upon the idea of going back to its derivation and substituting *conjugium*, along with an adjective where it has the mystical sense. But this seemed to me very disconcerting and disturbing. I would be very grateful for suggestions of better expressions. I am not at all concerned about defending my translation, but rather bringing it nearer to perfection. (1826: 254–8).

These remarks reveal the experienced translator – the man who knows better than many critics the difficulties facing his work. Schlegel admitted frankly his own uneasiness at the equivalents he found for the term *yoga*. As befits a true scholar, he declared himself ready to test and use all suitable suggestions for correction and improvement. The various points of view presented in this discussion now lead us to consider the problem first from the perspective of present-day linguistics and then from the perspective of Humboldt's philosophy of language.

According to the statements that have been made, three methods of translation can be distinguished.

1. The first method is what I would call 'refractive translation'. Here a complex expression or concept in the source language is rendered, according to context, by various expressions in the target language, or

split up into its semantic features. This procedure may give a closer correspondence to the specific sense of a particular passage of the text, but the unity of the source concept is liable to be destroyed.

2. The second method could be called 'convergent translation'. In this case several near-synonymous expressions or concepts in the source language are captured in one expression or concept in the target language for the nuances in the source language. This may be necessitated by the circumstance that there are no equivalents in the target language. The richness of the content of the original would, however, be destroyed and a paler image of the original offered in its place. This can only be prevented by the translator trying to enrich the target language by the creative use of language through neologisms. These may have an alienating effect at first, but they also bring us closer to unusual ways of thinking.

3. The method of 'indirect translation with contextual assistance' can also be considered. In this case the expression or concept in the source language which is deemed untranslatable is retained as the original foreign word, in the hope that its context may make its meaning obvious and clear.

The first method is Schlegel's. Hegel interprets it as a species–genus relationship, that is to say a logical representation of the *differentiae specificae* in relation to the shared *genus commune* of the term in the source language. Bilingual dictionaries deal with their definitions of individual lemmata in much this way. But anyone faced with choice also has the agony of choosing. Anyone with a limited command of a foreign language will know this difficulty only too well from using dictionaries. The second method is rarely followed. The third method is frequently used, but basically it gives a false impression of respect for the source language, since the whole passage translated is by no means unproblematic. Here, too, we are dealing with attempts at translation which are sometimes no more correct than a translation of the central term would have been.

But what can be done in this situation? If we adopt Humboldt's view of language, then every language contains a specific world-view (*Weltansicht*); in this world-view the extra-linguistic world in the broadest sense is transformed into language in a particular way. Extralinguistic reality is transformed into linguistic structures. The whole vocabulary shows the world from a linguistic point of view. Every word has its own place and value within this system. It is rare for the identical system to be found in another language. Translating is, therefore, continuous transposition from the world-view of one language into that of another. In the case of a philosophical didactic poem such as the *Bhagavadgita*, we must expect that terms in the system of values of the (ideological) *Weltanschauung* or religion which it expounds will have further specific contextual values. A one-to-one correspondence in such a translation is anyway out of the question. How we should now proceed will depend not least on the aim of the translation. Should we want to offer the target group of readers merely an impression of the foreign document, should we want to convey to them merely the 'story' and the attendant circumstances, it will be sufficient to make a translation which contains just one equivalent of the original expression. If we are dealing with more demanding readers, 'refractive translation' offers advantages, but only if the original term can still be identified. This can be done by adding it in brackets. Such bracketed additions are at all events advisable in doubtful cases. A further possibility would be a comment added to the text in all cases where particular nuances in meaning need to be noted. The 1969 edition of the *Bhagavadgita*, with the Sanskrit text and English translation, compiled by a team, made particular use of this method. We can ascertain that in the case of the term *yoga* most translators decided on one term, unless they simply chose to leave the original term as it was. An overview of fourteen translations which I have consulted is given in table 2 (for bibliographical detail see the Appendix). This should ideally be supplemented by an analysis of the translated items in terms of semantic features and an analysis of the word-formation patterns together with the semantic implications inherent in them. Space unfortunately does not permit this, but the results of such an analysis, however difficult to verify, would be important in deciding on individual words.

If we consider all the expressions in, for example, German that are suitable for a 'refractive' translation of *yoga*, the spectrum of variants is so broad that intellectual unity is virtually lost. This can lead to total confusion as becomes even more apparent if one translates the expressions resulting from this 'refractive' method into yet another language. This would result in further divergences, and so on *ad infinitum*. Though most western readers will not attach such importance to the *yoga* concept that they want to spend a long time racking their brains over translating it, there are nevertheless also some concepts that are much closer to our western Christian tradition which present the same problem to the translator.

I need only mention the Greek concept *logos*, which is present in Aristotle's definition of man as *zóon logon échon* (the living being who is in possession of *logos*) and again also in the New Testament, and in particular in the Gospel according to St John, where it is said: *en archê ên ho lógos*, 'in the beginning was the *logos*'. But what is *logos*? Every Greek dictionary offers a wide spectrum of expressions that can stand for *logos*, but which nevertheless do not exhaust the concept. It is important to remember that intellect and reason, reasoning power and reflection at least, but speech, word and discourse (in other words language) as well are contained in the word *logos*. This is significant for both Aristotle's use of the word and its use

Table 2. *Overview of the various translations of* yoga/yogi(n) *in the 6th canto, which is dedicated to the theory of* yoga

	Yoga	Yogi(n)
Wilkins 1784	Yōg: (practice) of devotion (divine) discipline spiritual union	Yōgēē: devout
Fr. Schlegel 1808	Frömmigkeit	Frommer
A.W. v. Schlegel 1823, ²1846	devotio	devotus
Langlois 1824	dévotion	dévot
W. v. Humboldt 1825	Vertiefung Insichgekehrtsein	
Hegel 1826	(abstraktive) Andacht	
Sastri 1897, ⁷1977 (with English commentary)	(Chapter heading: renunciation in action) Yoga union (6th discourse: Yoga by meditation)	Yogin
Garbe 1905	Yoga Versenkung	Yogin (ein Ergebener) (a devoted one)
Deussen 1911	Yoga	Yogin (Hingegebener, ein sich Anschickender) (Devotee, a person preparing himself)
	(6th canto: devotion to self-conquest/ātma-śaṃyama-yoga)	
Edgerton 1952	discipline (of action) (chapt. 6, discipline of meditation)	possessor of discipline, man of discipline, disciplined man
Arnold (in Edgerton, part 2)	Yôga religion, true piety, holiness	Yôgin
Senart 1944	Yoga	Yogin
Goyandka (and staff of the Kalyana Kalpataru) 1969 (with detailed English commentary)	Yoga (with commentary) (Chapt. VI: yoga of self-control)	Yogi (with commentary)
Zaehner ²1972 (paraphrases and comments)	spiritual exercise practice way of integration integration of the self act-of-integration sameness-and-indifference	man of integration man of spiritual exercise athlete of the spirit
v. Schroeder 1979, ²1980	Andacht, Andachtübung	Yogin
Bolle 1979	(liturgical) discipline (of the self)	man of discipline
Rivière 1979	yoga	yogin

in the Bible. The Latin translation of the sentence from St John's Gospel is *In principio erat verbum*, and the German equivalent *Im Anfang war das Wort* ('In the beginning was the Word'). This is certainly a narrowing of the Greek meaning. Talking of the word of God accentuates the linguistic component in a one-sided manner. A check of the entries under *verbum* in a Latin–German dictionary will yield considerably fewer German expressions than under *logos* in a Greek–German dictionary. The narrowing is thus indisputable. But nobody would be willing to abandon the familiar translation of *logos* as 'Wort' or 'Word' on this basis alone, especially since it reveals a deep meaning if the power of language to constitute sense and to constitute object is fully recognized. But it is unquestionable that talking about the 'Word' of God implies an anthropomorphic view of God.

Translating means having the courage to compromise. Every individual case calls for separate examination and decision. How it will be resolved depends on the type of text, the intention of the translator and the target group of readers. I have tried to show how an historic argument among scholars was sparked off by an Indian didactic poem and has given us insight into the problem of translation. I hope also that some light has been thrown indirectly on the relationship between Humboldt, Hegel and Schlegel, but here much still remains to be done.

As I have already mentioned above, it was my study of Humboldt which led me to examine the problems associated with translation. I would like to conclude this paper with a brief outline of Humboldt's philosophy of language and to give some indication of just how the problems of translation dealt with here are to be related to his system.[4] I have attempted to appraise Humboldt's contribution to linguistics and the philosophy of language in a number of publications (Gipper 1965, 1968, 1976) and would, indeed, go so far as to claim him as the true founder of modern linguistics. There can be no doubt that he contributed to laying the theoretical foundations of general linguistics, a fact which has for long been overlooked. After Humboldt's death the field came to be dominated by comparative and historical linguistics which concentrated rather more on the question of the common origin of the Indo-European languages and the sound-laws governing their development (see Gipper & Schmitter 1979: 77–129). With the twentieth century came the ubiquitous rise of the various forms of European and North American structuralism and most recently the sweeping success of Chomsky's transformational–generative grammar. In the American taxonomic linguistics of the Bloomfieldian school in particular, with its neo-positivistic outlook and concentration on the formal aspect of languages, there was no longer any room for Humboldtian views. It would, however, have been perfectly possible to make a renewed link with Humboldt by way of de Saussure's concept of linguistic system and his emphasis on linguistic units of structure each with its own 'value' (*Stellenwert*, *valeur*). Internationally the Humboldtian tradition had hardly any impact. The same applies to the school of language typology of Steinthal, Finck, Lewy and Lohmann, and to the so-called Neo-Humboldtians, led by Weisgerber, whose content-orientated grammar was conceived in an entirely Humboldtian spirit. Only when Chomsky attempted to link his generative principle with Humboldt's concept of *enérgeia* did Anglo-Saxon linguistics again take notice of Humboldt. The fact that Chomsky misunderstood him in significant passages does not change this fact.

Humboldt thus has still to be rediscovered at an international level. His brother Alexander, the great naturalist, is in fact still the better known of the two, especially in the New World where he is sometimes confused with Wilhelm. That a Prussian diplomat and statesman of the turbulent Napoleonic era should make a significant contribution in a subject as recondite as linguistics is simply not the kind of thing one would expect.

The importance of Humboldt's work in the philosophy of language can be demonstrated by examining three basic principles. These also show just how closely the problem of translation is bound up with them.

The first of these principles is that every natural language is a separate organism, which differs from all other languages not only in having unique grammatical structures, but above all in having specific semantic structures. Humboldt says that linguistic diversity is not a matter 'of sounds and signs' but 'of world-view' ([1820] 1905: 27). This important insight has often been misunderstood and dismissed as idealistic speculation. But it is in fact readily verifiable. Any act of translation from one language into another demonstrates that the main difficulty lies not in the grammatical structure but in the semantic content. One cannot simply translate word for word, one must carry over the text of the source language into a different linguistic perspective, that is to say into a different mental structure. The underlying reason for this difficulty resides in the fact that each language encapsulates its own *Weltansicht*, a term which is, however, not readily translatable into other languages. The Amerindianist Whorf who, although ignorant of the work of Humboldt, developed similar ideas, spoke of a language's 'view of the world'. If one is to avoid misunderstanding one must not confuse this with certain related concepts. These are, in German, *wissenschaftliches Weltbild* (scientific model of the world, for instance that of Copernicus, Kepler, Galileo or Einstein) and *ideologische Weltanschauung* (ideology, such as Marxism, capitalism, religions, etc.). By comparison with these 'epiphenomena', the linguistic world-view of Humboldt, which Weisgerber prefers to call *sprachliches Weltbild* (linguistic model of the world), is an underlying a priori phenomenon, the precondition which makes possible all forms of 'secondary cognition' (Gipper 1978). The sensible world is conceptualized in a specific manner in each language, which contains a specific internal organization of the vocabulary and specific syntactic structures. The speakers of a language do not realize this as long as they only know and use their own mother tongue. As soon, however, as they learn a foreign language they notice this diversity with every step they take. The underlying cause of this is, however, not normally realized. The world-view character of language can only be made explicit by means of linguistic analyses.

The second basic principle of Humboldtian philosophy concerns 'the nature of language', that is to say its fundamental character. He says that language is not object (*Werk, érgon*), it is activity (*enérgeia, Tätigkeit*) (Humboldt 1907a: 46); it is not a static product but a process of continuous generation. Language must be constantly recreated, not only in each concrete speech act but also as 'the necessary prerequisite for the thought of the individual even in total isolation' (1907b: 155). This principle is concisely expressed in Humboldt's statement that language is 'the eternally repeated work of the mind which consists in enabling articulated speech to express thought'. It will be seen that what is meant here is something different from the mere generation of sentences according to specific syntactic rules as envisaged by Chomsky. We are dealing rather with a fact of anthropology, namely that when a human being acquires a specific language he constantly produces by means of this mother tongue thoughts which bear the hallmark of the structure of that language. Here too the problem of translation plays a key role in demonstrating the correctness of this statement.

The third of these basic principles is that of *the inner form of language*, probably the most controversial concept of Humboldt's philosophy of language (1907a: 86–97), no doubt because Humboldt failed to make it sufficiently explicit. What is meant by inner form must therefore be inferred from Humboldt's work as a whole. One must in the first place realize that it is not only the grammatical component of language that has a distinct structure, but that the semantic, or content side also has a specific conceptual structure. The semantic analysis of a language reveals that all meaningful elements, from the morpheme to the sentence, are structured according to specific thought principles or, at the very least, that languages follow specific strategies in processing thought. Humboldt refers to these inner tendencies of conceptualization by means of the term 'inner linguistic form'. In order to make this concept more explicit, one could use the term 'language style' (*Sprachstil*), as opposed to 'individual style' (*Individualstil*). Every act of translation shows clearly that such tendencies do in fact exist, and that it would be worthwhile to investigate them more closely.

The above three basic principles concern the character of human language in general (Saussure's *langage*) as well as the specific character of each individual language (*langue*). For Humboldt the universality of human language as an anthropological fact lies beyond all shadow of doubt. For the daily lives of human beings the actual diversity of the existing languages is, however, more important, because it is here that the culture-determined

HELMUT GIPPER

diversity of nations and of language communities is revealed. Humboldt was therefore right to insist that research into linguistic diversity should be the major task of linguistics.

The problems of translation provide a key to the understanding of Humboldt's concept of language. For here it is shown in all clarity that languages differ not only in form but also in content. That this is so even in the case of such closely related languages as English and German is apparent from the problems raised by the translation into English of the present essay. Quotations from Humboldt, Hegel and Schlegel are not easily intelligible even to the German reader, and their translation into English has proved still more difficult. This strikingly corroborates at the practical level what Humboldt postulated on the theoretical plane. Thus the present contribution, which has attempted to interpret each act of translation and comprehension as a process of linguistic accommodation, brings us to the very centre of Humboldt's philosophy of language.

APPENDIX. TRANSLATIONS OF THE *BHAGAVADGITA*

a) Wilkins, Charles (trans.): *The Bhagvat-Geeta* (1785). Translated with notes, by Ch. W. Facsimile reproduction with an introduction by George Hendrick. Gainesville, Florida: Scholars' Facsimiles & Reprints 1959.

b) Schlegel, Friedrich: *Ueber die Sprache und Weisheit der Indier. Ein Beitrag zur Begründung der Alterthumskunde von Friedrich Schlegel. Nebst metrischen Uebersetzungen indischer Gedichte.* Heidelberg: Mohr & Zimmer 1808.

c) Schlegel, August Guilelmus a: *Bhagavad-Gita, id est sive Almi Krishnae et Arjunae Colloquim de Rebus Divinis, Bharateae Episodium.* Textum recensuit, adnotationes criticas et interpretationem latinam adiecit A.G. a Schlegel. Bonn: Weber 1823.

d) Schlegel, August Guilelmus a: *Bhagavad-Gita, id est,* etc. Editio altera auctior et emendatior cura Christiani Lasseni. Bonn: Weber 1846.

e) Sastri, Alladi Mahadeva (trans.): *The Bhagavad Gita.* With the commentary of Sri Sankaracharya. Translated from the original Sanskrit into English by A.M.S. Madras: Samata Books, 7th edn. 1977 [1897].

f) Garbe, Richard (trans.): *Die Bhagavadgîtâ.* Aus dem Sanskrit übersetzt. Mit einer Einleitung über ihre ursprüngliche Gestalt, ihre Lehren und ihr Alter von R.G. Leipzig: Haessel 1905.

g) Deussen, Paul (trans.): *Der Gesang des Heiligen.* Eine philosophische Episode des Mahâbhâratam. Aus dem Sanskrit übersetzt von P.D. Leipzig: Brockhaus 1911.

h) Edgerton, Franklin (trans.): *The Bhagavad Gita.* Translated and interpreted by F.E. Part 1: Text and translation. Part 2: Interpretation and Arnold's translation. Cambridge, Mass.: Harvard University Press; London: Cumberlege, Oxford University Press 1952; first published Chicago and London 1925.

i) Senart, Emile (trans.): *La Bhagavad-Gîtâ.* Traduite du Sanskrit avec une introduction par E.S. Paris: Les Belles Lettres 1944.

j) Goyandka, Jayadayal [ed.]: *Śrīmad Bhagavadgītā.* With Sanskrit text and English

translation. Translated into English by the editorial staff of the Kalyana-Kalpataru. Gorakhpur: Gita Press 1969.
k) [Mahabharata]: *The Bhagavad-Gita*. With a commentary based on the original sources, by R.C. Zaehner. Oxford: Clarendon Press 1969, 2nd edn. 1972.
l) Schroeder, Leopold von: *Bhagavadgita. Des Erhabenen Sang*. Düsseldorf, Cologne: Diederichs 1978, 2nd edn. 1980.
m) Bolle, Kees W.: *The Bhagavadgītā. A new translation*. Berkeley, Los Angeles, London: University of California Press 1979.
n) Rivière, Jean M.: *La Sainte Upaniṣad de la Bhagavad Gītā*. Introduction, commentaire et texte traduit du sanskrit par J.M.R. Milan: Archè 1979.

NOTES

1 I would like to express my gratitude to Mr. T.I. Rhodes for the translation of the German text as well as to Professor P.B. Salmon, the editors and the publishers for their help with the revision of the English text.
2 The Sanskritists' argument over the origin, age and homogeneity or heterogeneity of the doctrine still continues, but must remain peripheral here.
3 See *Katalog der von August Wilhelm von Schlegel nachgelassenen Büchersammlungen*, Cologne & Bonn 1845. Reprint Munich: Omnia-Minireprint 1977 p. 49. For this reference I am indebted to the resourcefulness of my colleague R.-H. Schneider, who was of great help to me in gathering material.
4 It was only after this paper had been completed that, through correspondence with the editors, I realized that a much more general account of Humboldt's views on language was what they had in mind. I have therefore added a brief outline of Humboldt's basic views and indicated how the translation issue treated here may be related to his philosophy of language. I hope it also serves to draw attention to the fact that Humboldt's relations with the great philosophers of his day urgently need clarification through further research.

REFERENCES

Cassirer, E. 1923. Die Kantischen Elemente in Wilhelm von Humboldts Sprachphilosophie. In *Festschrift P. Hensel*. Greiz: Ohag.
Colebrooke, H.T. 1824. On the philosophy of the Hindus. *Transactions of the Royal Asiatic Society* 1, 19–43. Reprinted in *Essays on the religion and philosophy of the Hindus*. London & Edinburgh: Williams & Norgate 1858.
Freese, R. 1955. *Wilhelm von Humboldt. Sein Leben und Wirken, dargestellt in Briefen, Tagebüchern und Dokumenten seiner Zeit*. Berlin: Verlag der Nation.
Gipper, H. 1965. Wilhelm von Humboldt als Begründer moderner Sprachforschung. *Wirkendes Wort* 15, 1–19.
    1966. *Sprachliche und geistige Metamorphosen bei Gedichtübersetzungen. Eine sprachvergleichende Untersuchung zur Erhellung deutsch–französischer Geistesverschiedenheit*. Düsseldorf: Schwann.

1968. Wilhelm von Humboldts Bedeutung für die moderne Sprachwissenschaft. In H. Kessler & W. Thoms (eds.) *Die Brüder Humboldt heute*, 41–62. Mannheim: Verlag der Humboldt-Gesellschaft.

1976. Individuelle und universelle Züge der Sprachen in der Sicht Wilhelm von Humboldts. In K. Hammacher (ed.) *Universalismus und Wissenschaft im Werk und Wirken der Brüder Humboldt*, 198–216. Frankfurt on Main: Klostermann.

1978. Sprachliches Weltbild, wissenschaftliches Weltbild und ideologische Weltanschauung. In J. Zimmermann (ed.) *Sprache und Welterfahrung*, 160–76. Munich: Fink.

Gipper, H. & Schmitter, P. 1979. *Sprachwissenschaft und Sprachphilosophie im Zeitalter der Romantik*. Tübingen: Narr.

Haym, R. [1856] 1965. *Wilhelm von Humboldt. Lebensbild und Charakteristik*. Reprint Osnabrück: Zeller.

Hederich, B. 1766. *Lexicon manuale Latino–Germanicum*. Leipzig: Gleditsch.

Hegel, G.W.F. [1825] 1970. Über die unter dem Namen Bhagavad-Gita bekannte Episode des Mahabharata von Wilhelm von Humboldt. In *Werke* vol. 11: *Berliner Schriften 1818–1831*, 131–204. Frankfurt: Suhrkamp.

Hegel, K. (ed.) 1887. *Briefe von und an Hegel*. 2 vols. Leipzig: Duncker & Humblot.

Humboldt, Wilhelm von. [1825] 1906a. Über die unter dem Namen Bhagavad-Gîtâ bekannte Episode des Mahâ-Bhârata. In *Gesammelte Schriften* V, 190–232; 325–44.

[1826] 1906b. Ueber die Bhagavad-Gita. Mit Bezug auf die Beurtheilung der Schlegelschen Ausgabe im Pariser Asiatischen Journal. In *Gesammelte Schriften* V, 158–89.

[1820] 1905. Ueber das vergleichende Sprachstudium in Beziehung auf die verschiedenen Epochen der Sprachentwicklung. In *Gesammelte Schriften* IV, 1–34. Berlin: Behr.

1907a. Ueber die Verschiedenheit des menschlichen Sprachbaues und ihren Einfluss auf die geistige Entwicklung des Menschengeschlechts. In *Gesammelte Schriften* VII, 1–344. Berlin: Behr; First version 1907b: *Über die Verschiedenheiten* . . . *Gesammelte Schriften* VI, 111–303. Berlin: Behr; *Linguistic variability and intellectual development* tr. by G.C. Buck & F.A. Raven. Coral Gables: University of Miami Press 1972.

Langlois, A.S. 1824. Bhagavad-Gita id est thespesion melos etc. A.G. de Schlègel. *Journal Asiatique* 4, 105–16; 236–52.

Leitzmann, A. (ed.) 1908. *Briefwechsel zwischen Wilhelm von Humboldt und August Wilhelm Schlegel*. Halle: Niemeyer.

Menze, C. 1985. Das indische Altertum in der Sicht Wilhelm von Humboldts und Hegels.

Scheller, J.J.G. 1804. *Lateinisch–deutsches Lexicon*, 5 vols. *Deutsch–lateinisches Wörterbuch*, 2 vols. 3rd edn. Leipzig: Fritsch.

Schlegel, A.W. 1826. Über die Bhagavad-Gita. Mit Bezug auf die Beurtheilung der Schlegelschen Ausgabe im Pariser Asiatischen Journal. Aus einem Briefe von Herrn Staatsminister von Humboldt. *Indische Bibliothek* 2, 218–58.

Slagle, U.W. 1974. The Kantian influence on Humboldt's linguistic thought. *Historiographia Linguistica* 3, 341–50.

9

AUGUST SCHLEICHER:
INDO-EUROPEANIST AND GENERAL LINGUIST

THEODORA BYNON

August Schleicher and his contemporaries occupied an intermediate slot between two generations which together comprised some of the most prominent scholars in the history of German linguistics. The preceding generation had included such famous names as Bopp, the Grimm and the Schlegel brothers and Wilhelm von Humboldt, whereas that which followed them included such 'Neogrammarians' as Brugmann, Osthoff, Delbrück, Leskien, Paul, Braune and Sievers. As an Indo-Europeanist Schleicher is acclaimed today for a number of bold innovations which were to lay the foundations of Neogrammarian methodology. As a general linguist, on the other hand, he has not met with the same level of approval, his ideas tending to be dismissed as mere 'glottogonic speculation' resulting from the uncritical application to language of the evolutionary theories which were then being developed in the field of biology. This division of his personality into 'Indo-Europeanist' and 'general linguist' is necessarily somewhat artificial, but it can be instructive to examine certain aspects of his work and thinking in these terms, for it would appear that the Indo-Europeanist in him may sometimes have been at odds with the general linguist.

Indo-European studies owe a lasting debt to Schleicher for introducing two new methodological devices. He was the first to 'reconstruct' forms of the parent language for the purpose of systematic historical comparison, and it was he who introduced the family tree model as a means of representing the historical changes which, through a process of gradual differentiation, eventually result in the creation of new languages. His *Compendium of the comparative grammar of the Indo-European languages* (1861–2)[1] was in his day accepted as the unrivalled textbook on the subject, running to four editions in fifteen years before being finally superseded by Brugmann's *Outline* (1886–92). It was a thoroughly up-to-date systematization of the existing knowledge of the time and, in addition to introducing a considerable amount of new material, especially from the Baltic and Slavonic languages, it was also the first attempt to present a systematic account of the historical phonology of the individual Indo-European languages. After his death in 1868 the *Compendium* saw two further editions, brought out jointly by his pupils August Leskien and Johannes Schmidt. In the preface to the last edition (1876) these stated that they had confined themselves to minor corrections and had refrained from undertaking a more fundamental revision, since, in view of the amount of rewriting that this would have entailed, the result would no longer have represented Schleicher's views. Although they did not specifically say so, it would appear that one substantive issue which then dominated current thinking was the number of vowels to be reconstructed for the parent language. Schleicher's assumption that Sanskrit, with its three basic vowels *a*, *i*, *u*, had preserved the original system was becoming increasingly suspect and the editors clearly saw that any revision of this would have profound repercussions on the rules governing vowel alternation (Jacob Grimm's *ablaut*), a topic to which we shall return.

From what has been said so far it might be deduced that Schleicher was a Neogrammarian in spirit if not in name. There is even the fascinating thought that, but for his untimely death, he might have become one. But would he in fact have done so? When he died in Jena in 1868 at the age of forty-seven he had been teaching comparative linguistics and German philology at the university there for more than ten years but had never been offered an established post. At the neighbouring University of Leipzig, which in the following decade was to become famous as the centre of the Neogrammarian movement, a chair in Slavonic philology had, however, been in the making for some years and Schleicher had well-founded hopes of being appointed to it. But he was not to live to see this ambition fulfilled, and in the event the post fell to his pupil Leskien (Dietze 1966: 46). It is tempting to speculate on what might have happened had it been Schleicher rather than Leskien who had gone to Leipzig in 1870. Would he have embraced the new doctrine? Or, like Georg Curtius, who had been his former colleague at Prague and who had subsequently moved to Leipzig, would he have remained aloof?

Three prominent members of the new movement, Brugmann, Osthoff and Leskien, were pupils either of Curtius or of Schleicher and it can be argued that they derived the essence of their methodology, as well as much of their knowledge of comparative Indo-European grammar, directly from these teachers. The generation gap, which has been given so much prominence, may thus perhaps have been exaggerated (Collitz 1886; Hoenigswald 1974). There were, however, two closely related theoretical issues which did sharply separate the two generations. The first of these was Schleicher's interpretation of languages as 'natural organisms' endowed with 'life'; that is to say, the widely held view that languages developed according to inherent laws which were not accessible to the intervention of the human will.[2] The other was the division of the 'life' of languages into two successive phases, a prehistoric period of 'growth' during which they develop increasingly complex structures, and a subsequent historical phase during which these complex structures 'decay'. Although Schleicher was not in fact mentioned by name, both these claims were the target of biting criticism in the 'manifesto' of the new Neogrammarian school (Osthoff and Brugmann 1878), which proclaimed that languages cannot be studied in isolation from the speakers who employ them and that, since the general conditions governing the transmission and use of language must have been identical at all times in the history of mankind, prehistoric language change could not have been different in principle from observable change – as Whitney was to put it a few years later: 'All expressions . . . are at present, and have been through the known past, made and changed by the men who use them; the same will have been the case in the unknown prehistoric past' (1885: 766).

This 'uniformitarian' position is, of course, methodologically unexceptionable. It does nevertheless raise the question as to whether, by basing a general theory of language change on their perception of Indo-European language history, the Neogrammarians did not in fact restrict the actual scope of enquiry into language change. This certainly would have been the opinion of Schleicher, for the basic mechanisms of sound change and analogy which they saw as governing language change were for him merely processes of language 'decay' which he saw as being balanced by corresponding processes of 'growth'. These growth processes were inferable for him not from the comparison of inherited substance as in Indo-European, but from the world-wide comparison of morphological form which for him fell within the domain of the general linguist, whose concern was the total range of structure found throughout all the languages of the world. Schleicher's hypotheses about language 'growth' derived from the work of the previous generation which had developed a theoretical framework of grammatical analysis based on linguistic typology. Humboldt and others had in fact hypothesized that any language in the world could be assigned to one of three (or perhaps four) basic structural types, namely isolating, agglutinating and flectional (with incorporating as a fourth possibility). They had interpreted this classification in evolutionary terms as a progression from isolation through agglutination to flection. Schleicher accepted this hypothesis, including the gradual development of complex forms from simple ones through agglutination. It was this 'growth process' aspect of his theory which the Neogrammarians came to reject as 'glottogonic speculation'.

It should, however, be noted that their decision to exclude language 'growth' from investigation was thought of at the time more as a temporary suspension than as a matter of principle. Sievers, for instance, lists a number of points which distinguish the Neogrammarians from the older school, and the first of these is that 'they were inclined more or less to abandon glottogonic problems as insoluble – if not for ever, yet for the present and with the scanty means that Aryan [Indo-European] philology alone can furnish' (1885: 782). Whitney, on the other hand, emphatically endorsed the agglutination theory albeit on the basis of evidence quite different from Schleicher's: 'By all the known facts of later language-growth, we are driven to the opinion that every formative element goes back to some previously existing independent word' (1885: 769). The subsequent historiography of the subject appears to have given little weight to statements such as these and to have endorsed the 'narrower' Neogrammarian position without qualification – perhaps, as has been suggested, because much of the history-writing in fact lay in Neogrammarian hands.

There were certainly good reasons at the time for the adoption of a sceptical attitude towards the agglutination theory, for Schleicher's latest presentation of it saw agglutination processes as preceding in time those of sound change and analogy. As already pointed out, 'growth' for him took place only during the prehistoric phase when languages were still 'young' and capable of word-building whereas 'decay' was restricted to the historical period after they had lost this power. This was an extreme interpretation of the views of his predecessors and more radical than the views of contemporary and subsequent adherents of agglutination. It is true that both the Schlegel brothers and Humboldt subscribed to the growth–decay model, although they had never stated it in quite such rigorous terms. Later scholars such as Whitney relied on evidence entirely compatible with the uniformitarian principle. So what, we may ask, made Schleicher see things in the way he did? We have no reason to believe that he himself was uneasy about his doctrine. He repeated it constantly in his many publications. On what then, did its attraction depend? It is usually assumed that the theoretical basis of the two-phase model of language evolution had come from the philosophy of Hegel, who associated 'language-building' with the 'natural' state of man and 'decay' with the loss of this state as a result of man's ability to reflect upon himself (see Streitberg 1897; Dietze 1966: 66f; Koerner 1983: xxxii–xl). Schleicher did indeed endorse Hegel's claim that 'the historical, as opposed to the prehistoric phase of language presupposes the existence of completed language, since man himself could not have as the goal of his unselfconscious mental activity the creation of language form and at the same time be mentally free to merely use language as a means of communicating self-conscious mental activity' (Schleicher 1869: 35). It would appear, however, that Schleicher adopted this theoretical stance rather by way of an explanation of his linguistic observations than as a blueprint for his actual research. Philosophical argument alone would never have satisfied him, especially as he excluded the philosophy of language from linguistics proper, insisting that this was an empirical science (*eine Beobachtungswissenschaft*).

It was in fact natural science rather than philosophy which was the major influence on Schleicher. We know that in his spare time he bred plants and that he was fully conversant with the biological literature of his time (see the references in his essay on Darwinism 1863). The concept of evolution was the explanatory principle of the day, not only in biology but also in the arts (Koerner 1983: xlv–xlvii). Schleicher believed that he found evidence for evolutionary processes in language through the systematic study of language types, since their synchronic and diachronic order could be shown to form a 'natural system' in the sense of the natural order of the biologist. Precisely what constituted for him a natural system, as opposed to an arbitrary classification, can be seen from a statement which, with only slight variation, recurs on several occasions in his writings, namely that 'that which is adjacent in the system is successive in history' ('was in der systematischen Betrachtung neben einander erscheint, das tritt in der Geschichte nach einander auf': 1850: 10; cf. Robins 1973: 39, 1979: 196 note 75; Koerner 1983: xxxv). This concept is clearly based on the fact that, in the *systema naturae* of biology, the arrangement of the phyla, genera and species of living beings by ascending order of structural complexity had also been found to reflect the order of their appearance in the geological record. We must remember, as Maher (1966) has pointed out, that Schleicher was operating with a pre-Darwinian teleological (progressionist) view of biological evolution (and in fact when later in life he came to read the German translation of *The Origin of Species*, he completely failed to appreciate its true significance; see Schleicher 1863). If, therefore, an analogous arrangement of morphological types according to increasing order of complexity could be devised for language, a *systema linguae* as it were, this would in his opinion at the same time represent the order in which they had evolved.

The linguistic system that Schleicher sought to construct, based on the ascending order of complexity of the word in the isolating, agglutinating, flectional and incorporating classes of language, would for him thus qualify as a 'natural system' if it could be demonstrated that it could accommodate any language and that the transitions between adjacent types were systematic in the sense 'that each higher class includes and supersedes the structures of the classes below it'.[3] Although Schleicher was inspired by a model which derived directly from contemporary natural science, this should not blind us to the fact that the specific arguments which he used in support of his hypothesis were entirely internal to linguistics and were firmly based on data drawn from the most recent studies of Indo-European and other languages. We will limit ourselves in what follows to this purely linguistic aspect of his work and will in particular seek to show how it was the separate roles of Schleicher as general linguist and as Indo-Europeanist which conspired together to impel him with a certain inevitability towards the theoretical position he was to adopt.

For Schleicher the most important aspect of linguistic form was the morphological structure of the word, that is to say the various forms that this takes in speech. For the purpose of describing the structure of these word-forms, seen as the basic constituents of sentences, he used the theoretical framework which had been employed in the previous generation for the morphological typology of languages. We find a clear account of the underlying principles involved in various places in his writings. We shall here follow that given in *The German language* (1869: 1–30). Schleicher defines language as the representation of the thinking process through the medium of sound, thought being considered to have two components, namely 'concepts' (*Bedeutungen*) and 'relations' (*Beziehungen*). The respective counterparts of these in language, where they have no existence independent of an associated phonic expression, are 'conceptual meaning' and 'relational meaning'. Conceptual meaning refers to the meanings of lexical bases or roots. Relational meaning refers to the semantic functions typically associated (in those languages which have them) with two kinds of affix: (1) lexical (or derivational) affixes, which are a means of building up a lexicon from a limited stock of bases in such a way that semantically related words are also formally related (English *boy*, *boyish*, *boyhood*; German *Stein* 'stone, *Steinchen* 'little stone', *versteinern* 'to turn into stone', *steinigen* 'to kill by stoning', etc.), and (2) grammatical (or inflectional) affixes which indicate the functions of words in sentences (Latin *rosam filiae dedit* 'he gave the rose to the girl', where *-ae* marks the indirect and *-m* the direct object; Sanskrit *agním īḷe* 'I praise Agni', where *-m* again marks the direct object). While conceptual and relational meaning are assumed to be universal properties of semantic structure, individual languages differ in the manner of their representation through the medium of sound. All languages give overt expression to conceptual meaning in the form of lexical roots or bases, but there is considerable variety in their manner of expressing relational meaning and some languages have no morphological means of expressing it at all.

Languages which do not physically attach the exponents of relational meaning to those of conceptual meaning, either because they do not represent the former overtly at all or because they express it by simply juxtaposing a base word functioning as the bearer of a conceptual meaning and another functioning as the exponent of a relational meaning (as for instance in Chinese, where 'stone' followed by 'child' means 'little stone'), are termed 'isolating' languages ('Class 1') on account of the 'isolation' (non-attachment) of their elements. When, on the other hand, the elements expressing relational meaning are physically combined with the root to form words and word-forms, they are termed 'conjoining' or 'agglutinating' languages ('Class 2'). In this class relational meaning is given overt expression but its exponents, while distinct from those of conceptual meaning, show a degree of formal resemblance to them. The resulting word is a linear succession or string of individual elements and may sometimes be of considerable length. Although in this class the semantic structure is directly reflected on a one-to-one basis in the formal structure of the word, this is still relatively unconstrained in so far as the nature and number of its elements is concerned. This is particularly so in the case of the so-called 'incorporating' languages, which exploit this absence of constraint to the utmost 'by permitting the word to be enlarged at the expense of the sentence' (1859: 18). Finally, the 'flectional' languages ('Class 3') impose strict constraints on the number, nature and arrangement of relational elements within the word. And, because they are able to express relational meaning by modifying the root itself through the use of *ablaut*,[4] they achieve 'maximum word unity' and represent relational meaning 'in a truly symbolic fashion'.

This classification of all languages into a restricted set of structural types, although adopted by Schleicher from his predecessors, had in fact been a fairly recent development. Like Indo-European comparative grammar, it owed its origin to the 'discovery' of Sanskrit by western scholars. It was clearly not simply due to chance that Friedrich von Schlegel was among the very first in Germany to acquire a knowledge of that language and was also the originator of this typology in its earliest version. The way in which the Indian grammarians, and following them European scholars, described Sanskrit must surely have suggested to Schlegel the profound contrast which he saw between the internal structure of the word-forms of that and of other ancient Indo-European 'flectional' languages on the one hand, and the word-structure of 'flectionless' languages such as Chinese, Basque, Arabic, Celtic and many American Indian languages on the other (F. Schlegel 1808: 45–50). For, while the flectional languages expressed relational meaning 'organically' by means of internal modification of the root, the flectionless languages did so 'merely mechanically' by simply juxtaposing the root and other elements of appropriate meaning and differed among themselves only with regard to the degree of cohesion between these various elements. These two original typological classes of Friedrich von Schlegel were subsequently expanded by his brother August Wilhelm into the familiar three by splitting the flectionless type into 'languages without grammatical structure', in which, as is the case in Chinese, words are incapable of formal modification, and 'languages which employ affixes to express the accessory meanings', as is the case in Turkish (A.W. Schlegel 1846: 158–9). The first of these were later to be renamed 'isolating', the latter 'agglutinating' languages. This was in essence the system adopted by Humboldt (1836: cxxxiv–cxlviii), except that he gave special attention to the problems raised by the highly complex word-structures found in 'incorporating' languages (Basque, Amerindian, etc.: 1836: clxviii–cxcvi), a group whose classification was also to cause Schleicher a good deal of trouble.

We have remarked that the impact of Sanskrit on western linguistics was as pervasive as it was because its study entailed exposure to a new model of grammatical description. Whereas traditional European grammar had simply grouped related word-forms together in paradigms, the Sanskrit grammarians split up words and word-forms into a lexical root[5] subject to internal modification (*ablaut*) and one or more affixes drawn from a closed set and attached to it in a fixed order. Humboldt had perceived very clearly the power (although also the artificiality) of this descriptive system 'whose essence resides in the fact that a limited number of root elements (*Wurzellaute*) underlying the entire vocabulary may, by means of additions and modifications, be applied to ever more specific and more complex concepts. The recurrence of the same base (*Stammlaut*), or at least the possibility of isolating this according to definite rules, and the regular way in which the modifying additions or internal modifications function, determine the implicit structural transparency of the language' ('die Erklärlichkeit der Sprache durch sich selbst': Humboldt 1836: cxxviii). Thus in Sanskrit the rules of *ablaut* (which was perceived by Schleicher, after the Indian grammarians, as a 'strengthening' of the root vowel achieved by adding an *a* in front of it in two successive operations) when applied to the three vowels *a, i, u* produce all the vowels that can occur in roots grouped into three *ablaut* sets, each with its exclusive series of vowels none of which occur in either of the other two sets:

(1) a, ā (a+a), ā (ā+a); for example root *vak-* 'to speak': *vi-vák-ti* 'he speaks', *vā́k* 'voice';

(2) i, ē (a+i), ai (ā+i); for example *vid-* 'to know': *vid-má* 'we know', *véd-a* 'he knows', *váid-ika-* 'Vedic';

(3) u, ō (a+u), au (ā+u); for example root *stu-* 'to praise': *stu-tá-* 'praised', *stó-ma-* 'praise', *stáu-mi* 'I praise'.

Given these constraints on the structure of the base and a closed set of relational affixes, all the words and word-forms in the language could thus in principle be generated by rule and each assigned a unique analysis. This integrated representation of formal and semantic relationships was felt by western scholars to achieve the closest possible approximation to the structure of thought (Humboldt 1836: xcvii).

Schleicher the Indo-Europeanist, quick to perceive the explanatory power of this system, carried it over into his reconstructed parent language in which forms were in fact even more transparent since they were not obscured by (morpho)phonological change. Schleicher the general linguist, on the other hand, must have realized that the descriptive apparatus developed for the highly complex word-structures of Sanskrit was equally capable of application to the simpler word-structures of the other language types. For, although he does not actually say so, it is clear that the method of analysing word-structure by means of formulae which he applied to the languages of the world is directly modelled on the Indian system. And it is these formulae which constitute the foundation of his attempt to construct a *systema naturae* for language based on the structure of the word. The fullest and most explicit exposition of his views on word-structure is contained in a paper entitled 'On the morphology of language' (1859). Already in the title his indebtedness to the natural sciences is plainly visible, for he deliberately borrowed from them the term 'morphology' (*Morphologie*) in order to refer to the non-phonological aspect of word-structure. As he saw it, a scientific analysis of the word must cover: (1) 'the sounds of which it is composed', (2) 'its form', and (3) 'its function and the functions of its individual parts, if it has these'. The first is the task of phonology, the third that of semantics (*Funktionslehre*). It is the second which is the task of morphology. He chose this new label in order to avoid employing the term *Formenlehre*, which was then being used for a method of morphological analysis which included the semantic description of the relational elements (1859: 35). Morphology, be it noted, for him excluded all aspects of meaning 'other than what is absolutely necessary in order to separate root from relational elements, and stem-forming from declensional and conjugational ones' (1859: 1).

The paper should be seen as Schleicher's attempt to place traditional typology on a scientific footing by proposing explicit analyses of word-structure. It has two main sections, headed respectively 'Aprioristic exposition of word-structure and description of it by means of morphologic-al formulae' and 'Application of the morphological system and its formulae to a number of languages'. In the first section Schleicher thus seeks to establish what word-structures are theoretically possible, irrespective of their actual attestation in real languages, and asks: (1) What morphological elements must be present, that is to say, what is the minimal structure of the word? (2) What morphological elements may be present and what are their possible permutations and combinations? Word-structure is represented by means of abstract formulae made up from a closed set of symbols. These are, together with their values (1859: 2):

A, B, C, etc.,	indicating lexical roots where these express conceptual meaning;
'A, 'B, 'C, etc.,	indicating lexical roots where these express relational meaning;
a, b, c, etc.,	indicating relational elements in the form of affixes;

α, β, γ, etc.,	indicating inflectional affixes when one wants to differentiate these from derivational ones;
A̡, B̡, C̡, etc.,	indicating the infixation of a relational element into a lexical root;
Aᵃ, Bᵃ, Cᵃ, etc.,	indicating flection in the sense of regular internal modification of the root (*ablaut*);
+	indicating juxtaposition without attachment.

This inventory of symbols is, it would appear, considered to comprise all the various types of morphological unit that are needed in order to cover all possible kinds of word-structure. It contains three sorts of root, namely simple (itself subdivided by function into conceptual and relational), infixed, and ablauting. It also contains affixes which can in turn be subdivided, if need be, according to their function into inflectional and derivational. If word-structure is constrained in such a way that, compounds excluded, a word must contain a conceptual root but not more than one and that this may be preceded, followed, or preceded and followed, by relational elements from a closed set taking the form either of roots or of affixes, then all theoretically possible word-structures may be generated and represented in formulaic terms. Schleicher does this, not in a haphazard fashion but by working his way systematically through his four language types arranged by order of increasing complexity from the isolating via the agglutinating and flectional to the incorporating class. This ordering of the language types follows the principle that 'in a natural system each higher class includes and supersedes the structures in the classes below it'. He then, in the second section of his paper, tests this purely aprioristic system against the actual word-structures of a number of languages.

Schleicher further imposed on his formulae the convention that direct sequences of the same kind of relational element are not given separate representation, so that either a single element or a sequence of such elements preceding the root are written in the same way ('A + A or aA according to the type concerned), the same principle being applied in the case of elements placed after the root; the simultaneous presence of both types of placement is, however, given overt representation ('A + A + 'B or aAb). He was enabled by this device to reduce the potentially very large number of possible formulae to a more manageable set. Thus, in the isolating type (Class 1) the simplest possible word-structure is a single root, or this may be accompanied by one or more relational elements which are identical in form to roots. Taking into account the three arrangements described and the convention regarding sequences, this yields a total of only four possible structures: A, 'A + A, A + 'A and 'A + A + 'B. In the agglutinating type (Class 2) there is no such formal identity between roots and relational elements, these having the form of affixes. Here Schleicher recognizes seven possible word-structures, determined by the position of the affixes and by whether the root is simple or infixed: aA, Aa, aAb; A_a, bA_a, A_ab and bA_ac. The characteristic feature of the flectional type (Class 3) is internal modification of the root (*ablaut*) as a means of conveying relational meaning. This class is seen by Schleicher as having two sub-groups, depending upon whether the ablauting root is combined with isolating structure (Class 3a), giving four possibilities: A^a, 'A + A^a, A^a + 'A and 'A + A^a + 'B or with agglutinating structure (Class 3b) with seven possibilities: aA^a, A^aa, aA^ab; A_a^a, bA_a^a, A_a^ab and bA_a^ac. Provided that *ablaut* is confined to conceptual roots, this yields a total of eleven possible structures, whereas if it is extended to relational roots, the total number is twice as many as in Class 3b, that is to say fourteen. It is only in the incorporating type (Class 4), which comes last because of the complexity of its structure, that the range of possible formulae becomes very large. In theory it includes the combined possibilities of all three previous classes. Schleicher estimates that all conceivable combinations would add up to about a thousand possible word-structures.

As we have already mentioned, Schleicher saw this system as 'natural' and therefore as having diachronic implications, 'adjacency in the system corresponding to successiveness in time'. He thus perceived significance in the transitions between the classes. In Class 1 lexical roots and relational elements are formally identical. In Class 2 there is no such formal identity, although roots and relational elements frequently show a degree of formal and semantic similarity. For Schleicher this indicates that affixes are historically derived from lexical roots, the transition from the isolating to the agglutinating type involving the formal reduction and attachment of those lexical roots which carry relational meaning. The systematic step in the transition from Class 2 to Class 3 is the addition of internal modification of the root (*ablaut*) as a means of conveying relational meaning. Schleicher retains the same set of symbols (a, b, c, etc.) for the relational affixes of the flectional class as he used for the agglutinating class, and we may thus assume that there was no doubt in his mind that these affixes have the same theoretical status as those of Class 2 and that they also derive historically from lexical roots.[6] The historical origin of the incorporating type he leaves open.

In the second section of the paper Schleicher compares this aprioristic set of possible language types and their associated word-structures with what is actually attested in the languages investigated by him. These languages are clearly intended to represent a sample of all extant languages. This comparison of the theoretically possible with the actually attested raised a number of issues. He first poses the question of whether in Class 1 languages the simplest possible structure A (the *Urform*) does in fact exist. He finds that it does, for instance in Ancient Chinese where a sentence may simply have the structure A B C. However, even at that early period such structures are rare since the language was already making frequent use of lexical roots with generalized meanings for the purpose of expressing relational meaning (for example *ši yl* 'small stone', cf. *ši* 'stone', *yl* 'child').

He next considers the question of transitions between classes. Two findings emerge here which would appear to confirm that the systematic arrangement of the morphological classes by increasing order of formal complexity is significant. The first of these is the observation that, although the structures of the agglutinating and the flectional classes (Classes 2 and 3) frequently co-occur, a combination of those of the isolating and flectional classes (Classes 1 and 3) does not appear to do so. Thus Class 3a, which combines the structures of Classes 1 and 3, does not seem to be empirically attested. Schleicher sees the reason for this 'gap' in the probable existence of a cause and effect relationship between affixation and internal modification, namely that internal modification is conditioned by affixation. One argument he gives in favour of this assumption is that *ablaut* without affixation, that is to say the structure A^a, seems to be rare in the languages of the world. The historical transition from A to A^a would thus have progressed through the intermediate stages A + 'A, Aa, and perhaps even A̧ (1859: 28), although it is true that certain word-pairs in Chinese, such as *lai* 'to come' as opposed to *laí* 'to invite, make come', are differentiated by tone alone. Such cases as this latter raised the question as to whether tonal distinctions expressing relational meaning should be interpreted as internal modification of the root, which would imply the occurrence of internal modification without affixation as a mechanism and hence the possibility of a systematic (and therefore historical) transition from Class 1 to Class 3. Schleicher argues against such an analysis on the grounds that, in Chinese at least, the representation of relational meaning by means of change of tone is not a regular pattern if measured against the regularity of *ablaut* in Sanskrit, where any given vowel is uniquely associated with just one series and where a given morphological category is consistently associated with a given vowel grade. The conclusion he draws from this is that the virtual non-occurrence of regular internal modification of the root in Class 1 and the marked rarity of internal modification without affixation in Class 3 appear to exclude the possibility of a direct transition from isolation to flection.

His second observation with regard to transitions between classes relates to the place of the incorporating languages (Class 4) within the system. We have already remarked that Humboldt had hesitated over the classification of these languages, in which the remainder of the sentence appears to be in apposition to the verb. On re-examining the limited evidence at his disposal, Schleicher placed these languages in the first instance between the agglutinating and flectional class because of the apparent absence in them of combinations with A^a. Thus, while structures such as 'A + aA, 'A + aA + 'B are attested, equally conceivable combinations with A³ (Class 3) do not appear to exist ('sind schwerlich zu finden'). This is the conclusion he reached in the 1859 paper. In a subsequent review of the question in his and Kuhn's journal (1861: 257), he prefers to treat them as a subgroup of Class 2 on the grounds that the mechanisms they employ in their word-structure do not exceed the combined possibilities of Classes 1 and 2.

Schleicher's findings that Class 3 languages nearly always contain the structures of Class 2 languages but never those of Class 1 and that there is no justification for the setting up of a fourth incorporating class, since its languages can be accommodated within Class 2, were interpreted by him as confirming his assumption that there has been an evolutionary progression of language from Class 1 through Class 2 to Class 3 and that Class 3 could not have developed directly from Class 1. He also found that all the actually existing word-structures of the language sample examined by him could readily be handled in terms of his formulae. In the absence of positive evidence then, his inventory of morphological units and three language classes could be seen to form a truly 'general' (i.e. universal) system in the sense that it can accommodate all languages and thus give an explicit account of constraints on word structure in general.[7] Read diachronically the system supported the 'agglutination theory' of the time (see Bopp [1824] 1972: 43–80, Humboldt [1822] 1905: 295–307). It is clear that Schleicher considered the transitions between successive types of word-structure to be just as systematic in their phase of language history as were the derivations of word-forms in individual Indo-European languages from their respective protoforms by means of the sound-laws in their phase. He attached considerable significance to his morphological formulae, comparing them to those of mathematics in that both could be 'put to work' (1859: 28). It would thus appear that in Schleicher's view the rules governing both phases of language history, namely that of evolutionary development through the three typological classes and that of decay which set in after the earliest stages of Indo-European, were both capturing significant generalizations. As we have seen, however, he saw these two diachronic processes as successive in time.

Anna Morpurgo Davies (1975: 635), who counts Schleicher among the few scholars of his time to have made a systematic distinction between typological and genealogical classification, draws attention to the fact that he did actually consider the theoretical possibility of two languages being genealogically related although belonging to two different typological classes. Such a situation was perfectly conceivable to him, since he rightly saw typological classification as determined by structure and genealogical classification by sound correspondences. He, however, rejected the possibility on empirical grounds: 'All languages which have so far been recognized as belonging to a single family agree also in their morphological form. The splitting-up of the parent language must thus have begun only after the evolution of the morphological form had already been completed' (1869: 31). His claim that genealogical relationship implies membership of the same typological class, and that the division into typological classes preceded the division into language families, was thus to him empirically based rather than made as a matter of principle. The sequential ordering of these two types of classification rested for him on two 'certainties' (*Gewissheiten*), namely that 'languages have developed in such a way that the higher forms have originated from lower ones' and that 'in the period during which we can observe them, that is to say in the historical phase, languages do not develop further; on the contrary, they decline'. He goes on to say: 'If we combine these two facts, the true state of affairs is self-evident. Evolution, that is to say the development of language-morphology, occurred during those periods of its life which lie before all history.' Only after this statement does Schleicher turn to Hegelian philosophy: 'We could equally well have reached this conclusion on the basis of the fact that nations with uncompleted languages cannot possibly play a role in history. . . . Language formation and history are human activities such that one takes over where the other has left off: they . . . never co-occur' (1869: 35). The 'objective proof' of this assertion Schleicher saw in the inverse relationship which holds between history and language form, namely that the richer and more formidable the history of a nation the faster its language decayed morphologically, as is shown by the example of the English.

It must be faced that the essential compatibility and complementarity of processes of growth and decay, in the sense that the rules governing the former were morphological in nature whereas those governing the latter were essentially phonological in nature, was not considered by Schleicher as a realistic possibility. In the last instance the entirely different nature of the data relating to these two domains, namely word-structure examined on a world-wide basis in the one and the successive shapes of inherited word-forms within the history of a single language family in the other, must have been a major factor in shaping his attitude as a general linguist on the one hand and as an Indo-Europeanist on the other.

Schleicher the Indo-Europeanist only perceived the gradual disintegration of the transparent morphological structures which he found in the reconstructed parent language and the earliest stages of the daughter languages, where there is a regular and systematic relationship between functional category and morphological element. In the 'classical' stages of these latter this structure had already given way to 'symbolic' exponency of the various categories. This can be seen for instance in the nominative singular forms of the present participle of the verb *túptein* 'to beat' in Greek (1850: 114), where masculine *túptōn*, feminine *túptousa* and neuter *túpton* show a typically 'symbolic' marking of gender. The formal relationship between these three is considerably more transparent, however, in their reconstructed protoforms where a single shared stem *tuptont-* and the affixation of overt gender (and case) markers give masculine *tuptont-s*, feminine *tuptont-ya* and neuter *tuptont* respectively. From these the later Greek forms are derived by means of 'the sound-laws which have general validity in Greek'. It is the sound-laws then which lead to the 'fusion and inseparability of the elements expressing conceptual and relational meaning' which we typically associate with the flectional language type. The very earliest stages of flectional languages are thus characterized by their speakers having 'a feeling for the functions of the individual parts of the word'. In the later stages, however, this feeling is progressively lost, so that eventually it is the whole word which may be said to carry these functions simultaneously. Schleicher illustrates this further development by comparing certain Latin verb-forms with their reflexes in Italian (1869: 64):

Latin *dīc-ō* 'I say'	>	Italian *dico* /diko/
dīc-it 'he says'	>	*dice* /ditʃe/
dīc-sī 'I said'	>	*dissi* /dis:i/
dīc-tu-s 'said'	>	*detto* /det:o/

In the modern Indo-European languages then, there is no longer that 'feeling for the individual parts of the word' and Schleicher does not propose any internal analysis of their word-forms. They are in fact the only languages which are systematically excluded from being assigned structural formulae in his universal system of word-structures. It is true that he considers them to be members of Class 3, but only by virtue of their past history and not on the basis of their present structure. Either he considered a morphological analysis to be impossible in their case or he did not consider it desirable. His general principle that 'in all known languages the root can be separated from the relational elements by means of scientific analysis' (1869:7) he simply does not apply where they are concerned. Schleicher's reason for treating the Indo-European languages in their 'decayed' state, and these alone, differently from all the others can only have been his knowledge of their history, the fact that their word-forms directly continue – but for the effects of sound-change – the kind of ancestral structures we have described for the earliest stages of Indo-European, each perfectly analysable and with a regular correlation between morphological elements and functional categories.[8] It would thus seem that here the factual knowledge of the Indo-Europeanist was seriously impeding the vision of the general linguist.

Schleicher was of course fully aware of the fact that these modern languages had compensated for their loss of 'synthetic' morphological structure by developing new 'analytic' devices for signalling relational meaning such as articles, obligatory use of subject pronouns, prepositional phrases, auxiliary verbs and word order. He also saw very clearly that these analytic devices showed a distinct similarity to those of the isolating languages, in that lexical items with generalized meanings had become function-words by a process of grammaticalization. And he naturally asked the question whether this development from synthetic to analytic structure did not in fact constitute a return to Class 1, so that the observed progression through the morphological types was simply a stage in a more comprehensive cyclical process. Curiously, he did not in fact conclude that this was the case. The visible structural similarities between English and Chinese, for example, did not in his eyes constitute evidence of the existence of such a cycle for two reasons. Firstly, he saw no positive evidence in the history of isolating languages such as Chinese that they ever possessed more complex word-structures in the past. Secondly, unlike Chinese and the other isolating languages, even the most decayed Indo-European languages such as English still retained at least vestiges of earlier *ablaut*. By virtue of these vestiges the modern languages of the flectional class with their analytic structures were thus to him still members of Class 3.

For Schleicher, as already for A.W. Schlegel and Humboldt before him, the division into analytic and synthetic structure is internal to Class 3 and membership of this class is restricted, as far as he is concerned, to the Semitic and Indo-European languages as the only ones which fully possess the defining feature of *ablaut*. Other potential candidates for Class 3 membership were refused admission on closer inspection: Ural–Altaic languages because their vowel harmony, despite its superficial similarity to *ablaut*, is phonologically conditioned and hence 'purely mechanical'; Chinese, as already mentioned, because of the irregular character of its tonal alternations; and languages such as Coptic and Tibetan because the conditions which govern their vowel alternations are not clearly discernible. As a preliminary solution pending further investigation, Schleicher suggested labelling their changeable roots as $\underline{A}$ etc. so as to distinguish them from regularly alternating ones which are labelled A[a]. Genuine flection was then for him restricted to Semitic and Indo-European, although he was fully aware of the limitations of his sources in this respect, especially those relating to Caucasian.

We have already mentioned that Schleicher saw *ablaut*, the defining feature of the flectional languages, through the eyes of the Sanskrit grammarians, namely as two degrees of 'strengthening' of the root vowel (*a*, *i*, or *u*) for the purpose of signalling relational meaning. He never abandoned this morphological interpretation, although already Bopp, and following him (although with some reservations) Humboldt, had held that the three basic vowels probably resulted rather from the 'weakening' of originally 'fuller' vowels or diphthongs under specific phonological conditions only partially accessible to reconstruction. For them, therefore, *ablaut* could not initially have had any morphological role. For Schleicher on the other hand, as for Jacob Grimm, the vowel grade (and in Germanic also the vowel shade) had symbolic function and was morphologically significant from the start. Curiously, the fact that one and the same *ablaut* grade should serve quite distinct functions (marking 'perfect' for instance as well as 'causative') did not worry him, whereas in the case of affixes he refused to accept a similar homophony, claiming that the single suffix *-tu- for instance, marking agent and action nouns, indicated the original non-differentiation of these two semantic categories. (Further complications, such as the existence of qualitative *ablaut* *e~*o alongside the quantitative one discussed so far, were of course only to come with the five-vowel system of the Neogrammarians.)

Schleicher must have been aware of Bopp's criticism of Grimm's 'mythical' views concerning *ablaut* (see Wyss 1979: 126, 145) and he was certainly aware of Humboldt's views on the matter. It is puzzling therefore that he, normally so thoroughly up to date in the scholarship of his day, should have been so conservative in this respect. One possible reason for his position on this point might be the fact that in the Semitic languages the morphological function of the vowels inserted into the consonantal root seems to be paramount and that here there appears to be no discernible trace of a phonological origin. He was also particularly conscious of the fact that in Semitic *ablaut* is frequently the sole marker of relational meaning so that A[a] alone is a frequent word-structure, whereas in Indo-European it normally only co-occurs with affixation and the structure A[a] is restricted on the whole to imperatives and vocatives. To Schleicher, however, these were quite unlike other word-forms in that they are not strictly syntactic constituents but more like 'verbal gestures' and thus outside the sentence proper. He considers the canonical structure of the Proto-Indo-European word to be A[a](a)α, that is to say one or more optional derivational suffixes followed by one or more obligatory inflectional ones.

Although Schleicher saw other criteria as a potential basis for classification, to him it was the morphology which was central to the grammar and within morphology the internal modification of the root was a basic distinguishing feature. We may wonder how he would have analysed Sanskrit had it come down independently of the analyses of the Indian grammarians. No doubt he would then have attributed less importance to internal modification of the root and seen Indo-European and Semitic as less unusual among the languages of the world. But, without the Indian grammarians' analyses, he would not have had at his disposal the descriptive framework which is the basis of his 'natural system of language' and upon which his morphological formulae depend.[9]

We have attempted in this discussion to examine Schleicher's thinking from two different angles, that of the Indo-Europeanist and that of the general linguist. Subsequently, at least in Germany, these two roles tended no longer to be united within a single scholar and often not even within the same department. It is possible that Schleicher's failure to integrate these two lines of enquiry may in fact have largely been responsible for creating this rift. For it would seem that from the Neogrammarians onwards Indo-European studies tended to espouse his empiricism to the extent of developing an oversensitivity towards theory ('speculation'), forgetting that there were issues such as the creation of new morphological form which had deliberately been left open for future research. It was easy in principle to replace Schleicher's two-phase model by a uniformitarian one. But in practice it proved difficult if not impossible to accommodate the creation of new morphology within the Neogrammarian framework. If agglutination processes were to complement sound change and analogy, they must necessarily conform to the relevant sound laws. But in fact there was usually some conflict and the possibility of mechanisms other than sound change and analogy being involved was never developed.

NOTES

1 German titles and textual quotations are always given in my own English translation. Information regarding existing English translations will be found in the References.

2 The 'organism' concept was part and parcel of the scientific metalanguage of the time and was all-pervasive in the arts as well as in science. In the linguistic domain Bopp, for instance, spoke, in what might be called typically Schleicherian terms, of languages being 'natural organisms' (*Naturkörper*) which come into existence following well-defined laws, develop according to an 'inherent vital principle' (*ein inneres Lebensprinzip*) and then 'die' (*sterben ab*) (Wyss 1979: 125; cf. Aarsleff 1982: 293ff). Here 'organism' clearly implies an inherent propensity for change whereas elsewhere Bopp uses the term more loosely, in the sense of 'structure' or 'system' (Morpurgo Davies 1986).

3 'Include and supersede' is my rendering of the Hegelian *aufheben* which, in ordinary language, means both 'to lift up' and 'to nullify, cancel'. In philosophical usage it combines the concepts of *negare*, *conservare* and *elevare*.

4 This ability of the root to 'inflect' was, at the time, held to be the defining characteristic of a flectional language. The relationship between this 'inner' inflection and 'inflection' in the sense of declension and conjugation, that is modification by means of affixes, was not systematically considered (see note 6 below). Because of this ambiguity we have on the whole avoided using the term.

5 It is true that the concept of 'root' was not entirely unknown at the time, having for instance been employed in the analysis of Hebrew and Arabic for several centuries. It had not, however, been applied in linguistic analysis in general.

6 Schleicher did not consider the alternative of a merely prosodic explanation of ablauting affixes. As regards the equal structural status and historical derivation of

affixes in agglutinating and flectional languages, his position differs sharply from that held by Friedrich von Schlegel, for whom the affixes of flectional languages had 'organically sprouted from the root as the centre of germination' whereas those of the non-flectional languages were 'merely mechanical additions'.

7 He took this universalist aim of covering all structural possibilities extremely seriously, and one of his early works, *The languages of Europe in systematic outline* (1850) even contains a section on Chinese since there was no European representative of the isolating language type.

8 Delbrück (1919: 99) draws attention to a statement from the *Compendium* (1861–2) which says that without a knowledge of 'the laws according to which languages change it is impossible to understand the forms of the languages under investigation, especially the present-day ones'.

9 The fact that he focused his attention on *morphological* form is perhaps less important than his wider methodological principle that functional analysis must be firmly based on formal distinctions. In one of his last major publications, devoted to 'the differentiation of noun and verb in their morphological form' (1865), he argues that the status of noun and verb as universal linguistic categories must depend on their formal differentiation. Finding that they are not in fact always morphologically differentiated, he denies their universality. The general principle that functional analysis must rest on formal distinctions has stood the test of time, although not of course the restriction to morphological form. The criterion of distribution was not, however, to come until much later.

REFERENCES

Aarsleff, Hans. 1982. Bréal vs. Schleicher: reorientation in linguistics during the latter half of the nineteenth century. In *From Locke to Saussure*, 293–334. London: Athlone Press.

Arens, Hans. 1955. *Sprachwissenschaft: der Gang ihrer Entwicklung von der Antike bis zur Gegenwart*. Freiburg & Munich: Karl Alber.

Bopp, Franz. 1972. *Kleine Schriften zur vergleichenden Sprachwissenschaft* (Gesammelte Berliner Akademieabhandlungen 1824–54) Leipzig: Zentralantiquariat der Deutschen Demokratischen Republik.

Brugmann, Karl. 1886–92. *Grundriss der vergleichenden Grammatik der indogermanischen Sprachen* 5 vols. Strassburg: Trübner; English translation by Joseph Wright et al., *Elements of the comparative grammar of the Indo-Germanic languages*, London: Trübner 1885–95; reprinted as vol. lxxxiv of Chowkhamba Sanskrit studies, Varanasi: Chowkhamba Sanskrit Series Office.

Christmann, H.H. (ed.) 1977. *Sprachwissenschaft des 19. Jahrhunderts*. Darmstadt: Wissenschaftliche Buchgesellschaft.

Collitz, Hermann. 1886. Die neueste Sprachforschung und die Erklärung des indogermanischen Ablautes. *Beiträge zur Kunde der indogermanischen Sprachen* 11, 203–42; reprinted in T.H. Wilbur (ed.), *The Lautgesetz controversy*. Amsterdam: Benjamins 1977.

Delbrück, Berthold. 1919. *Einleitung in das Studium der indogermanischen Sprachen*. 6th edn. Leipzig: Breitkopf & Härtel.

Dietze, Joachim. 1966. *August Schleicher als Slawist*. Berlin: Akademie-Verlag.

Hoenigswald, Henry M. 1974. Fallacies in the history of linguistics. In Dell Hymes (ed.) *Studies in the history of linguistics*. Bloomington: Indiana University Press.

Humboldt, Wilhelm von. [1822] 1905. Über das Entstehen der grammatischen Formen und ihren Einfluss auf die Ideenentwicklung. In *Gesammelte Schriften* vol. IV, 285–313. Berlin: Behr.

   [1836] 1960. *Über die Verschiedenheit des menschlichen Sprachbaues und ihren Einfluss auf die geistige Entwickelung des Menschengeschlechts*. Facsimile reprint. Bonn: Dümmler; *Linguistic variability and intellectual development* translated by G.C. Buck & F.A. Raven. University of Pennsylvania Press 1972.

Koerner, Konrad E.F. 1981. Schleichers Einfluss auf Haeckel: Schlaglichter auf die wechselseitige Abhängigkeit zwischen linguistischen und biologischen Theorien im 19. Jahrhundert. *Nova acta Leopoldina* New Series 54, No. 245, 731–45.

   1982. The neogrammarian doctrine: breakthrough or extension of the Schleicherian paradigm? In J. Peter Maher, Allan R. Bomhard & E. F. Konrad Koerner (eds.), *Papers from the 3rd International Conference on Historical Linguistics*. Amsterdam: Benjamins, 129–52.

   1983. The Schleicherian paradigm in linguistics. In Schleicher 1983, xxxii–lxii.

Maher, J. Peter. 1966. More on the history of the comparative method: the tradition of Darwinism in August Schleicher's work. *Anthropological Linguistics* 8, 1–12.

   1983. Introduction. In Schleicher 1983, xvii–xxxii.

Morpurgo Davies, Anna. 1975. Language classification in the nineteenth century. In T.A. Sebeok (ed.) *Current trends in linguistics* 13: *Historiography of linguistics*, 607–716.

   1986. 'Organic' and 'organism' in Franz Bopp. In H.M. Hoenigswald & L. Wiener (eds.), *Biological metaphor and cladistic classifications*. Philadelphia: University of Pennsylvania Press.

Osthoff, Hermann & Karl Brugman. 1878. Vorwort. *Morphologische Untersuchungen* 1, iii–xx; English translation in W.P. Lehmann, *A reader in nineteenth century historical Indo-European linguistics*, chapter 14. Bloomington: Indiana University Press.

Robins, R.H. 1973. *Ideen- und Problemgeschichte der Sprachwissenschaft*. Frankfurt on Main: Athenäum.

   1978. The neogrammarians and their nineteenth century predecessors. *Transactions of the Philological Society* 1978, 1–16.

   1979. *A short history of linguistics*, 2nd edn. London: Longman.

Schlegel, August Wilhelm von. 1846. Observations sur la langue et la littérature provençales. In E. Böcking (ed.) *Oeuvres écrites en français*, vol. 2. Leipzig.

Schlegel, Friedrich von. [1808] 1977. *Über die Sprache und Weisheit der Indier*. (New edition with an introductory article by Sebastiano Timpanaro) Amsterdam: Benjamins.

Schleicher, August. 1848. *Zur vergleichenden Sprachengeschichte*. Bonn: H.B. König.

   [1850] 1983. *Die Sprachen Europas in systematischer Übersicht* (New edition with an introductory article by Konrad Koerner) Amsterdam: Benjamins.

1859. Zur Morphologie der Sprache. *Mémoires de l'Académie des Sciences de St-Pétersbourg* series 7, vol. 1, no. 7, 1–38.

1861. Zur Morphologie der Sprachen. *Beiträge zur vergleichenden Sprachforschung auf dem Gebiete der arischen, keltischen und slavischen Sprachen* 2, 256–7.

1861–2. *Compendium der vergleichenden Grammatik der indogermanischen Sprachen.* 2 vols. Weimar: Böhlau; *A compendium of the comparative grammar of the Indo-European, Sanskrit, Greek, and Latin languages* (translated from the third German edition by Herbert Bendall) London: Trübner 1874–7.

1863. *Die Darwinsche Theorie und die Sprachwissenschaft: offenes Sendschreiben an Herrn Dr. Ernst Häckel.* Weimar: Böhlau; reprinted in Christmann 1977, 85–105.

1865. Die Unterscheidung von Nomen und Verbum in ihrer lautlichen Form. *Abhandlungen der Königlich-Sächsischen Gesellschaft der Wissenschaften* 10, Philologisch-historische Klasse 4, 5; 497–587.

1869. *Die deutsche Sprache.* 2nd edn. Stuttgart: Cotta.

Schmidt, Johannes. 1890. Schleicher, August S. In *Allgemeine Deutsche Biographie* vol. 31, 402–16. Berlin: Duncker & Humblot.

Sievers, Eduard. 1885. Philology, part II: Comparative philology of the Aryan languages. In *Encyclopaedia Britannica* 9th edn. Edinburgh: Adam & Charles Black; vol. XVIII, 781–90.

Streitberg, Wilhelm. 1897. Schleichers Auffassung von der Stellung der Sprachwissenschaft. *Indogermanische Forschungen* 7, 360–72.

Timpanaro, Sebastiano. 1977. Friedrich Schlegel and the beginnings of Indo-European linguistics in Germany (English translation by J.P. Maher). In Schlegel, F. 1977, xi–lvii.

Whitney, William Dwight 1885. Philology, part I: Science of language in general. In *Encyclopaedia Britannica* 9th edn. Edinburgh: Adam & Charles Black; vol. XVIII, 765–80.

Wyss, Ulrich. 1979. *Die wilde Philologie: Jacob Grimm und der Historizismus.* Munich: Beck.

10

KARL BRUGMANN AND LATE NINETEENTH-CENTURY LINGUISTICS

ANNA MORPURGO DAVIES

In his 1882 report to the Philological Society Henry Sweet observed:

Passing from general principles to the detailed investigation of each Arian language separately, one is simply appalled by the vast mass of undigested, scattered, and conflicting investigations the student has to try and master. Schleicher's *Compendium* is now so utterly antiquated that no one thinks of using it except for the sake of its word-lists and inflection tables, and in the present revolutionary state of all things philological, it is hopeless expecting any real philologist to make himself the butt of his fellows by attempting to supersede it. (H. Sweet 1882–4: 109)

In 1886, two years after Sweet's words appeared in print, the first volume of a new *Grundriss der vergleichenden Grammatik der indogermanischen Sprachen* appeared in Strassburg from the press of Trübner. By 1892 the three remaining parts had appeared and in 1897 a second edition started to be published. Karl Brugmann (1849–1919), the author of the *Grundriss*, may well be the most representative linguist of the late nineteenth century, though some qualifications are needed. Sociologically Brugmann is wholly representative – intellectually he both is and is not. The distinction calls for further explanation.

The organization of linguistics as we now know it, its insertion into a university system ready to provide it with financial and administrative support, its establishment as a proper academic subject equally recognized by laymen, publishers and academies – all these date from the nineteenth century. A modern department of linguistics in, for example, an American university, is not too remote in its *modus operandi* from a *Sprachwissenschaftliches Seminar* or *Institut* found in a German university of the late nineteenth century or early twentieth century. In their turn those Seminars or Institutes were founded by scholars who had no hesitation in acknowledging that their work depended on work done in the first part of the century and in denying any continuity with earlier linguistic thought. Similarly, the periodicals in which modern linguistic articles are published either were founded in the nineteenth century (*Bulletin de la société de linguistique de Paris*,

Transactions of the Philological Society, (Kuhns) Zeitschrift für vergleichende Sprachforschung, (Paul und Braunes) Beiträge zur Geschichte der deutschen Sprache und Literatur, Indogermanische Forschungen, Archivio glottologico Italiano, etc.) or were modelled at a later stage on their nineteenth-century predecessors. The first linguistic societies (*The Philological Society*, the *Société de linguistique de Paris*) are nineteenth-century foundations; other societies have been founded since, but this has been done in full awareness of the link which joined them to the earlier groups.

Against this background my earlier distinctions may be more comprehensible. Among linguists Brugmann belongs to the first, or at most, the second generation of scholars who, if intellectually able, had good reasons to hope that their work would be supported by a university or an institution of learning and who could from the start aim at an academic career with a roughly predictable development. His curriculum is paradigmatic.[1] Born from good middle-class, but not academic, parents in Wiesbaden in 1849, he studied at the local *Gymnasium*, and then read classics first at the University of Halle and afterwards at that of Leipzig (from 1868). There he remained, except for a short period in Bonn, where he took the *Staatsexamen* in 1872, and for his probation year as teacher in the *Gymnasium* of his native city. Back in Leipzig he first became a teacher in the *Nikolaischule*, one of the most famous German schools, and then a young *Privatdozent* in Sanskrit and comparative linguistics (from 1877) and the holder of an Assistantship in the *Russisch-philologisches Seminar*, a university institution which after Ritschl's death was directed by Justus Lipsius and taught classics to people of Russian and Slavic origin. He became *Extraordinarius* in 1882, the year in which he married. He then spent less than three years at Freiburg im Breisgau as *Ordinarius* in the new chair of comparative linguistics and Sanskrit (1884–7) but soon was called back to the newly named chair of *Indogermanische Sprachwissenschaft* (Indo-European linguistics) in Leipzig – a chair which he held until his death. Official recognition frequently came his way: he was a member of seventeen academies and an honorary doctor of Princeton and Athens. Public events did not have a great impact on his life; his one attempt to fight for his country in the Franco–Prussian war was frustrated by poor eye-sight. At his funeral a Leipzig colleague commented that Brugmann's life had been the typical life of the German scholar, poor in external vicissitudes, but rich *im inneren Erleben und stillen Glück* (in inner life and quiet happiness) (Förster 1918: viii). From a modern point of view, it is not an exciting life nor one which would interest a potential biographer. Yet from the point of view of the history of linguistics this career pattern, however trite, is worth rehearsing because it contrasts so remarkably with that of earlier linguists. Even if we think of Germany only and of people whom Brugmann was proud to consider his predecessors, the contrast is obvious. By all accounts W. von Humboldt

(1767–1835) is an exception: a great man of letters, an aristocrat, a founder of universities, but also a man who did not need to earn his living and who owed his fame as much to his political activity as to his written works; a Prussian minister, an ambassador to the Court of St James who spent his spare time learning Sanskrit. Yet even the somewhat more conventional Jacob Grimm (1785–1863) and Franz Bopp (1791–1867) had very different career patterns from Karl Brugmann. Both of them – in spite of their different social backgrounds – had to find patrons and benefactors who could allow them to pursue their studies; neither of them had the benefit of a complete and regular university education in their subject; neither of them could reckon from the start on eventually belonging to the conventional world of university promotion and university chairs. Each ended his life covered in academic honours which match those received by Brugmann some fifty or more years later. The beginning was different. Jacob Grimm, after a series of disparate activities, had his first university teaching position at Göttingen in 1829 when he was forty-four, and even this did not last. Eight years later, together with others, he was dismissed and told to leave the country because he had refused to swear an oath of allegiance to the King of Hanover who had dissolved the Parliament and revoked the constitution. It was not until 1841 that he settled in Berlin as a member of the *Berliner Akademie der Wissenschaften* (Berlin Academy of Sciences) with a guaranteed stipend and the right to give lectures. Bopp, on the contrary, obtained his first teaching position in Berlin in 1821, when he was thirty, but no doubt this was due to Humboldt's immense influence and to his firm belief in the importance of Sanskrit, which Bopp had taught him in London. Until then, however, he had led a somewhat erratic life between Germany, Paris and London, supported in turn by Windischmann, who was his *Gymnasium* teacher, but also belonged to the inner circles of the German romantics, and by the odd grant from the King of Bavaria. He had failed to obtain a post in Sanskrit at Würzburg because the faculty of philosophy believed that Sanskrit was a 'luxury item' (Leskien 1876: 145).[2] By contrast Brugmann's career pattern was one which most of his contemporaries shared – nor is this surprising. At the beginning of the century no German university had a chair of linguistics; if we leave aside the first Sanskrit chair, created for A.W. Schlegel in 1818 at Bonn, Bopp's position in Berlin was the first such appointment, and even then the specification of his chair (*Orientalische Literatur und allgemeine Sprachkunde* – Oriental literature and general linguistics) was not as innovative as it looks (Wackernagel 1904: 202). In the late 1890s most of the twenty German universities had appointments in comparative linguistics or related subjects in their faculties of philosophy. A relatively small university like that of Freiburg (which during the 1880s had no more than 270 students on average in its faculty of philosophy, a faculty which included all arts and all sciences) was able to create a new chair for comparative linguistics and Sanskrit, while at the same time it also had professors who taught Germanic linguistics (Paul) and Romance philology (Neumann), and someone who taught Sanskrit (Holtzmann) first as a *Privatdozent*, then as an *Extraordinarius*. In the summer term of 1887 a much larger university like Leipzig (with an average of more than 1,000 students in the faculty of philosophy) provided linguistic teaching in Slavonic philology (Leskien), Sanskrit and Celtic (Windisch), comparative linguistics (Brugmann), general linguistics (G. von der Gabelentz). *Ausserordentliche* professors taught Sanskrit (Lindner), phonetics (Techmer), Germanic philology (Kögel), Romance philology (Koerting), Armenian philology (Wenzel), etc. These were scholars who were very much *au fait* with comparative linguistics, as were (in the university of Georg Curtius) some of the classicists.[3] By 1902 all German universities had an official position in comparative linguistics (Wackernagel 1904: 206).

In this context, Brugmann is representative in two ways. First because, as we have seen, he shared the career pattern of his contemporaries which differed so dramatically from that of his predecessors; secondly because his prestige became so immense that already when he was in his forties he came to be treated as the 'main' linguist, the 'representative' linguist. In 1893 the editor of an authoritative two-volume book about German universities found it useful to commission two chapters about '*Indische Philologie*' (Indic philology – as distinguished from '*Orientalische Philologie*' – Oriental philology) and about '*Vergleichende (indogermanische) Sprachwissenschaft*', '*Allgemeine Sprachwissenschaft*' and '*Slavische Philologie*' (comparative (Indo-European) linguistics, general linguistics and Slavic philology) respectively. The second chapter was written by Brugmann (1893). Years later (1912) the executive committee of a new *Indogermanische Gesellschaft* which was meant to further the study of 'Indo-European languages and culture, and of general linguistics' consisted of four scholars: Brugmann (Leipzig), Wackernagel (Göttingen), Streitberg (Munich), and Thumb (Strassburg) (Thumb 1913: 254); they were obviously chosen as the most representative linguists in Germany but two of them had been Brugmann's students (Streitberg and Thumb). In the forty or so years in which Brugmann held his chair at Leipzig that university not only kept the extraordinarily high reputation it had acquired in linguistics first with Georg Curtius and then with Leskien, but in practice became the obvious training ground for German and foreign linguists. Joseph Wright, the English dialectologist, studied at Leipzig and ended up translating into English the first edition of the *Grundriss* (Wright 1888); later, Leonard Bloomfield went to Leipzig too. There is little doubt that the combination of Brugmann, Leskien, and Windisch on the one hand, and Wundt on the other was largely responsible for Leipzig's attractiveness as a centre of linguistic studies, but among these scholars Brugmann was the most influential for those interested in language. Of him one can say what has been said of Bloomfield (Hymes & Fought 1975: 103), that he became 'the symbol for an entire period' – with all the complications that this poses for historiography.

What is the intellectual side of the coin? How do we envisage Brugmann's intellectual progress? Where does he stand in the development of linguistic thought? The first impression – one that his contemporaries might have shared – is that we are dealing with a young revolutionary, a hot-headed young Turk who turned into an archetypal member of the establishment. First, we meet a young man in his twenties who risks his career in order to publish one or two controversial articles in the periodical which he coedits with his teacher, is officially reproached and repudiated and does not apologize, but joins forces with a somewhat older contemporary to create a new periodical, reasserting with vehemence and considerable arrogance the same principles and the same conclusions – a man whose work and strong methodological statements created an apparently unbridgeable division among all contemporary linguists. Later, we find a peace-loving scholar, a great systematizer, the author of some 400 books and articles, someone whose genius was seen to consist in his diligence and working stamina (Kretschmer 1920: 256), but also someone who gave to a later generation the impression that the basic principles of linguistics had been found a long time earlier and that all that was needed was to apply them again and again (Hoenigswald 1980: 23). Common characteristics of the two phases are inexhaustible energy and humourless diligence. How correct is this picture?

The revolutionary phase coincides with the beginning of the so-called *junggrammatische Richtung*.[4] The articles which angered Georg Curtius, Brugmann's teacher and one of the most influential linguists of the period, concerned highly technical questions of Indo-European reconstruction; one (Brugman 1876a) argued for the attribution to Indo-European of a vocalic [ṇ] sound, the other (Brugman 1876b) discussed the inflection of a noun type (the *r*-stems) and also gave reasons for reconstructing for Indo-European a set of vowels which made the parent language much closer to, for example, Greek than to Sanskrit, thus destroying one of the accepted views about the development and branching of the Indo-European family. This was not all; in both articles, which conspicuously lack the clarity which marked the older Brugmann's productions, there were, admittedly in footnotes, long methodological discussions. The principles advocated were later repeated with greater clarity and greater emphasis in the 1878 preface to the *Morphologische Untersuchungen*, the real manifesto of the movement (Osthoff & Brugman 1878), signed by the two editors but written by Brugmann alone. These principles were: a) the methodology used in the study of language must be explicit and must be based on a different conception of language from that popularized by Schleicher; language cannot be an organism which develops according to laws of its own independently of the speakers;

historical linguistics is a form of history, not a form of science, b) we can understand how languages change only if we observe how change occurs in present-day languages and assume that the same types of development apply to all phases of linguistic history (the uniformitarian principle), c) sounds change according to 'mechanical' laws which in principle suffer no exception, nor is the speaker conscious of the progress of sound change (the regularity principle), d) analogy, which is determined by psychological factors, is one of the main causes of language change, now and at all stages. This is a crude summary of the manifesto, though less crude than the one which has become familiar through the polemical stance of its adversaries and the overemphatic claims of partisans. The former either dismissed a) and b) as trivial, or found them unpalatable, or did both, though for the most part they saw no reason to discuss the two points, since they were not relevant – or so they thought – to the technical work of the comparative linguist; they found c), the regularity principle, both old hat (had not Schleicher and Curtius himself been constantly in favour of a more rigorous application of sound-laws?) and wildly exaggerated (the exceptions to sound-laws were obvious); as for d), they found it difficult to accept that analogical change (*falsche Analogie* or *Formübertragung*) could occur in the earliest stages of language or could be more than a *pis-aller* explanation for changes which were not really understood. They were also, and rightly, irritated by the somewhat woolly dualism between 'mechanical' sound-laws and 'psychological' analogy. Some of the partisans did not fare much better; most of them concentrated on c) and used it both as a *cri de guerre* and as a password which would instantly distinguish friends from foes.[5]

The young Brugmann was not alone in his views; in the mid-1870s they had been formulated by a group of Leipzig people in their twenties and early thirties: among others there were the Slavist Leskien, the most senior, who was already an *Ordinarius*, the classicist and Indo-Europeanist Osthoff, the Sanskritist and Celtologist Windisch, the Germanist Braune, the Orientalist Hübschmann, and a frequent visitor, Karl Verner (Brugmann 1909: 219). They formed a sort of coterie which indulged in frequent outings and discussions, in sharp criticism of other work, and in a series of arrogant statements: the subject needed to take a new direction and they were going to show the way. The phenomenon is not unique. Writing of a lively and very successful group of Oxford philosophers in the late 1930s, of their self-centred attitude, and of their assumption that no one existed 'outside the magic circle', Isaiah Berlin (1980: 115) concludes: 'This was vain and foolish and, I have no doubt, irritating to others. But I suspect that those who have never been under the spell of this kind of illusion, even for a short while, have not known true intellectual happiness.' This – one understands from the literature of the period – was the atmosphere in which the *Junggrammatiker* lived. They felt, and partly were, revolutionary; in their mind – and this is perhaps the most striking fact from a modern point of view – it was equally important to have the 'right views' about the number and nature of vowels to be attributed to Indo-European and to be ready to reconsider from the beginning the view of language which their textbooks (and here again Schleicher's *Compendium* was the most important) had promulgated. They felt, nor does it matter whether this was true or not, that they had new things to say both about the techniques and about the theory, and that there was no distinction between the two; they also felt, perhaps misguidedly, that they were at long last joining the two strands of linguistic thought which their predecessors had separated: the tradition of philo-sophical thought about language (as they would have put it) and the concrete work of comparison and reconstruction, whose origins they saw in the early nineteenth century.[6] Finally, they felt daring and courageous; in the gossipy intrigue-ridden atmosphere of German universities (Gilder-sleeve 1884: 354) too uncompromising a stance might have damaged their career prospects.

This is not the place to discuss how original the Neogrammarians were (Robins 1978); in their opposition to Schleicher's conception of language as an independent organism they obviously had predecessors both in Germany (Steinthal) and outside (Madvig, Whitney, Bréal, Ascoli, etc.); their uniformitarian views were also common to many of the people I have just mentioned (Aarsleff 1979; Christy 1983); the importance of analogy had been previously recognized by a number of people again in Germany and outside (Morpurgo Davies 1978: 39, 46, 57). Schuchardt (1885), in the most intelligent of the anti-Neogrammarian pamphlets published at the time (Fought 1982), had no hesitation in stating that the only new principle was the regularity principle (which he wanted to attack) – yet, as we have seen, even this limited claim to originality was not generally accepted. If so, both the challenging tone of the manifesto and the violence of the polemics it provoked are hard to understand. However, two points need to be stressed. The first is the general antitheoretical and antimethodological mood of contemporary German linguistics, which made any strong methodological statement, such as those included in the preface to the *Morphologische Untersuchungen*, singularly distasteful to the reader. The causes were manifold. Some were related to the intellectual climate of the period, which was more data- than theory-oriented. Others were intrinsic to the subject: the obvious successes had been reached independently of methodological and theoretical discussions and sometimes in spite of them: Bopp's importance, for instance, was due to his 'concrete' results; his original aim of demonstrating that the earlier phases of language reflected the logical structure of thought had not been achieved. Still others are probably to be seen in the close link which had always existed between comparative linguistics and classical studies; most of the Neogrammarians and their opponents had been trained as classicists and classicists were (and to a large extent still are) reluctant to indulge in methodological discussions. Ritschl, the great Latinist, who, after his Bonn successes, had been largely responsible for resurrecting classical studies at Leipzig, had explicitly stated it in the fourth of the ten commandments which he and Lehrs had composed (partly in jest) for the benefit of classicists: 'Du sollst den Namen Methode nicht unnütz im Munde führen' (Thou shalt not take the name 'Method' in vain) (Ribbeck 1879–81.2: 450). Among Ritschl's pupils there were Georg Curtius, Schleicher, Schuchardt, Sievers, Joh. Schmidt, Clemm, Windisch, Meister, Brugmann, Cauer. If we added here the list of Curtius' pupils we would obtain an almost complete roster of German linguists of the second part of the nineteenth century. Karl Brugmann, who had been a devoted member of both Ritschl's and Curtius' seminars, must have felt very strongly indeed if he had allowed himself to break the fourth commandment.

A second reason for the violence of the anti-Neogrammarian reactions is again linked to the 'concrete' nature of the questions discussed by the contemporary German linguists. In spite of their methodological statements Brugmann and his group were as data-oriented as the others. All the five volumes of the *Morphologische Untersuchungen*, edited and written by Osthoff and Brugmann, consist of articles about specific problems in the historical grammar of Indo-European and the Indo-European languages. Often enough the conclusions reached by the two authors differ from those of their predecessors; this is to be expected, but what must have been difficult to bear for those whose favourite views were attacked was the statement, repeated on all possible occasions, that the new conclusions entirely depended on the correct application of the new principles.[7] Consider, for instance, Brugmann's discussion of the origin of the verbal endings in Indo-European. The standard view, after Bopp, Schleicher and Curtius, was that they were pronouns which somehow had been joined to a preceding verbal stem. For the first person singular active Schleicher (1871: 647f, 653ff) reconstructed a *ma* pronoun which appeared in a weakened *mi* form in e.g. Sanskrit *ásmi*, Greek *eimí* 'I am', Sanskrit *bhárāmi* 'I carry'; was lost in Greek *phérō* 'I carry'; lost the *m* in the Greek perfect *léloipa* 'I have left' from a supposed *leloipma*; lost the *a* in Greek *épheron* 'I was carrying' with later change of *m* to *n*, and lost both final *a* and *m* in the Greek aorist *étupsa* 'I beat' (presumably from -*ama*). For the second person singular he reconstructed *tva* 'thou' which yielded the Greek 'present' -*si* and -*eis*, 'past' -*s*, and 'perfect' -*tha*. None of these phonetic changes, except for that of final *m* to *n*, is parallelled in any other Greek form. Brugman(n) (1878a: 133–50; cf. 1886–92.ii.2: 1335–45; 1904a: 588–90; 1897–1916.ii.3: 583–99; 1921) reconstructs four different endings of first person: 'present' -*mi* and -*ō* (same function, different types of verbs); 'past' postvocalic -*m* (> Gr. -*n*) and

postconsonantal -ṃ (> Gr. a); perfect -a. Sanskrit -āmi in bhárāmi (< *-ōmi)
owes its form to the contamination of -ō and -mi verbs. For the second
person he reconstructs 'present' -si, 'past' -s, perfect -tha. The reason? Only
in this way can we account for the attested forms without postulating sound
changes for which no other evidence is available. The consequences? The
second person endings and some of the first person endings show no
obvious similarity with the pronominal forms; hence it is not legitimate to
assume that all personal endings are of pronominal origin. Is a different
origin plausible? Brugmann's answer is that, if we look at the history of
attested languages, we see that verbal endings have a multiplicity of origins:
nominal forms, analogical remodelling of pre-existing endings, pronominal
suffixes, etc. There is no reason to assume that the parent language, for
which presumably we can reconstruct only a late phase, that is, a phase
which was in itself the product of a long historical development, was
different: a clear-cut example of application of the four principles mentioned
above – and one which was bound to irritate because it cut across a series of
lengthy arguments which had been pursued for some seventy years (cf.
Curtius 1885: 147ff; Delbrück 1880: 61ff, 96ff). Moreover, the conclusions led
to some form of retrenchment: Max Müller (1866: 244), to take just one
example, had argued that future work was likely to account (mostly in
compositional and pronominal terms) for the origin of all grammatical
forms; thanks to 'careful inductive reasoning . . . in the end grammatical
analysis will become as successful as chemical analysis'. Essentially
Brugmann and the others were saying that that was not a real possibility:
reconstructed Indo-European is just a stage of language like all others. Was
this not a betrayal of the whole discipline?[8]

Between the early 1880s and the early 1890s, in addition to innumerable
reviews and a large number of articles, Brugmann coedited and to a large
extent wrote three more volumes of *Morphologische Untersuchungen* (1880,
1881, 1890), compiled an edition and a descriptive grammar of Lithuanian
legends and folk songs, the result of field work which almost doubled the
material then available for the language (Leskien & Brugman 1882),
answered the anti-Neogrammarian criticism with a book 'On the present
state of linguistics' (1885a), founded and coedited an influential new
periodical, the *Indogermanische Forschungen* (1892ff), and wrote for Müller's
Handbuch a fundamental historical grammar of Greek; the first edition
appeared in 1885 but in 1889 Brugmann produced a completely rewritten
edition of almost double the size. In 1892 he completed the four parts of the
Grundriss (1886–92), which presupposed a first hand acquaintance with all
ancient Indo-European languages and what had been written about them (a
second and fully rewritten edition appeared between 1897 and 1916). The
amount of authoritative work done in a relatively short period is almost

incredible – it is of course what made Brugmann a 'member of the establishment'. To the modern Indo-Europeanist the very name of the *Grundriss* may conjure up the image of a lengthy unoriginal compilation which must be used because nothing has ever superseded it, but should also be attacked because it stands for dull respectability. If this is so now (and I doubt it) certainly it was not so at the time. The only immediate predecessor of the *Grundriss* was Schleicher's *Compendium* and, as Henry Sweet had pointed out (see above), no part of the *Compendium* was any longer acceptable: in Indo-European studies everything was in a state of flux. How much this was felt when the *Grundriss* came out emerges from the words of Wilhelm Streitberg who was twenty-two when the first volume appeared; in 1921 he wrote:

> One must have lived in that great period of the development of linguistics to be able to understand what impression this first volume made. Even today I still feel the joy which took hold of me, as a very young student, when on an autumn evening I found the first volume on my desk; I can still see myself breathlessly turning page after page till terribly late at night, incapable of extricating myself from the fascination [*Zauber*] which emanated from the book. (Streitberg 1921: 33*)

Brugmann's achievement did not consist only in discovering or collecting the right answers to the old problems; he had to find out what the problems were because they were no longer the same – and I speak of 'concrete', not of theoretical problems. Consider a trivial example, once again from the history of the personal endings: for Max Müller (1862: 272; 1866: 304) and Schleicher (1871: 656) the *ta* demonstrative in a weakened form yielded in Indo-European the third person singular ending *ti*; this, they assumed, became *si* through a normal change of Greek and then, through another normal change, intervocalic *s* was lost; hence *phereti* > *pheresi* > *pherei* 'he carries'. Brugmann could not accept the conclusion because in Greek all instances of *si* < *ti* are preserved; it is only inherited intervocalic *s* which is lost. Hence the origin of *pherei* becomes a serious problem, which Brugmann tried to solve at different times in different manners (1878a: 173–9, 1886–92.ii.2: 1347–8; 1904a: 590f; 1897–1916.ii.3: 582; Brugmann & Thumb 1913: 397f, etc.); whatever the solution (and a generally accepted solution has not yet been found) the form could no longer be used as positive evidence for a pronominal origin of the endings. On the other hand the objections to the old view presupposed a number of important assumptions about the relative chronology of sound change, the ordering of rules, and so on. More important still, the regularity principle was in fact compelling the Neogrammarians and their followers to test all observable instances of linguistic change against a definite parameter: each instance had to be classified as either 'sound-change' or 'non-sound-change', depending on the existence or otherwise of regular sound correspondences between the old and the late form. Thus the shift from *ebherom to Greek épheron was an example of 'sound-change' (in Greek regularly *bh > ph and *-m > -n) but Greek pherei could not be derived from *bhereti through sound-change since -ti does not regularly become -i. If the shift was not an example of sound-change, further classification was needed: analogical change, dialect borrowing, any other type?[9] New problems arose and these, both at a general and a specific level, were the problems which the Grundriss had first to recognize and then to tackle.

The Junggrammatiker in general and Brugmann in particular have often been accused of ignoring the systemic aspect of language. This may be true – though not always – in their study of sound-change, but when they considered analogical change the position was entirely different. Here, they saw, and saw very clearly, that no item could be studied in isolation. Any discussion of specific examples of analogical change presupposed a reconstruction of the relevant états de langue and an analysis of the intricate web of relationships (phonetic, grammatical and semantic) in which the linguistic form considered was included. At this stage we are not too remote from the distinction between synchrony and diachrony which Saussure was to make famous (Jankowsky 1976) and from the structural conception of language which we also associate with the name of Saussure. A number of points confirm that this is so in Brugmann's work. On the one hand we have not one (Lieb 1967; Koerner 1975: 784) but numerous references to statistisch ('statistic'/static) methods of analysis; the adjective is used jointly or synonymously with beschreibend (descriptive) (Brugman(n) 1875: 651; 1884b: 1363; 1885a: 18; 1887; 1892: 15, etc.), is contrasted with sprachgeschichtlich (historical/diachronic) (1884b: 1363; 1887) or historisch (historical) (e.g. 1892: 15), and is by no means meant in the pejorative sense which one might expect (e.g. 1875: 651). More important, however, than mere terminology is the way in which Brugmann argues in specific cases for the need to distinguish between, for instance, an etymological account of the segmentation or meaning of some forms and the actual segmentation or meaning which we must attribute them at a particular linguistic stage. Thus both in the first and (at greater length) in the second edition of the Grundriss Brugmann (1886–92.i: 14–19; 1897–1916.i.1: 32–40) makes much of the distinction between elements which we want to segment because they were originally free forms, such as the heit (hood) of German Mannheit (manhood), and elements which we segment on 'psychological' grounds, such as the various morphs of Greek pa-ter-es 'fathers', where -es indicates nominative plural. Similarly, Leo Meyer is attacked (1884a) for his incapacity to recognize that forms like Greek apneustos 'breathless' (instead of the expected *apneutos) owe their -stos termination to the analogy with adjectives where -tos was added to an s- stem; at the same time, however,

Brugmann states that, if it is really necessary to segment (*secieren*) such forms as *agnōstos* 'unknown' or *apneustos*, it is better to analyse them as *agnō-stos*, *apneu-stos* etc. than as *agnōs-tos* etc., even if *-tos* is the older suffix, because 'im Sprachbewusstsein' (in the speaker's linguistic intuition) there was by then a *-stos* suffix as well as a *-tos* suffix. In the same review he argues against treating roots as original free forms. All that we can say, he maintains, is that some phonetic sequences are treated as units from a morphological point of view since they may be compared with similar sequences: *bher-* in Greek *pherō* 'I carry' (<*bherō*) as *der-* in Greek *derō* 'I skin'. We now realize that just like 'statistisch' ('statistic'/static), terms like 'psychologisch', 'Sprachbewusstsein' (linguistic intuition), 'Sprachgefühl' (linguistic feeling) can be used to refer to a synchronic analysis of linguistic facts. Yet, the psychological terminology also presupposes some form of structural approach. One could quote striking formulations such as that of Brugmann (1904a: viii) according to which language is a highly complex human activity 'bei der die verschiedenartigsten Faktoren in gegenseitiger Abhängigkeit zum Ganzen zusammenwirken, bei der im Grunde alles durch alles bedingt ist' (in which the most varied factors work together in mutual dependence on the whole, in which fundamentally everything is determined by everything else),[10] but they are probably less significant than the concrete examples of application of structural principles. In an attack against an earlier book by Leo Meyer, Brugman (1880: 977) takes issue with the statement that some Greek imperatives, *ithi* 'go', *stēthi* 'stay', are neither aorists nor presents, that they are not marked for duration. This, he argues, may have been true in origin but it does not follow that it is true at a later period; it is far more normal that forms of whatever origin which come to belong to a linguistic system differently organized from the original one modify their meaning and function accordingly. In ignoring this, Meyer is guilty of a common *Grundfehler* (basic mistake). In his inaugural lecture in Freiburg, Brugmann (1885a: 22f) was even more explicit in the discussion of that basic mistake: language is not something which exists outside the speakers; all linguistic elements are linked in our psychic organization, our linguistic perception. It is impossible from this point of view to distinguish between old and new linguistic forms; there are no Indo-European forms in Greek or Latin or in any other Indo-European language; in Greek there are only Greek forms, in Latin Latin forms, and so on, because in any language what is inherited has become something new and specific: 'the whole organism of the representations [*Vorstellungsgruppen*] which exist in our consciousness has been repeatedly altered and consequently the position of each individual element has changed'; we ought not to treat language as if it were a 'mere aggregate of words'.

The old organic conception of language has been seen (by Cassirer 1945, for instance) as a pre-form of structuralism – and there is little doubt that for some scholars at least it fulfilled exactly that function – and other functions too (Morpurgo Davies 1986). In Brugmann (and obviously in Paul) the awareness that linguistic elements are interdependent and cannot be treated in isolation has not disappeared but if anything has become stronger. Only it has a new justification: it is based on a psychological view of language as something which cannot exist independently of the speaker, and, as Brugmann would have put it, of his association processes.[11] Analogy is based on these association processes, and analogy, as is now clear, is envisaged as a major force, responsible both for language creativity as a purely synchronic process and for language change. On the one hand it accounts for analogical creation – for the creation of new forms, new sentences etc., and on the other for analogical change – for the replacement of old forms or constructions with new forms and constructions (cf. e.g. Hoenigswald 1978, Morpurgo Davies 1978). The latter is what the historical linguist is most interested in, but the latter cannot be separated from the former. The result is that in the concrete work of Brugmann or Brugmann-like linguists both synchrony and diachrony play a necessary part – nor is there any sign that the two were confused. If a greater role is played by diachrony it is because, in agreement with Paul and most contemporary linguists, Brugmann attributes explanatory power to historical study alone (Kiparsky 1974). Yet it is this constant awareness of the systematic nature of the linguistic fact which accounts for the systematic nature of Brugmann's work; in all his opus there is a general reluctance to investigate facts in isolation.

Let us now return to Brugmann's conventional image. How correct is the view that I described earlier? Did he really change from a young revolutionary into a member of the establishment; did he really assume that all problems of method and theory had been solved in the 1870s? The answer to the first question is that certainly his status changed in the way indicated but any comparison with a rabid young leftist who betrays his youthful convictions to enjoy middle-aged comforts is misplaced. Brugmann did abandon his polemical stance but not his convictions – nor was there any reason to change them since they became commonplace.[12] No one tried to resurrect Schleicher's concept of *Glottik* as a science or of language as an independent organism; consciously or unconsciously uniformitarianism was accepted, at least among specialists. The debate about sound-laws largely concentrated on the formulation and the rationale of the statement but for a while at least the procedures followed in historical study and reconstruction, Brugmann's main concern, did not greatly differ from scholar to scholar. Indeed the beginning of this convergence is earlier than the 'coming out' of the *Junggrammatiker*.[13] Discussion about analogy continued, but no one doubted its importance. In Indo-European studies

Brugmann's *Grundriss* in its two successive editions and in its shortened version (Brugmann 1904a) became the standard text and Schleicher's *Compendium* was entirely abandoned. A success story – nor did Brugmann live to see the shift in interests from diachronic to synchronic and theoretical linguistics which was partly determined by Saussure's *Cours*. But should we infer that between the late 1870s and the late 1910s no change occurred and Brugmann's thought remained stagnant? His contemporaries recognized in his work an increasing interest in syntax and in semantics (Förster 1918: x), and it is noticeable that syntactic and semantic problems loom large in the work of the last twenty years. The new edition of the *Grundriss*, which was not completed, did not separate study of forms and study of functions as the earlier edition had done. In this, Brugmann was following the model of his own Greek grammar which included a syntactical part and of the *Kurze vergleichende Grammatik* (1904a) where he had justified his undertaking with the observation (quoted above) that in language 'everything depends on everything else'. The monographs on the nature of composition (1900), on the demonstrative pronouns (1904b), on the numerals (1907), on differences in sentence formation (1918), on the simple sentence (1922), all belong to the late period, together with a number of semantic studies. The approach is the historical–comparative one which we recognize in the earlier work and the aim is again that of reconstructing Indo-European and understanding the changes from Indo-European to the attested languages; what is new is an attempt at offering both definitions and preliminary generalities before the historical work starts. Obviously we recognize everywhere the influence of Delbrück, the author of the three volumes on syntax (1893–1900) which were added to the first edition of the *Grundriss*. But what matters is the change in attitude. A review of Delbrück (1893–1900.1) published in 1894 by Streitberg, Brugmann's pupil, is representative of a widely spread set of reactions, which at some stage may well have been shared by Brugmann himself. There Streitberg (1894: 176) reaffirmed that the final aim of all serious work must be to clarify the historical development, i.e. [sie] 'auf Gesetze zurückzuführen' (to reduce it to laws). And he continued: 'the naked fact is indifferent; it becomes valuable when we are able to insert it into a system, thus validating and understanding it'. This, he argued, may explain why the study of phonology and morphology is privileged; for syntax we have not yet gone beyond the mere statement of facts; the password which will open the entrance to the *Zauberberg* (magic mountain) is still escaping us. By 1904 the older Brugmann had realized, as the young Streitberg had not, that even the standard historical work about phonology and morphology presupposed some syntactical notions and that, both if they were wrong and if they were right, it was better to make them explicit than to ignore their existence. In the second edition of the *Grundriss* Brugmann had found it useful to introduce some general account of articulatory phonetics, largely based on Sievers' manual. A similar attempt is made for some syntactical concepts: the second volume starts with a discussion of what is meant by *Satz* 'sentence' and with the statement (admittedly common to Paul and Delbrück) that the sentence is theoretically prior to the word. Some of the arguments reappear in Brugmann 1918 (which would repay much closer study) and in the posthumous book about the syntax of the simple sentence (Brugmann 1922), which was meant to be a part of the *Grundriss*. For the student of sound-change a basic knowledge of phonetics is indispensable; similarly, the mature scholar came to recognize that morphological and syntactic change cannot be studied without dedicating some thought to the basic foundations of morphology and syntax. In this he certainly foreshadowed later developments in linguistics.

The contrast between the preface to the *Morphologische Untersuchungen*, the first, and the second edition of the *Grundriss* is interesting in other ways too. The first edition of the *Grundriss* offers almost no general statements; the second contains a chapter about *Lautgesetze* (1897–1916.i.1.: 63ff) written in a very different tone from the relevant part of the manifesto. No mention is made of the 'blind necessity' of sound-laws and of their mechanical–physiological nature; more interestingly, Brugmann now realizes that 'pure' dialects and 'pure' linguistic communities do not exist; everywhere there is a degree of linguistic mixture. If so, a sharp definition of the regularity principle is impossible. Yet, Brugmann argues, that should not induce us to reject it, since the results of its application are obvious; rather, we must acknowledge that we know nothing about the ultimate causes of sound-change, and little about the manner in which it develops.

I mentioned earlier that intellectually Brugmann is not wholly representative. This is partly because the amount and the importance of the work he did is unique, but mainly because a serious reading of his works does not confirm the most generally accepted image. In his assessment of the German contribution to comparative linguistics Meillet (1936 [1923]: 159) acknowledged that 'l'édifice solide de la grammaire comparée des langues indo-européennes, des langues romanes, des langues germaniques, a été fondé par les Allemands, et construit, en très grande partie, par des savants allemands' (the foundations of the comparative grammar of the Indo-European languages, of the Romance languages, of the Germanic languages, were laid down by the Germans, and the edifice itself, in all its solidity, was also built for the most part by German scholars). Yet he also wrote that: 'Le défaut fondamental des travaux allemands est que les faits y sont trop considérés en eux-mêmes et que trop souvent les auteurs semblent satisfaits quand ils ont fait la critique des sources et rangé les données dans des cadres à peu près constants' (The basic defect of German works is that the facts are looked at too much on their own and that all too often the authors seem to be content to produce a critical examination of the sources and a classification of the facts according to an almost fixed model). It is likely that the works he had in mind were Brugmann's books or the Brugmann-like manuals to which he had referred earlier in the same article; if the former is true, this is perhaps an occasion on which it is possible to disagree with Meillet. What is absent in Brugmann, in contrast with some of his followers or imitators, is the stolid satisfaction of the man without problems. He did not have the intellectual elegance which characterized Saussure or Meillet, nor did he have, as did Meillet, an instinctive feeling for the links between cultural and linguistic facts, or for the social nature of language, but he had the constant urge to consider and reconsider what the problems were, to vary their formulation and his own solutions, to emphasize rather than bypass the difficulties. He also realized that his subject had reached a stage at which it was necessary to deal with it in its entirety. He was no great theoretician, but he succeeded in making clear to an antitheoretical generation that even the most technical work depends on definite assumptions which need to be spelled out before they can be accepted or rejected – above all he had the courage and the stamina to put his views to the test in a monumental book which is still the most complete historical account available of a language family.

NOTES

1 The most detailed account is that in Streitberg (1921); less useful, but worth reading are Förster (1918), Streitberg (1919a), Kretschmer (1920), Devoto (1930), Sommer (1955). For a list of Brugmann's writings see Streitberg (1909 and 1919b). The Brugman family adopted the Brugmann spelling of its name in 1882 (Streitberg 1919a: 143).

2 For W. von Humboldt cf. most recently P. Sweet (1978–80); for Grimm's earlier activity cf. Ginschel (1967) and for a general bibliography about him see Denecke (1977); for Bopp see Lefmann (1891–7).

3 Basic information and statistical data about the German universities can be found in Lexis (1893 and 1904); for Leipzig in particular cf. Leipzig (1909); for the names and basic biographical data of all Leipzig professors see Leipzig (1961). For our period, lists of lectures and lecturers in German universities were regularly printed in the *Literarisches Centralblatt*.

4 The bibliography about the *Junggrammatiker* or, in the current mistranslation, Neogrammarians (for the name see Pedersen 1983: 79f) is now immense: for it cf. Morpurgo Davies (1975: 644–7), but add at least Vennemann & Wilbur (1972), Koerner (1975: 659–92), Jankowsky (1976), Wilbur (1977), Robins (1978), Hoenigswald (1978), Christy (1983).

5 Joseph Wright may serve as an example. His enthusiasm was such that as late as 1890 he could end – abruptly – a letter to a student, who later became his wife, with the words: 'Die Junggrammatiker sollen leben!' (E. Wright 1932.1: 197); he

also wrote to the same student that 'the dialect of Wellington has some very important sound-laws' (*ibid*. 187) and that 'Phonology corresponds to Pure Mathematics and Accidence to applied (mixed) Mathematics' (*ibid*. 202). In 1886 he spent his holidays with a German colleague and they 'discovered almost daily new sound-laws and etymologiés' in his native dialect (*ibid*. 85). All this is naive, to say the least, but we may ask whether in the late nineteenth century J. Wright would have started his very useful work on English dialects if he had not learned, at the Neogrammarians' feet, that the scholarly study of living languages was both respectable and essential.

6 Cf. for example, Brugmann 1885a: 38f (with an interesting reference to Schuchardt). In fact this was not meant as a return to the seventeenth- and eighteenth-century tradition of linguistic thought; in concrete terms it simply meant that linguists were advised to read Whitney, Steinthal, and perhaps Steinthal's version of Humboldt.

7 To say that the main or only principle maintained by the *Junggrammatiker* is that 'the laws of sound-change admit of no exception' (cf. Fiedler ap. E. Wright 1932.1: 87) is historiographically wrong, though this was the interpretation of the controversy given by most of the contenders – and by their descendants; yet at the moment there is a real risk that we may be going too far in redressing the balance and we may underrate the importance of a strict application of the regularity principle in the concrete historical work of the time (cf. Hoenigswald 1978: 21). We are no longer trained to see reconstructions such as those found in Schleicher's *Compendium* (1871) and discussed below, with the result that we tend to forget the impact that the new reconstructions must have had on the specialists.

8 This 'dogmatic' scepticism (H. Sweet 1882–4: 108) was as important as the other views, and as strongly expressed. From the height of his twenty-nine years of age Brugman (1878b) felt free to advise a young scholar to refrain from speculations about the 'embryonic' period of Indo-European – all the more free, as he pointed out, because in the past he himself had come close to joining the 'Secte der Glottogonologen' (the sect of the glottogonists). Later (1881: 127) he pleaded against Fick's pupil, Bechtel, for a judicious use of the *ars nesciendi*: 'man hat bisher allzu viele in grauer indogermanischer Vorzeit spielende sprachhistorische Romane zu lesen bekommen, um nicht zu der Erkenntniss zu gelangen, dass nüchterne Zurückhaltung gegenüber den glottogonischen Hypothesen das einzige Mittel ist, um unserer Wissenschaft ihren Character als Wissenschaft zu wahren' (we have had to read too much linguistic fiction set in the misty prehistory of Indo-European, and we are now obliged to realize that a sober avoidance of all glottogonic hypotheses is the only possible way to preserve the scientific character of our discipline).

9 I accept here the point often made by Hoenigswald (most recently 1978: 25) that the regularity principle is in essence a tautology; the only way we have of distinguishing between sound-change and, for example, morphological or semantic replacement is to state that sound-change is regular. This does not exempt us from asking why this tautology is so essential to our understanding of language change.

10 What is the connection, if any, between this type of formulation and Meillet's

(1903: 407) view of language as a system 'où tout se tient' (where everything depends on everything else) (Szemerényi 1980: 160–2)?

11 We do not really know what 'psychological' meant for Brugmann; what was he referring to when he wrote to Ascoli in 1887 (Gazdaru 1967: 58) that the great Neogrammarian controversy had not centred so much on questions which concerned the link between linguistics and *Sprachphysiologie* (linguistic physiology) as much as on questions which had to do with the relationship between *Einzelforschung* (individual research) and psychology? Does this just mean that analogy is more important than sound-change? And what did Kretschmer (1920: 256) mean when he referred to Brugmann's death as signalling the end of an era which had seen the foundation and development 'der psychologischen Methoden der Sprachwissenschaft' (of psychological methods in linguistics)? How much did Brugmann really owe to his Leipzig colleague W. Wundt, the founder of experimental psychology? Streitberg (1921: 37*) thought that, for instance, Brugmann's work on the demonstratives (1904b) showed the influence of Wundt's *Völkerpsychologie*, but in my view it simply shows the influence of the data about non-Indo-European languages collected by Wundt (1900) in *Die Sprache*. Brugmann (1897–1916.i.1: 67) certainly accepted from Wundt (1886) his view of the regularity principle as a logical postulate, but this had little to do with psychology, and he seems to be much closer to the theory of psychology as psychology of the individual adopted by Paul (and Delbrück) than to the *Völkerpsychologie* of Wundt (cf. Esper 1968: 1–81; 1973). For the early period cf. Brugman (1879: 322): 'It is indifferent for our assessment of the psychological process whether such an innovation has been accepted only by isolated individuals and remains limited to their speech or becomes the general norm in the linguistic community.'

12 As early as 1882 Brugman (1882) argued in a review that the name 'Junggrammatiker' ought to be avoided because it reminded one of contrasts in linguistics which by then had mostly been settled, at least in matters of substance rather than of personalities, and, one hoped, would be totally settled under both aspects in the not too remote future.

13 Cf. Kiparsky (1974: 340f). A typical example is provided by the history of the so-called *Palatalgesetz* or Collitz's Law, which demonstrated that the Sanskrit vocalic system had undergone profound changes and could not represent the earliest state of affairs: the law was discovered in the mid-1870s more or less at the same time, and probably independently, by a number of scholars: K. Verner, F. de Saussure, Johannes Schmidt, H. Collitz, E. Tegnér, W. Thomsen (Collitz 1886: 1; Osthoff 1886: 14–20; cf. Pedersen 1983: 69; Wilbur 1977: lxxxiv–lxxxviii); the first two could count as Neogrammarians or pro-Neogrammarian (at the time this was true for Saussure), the second two belonged to the opposite party, but both sides acknowledged the importance of the finding and argued for it in similar manner. In this instance acrimony arose, but only because of priority questions.

168 ANNA MORPURGO DAVIES

REFERENCES

Aarsleff, H. 1979. Bréal vs. Schleicher: linguistics and philology during the latter half of the nineteenth century. In H.M. Hoenigswald (ed.) *The European Background of American Linguistics*, 63–106. Dordrecht: Foris.

Berlin, I. 1980. *Personal impressions*. London: Hogarth Press.

Brugman, K. 1875. Review of G. Koffmane, *Lexicon lateinischer Wortformen*, Göttingen 1874. *Literarisches Centralblatt*: 651–2.

1876a. Nasalis sonans in der indogermanischen Grundsprache. *Curtius' Studien* 9: 256–338.

1876b. Zur Geschichte der stammabstufenden Declinationen. Erste Abhandlung: Die Nomina auf -*ar*- und -*tar*-. *Curtius' Studien* 9: 361–406.

1878a. Zur Geschichte der Personalendungen. *Morphologische Untersuchungen* 1: 133–86.

1878b. Review of K. Penka, *Die Nominalflexion der indogermanischen Sprachen*. Wien 1878. *Literarisches Centralblatt*: 1040–2.

1879. Review of H. Ziemer, *Das psychologische Moment in der Bildung syntaktischer Sprachformen*. Colberg 1879. *Literarisches Centralblatt*: 401–2.

1880. Review of L. Meyer, *Griechische Aoriste*. Berlin 1879. *Literarisches Centralblatt*: 976–8.

1881. Review of F. Bechtel, *Ueber die Bezeichnungen der sinnlichen Wahrnehmungen in den indogermanischen Sprachen*. Weimar 1879. *Literaturblatt für germanische und romanische Philologie*: 126–8.

1882. Review of H. Ziemer, *Junggrammatische Streifzüge im Gebiete der Syntax*. Colberg 1882. *Literarisches Centralblatt*: 401–2.

Brugmann, K. 1884a. Review of L. Meyer, *Vergleichende Grammatik der griechischen und lateinischen Sprache*. Berlin 1884. *Literarisches Centralblatt*: 1027–8.

1884b. Review of A. Leskien, *Der Ablaut der Wurzelsilben im Litauischen*. Leipzig 1884. *Literarisches Centralblatt*: 1362–3.

1885a. *Zum heutigen Stand der Sprachwissenschaft*. Strassburg: Trübner.

1885b. *Griechische Grammatik*. In I. Müllers *Handbuch der klassischen Altertumswissenschaft* II: 1–126. Munich: Beck.

1886–92. *Grundriss der vergleichenden Grammatik der indogermanischen Sprachen*. Strassburg: Trübner.

1887. Review of J. van Leeuwen & M.B. Mendes da Costa, *Der Dialekt der homerischen Gedichte*. Leipzig 1886. *Literarisches Centralblatt*: 21–2.

1889. *Griechische Grammatik*. In I. Müllers *Handbuch der klassischen Altertumswissenschaft*. Second edition. II: 1–236; 897–910.

1892. Review of R. Kühner & F. Blass, *Ausführliche Grammatik der griechischen Sprache* I. Hanover 1890. *Indogermanische Forschungen. Anzeiger* 1: 116–18.

1893. Vergleichende (indogermanische) Sprachwissenschaft. Allgemeine Sprachwissenschaft. Slavische Philologie. In Lexis (1893): 536–45.

1897–1916. *Grundriss der vergleichenden Grammatik der indogermanischen Sprachen*. Second edition. Strassburg: Trübner.

1900. Ueber das Wesen der sogenannten Wortzusammensetzung. *Berichte über die*

Verhandlungen der Sächsischen Gesellschaft der Wissenschaften zu Leipzig. Phil.-hist. Klasse: 359–401.

1904a. *Kurze vergleichende Grammatik der indogermanischen Sprachen*. Strassburg: Trübner.

1904b. *Die Demonstrativpronomina der indogermanischen Sprachen* (Abhandlungen der phil.-hist. Klasse der Königlich Sächsischen Gesellschaft der Wiss., 22: 6). Leipzig: Teubner.

1907. *Die distributiven und die kollektiven Numeralia der indogermanischen Sprachen.* (Abhandlungen der phil.-hist. Kl. der kgl. Sächsischen Gesellschaft der Wiss., 25: 5). Leipzig: Teubner.

1909. Hermann Osthoff. *Indogermanische Forschungen. Anzeiger* 24: 218–23.

1918. Verschiedenheiten der Satzgestaltung nach Massgabe der seelischen Grundfunktionen in den indogermanischen Sprachen. *Berichte über die Verhandlungen der Sächsischen Gesellschaft der Wissenschaften zu Leipzig. Phil.-hist. Klasse* 70: part 6. Leipzig: Teubner.

1921. Zur Frage der Personalendungen des indogermanischen Verbums. *Indogermanische Forschungen* 39: 131–9.

1922. *Die Syntax des einfachen Satzes im Indogermanischen*. Berlin: De Gruyter.

Brugmann, K. & Thumb, A. 1913. *Griechische Grammatik*. Munich: Beck.

Cassirer, E. 1945. Structuralism in modern linguistics. *Word* 1: 99–120.

Christy, C. 1983. *Uniformitarianism in linguistics*. Amsterdam: Benjamins.

Collitz, H. 1886. Die neueste Sprachforschung und die Erklärung des indogermanischen Ablautes. *Beiträge zur Kunde der indogermanischen Sprachen* 11: 1–40.

Curtius, G. 1885. *Zur Kritik der neuesten Sprachforschung*. Leipzig: Hirzel.

Delbrück, B. 1880. *Einleitung in das Sprachstudium*. Leipzig: Breitkopf & Härtel.

1893–1900. *Vergleichende Syntax der indogermanischen Sprachen*. (Grundriss der vergleichenden Grammatik der indogermanischen Sprachen iii.1.2.3.) Strassburg: Trübner.

Denecke, L. 1977. *Jacob Grimm und sein Bruder Wilhelm*. Stuttgart: Metzler.

Devoto, G. 1930. Brugmann, Karl. In *Enciclopedia Italiana*. Roma: Istituto Treccani. VII: 963.

Esper, E.A. 1968. *Mentalism and Objectivism in Linguistics*. New York: Elsevier.

1973. *Analogy and Association in Linguistics and Psychology*. Athens (Georgia): University of Georgia Press.

Förster, M. 1918. Erinnerung an Karl Brugmann. *Indogermanisches Jahrbuch* 6: vii–x.

Fought, J. 1982. The reinvention of Hugo Schuchardt. *Language in Society* 11: 419–36.

Gazdaru, D. 1967. *Controversias y documentos lingüísticos*. Buenos Aires: Universidad de la Plata.

Gildersleeve, B.L. 1884. Friedrich Ritschl. *American Journal of Philology* 5: 339–55.

Ginschel, G. 1967. *Der junge Jacob Grimm (1805–1819)*. Berlin: Akademie-Verlag.

Hoenigswald, H.M. 1978. The *annus mirabilis* 1876 and posterity. *Transactions of the Philological Society*: 17–35.

1980. A reconstruction. In B.H. Davis & R. O'Cain (eds.) *First Person Singular*, 23–8. Amsterdam: Benjamins.

Hymes, D. & Fought, J. American Structuralism. In Sebeok (1975): 903–1176.

Jankowsky, K.R. 1976. The psychological component in the work of the early

Neogrammarians and its foundation. In W. Christie Jr. (ed.) *Current progress in historical linguistics*, 267–82. Amsterdam: North Holland.

Kiparsky, P. 1974. From Paleogrammarians to Neogrammarians. In D. Hymes (ed.) *Studies in the History of Linguistics*, 331–45. Bloomington: Indiana University Press.

Koerner, E.F.K. 1975. European Structuralism: early beginnings. In Sebeok (1975): 717–827.

Kretschmer, P. 1920. Nekrolog von Prof. Karl Brugmann. *Almanach der Akademie der Wissenschaften in Wien* 70: 256–61.

Lefmann, S. 1891–7. *Franz Bopp, sein Leben und seine Wissenschaft*. Berlin: Reimer.

Leipzig 1909. *Festschrift zur Feier des 500-jährigen Bestehens der Universität Leipzig*. Leipzig: Hirzel.

1961. *Karl-Marx-Universität Leipzig. Bibliographie zur Universitätsgeschichte 1409–1959*. Leipzig: VEB Verlag.

Leskien, A. 1876. Franz Bopp. In *Allgemeine deutsche Biographie* 3: 140–9. Leipzig: Duncker & Humblot.

Leskien, A. & Brugman, K. 1882. *Litauische Volkslieder und Märchen*. Strassburg: Trübner.

Lexis, W. 1893. *Die deutschen Universitäten*. Berlin: Asher.

1904. *Das Unterrichtswesen im deutschen Reich*, vol. 1. *Die Universitäten*. Berlin: Asher.

Lieb, H.H. 1967. 'Synchronic' versus 'diachronic' linguistics; a historical note. *Linguistics* 36: 18–28.

Meillet, A. 1903. *Introduction à l'étude comparative des langues indo-européennes*. Paris: Hachette.

1936. *Linguistique historique et linguistique générale*, vol. II. Paris: Klincksieck.

Morpurgo Davies, A. 1975. Language classification in the nineteenth century. In Sebeok (1975): 607–716.

1978. Analogy, segmentation, and the early neogrammarians. *Transactions of the Philological Society*: 36–60.

1986. 'Organic' and 'organism' in Franz Bopp. To appear in H.M. Hoenigswald & L. Wiener (eds.), *Biological metaphor and cladistic classification*. Philadelphia: University of Pennsylvania Press.

Müller, Max. 1862. *Lectures on the science of language*. 2nd edn. London: Longman, Green, Longman & Roberts.

1866. *Lectures on the science of language*. 5th edn. London: Longman, Green & Co.

Osthoff, H. 1886. *Die neueste Sprachforschung und die Erklärung des indogermanischen Ablautes*. Heidelberg: Petters.

Osthoff H. & Brugman, K. 1878. Vorwort. *Morphologische Untersuchungen auf dem Gebiete der indogermanischen Sprachen* 1: iii–xx.

Pedersen, H. 1983. *A glance at the history of linguistics*. Amsterdam: Benjamins.

Ribbeck, O. 1879–81. *Friedrich Wilhelm Ritschl*. Leipzig: Teubner.

Robins, R.H. 1978. The neogrammarians and their nineteenth-century predecessors. *Transactions of the Philological Society*: 1–16.

Schleicher, A. 1871. *Compendium der vergleichenden Grammatik der indogermanischen Sprachen*. 3rd edn. Weimar: Böhlau.

Schuchardt, H. 1885. *Ueber die Lautgesetze. Gegen die Junggrammatiker.* Berlin: Oppenheim.

Sebeok, T.A. (ed.). 1975. *Current trends in linguistics, 13: Historiography of linguistics.* The Hague: Mouton.

Sommer, F. 1955. Brugman(n) Karl. In *Neue deutsche Biographie* 2: 667. Berlin: Duncker & Humblot.

Streitberg, W. 1894. Review of B. Delbrück, *Vergleichende Syntax der indogermanischen Sprachen.* 1. Strassburg: Trübner. *Indogermanische Forschungen. Anzeiger* 3: 175–82.

1909. Karl Brugmanns Schriften 1871–1909. *Indogermanische Forschungen* 26: 425–40.

1919a. Karl Brugmann. *Indogermanisches Jahrbuch* 7: 143–8.

1919b. Karl Brugmanns Schriften. 1909–19. *Indogermanisches Jahrbuch* 7: 148–52.

1921. Worte zum Gedächtnis an Karl Brugmann. *Berichte über die Verhandlungen der Sächsischen Akademie der Wissenschaften zu Leipzig. Phil.-hist. Klasse.* 73 2: 25*–40*.

Sweet, H. 1882–4. Report on general philology. *Transactions of the Philological Society*: 105–15.

Sweet, P.R. 1978–80. *Wilhelm von Humboldt: a biography.* Columbus: Ohio State University Press.

Szemerényi, O. 1980. About unrewriting the history of linguistics. In G. Brettschneider & C. Lehmann (eds.) *Wege zur Universalienforschung (Festschrift H. Seiler)*, 151–62. Tübingen: Narr.

Thumb, A. 1913. Das erste Jahr der Indogermanischen Gesellschaft. *Indogermanisches Jahrbuch* 1: 245–59.

Vennemann T. & Wilbur, T.H. 1972. *Schuchardt, the Neogrammarians and the transformational theory of phonological change.* Frankfurt on Main: Athenäum.

Wackernagel, J. 1904. Vergleichende Sprachwissenschaft. In Lexis (1904): 202–7.

Wilbur, T.H. 1977. *The Lautgesetz-Controversy.* Amsterdam: Benjamins.

Wright, E.M. 1932. *The life of Joseph Wright.* London: Oxford University Press.

Wright, J. 1888. *Elements of the comparative grammar of the Indo-Germanic languages by Karl Brugmann.* Volume I translated by J. Wright. London: Nutt.

Wundt, W. 1886. Ueber den Begriff des Gesetzes mit Rücksicht auf die Frage der Ausnahmslosigkeit der Lautgesetze. *Philosophische Studien* 3: 195–215.

1900. *Völkerpsychologie. Eine Untersuchung der Entwicklungsgesetze von Sprache, Mythus und Sitte.* I, *Die Sprache.* Leipzig: Engelmann.

11

NINETEENTH-CENTURY LINGUISTICS
ON ITSELF

HENRY M. HOENIGSWALD

The historiography of any discipline has its well-known and obvious twofold attraction and twofold challenge:[1] it calls for competence in the history of scholarship and science, and it also calls for a very special kind of competence in the subject field – the ability not only to contribute to it, but to see it with detachment as well. The degree to which this double requirement has been filled must vary greatly across the *globus intellectualis*. In linguistics we have original and sensitive studies, most of all in the work of Robins, but it seems that collectively we are still at the beginning. Aarsleff (1982: 312–16) complains about our inability to get away from inventors, forerunners, and other holders of priority and, in general, from our Whiggishly naive (though not always innocent) apologetic linearities. These, he says, are not history, and he is right. But what, aside from good intentions, is the remedy?

We might do worse than start cultivating a bit of detachment, not only with regard to our positive work but with regard to our historiographic efforts, too. Let us ask how we customarily approach those efforts.

It could be put this way. There is (1) *language*, our primary subject matter. There is (2) conduct with respect to language, which includes *linguistics* and many other things besides. There is (3) talk *about linguistics*. Moreover, *linguistics* has (4) a *history*, and so does the *talk* about linguistics have (5) a *history*. All of these have entered into the discussion. All repay study, none merits neglect. But they should not be confused. The only excuse for going through the present pedantic exercise is that they often *are* confused, and that the confusion is a source of trouble.

In fact, the exercise is not quite at an end. We must hint more fully at what is meant by the second category (2). Linguistics is only an explicit scientific endeavour, and there are other modes of conduct in the face of language, including some technological ones: there is reduction to writing, translating, teaching; folklore about meaning, etymology, language classification; and what not. Linguistics, technology, or folklore are not at all the same thing as the reflection about them (3) where such questions are asked as 'What is an etymology?', 'What is required of a translation?', 'What is meant by descent and how is it determined?', 'What is the so-called comparative method?'. Consequently, that part of the history of conduct which includes one kind of history of linguistics (4), would be analogous, say, to a history of physics which goes to the trouble of describing and analysing experimentation, while another kind (5), which deals not with substantive work (2) but with generalizations (3) only, is not unlike a history of physics (if there were one) in which only the beliefs of physicists are considered but not what physicists do.

In choosing its topics, a proper history of linguistics would, we submit, subordinate reflection to execution, philosophizing to problem-finding and problem-solving, and, to use a specific illustration, the 'theory' of sound-change to the ways in which practitioners came to identify and treat 'sound-changes'. Yet, subordination is not suppression. The very relation between the activities of linguists as performed and the ways in which they are discussed is a subject to fascinate anyone who worries about the pitfalls of self-description and who knows that they create an ever-present problem in intellectual history – if for no other reason than that they become influential outside the field. The valid generalizations, whatever the terminology – that is to say, the useful generalizations – are those which have an operational content. For example, the 'comparative' method of reconstructing the phonological shapes of morphs attained its consistency and reliability through a long process of trial and error. It can, and should, be formulated in terms of its workings, and ought precisely not to be characterized in some common-sense fashion as a 'comparison' or a discovery of 'resemblances'.[2] In other words, the difference between the two kinds of history ((5) and (4)) dwindles as improper generalizations are replaced by adequate ones. The improper ones remain a valid subject for students of intellectual folklore, and they are indispensable to an understanding of intellectual biography, which is a crucial part of the history of learning. Creative scholars do not always step back to contemplate their handiwork; in fact, in some fields of endeavour there is an honourable tradition in favour of avoiding such activities. The drawback is that even the most austere members of the profession have had difficulty, in moments of reflection, reconciling their imperfectly formulated, fragile creative experience with the ideological baggage that encumbers their preconceptions (Hoenigswald 1978: 22). This can be intriguing when we see familiar metaphorical or commonsensical concepts being filled with new technical content, and especially when we see it happen unbeknownst to the actors on the stage. Descent, to name an example, is an old metaphor, seemingly irreducible. Under the competent hands of our forebears it acquired its alternative status as a particular configuration in the operation (a better word than 'application') of the 'comparative' method. The reason for thinking so is the most convincing one imaginable: this is how specific controversies ('is French really a descendant of Classical Latin?') have long been decided (Hoenigswald 1977: 168–78).

We are all familiar with the notion of the nineteenth century as the heroic age of linguistics, though, by now, we are equally familiar with its rejection. In accordance with what we have been sketching here, it deserves study in its own right. We would like to know how it came about and why it has, or had, a hold so strong that revisionist attack used to be possible against particular details only, as for instance when it was pointed out that Rask, not Grimm, 'discovered' the Germanic consonant shift. Our purpose is not to deflate it and to replace one mythology by another but to understand it a little better. We shall concentrate on a few high points: on the Humboldt–A.W. Schlegel correspondence, mostly from the 1820s (Leitzmann 1908), on Benfey's *Geschichte der Sprachwissenschaft* of 1869, on Delbrück's *Introduction* of 1880 (Delbrück 1882), on some direct by-products of the Neogrammarian controversy (Wilbur 1977; Christmann 1977), and on Pedersen, in the title of whose book linguistics and the century which was then just past were solidly married (Pedersen 1931). Even as a sample, this selection is meagre. A full study would require the thorough use not only of scholarly publication but especially of correspondence. Only a point of view can be ventilated here, and a few questions formulated.

It would be impossible to begin without Sir William Jones, and wrong to ignore the Finno-Ugricists sponsored by Göttingen. Aarsleff, Jones' champion, observes that Jones was not interested in language as such and had always, with Dr Johnson, 'considered languages as the mere instruments of learning . . ., improperly confounded with learning itself' (Aarsleff 1967: 121). This, of course, puts him squarely in an ancient and flourishing tradition in which Schlözer, the Göttingen historian and economist and expert on eastern history and geography likewise moved. Within that tradition it was a debatable point whether languages should only be classified 'by vocabulary' (etymology, as then understood) or also 'by grammar'. Both Sajnovics (1770: 92), the author of the treatise known as the *Demonstratio idioma Hungarorum et Lapponum idem esse*, and Jones stress the importance of 'grammar' – 'both in the roots of verbs and in the forms of grammar' says Jones – and they are not the only ones. It is not quite clear whether Jones refers to what we would call grammatical structure in the abstract or to morphs that happen to have 'grammatical' rather than lexical meaning (affixes, particles and so on). It is perhaps interesting that he does not ask the question. Something that has to be understood about Jones is that his use of language characteristics, in the famous 'philologer passage' and elsewhere is aprioristically based on such propositions as that languages possessed of 'wonderful structure', of 'perfection', 'copiousness' (of vocabulary?), and 'refinement' cannot be ancestral (Hoenigswald 1974: 349 with n.4). Not unnaturally, the rest of the famous paragraph, with its vaguely algorithmic sound ('stronger affinity than could possibly have been produced by accident . . . so strong . . . that no philologer could examine them . . . without believing . . .'), was taken to have presaged the course which the academic profession of Indo-European comparative linguistics was to follow. While Jones was not 'the discoverer' of comparative language study, he was effective, as Aarsleff observes, because he was an authority on matters Asian, because his account fitted into a systematic scholarly framework, and indeed because he had the 'foresight' to found a learned society, an establishment. To say that 'he created a method', however, is dangerous, since it was not the method elaborated and cherished by a very different establishment – namely that of the academic discipline, especially in Prussia where it was part of a profound educational revolution, what with the setting up of the *Seminare* in the teaching of the humanities and other innovations (Aarsleff 1982: 315). Thus, together with the Göttingen scholars who had been themselves the beneficiaries of the special innovative extra-Prussian atmosphere at that unique place, Jones became and remained the quintessential precursor, destined to be forever judged according to the lights of the professionals of a much later day. One would like to know, as a matter of fact, who first put Jones on his pedestal (if it was not simply Theodor Benfey) with the quotation, out of context, of the 'philologer passage' in a ritual destined to be re-enacted with deadly monotony countless times.[3]

When, then, does 'method' rear its head? The question cannot be answered in terms of invention *ex novo*, and certainly never in terms of the invention of a procedure antedating its application. Yet we get glimpses. There is an interesting passage in an 1822 letter written by none other than Wilhelm von Humboldt to August Wilhelm Schlegel. The retired but still powerful reformer of the Prussian universities gives the recently appointed Bonn Professor his views on the role of 'grammar' in the determination of language relationship (Leitzmann 1908: 50–2). But Humboldt transforms that traditional article of faith into something quite different, and he does so by making a distinction which palpably reflects observable scholarly behaviour when it is guided by a step-by-step concern for coherent and concrete results. When it comes to grammatical structure, says Humboldt, one must distinguish (1) that which rests exclusively on ideas and concepts and can be discussed perfectly well without reference to a single sound of the language (e.g. whether the language has verbs proper or is built in such a way as to allow any word to function as a verb), (2) the nature of the devices used to denote such grammatical distinctions as are provided for (e.g. affixes, alternations, reduplication), and (3) the 'real sounds' of the grammatical elements (e.g. the negative *a-* in Sanskrit and in Greek). His conclusion is remarkable: the last-named criterion (3), he says, is the most probative in deciding for (or against) relationship 'because it is the most specific' ('weil er der speziellste ist'). In other words, it is the least abstract variety of grammar that is the most important – the one that bears, in Humboldt's admirable formulation, a close resemblance to the transmission of real words and belongs with the lexical aspect of language. There is, incidentally, no mention here or elsewhere in this sober and substantial correspondence, of Jones, except as a translator of texts – a fact that gives substance to the impression that the alleged founding of Indo-European linguistics by Jones had no particular reality in the concrete history of scholarship (*pace* Szemerényi 1980: 152). On the other hand, if there is true, systematic precursorship, we find it in the Humboldt letter. With perfect insight, the 'grammatical argument' in its more uncompromising forms is made suspect, the century's abiding preoccupation with the phonological reconstruction of morphs has become visible in outline, and along with it the distinction between a genetic and a typological classification. What is even more remarkable is that this interpretation applies directly only where it counts, namely to the substantive work as we have it in the great handbooks and dictionaries. On the loftier levels of secondary discussion, the thought that 'structure cannot be borrowed' or 'is not borrowed easily' took much longer to discredit and was capable of misleading great linguists, without, to be sure, ever interfering with their real contributions (see now Emeneau 1980: 57). However this may be, Humboldt's position is of a piece with Pott's celebrated words of praise for Grimm for having restored the 'letters' to their dignity, to the deserved detriment of 'many a philosophical system of philology' (Pott 1859–76: 1, XII).

When Theodor Benfey published his *Geschichte der Sprachwissenschaft und orientalischen Philologie in Deutschland, seit dem Anfange des 19. Jahrhunderts mit einem Rückblick auf die früheren Zeiten* in 1869, six years after Jacob Grimm's death and one year after Schleicher's, the institution of comparative linguistics was in full working order in Germany and in many other parts of the world, and so was its in-house history to which Aarsleff (1982: 313) alludes so sardonically. Aside from Max Müller's remarks,[3] Benfey has the immense merit of having first codified it – Raumer's *History of German philology* came a year later (Morpurgo Davies 1975: 608).

Benfey found the scope of his work circumscribed by an editorial plan; it was to be a volume in a History of the sciences in Germany (Modern period) sponsored by the Royal Bavarian Academy. He tells us that he sees nothing wrong with the restriction in time and place. Brief though the period covered may be – six or seven decades – its relative importance is so overwhelming as to make the 3,000 years or so that precede it – Benfey of course knew a great deal about the Indian grammarians – a mere preparation for it. That preparatory period is one of error and, at best, failed starts. The most recent period, on the other hand, is in possession of an entirely new dispensation; the object of linguistics can now be defined with certainty, and though our ultimate destination may still be remote, we are assured of attaining it by the unerring pursuit of the right direction. Therefore, the temporal constraint is not artificial. The geographic restriction is likewise justifiable, for linguistics is a German affair. After all this is said the author, to give him his due, proceeds to give us his 312-page introductory (that is pre-nineteenth-century) history, replete with information about Hindu grammar, Arabic and Jewish medieval philosophy of language, early grammar-writing, and many other subjects. The main section is only less than twice as long as the introduction.

Much of our perpetual *fable convenue* is Benfey's; but where the later line became stale and repetitive, Benfey is fresh and vigorous because he is in contact with the sources. His data are not yet copied from secondary writing. He constantly refers to the riches of the Göttingen library, occasionally complaining of its minor shortcomings. The standbys of the official history as we know it are found here: Sassetti on Sanskrit, Ludolf on grammar, Christian Kraus with his review of the Pallas dictionary, Sir William Jones, and others. His choices were excellent.

One of the important motifs in Benfey's view of history is that of the fundamental break between the 'older' and the 'recent' linguistics; between the precursors and the founders. *Mithridates* was concluded a year after Bopp's *Conjugationssystem*, 'the first work to be totally imbued with the spirit of the new linguistics'; in this sense *Mithridates* marks the end of the older linguistics (Benfey 1869: 272). Humboldt, 'properly speaking' already belongs on this side of the dividing line. One wonders why Horne Tooke is singled out for a special role: he is declared to have led a victorious battle against old views with old methods and to have therefore deserved to be called the last of the old linguists; but, so Benfey continues, there are other reasons why he might with equal right be placed in the vanguard of the new era. Among these are his generally critical attitude with regard to universal and philosophical grammar, his tendency (on which Robins has remarked) toward formal rather than metaphysical or content-oriented definition, and, above all, his method of explaining affixes as the remnants of independent words (Robins 1967: 156). It is a little puzzling to see such emphasis given to an idea which was not particularly original, even on the surface, until we remember what Bopp's morphology meant for observers like Benfey. Except for his lack of acquaintance with Sanskrit, Horne Tooke could pass for a predecessor of Bopp, and that was enough.

Benfey's observations on Horne Tooke fit into a lengthy and interesting discussion of the two issues which in his eyes need to be identified before it is possible to go on with the principal business on hand, and to have seen them so clearly is no doubt another feather in Benfey's cap. One is that of philosophical grammar, where the argument culminates in the pretty *aperçu* that according to the new linguistics it is precisely in the specific grammars that there is nothing 'arbitrary' (nothing not governed by 'laws'), while the purported eternal verities of general grammar turn out to be 'arbitrary' figments of the imagination (Benfey 1869: 301). The other is the question of the 'origin' of language. The two are connected inasmuch as (some) general grammarians treat that problem or pseudo-problem as if the inventors of language 'had possessed language before it was formed'. It is worth remarking (although of course it is only to be expected) that there is no hint of the conversion to the de-facto uniformitarianism which, to us, is perhaps the most profound characteristic of nineteenth-century linguistics (Aarsleff 1982: 316). Clearly, the outlawing of discussions on the origin of language is nothing but an extreme, sloganeering expression of the rejection of non-uniformitarian reconstruction in general. Reconstructed languages must be the same in kind (if not in their accidental properties) as observed ones, and for this reason cannot have, or approach, the condition of a non-language. The term, uniformitarianism, was not then known outside of geology; but that the principle itself, which had taken such firm hold, could still not be raised to the level of consciousness, is an excellent illustration of the tension between real but unformulated working principles on the one hand, and cant on the other.

Another standard item of our official historiography, mentioned earlier, also goes back to Benfey: it is the quotation from August Friedrich Pott's *Etymologische Forschungen* in which the author praises Jacob Grimm for 'reinstating the letters in their natural rights which had hitherto been curtailed by linguistic science' (Pott 1859–76: 1, XII; Delbrück 1882: 33–4). Again, it must be said that the selection of this remark testifies to Benfey's instinctive understanding of what is important in the history of real linguistics. In spite of the lip-service which continued to be paid to 'grammar' as the presumably superior factor, phonology had to be developed to the point where the historical weaknesses of arbitrary etymology were overcome. Pott was independent enough, and pugnacious enough, to formulate the issue in 1833. From then on the content of 'comparison' had shifted decisively from 'grammar' to sounds, that is, to the phonological shapes of forms, regardless of the persistence of a formidable amount of pious wishing to the contrary. Rask is of course hardly mentioned in this context, though he is highly lauded in another (Benfey 1869: 619).

Like others after him, Benfey gives a central position to Bopp. It is clear that this has as much to do with institutional history (Bopp was called to Humboldt's Berlin as early as 1822) as with other factors. Whatever the objective justification, the identification of Bopp as the leader of 'scientific linguistics' has remained a corner-stone of our historical view of ourselves. But there is more here than mere identification. Apparently Benfey (1869: 474) is the originator of the school of thought according to which Bopp's work is an amalgam of two or three different elements, the relation among which remains to be interpreted. He sees it as hierarchical: Bopp's ultimate goal was the 'origin' of the grammatical forms of Indo-European; 'comparison' is a way of reaching that goal because comparison permits the recovery of 'basic forms'; the 'sound-laws' are the instruments of comparison. Much is obscure here. In particular, it is not clear, just how Benfey pictures Bopp's method of 'comparison'. What is interesting is that while 'origin' (meaning the discovery of 'yesterday's syntax' in 'today's morphology') was probably intended in a non-uniformitarian fashion, 'sound-laws', even when we allow for the fact that a good many of these were morphophonemic alternations rather than chronological replacements, could be seen, from Benfey's vantage point, as uniformitarian. But to what extent did Benfey think that Bopp's 'comparison' was already, or at least in embryo, what Schleicher had more recently made of it? No doubt his idea of 'comparison' was not such as to require a precise description of how it is carried out.

In fact, Benfey's methodological chapter (1869: 556–73) raises more questions than it answers. In any event it is less what perhaps it purports to be, namely a summary of collective achievement (?) – and hence less historiography – than it is an exposition of the author's system – hence stuff for history itself so far as we are concerned. This system has three internal and two external components, or rather topics, which we might paraphrase as (1) synchronic and, where possible, diachronic description of one language in a family, (2) a static depiction of the ancestor language as reconstructed, and (3) a downward presentation, complete with intermediate stages, of the prehistoric interval between ancestor and descendant. The remaining two concern the family as a whole: (4) is the ancestor in some relationship, 'genetic' or 'morphological' (typological), with other ancestors; and (5) what does all this contribute to our understanding of universals ('die Idee und Aufgabe der Sprache überhaupt')?

To return to Benfey as a historian rather than as a subject of history, it is only fair to pay tribute to his splendidly written *bibliographie raisonnée* of the enormous factual output of the time on which he writes. He remains polite and respectful – too respectful, one feels – when he confronts the kind of general, interpretative writing which is not congenial to him but which he cannot dismiss, given the undiminished production in this field, as excusably pre-scientific. He is, in other words, becoming enmeshed in the unacknowledged state of disorder and incomprehension between practice and preachment which had reached such depths at the time and for which the profession has paid so dearly ever since. Those who think that the history of linguistics has an obligation to concentrate on preachment may find only scandal in Benfey's two-line mention of Schleicher's *Darwinian theory* (1863) in the course of a brief (and possibly somewhat hasty) final chapter entitled 'Sprachwissenschaft überhaupt' (Benfey 1869: 803). He was interested in other things, though his disagreement with Schleicher on certain specific areas did not keep him from citing him with respect and implicit approval as long as the issues were well controlled by subject matter.

Berthold Delbrück's *Einleitung in das Sprachstudium* (1882) appeared while Benfey was still alive, and after a turbulent decade had passed. There was still a time lag; in the body of his text Delbrück has caught up with Schleicher's theorizing and with Johannes Schmidt (1872); Leskien as well as Osthoff and Brugmann appear in footnotes, while Verner is not mentioned. The first, historical part begins with a chapter on Bopp which in turn starts with Jones and the philologer passage and is quite directly indebted to Benfey in other ways as well. To Delbrück, who is younger by a generation, Bopp is no longer a live influence. In discussing him, Delbrück makes the distinction between his 'explanatory' and his 'comparative' work. The former – Bopp's agglutination theory in its successive, more and more anti-Schlegelian stages – did not spontaneously arise as the natural consequence of his comparison, but from a composite of other sources: observation, to be sure, but also traditional motifs, such as the 'prejudice in favour of the threefold nature of the parts of speech, which seems to have first given rise to the idea that the substantive verb is to be recognized in the shape of the various s's in the verbal forms', the transmitted theory to the effect that roots are necessarily monosyllabic, and 'the tradition derived from Hebrew grammar, that we have to recognize affixed pronouns in the personal suffixes of the verb' (Delbrück 1882: 16). As for the other, the 'comparative' wing of Bopp's edifice, Delbrück seems to be saying that Bopp's 'comparison' is meant to distinguish retention from innovation (as is our late-nineteenth-century 'comparative' method). His criterion lies in the 'mechanical laws' of syllable-weight and the like which tell us what is organic and therefore retained, what inorganic and hence innovated or rather decayed – an idea which Delbrück criticizes both because it is factually untenable and self-contradictory. Of Bopp's 'physical' laws he says, however, that they are indeed sound-laws, except that they are not mandatory or 'regular'.

An important chapter in Delbrück's book deals with August Schleicher. Delbrück is ambivalent with regard to Schleicher's naturalism which he does not take quite seriously. His discussion of Schleicher rightly turns on the *Compendium* (Schleicher 1861–2), and it is perhaps characteristic that the Darwinism tract is not even mentioned. There is an effort to establish continuity from Bopp to Schleicher; but the true value judgement is visible when Delbrück exclaims: 'What a stately appearance Schleicher's Lautlehre [phonology] presents, occupying, as it does, half of the whole *Compendium*, compared with Bopp's scanty and unevenly written chapter' (Delbrück

1882: 47). The comparison is not merely quantitative, for Schleicher's bulk is only the quantitative expression of the same striving for the new ideal of total accountability (to use Hockett's phrase) to which we owe his much-maligned proto-Indo-European fable. By a close interpretation of Schleicher's procedure, Delbrück shows that Schleicher saw how 'the parent speech' was no longer an ideal identity against which the reconstructions could be tested, but emerged as that which was simply and starkly defined as the collection of all reconstructions; nothing more nor less.

The final chapter in the historical part of Delbrück's work (so designated in the Table of Contents) is entitled 'New endeavours' and consists of a discussion of contemporary doings. The catalogue of subjects is no surprise; phonological reconstruction comes to the fore and 'glottogonic' hypothesizing such as is embodied in the agglutination theory is abandoned. That is, since there is, strictly speaking, no comparative method for the 'reconstruction of grammar', all that can be attained is the phonological reconstruction of forms and paradigms.[4] Their Boppian 'explanation' can only be an explanation of these reconstructed forms, and it is never an 'explanation' of say, Greek or Sanskrit forms (such an explanation would compete with, and would often simply be contradicted by, the comparative method proper). It can, therefore, only be an 'explanation' of proto-Indo-European forms. But there are two objections to it: it cannot be 'proved' by the standards which the comparative method had helped develop in the field of phonology (reconstruction of morphs) and precisely for this reason must be rejected on the generally accepted uniformitarian grounds. This, at least, seems to be what emerges from those tentative pages. Delbrück concludes by calling attention to the issues of the day: the Neogrammarian concept of exceptionlessness, and the increased role of analogy as the factor which makes the Neogrammarian conception of the sound-law acceptable in the cases in which that conception seems to offend common sense.

Thanks to Christmann (1977) and Wilbur (1977) we have easy access to the products and byproducts of the Neogrammarian controversy. While it is not our principal purpose to judge its merits, it may nevertheless be helpful to remember what it was about and how it was settled, if it ever was. The formula that sound-laws operate without exception could become a subject for controversy only so long as it was held that the identification of a change as a sound-change was one thing and the finding of such a sound-change to be either with or without exceptions another; the Neogrammarian claim being that sound-changes are always discovered to be without exception. Since there is much to be said about this even at this late date, a reference to one thoughtful and telling elaboration will have to suffice: it was Karl Brugmann who found it necessary to say, more specifically than August Leskien, that sound-change, 'insofar as it goes forward mechanically' suffers no exception (Hoenigswald 1978: 31, n.1). The proviso added here carries as clear a hint at circularity as one could wish. The circularity, to be sure, is not of the vicious variety, for if we understand 'mechanically' not in its (by then completely obsolete) Boppian sense but as meaning 'phonologically' (that is: 'without regard to meaning'), we are told that replacements that are, as we would now say, phonologically statable ('regular' or, if you will, 'exception-free') are called sound-changes. What is worth more than the circularity itself, acknowledgement of which simply serves to clear the air, is the implication that the partitioning of replacements into sound-changes and non-sound-changes is useful, that 'sound-changes' are historically and sociolinguistically capable of particular interpretations (substratum, hypercorrection, etc.), and, best of all, that they may be regarded as diagnostic for the recognition of innovation, as contrasted with retention. One of the more pointed corollaries would have to be that so-called sporadic sound-change is not sound-change within the meaning of that term (Hoenigswald 1977: 182–3).

Naturally, it was not to be expected that things would be seen in that light, though an excellent case could have been made for the proposition that data were, and had been for some time, treated in just this way. It was, therefore, only fair that scholars like Curtius and Ascoli, taking offence at the tone of the claims which were made, pointed to examples of that treatment in their own work and in that of scholars of the immediate past like Schleicher. Curtius' famous tract *Zur Geschichte der neuesten Sprachforschung* [1885] (in Wilbur 1977) is so valuable for our purposes because it is so explicit on metahistory. His roseate view of the intellectual past ('For sixty years Indo-European linguistics developed evenly and without major internal contradiction. . . . In 1866 our science observed its fiftieth anniversary while its founder, Franz Bopp, was still living') and his lament on the contemporary state of affairs – he quotes, with near-approval, Johannes Schmidt's reference to the 'catastrophe'[5] which had occurred – form a deeply-felt contrast. Most helpfully for posterity, he puts his finger on the four crucial topics: sound-laws, analogy, the Indo-European vocalism, and the 'origin' of the (inflected) forms of Indo-European. What strikes us as peculiar in this list is its heterogeneity, or rather the absence of any recognition that the list, while it may be representative of the Neogrammarians' work, is indeed heterogeneous. This suggests a further question which we ask precisely because we are interested in the relationship between what is said and what is only implied and taken for granted. This admittedly naive question concerns what surprising omissions we might notice if we put ourselves in Curtius' shoes without trying – not that we could even if we did try – to rid ourselves of hindsight or of our own peculiar conditioning. To make an arbitrary selection: Verner's discovery, to which Bloomfield ascribes such a central function in the formation of Neogrammarian thought because it seemed to him to be the culmination of the gradual solution of the Grimmian 'exceptions', is not mentioned at all by Delbrück, and mentioned with proper but casual appreciation by Curtius. And the acceptance of uniformitarianism together with the problems it raised is treated only indirectly where one might expect treatment, namely under Curtius' fourth heading. Curtius' penchant for the Boppian continuity prevents him from seeing (whatever his formulation would have had to be) the difference between (1) the legitimate reconstruction of a proto-Indo-European structure which turns out to be typologically different from many of the descendants (say, a phoneme inventory with ə, or an eight-case noun morphology), (2) internal reconstruction backward from reconstructed 'late' Indo-European, undertaken by a statable procedure (if there is one) and without concessions to non-uniformitarian beliefs in growth and decay and their alleged specific manifestations, and (3) a very different sort of internal reconstruction where non-uniformitarian assumptions are indeed allowed and where such questions as that concerning an either necessary, or only contingent, coincidence between the step from one epoch to another and the breaking-up of the ancestral speech community into descendant language communities present themselves. That we do not quite know – except from the way substantive problems are handled – where Curtius 'stands' is not our concern at this moment. But it is interesting to realize that the rise of uniformitarianism (as we would elect to call it) was not yet a central tenet of official historiography.

Wilbur's analysis makes it clear that the great controversy was more a matter of current events than of history and that those current events were quite naturally not seen with the historian's detachment – a circumstance we should remember whenever we feel tempted to use polemical formulations as primary sources. Nor is the protagonists' decision for or against a melodramatic rather than a conciliatory tone necessarily the result of historical zeal, even if reflections on the past are what is ostensibly offered. Brugmann (in Wilbur 1977: 125) defends himself and his companions-in-arms against Curtius' charge of a 'break with the past' by expressing the view that it was Curtius himself, as well as Schleicher, who had already moved in the same direction.

If we do not find what we are looking for in the Neogrammarians' debate the fault is altogether ours, as we approach their utterances with expectations that are absurdly wrong. Just as it would be arrogant to blame Jones for not having said what certain later readers imputed to him, so we cannot hope to find a history of ideas in a setting where not historiography but the uses of history loom so large as to make any other expectation patently unreasonable. It must be said again, however, that a narrative that oscillates between reporting a succession of so-called breakthroughs and tracing a steady, linear accumulation of evidence, both in the service of the attainment of perfection, will not escape the pitfalls of apologetic, Whiggish history-writing. What such a narrative lacks is, among other things, a sense of the choices as they existed at those particular times in the past, and the realization of the vast danger of misunderstanding as those choices alter while the terminology, more often than not, stays put.

One suspects that Hermann Collitz, perhaps alone among the giants of his generation, had a more truly historical view of the past and present of linguistics. His incentive for expressing it was, to be sure, just as polemical as that of others – he wished to break a lance for Johannes Schmidt against what he considered offensive attacks. In the course of his argument he makes a declaration the very tone of which makes the reader prick up his ears: 'Once and, so far as I know, only once since comparative linguistics has existed was it essentially transformed, namely, by Schleicher, who was the first to attempt to reconstruct the ancestor language' (of the Indo-European family) in detail, and so on (Collitz in Wilbur 1977: 206). Two things are remarkable here. One is the fact that the pronouncement is made about linguistics, and not, biographically, about a figure in linguistics – an outward manifestation, but a fitting one, of the criterion whereby to measure the function of scholarly personality. The other is negative and very striking: Schleicher's naturalism, that famous propensity which troubled everybody so badly, is hardly noted – rightly so, because it did not matter. There was no way in which biologistic fantasy could interfere with Schleicher's technical work. Where Scherer (in Christmann 1977: 182–3) had 'no doubt that the Darwinian model can be useful to linguistics', Collitz did not bother.[6]

Holger Pedersen's *Sprogvidenskaben i det Nittende Aarhundrede* of 1924 appeared in English in 1931, but it belongs in the nineteenth century, and not only in the sense that it deals with that century. The translator rightly considers that what Pedersen had in mind was not the past but the present ('the past century and a quarter'). It is very characteristic of this work, which has been called 'not unfair' though 'unbalanced',[7] that not only does it not so much as mention Baudouin de Courtenay and Kruszewski – this almost goes without saying – but not even Jost Winteler's *Kerenzer Mundart* (1876), which ought to have been well within its purview – and which has, incidentally, meanwhile attained canonic standing (Bloomfield 1933: 331; Hoenigswald 1978: 20). Pedersen was apparently so convinced that nineteenth-century linguistics is linguistics itself that he did not even feel the ordinary rhetorical urge to conclude his survey ('The methods of comparative linguistics; . . . the older period; the new period . . .') with an envoi of prospects for the future. But then Pedersen does have the great merit of concentrating, especially when it comes to the end of the century, on the technical controversies in Indo-European phonology, complete with their methodological aspects. That he does so largely under the guise of describing the prodigious achievement whereby factual knowledge (of languages, texts, and external histories) was enlarged is all to the good because, whatever the intent, it does discourage the thought that those controversies arose only as new philosophies were applied. It also shows by example that it is only through the controversies and not by ordinary common-sense interpretation that principles, slogans, and generalizations can be understood.

This, of course, is not said in so many words. As Pedersen looks back he sees two periods, one starting with Bopp's comparative grammar and ending with Schleicher's *Compendium* (Pedersen 1931: 240–310).[8] The placing of the endpoint is symptomatic; Pedersen pretends not to be impressed by Schleicher's striving for the all-inclusiveness of reconstruction, and of course, he objects to Schleicher's editorial asides on the possibility of exceptions to sound-laws, and to his organismic fugues. However, as Pedersen returns to the *Compendium* a few pages later (1931: 266–72), he praises it: 'it seems rather modern' (!); the reconstructions are 'precise' – a meaningful term, as we have seen; the necessity of such precise reconstructions having been stated before, Schleicher actually carried them out; he demonstrated that such questions as whether Sanskrit is ancestral or collateral to the other languages of the family are decided by the reconstructions themselves; some of Schleicher's etymological errors can be seen as errors in Schleicher's own terms, that is, they are inconsistencies about which there can be an explicit argument.

By the time the second period is reached, the principles are safe, and Pedersen's virtuosity in summarizing the important material controversies (such as the vocalism question and the intimately related problem of palatalization in some daughter languages) comes into its own. His exposition then naturally turns to the subject of analogy. It is his view that 'certain striking irregularities were got rid of not by discoveries in the history of sounds [not by refining sound-laws in the manner of Verner] but by . . . *theoretical inquiry* [author's or translator's emphasis]'.[9] This is one of the rare instances in which the issue of the relationship between practice and stated theory is faced historiographically. Here as in other cases one would have to distinguish between the terms (analogy, analogic change, *Systemzwang* [pressure from the system], form association . . .) and the operational use of the concept *avant la lettre*. Indeed to what extent, if any, did scholars before the days of Scherer show a preference for morphologically isolated forms in the working out of their sound laws?

What, then, is our historiographical heritage, as exemplified by these contemporary sources, like? It is, first of all, heavily weighted in the direction of historical and 'comparative' work – somewhat more so than was the period itself. In his description of the latter part of the century, Pedersen, who may after all be seen as the conscientious, authoritative custodian of that heritage, goes beyond such work only where he gives vent to his enthusiasm for phonetics. There are no inklings of a feeling for early structuralism: Nikolaus Finck is represented only by his work on Gypsy and by *Sprachstämme* (1909a) but not by his important *Haupttypen des Sprachbaus* (1909b) and Saussure only (and deservedly) by the *Mémoire* (1879) and other Indo-Europeanist studies but not by the *Cours* (1916). Secondly, our historiography is permeated by a far too credulous and straightforward view of the relation between our 'procedures . . . [which, in Leonard Bloomfield's words] are simply necessary things, carried on without much comment until they are systematized'[10] and their systematization. In that view the relation is such that the practitioner, who, after all, must be credited with knowing more about his business than anyone else, can therefore *ipso facto* discuss it with detachment. Few would make such pronouncements about, let us say, art, including sensitive artists themselves.

More recent historiographical studies such as those of Robins (1967) and Mounin (1967) have set the stage for an approach in which the area that lies between the mastery of the phenomena and the analysis of that mastery becomes the central topic. In part this is no doubt because the style of synchronic linguistics has moved towards greater formalization and axiomatization. Even for those historiographers who are not naive about precursorship, linearity, and the apologetic utilization of history, systematic orientation will necessarily and legitimately determine attitudes. We have alluded to the reinterpretation of concepts like ancestry-and-descent and 'regular' sound-change as salutary circularities; the reinterpretation might guide us as we investigate the early appeals apropos of case work to those concepts as well as the early attempts at formulating their essence. The century closed, in the view of some of the observers, with 'analogy' holding the centre of the stage. It could be argued that there was something wrong with a definition of analogic change in which it was simply regarded as a counter-agent to sound-change and that, perhaps, it would have been better to ask first what formal properties analogic changes have and under what particular formal conditions they pose a danger to the recognition of 'sound-changes'.[11]

Just as the understanding of the history of linguistics, including that of nineteenth-century linguistics, is essential to our own efforts, so we need to understand why our professional forebears had to see themselves and their antecedents as they did.

NOTES

1 *Current trends in linguistics*, vol. 13 (1975), entitled *Historiography of linguistics*, is a historiography of linguistics, that is, a work about the history of linguistics. It is not a work about the historiography of linguistics.

2 Hoenigswald (1963), where it is pointed out that J. Vendryes may have been the first to find it necessary to warn against terminological confusion.

3 Max Müller (1861) quotes the passage, which had remained well known, but it is clearly not yet a set piece.

4 The comparative method in the narrower sense of the word allows triangulation, because it can appeal to semantic identity. Thus 'the word for father' can be phonemically reconstructed but the operation cannot be repeated on the higher level because there is no still higher level to appeal to. Thus, there is no comparative method in the technical sense for syntax and semantics, which is not to say that there are no methods of reconstruction.

5 It is not quite certain just what was meant by 'catastrophe'.

6 Scherer, incidentally, understood the general importance of geological uniformitarianism. Collitz' reticence recalls Delbrück (1882: 47) but his special interest in Schleicher makes it more striking.

7 Wells 1974: 436.

8 Actually, August Fick is still included (Pedersen 1931: 272–3).

9 Pedersen (1931: 290). See the penultimate paragraph.

10 Hockett 1970: 425.

11 Wilbur (1977: xxxviii) quotes from Ferdinand Masing (1883: 21) to the effect that 'sound-laws operate without exception, and formations the shape of which cannot be explained through sound-laws are analogical formations'.

REFERENCES

Aarsleff, Hans. 1967. *The study of language in England*. Princeton: University Press; 2nd edn. London: Athlone Press 1983.
   1982. *From Locke to Saussure*. London: Athlone Press.
Benfey, Theodor. 1869. *Geschichte der Sprachwissenschaft und orientalischen Philologie in Deutschland*. Munich: Cotta.
Bloomfield, Leonard. 1933. *Language*. New York: Allen & Unwin.
Brugmann, Karl [1885]. Erwiederung [sic] auf Georg Curtius Schrift 'Zur Kritik der neuesten Sprachforschung'. In Wilbur 1977.
Christmann, Hans Helmut. 1977. *Sprachwissenschaft des 19. Jahrhunderts*. Darmstadt: Wissenschaftliche Buchgesellschaft.
Collitz, H. [1886]. 'Die neueste Sprachforschung und die Erklärung des indogermanischen Ablautes'. In Wilbur 1977.
Delbrück, Berthold. 1882. *Introduction to the study of language*, translated by E. Channing. Leipzig: Breitkopf & Härtel.
Emeneau, Murray B. 1980. *Language and linguistic area*, edited by A.S. Dil. Stanford: Stanford University Press.
Finck, Nikolaus. 1909a. *Die Sprachstämme des Erdkreises*. Leipzig: Teubner.

188   HENRY M. HOENIGSWALD

1909b. *Haupttypen des Sprachbaus.* Leipzig: Teubner.
Hockett, Charles F. (ed.) 1970. *A Leonard Bloomfield anthology.* Bloomington and London: Indiana University Press.
Hoenigswald, Henry M. 1963. On the history of the comparative method. *Anthropological Linguistics* 5: 1–11.
    1974. Fallacies in the history of linguistics. In Dell Hymes (ed.) *Studies in the history of linguistics,* 346–58. Bloomington & London: Indiana University Press.
    1977. Intentions, assumptions, and contradictions in historical linguistics. In R.W. Cole (ed.) *Current issues in linguistic theory,* 168–94. Bloomington & London: Indiana University Press.
    1978. The annus mirabilis 1876 and posterity. *Transactions of the Philological Society* 1978: 17–35.
Leitzmann, A. (ed.) 1908. *Wilhelm von Humboldts und A.W. Schlegels Briefwechsel.* Halle: Niemeyer.
Masing, Ferdinand. 1883. *Lautgesetz und Analogie in der Methode der vergleichenden Sprachwissenschaft.* St Petersburg: Verlag der Kaiserlichen Akademie.
Morpurgo Davies, Anna. 1975. Language classification in the nineteenth century. In Sebeok 1975, 607–716.
Mounin, Georges. 1967. *Histoire de la linguistique.* Paris: Presses Universitaires.
Müller, F. Max. 1861. *Lectures on the science of language.* London: Longman Green.
Pedersen, Holger. 1931. *Linguistic Science in the nineteenth century,* translated by John W. Spargo. Repr. as *The discovery of language.* 1962. Bloomington: Indiana University Press.
Pott, August Friedrich. 1859–76. *Etymologische Forschungen.* Lemgo and Detmold: Meyer.
Robins, R.H. 1967. *A short history of linguistics.* London: Longman.
Sajnovics, Joannes. 1770. *Demonstratio idioma Hungarorum et Lapponum idem esse.* Tyrnavia, Collegium Academicum S.J.
Saussure, Ferdinand de. 1879. *Mémoire sur le système primitif des voyelles dans les langues indo-européennes.* Repr. in *Recueil des publications scientifiques de Ferdinand de Saussure.* Geneva: Sonor 1922.
    1916. *Cours de linguistique générale.* Critical edition by R. Engler. Wiesbaden.
Schleicher, August. 1861–2. *Compendium der vergleichenden Grammatik der indogermanischen Sprachen.* Weimar: Böhlau.
    1863. *Die Darwinische Theorie und die Soprachwissenschaft.* Weimar: Böhlau.
Schmidt, Johannes. 1872. *Die Verwandtschaftsverhältnisse der indogermanischen Sprachen.* Weimar: Böhlau.
Sebeok, T.S. (ed.) 1975. *Current trends in linguistics 13: Historiography of linguistics.* The Hague: Mouton.
Szemerényi, Oswald. 1980. About unrewriting the history of linguistics. In *Wege zur Universalienforschung,* edited by G. Brettschneider & C. Lehmann. Tübingen: Narr.
Wells, Rulon. 1974. Phonemics in the nineteenth century. In Dell Hymes (ed.) *Studies in the history of linguistics.* Bloomington & London: Indiana University Press.
Wilbur, Terence H. (ed.) 1977. *The Lautgesetz controversy.* Amsterdam: Benjamins.
Winteler, Jost. 1876. *Die Kerenzer Mundart des Kantons Glarus.* Leipzig & Heidelberg: Winter.

12

EUROPEAN LINGUISTICS
IN THE TWENTIETH CENTURY

GIULIO LEPSCHY

This article is divided into three sections. The first presents an outline of some of the main theoretical developments in twentieth-century linguistics, the second an examination of some of its other achievements, including descriptive and historical linguistics, and the third a discussion of some of the problems which concern linguistic historiography and its relevance for linguistic research.

1. What are the main events in European linguistics in the twentieth century? The answer may appear to be obvious, and it is one on which most of the surveys of modern linguistics agree (see the bibliography quoted in Lepschy 1982, to which I refer also for many of the works mentioned in what follows). At the beginning of the century we find, in Geneva, a figure often considered the father of modern linguistics, Ferdinand de Saussure. As a young man he had been (1876–80) at the heart of the German tradition of comparative philology, meeting in Leipzig the main Neogrammarians, and had then produced that *Mémoire* on the Indo-European vowel system which still strikes the reader as one of the most extraordinary linguistic treatises ever written for power of abstraction and explanatory insights. After that he taught in Paris, influencing Meillet, and through him the whole school of French sociological linguistics. Finally, in Geneva, he became more and more preoccupied with the theoretical foundation of linguistics. He gave three courses in general linguistics (1907–11). After his death in 1913 the notes taken at these courses by some of his listeners, together with his own lecture notes, were used by some of his former colleagues and pupils to produce a text which, until the appearance of Chomsky's work, can be considered the most influential book in modern linguistics.

The book's appearance was not a bombshell (in 1916, the year of its publication, Europe was being devastated by less metaphorical explosions), but its effect was nonetheless all pervasive, and contributed to the shaping not only of linguistics, but also, through the structuralist movement, of a whole way of perceiving the world, an intellectual stance which is central for an understanding of contemporary culture.

The way in which this happened deserves to be investigated on its own merits as an episode of intellectual history, particularly if one considers the circumstances in which the book was put together, and that only in recent decades has serious work been devoted to the relation between the published synthesis, the notes on which it was based, and the nature of what Saussure actually said and thought (see Godel 1957, and Engler's 1967–74 synoptic edition of the *Cours* side by side with the relevant manuscript material). Saussure's personality, his cultural background, and his intellectual history remain enigmatic, notwithstanding the excellent contributions of many scholars, from Koerner (1972, 1973) to De Mauro's formidable commentary to the *Cours* (1972). Whatever may have been its real intellectual development and internal organization, Saussure's thought was absorbed and made its impact mainly through some striking pairs of interconnected antithetical notions. These are: synchronic versus diachronic, *langue* versus *parole*, syntagmatic versus paradigmatic, signifier versus signified. I shall briefly deal with these pairs in turn.

Synchronic versus diachronic: these terms refer not so much to aspects of language as to perspectives; it is possible to study the evolution of language, as comparative philology had done, identifying in the historical study the only possible scientific investigation. Against this prevalent historicist view, Saussure stated that it was also possible to study language synchronically, from the point of view of the system at work at any given period; even though language is changing all the time, the people who use it are not aware of this, and it functions, from the angle of linguistic consciousness, as if it did not have a past or a future, but purely on the basis of its present structure. Saussure introduced here a comparison with a game of chess: at any given stage the relative value of the individual pieces, and their possible moves, depend exclusively on the situation on the board at that particular point, and not on what has gone on beforehand; the moves through which the present state has been reached are irrelevant, and a player who comes to the board at this time is at no disadvantage compared to the one who has followed (or made) all the moves and therefore knows the history of that game.

Disregarding the fact that the comparison is here not fully appropriate (as there are certain moves, like castling, or taking a pawn *en passant* which are allowed by the rules of chess depending on certain previous moves), the distinction was in the air at the time. Economists and sociologists were analyzing society as a system of forces; on the one hand one can perceive here a distancing from historicist views according to which to know something means to know how that something was formed; on the other hand Saussure's dichotomy can be related to the one, present in the tradition of historiography, between historians and antiquarians (see Timpanaro 1963).

Even the terms used by Saussure are not, strictly speaking, neologisms; *syn-* and *dia-* were of course Greek prefixes widely used in scientific terminology, and opposed to each other in pairs like 'synaloepha' versus 'dialoepha', 'synaeresis' versus 'diaeresis', 'systole' versus 'diastole', etc. Formations like 'synchronism', 'synchronal', 'synchronous', and so on have a long history in European languages, as a glance at the OED will confirm; here one also finds 'synchronic' attested in 1833, and 'synchrony' in 1840. *Dia-* was also available, with the meaning 'through', to form scientific compounds like 'diagenesis' (1886), 'diageotopic' (1880), 'diahydric' (1883), 'diapositive' (1893); it is worth remembering that the OED gives 'diachronic', calling it a nonce-word, with a quotation of 1857, and defines it as 'lasting through time, or during the existing period'.

The novelty was the explicit introduction of this dichotomy in linguistics, since comparative philology had imposed the assumption that a scientific study of language had to be historical. By stressing the separation of the two viewpoints, and the legitimacy, even the primacy of the synchronic approach, Saussure, while he unwittingly gave respectability again to the long tradition of linguistic study up to the nineteenth century, was clearly conforming to the systematic, unhistorical bias of many natural sciences of the time. The rigid separation of the two viewpoints, synchronic and diachronic, is, however, not without its own difficulties for linguistics. There are questions of morphology, for instance, which seem to cry out for a diachronic rather than a synchronic account: if somebody asks why the plural of Italian *uomo* is *uomini* rather than *uomi*, he is more likely to be satisfied by an etymological explanation than by the attempt to fit that plural within the synchronic pattern of Italian noun inflection. Moreover, in the description of the semantic system of a language it is not easy to banish the conditions of previous periods, which have not only *changed into* the present ones, but also *coexist with* them, owing to the fact that works from the past, embodying prior semantic systems, are still part of our own culture. It may, in this context, be relevant to recall that it was a contemporary of Saussure, the illustrious Scottish scientist J.A. Ewing, who studied certain effects of metal stress, magnetism, etc. which depend not on the present state of the system, but on conditions prevailing *before* such effects manifested themselves; he introduced in 1881 the technical term 'hysteresis' for this phenomenon, which is defined in the OED as 'any dependence of the value of a property on the past history of the system to which it pertains'. This seems to me a notion which linguists could profitably take into account.

Langue versus *parole*: this dichotomy proved to be one of the most problematic in its implications and one of the most recalcitrant to definition. It could be used as a classic illustration of the difficulty one has in trying to distinguish linguistics (the study of language) from the history of linguistics (the study of what people have thought about language). It seems obvious that one cannot offer cut and dried 'technical' definitions of what these terms mean in Saussure's usage, as he was developing certain notions which are appropriately, but also approximately, designated by terms which carry with them the history of their usage within the French language and within French culture. In English there is no obviously equivalent pair of terms. *'Parole'* refers to the act of speaking, to the individual linguistic events which take place when somebody says something; *parole* is concrete, individual, specific, related to particular circumstances. 'Speech' is a possible rendering in English, but it is unfortunate as it may also correspond to the general faculty which Saussure calls *'langage'*; 'speaking' is another possibility, but it is heavier and less idiomatic than *'parole'*. *Langue* implies the collective and social side, as against the individual, the code as against the message; in other words the general system on the basis of which the individual act of speech can be understood, the abstract as against the concrete – with a distinction that can be related to the Galilean model: a set of abstract, mathematical rules which explain the individual instance of the fact in question, even though each specific event will take place in a way which is determined also by *other* factors: the law of falling bodies is explanatory just because it is abstract, while the way in which an individual object falls will also depend on a series of other factors such as the friction of the medium. It has been suggested that the distinction between *'langage'* and *'langue'* corresponds to the one conveyed in English by the absence of the article ('language' for *'langage'*) and its presence ('the language' for *'langue'*) (Saussure 1983: xiv), but this solution has the disadvantage that 'the language' (apart from being syntactically awkward in many contexts where there is no previous reference to a language) does not satisfactorily account for the distinction between *langue* and *parole*, given that the two terms, and not just the first one, refer to what goes on in any (unspecified) individual language. The distinction between the collective and the individual aspect has been related to the debate current within sociology at the time about the place of 'social facts' as analysed by E. Durkheim, and individual ones, as presented by G. Tarde; but of course the tension between what belongs to society (the community, the nation, and so forth) and what to the individual, in language, was a commonplace of linguistic research, and had been for a long time.

Apart from the methodological question of the place of abstract rules of a formal nature in scientific explanation, there is the choice of what is the proper object of linguistic investigation: individual *texts*, spoken or written (as was the case for philology, in the tradition of textual criticism), or *languages* (as was the case for comparative philology) of which any individual text would be considered a more or less accidental, inevitably incomplete realization. This can be related to the discussion on the generalizing versus individualizing character of science, or to the distinction between nomothetic and idiothetic disciplines.

Syntagmatic versus paradigmatic: the terms Saussure used were in fact 'syntagmatic' and 'associative' ('paradigmatic' for the latter was introduced by Hjelmslev). This is obviously connected to the previous distinction, in the sense that *parole* is syntagmatic, *langue* paradigmatic. Syntagmatic relations are *in praesentia*, they apply between elements which appear in the message (like the article and the following noun, the consonant and the following vowel); paradigmatic relations are *in absentia*, as they apply between elements which belong to a set or an inventory (as in the paradigm of noun declensions and verb conjugations in the grammars of classical languages). The distinction is comparable to the one fashionable in nineteenth-century psychology in the field of association of ideas: a word like 'read' can be associated to 'book', by contiguity (*in praesentia*), or with 'write' by similarity or dissimilarity (*in absentia*). An attempt can be made to construct the whole description of language through the relation between these two categories, building up paradigmatic systems on the basis of different syntagmatic relations (for instance, the inventory of the items that can occur between two consonants in an English monosyllable of the structure C–C would consist of the class of the English vowels). One of the problems which Saussurean linguistics left open concerns the status of syntactic rules, that is, the identification of those paradigmatic patterns which control the construction of sentences, instead of leaving the latter to the more individual and unstructured domain of *parole*. But before the appearance of generative linguistics the status of syntax in a general theory of language was normally unclear.

Signifier versus signified: the terms used by Saussure were '*signifiant*' and '*signifié*'. As we noted above for '*langue*' and '*parole*', it is difficult to separate the exact meaning of these terms from the way they have been used within their cultural tradition. The English term 'meaning' is a particularly tricky one in this context, as it may correspond to either of the French terms: a word meaning (*signifiant*) x, has x as its meaning (*signifié*). The term 'sign' is also ambiguous, as it may be used for the signifier, or for the union of signifier and signified. Apart from the ungainly expressions 'signifier' and 'signified', the Latin terms '*signans*' and '*signatum*' have also been proposed. This dichotomy is the one which is the most specifically linguistic (or rather, semiotic) of the four. Whereas the first three found their counterparts in other sciences, this applies only to semiotic objects, which are defined by their being used 'for' something else, or by having two aspects (or sides, or planes), one being the expression (*signifiant*) – the word 'cat' has a *signifiant* which consists of a voiceless velar stop, followed by an open front vowel and by a voiceless alveolar stop (or, in writing, by the letters 'c', 'a', 't' in this order); and the other being the content (*signifié*) – what the word 'cat' means, with reference to the animal it denotes (the cat) or to the set of categories which define it, or to the mental and psychological counterpart of these features, or to the cultural associations which have grown around the notion within certain traditions. Saussure was keenly aware of the 'semiotic' character of language, and in fact saw linguistics as one section of a more general science called '*sémiologie*'; 'semiology' and 'semiotic(s)' are some-times used as synonyms, sometimes they are distinguished by referring the former to the French tradition grown out of Saussure's theories (with implications for literary criticism, and for a critique of society and ideology in general); and the latter to a more logical study of signs, which goes back at least to Locke, and has been developed particularly by Peirce (see Jakobson 1975a).

Out of this Saussurean heritage which has shaped the whole of European linguistics in our century several schools have developed, which recognize explicitly their connections with it. We can recall the Geneva School of the immediate colleagues and followers of Saussure, with scholars like Bally and Sechehaye, and then Frei, Godel, and Engler. Particularly memorable are the attempts by Bally to create a stylistics based on the expressive aspects of certain usages, and the elaboration by Godel and Engler of questions of Saussurean theory such as syntagmatics (see Godel 1969).

The Prague Circle, which flourished in the thirties, was enlivened by the figures of two formidable Russian scholars, who are among the greatest of our century, Trubetzkoy and Jakobson. Trubetzkoy's work is central to the creation of phonological theory, and his posthumous *Grundzüge* (1958) are still one of the monuments of twentieth-century linguistics. (It is owing to the Prague Circle that the term 'phonology' became established with the meaning which is still prevalent today; the sense which was previously more common was that of the historical study of sound-change.) Here the Saussurean dichotomies are linked to each other: phonology is the study of the signifier (rather than the signified), within *langue* (rather than *parole*), mainly from a synchronic viewpoint. The basic unit of phonology, the phoneme, is identified through the exchange of one minimal element of a signifier for another, which is connected to an exchange in the signified; that is, with a resulting difference in intellectual meaning. The theory of phonological analysis has roots which go back not just to Saussure, but also to Slavic predecessors (in particular Baudouin de Courtenay). Trubetzkoy elaborated with particular vigour the notion of phonological oppositions, which Jakobson developed in an original way as the theory of binary distinctive features (which was to be incorporated into the phonological component of a generative grammar). Very early on Jakobson also produced with great originality a set of hypotheses on historical phonology, and stimulated the most fruitful interdisciplinary cross-fertilization, bringing his brilliant linguistic intuitions to bear in different areas, from child language acquisition and aphasic disturbances to information theory, semiotics and poetics (see Jakobson 1962–85).

Another development of Saussurean theories took place in the Circle of Copenhagen where Hjelmslev (1959, 1961, 1973) developed his theory of glossematics, based on a systematic coupling of the two dichotomies of expression (signifier) versus content (signified), and of form (*langue*) versus substance (*parole*), to produce the fourfold partition into expression form and content form, expression substance and content substance: the former two are abstract entities of *langue*, and the latter two are their manifestations in *parole*. Perhaps the most original contribution of this effort has been the stress put on the notion of content form, and therefore on the possibility of a structural semantics, of a formal study of meaning. Another feature of glossematics which is related to Saussurean notions is the systematic elaboration of the syntagmatic versus paradigmatic dichotomy, with the attempt to develop a whole algebra of language, a set of functions, designated by different terms, which variously link and define, at each level, relevant individual units through their syntagmatic and paradigmatic relations.

Another School, which derives ultimately from Saussure, has taken shape around the work of André Martinet in Paris, a linguist who has carried forward many of the findings of the Prague Circle, extending them in the direction both of diachronic research and of syntactic investigation; this trend has been given the label 'functional linguistics', and through the description of various languages has injected a sense of realism into the discussion of linguistic problems which was welcome to those scholars who felt that the methodological theorizing of structural linguistics had moved too far into stratospheric regions of abstract reasoning and had lost contact with concrete problems of language as it is in fact used in everyday life (see Martinet 1962, 1964).

2. I said at the beginning of the previous section that there may appear to be an obvious answer to the question of what the main events are in European linguistics in our century. But a quick glance at the most important trends which can be related to Saussurean thought, and which occupy pride of place in most surveys of modern linguistics, is sufficient to convince one that the situation is far more complex. To begin with, there are trends like that of the group of linguists in Britain influenced by J.R. Firth, occupying a conspicuous position in a panorama of structural linguistics and being more indirectly related to Saussure; an original development, against this background, has been the grammatical theory of Halliday, which has proved singularly influential owing to its provision of a consistent theoretical framework and of categories which allow one to tackle complicated syntactic and stylistic phenomena (see bibliographical refer-

ences, also for the rest of this section, in Lepschy 1982, 1984). Then there are other trends, influenced directly by Saussure, which are not normally considered to belong in the development of structural linguistics: one can recall for instance the French School of sociological linguistics represented in the first place by the great comparativist Meillet, and with a different slant by Vendryes, whose book *Le Langage* (1921) was widely influential, and later by M. Cohen, in whose work there is a rather schematically adopted Marxist orientation. There are also other trends and individual scholars to be taken into account, from Guillaume to two of the most eminent comparative philologists of our century, Kuryłowicz and Benveniste, who have also contributed to the progress of linguistic theory in a context that can be considered structuralist in a general sense. Both produced, with their hypotheses on Indo-European laryngeals and the primitive structure of the root, insights which were within the path masterfully traced by Saussure's *Mémoire* (Kuryłowicz 1935; Benveniste 1935), and both went on to develop their ideas in a series of works which constitute the foundation for contemporary studies in Indo-European comparative grammar.

But as one goes on looking at what has happened in European linguistics in our century, one inevitably realizes that the nature of one's account must depend on one's notion of what should be legitimately considered to belong to the field of linguistics. Some generativists have a curious idea that scientific linguistics begins with Chomsky's work, and since some of the best and most faithful followers of Chomsky are active in Europe, they would concentrate, for instance, on linguists who attend the GLOW (Generative Linguistics in the Old World) meetings. But it inevitably is (and was in the past) possible to have different views. At the turn of the century a lot of enthusiasm was aroused by Croce's theory of 'estetica come scienza dell'espressione e linguistica generale' (aesthetics as the science of expression and as general linguistics), which inspired Romanists like Vossler and Bertoni, but also, with results of varying interest, real linguists like Bartoli and Spitzer; this historicist view was particularly influential in Italy, where it was instrumental in shaping the work of the finest linguistic personalities of the century, like Terracini and Devoto, who tried to reconcile the subjective and creative side of language with its socially institutionalized historical systematization.

Other scholars may look on the development of linguistic geography as one of the main achievements of twentieth-century European linguistics, with the production of the great national Atlases, such as the French (1902–10) and the Italian (1928–40) ones, which for the first time allowed one to have a detailed overview of the extraordinary range of surprising variation found in areas previously thought to be reasonably well known (with important implications also for historical linguistics).

Others may look at the increase in factual knowledge produced by the great grammars and dictionaries published in our century: to mention just some examples, from Jespersen's English grammar to Schwyzer's Greek one, from the OED, completed in 1928, to the *Thesaurus Linguae Latinae*, and, among etymological dictionaries, from the Romance one by Meyer-Lübke to the French one by Wartburg. Still others may wish to concentrate not on new or better descriptions of accessible languages, but on the discovery or decipherment of previously unknown ones, and therefore find the most important developments in European linguistics in the interpretation of Ugaritic, of cuneiform Hittite, of Hittite hieroglyphic, of Linear B, or, more recently, of the archives of Tell Mardikh.

Philosophers of language and semioticians may want to concentrate on other aspects, and find that the most important developments in linguistic theory in our century are marked by the works of B. Russell, or Wittgenstein, or Austin; or perhaps of Barthes, Lacan, and Althusser, who with Lévi-Strauss, Foucault and others are at the heart of the structuralist movement, this being a cultural trend which is of course related to structural linguistics, but goes far beyond it in its implications. They all took, directly or indirectly, elements of Saussurean origin, grafting them onto different traditions, such as those of psychoanalysis or Marxism.

3. A final point is perhaps more controversial and troubling than the ones mentioned in the previous section. It concerns not so much the relative importance of different areas of linguistic research, in a historical account of the discipline, as the very nature of linguistic historiography. Here I should like to consider two different aspects. One is related to the kind of historical analysis and interpretation that can be considered satisfactory. It seems to be clear that a précis of different scholars' theories and hypotheses is not sufficient; what one would want is an account which conforms to the standards normally required for historical research, one which tries to make sense of the works under discussion in the context of the cultural and social background in which they originated (see Malkiel and Langdon 1969 for a statement of this requirement). In many cases, like those of Trubetzkoy and Jakobson, the conditions in which they worked seem to cry out for this kind of connection to be established: the former a Russian prince, uprooted first in the turmoil of the Soviet revolution, later under the shadow of the growth of Nazism, dedicated to the curious political movement of Eurasianism; the latter a Russian Jew, involved with Futurist and Formalist initiatives, escaping from one country of Europe to another, before finally reaching America in 1941: it is difficult to see how their ideas about language, its relation to society and nationality, the character of dialect mixtures, the definition of Indo-European (a topic which was always heavily charged with political and ideological overtones), could fail to be connected with the dramatic nature of what was happening in Europe at the time (see the precious collection of Trubetzkoy's letters in Jakobson 1975b). But the same

applies to a linguist whose life was, on the surface, more uneventful, like Saussure. It is clear that a biography would be precious: notwithstanding the meritorious efforts of many scholars, from Godel and Engler to De Mauro and Koerner, we still know far too little about Saussure's intellectual history, his personal life, his friends and correspondents, the books he read. The rumours about skeletons in his cupboard make this need more acutely felt. There is considerable disagreement about the roots of many of his ideas, which some scholars prefer to see as independent developments within the tradition of linguistic thought and others try to connect with what was going on at the time in the wider field of philosophical and sociological discussions. A recent attempt has been made to link Saussure's statements about the negative, oppositional, differential character of linguistic entities with a debate then going on among methodologists of science, and in particular with discussions on the foundations of physics and mathematics, in which it was stated that scientific observations create or determine their own objects, rather than being determined by them (see Rijlaarsdam 1978): it is noteworthy that these suggestions remained hypothetical and superficial, in the absence of relevant information about what Saussure was actually reading, with whom he was discussing ideas, when and in what circumstances. This sort of background information would also help us to assess other suggestions which at present remain rather gratuitous, such as the one that the notion of *langue* is determined by the ideology of a uniform national language, a myth enacted and enforced by the French bourgeoisie after the revolution as part of its policies directed towards the consolidation of a modern unified nation state. Knowing more about Saussure's culture would allow one to articulate this hypothesis more concretely and precisely. There would in any case remain the question of the scientific validity of the notion of *langue*, as an objective cognitive achievement, as an increase in knowledge, irrespective of the historical conditions which may have triggered its discovery and affected the form it assumed.

Something similar could be said of new achievements in the fields of physics and mathematics, and this leads to the second point I wanted to make, which concerns the status of linguistics as a science, from the point of view of linguistic historiography. There are areas in which a historical account of the discipline can come right up to the present without special difficulties being introduced, apart from the ordinary one of detached judgement, which may be harder to achieve the nearer one gets to the present. A history of literature can give, in principle, the same sort of account for the works of Chaucer, Shakespeare, or Tom Stoppard. Normally, by writing a history of literature one is not producing a literary work – or rather, the work one produces is not necessarily of the same kind as those which form its object (although in some cases this may happen, as one can legitimately consider De Sanctis's History of Italian literature as part of that literature). Similarly for ordinary historical work: it is possible to argue that the basic methodological problems are the same if one is writing about the Peloponnesian war, the First World War, or the Falklands war; in each case one has to examine and assess certain sources and to try to understand complex facts within their contexts. And, of course, writing about these wars is different from fighting them, even though writing a historical work is also a way of contributing to shaping current events, and so part of making contemporary history.

With physical and mathematical sciences the situation seems to be different, in the sense that studying the history of a discipline is not the same as studying the discipline itself, and this latter is normally done using the works of the most recent practitioners, who have in a way superseded their predecessors. For many modern linguists, their field is in the same category: if you want to study the history of linguistics you can start with Robins's *Short History* (1979), and the texts he discusses in it, if you want to study linguistics, you can start by reading his *General Linguistics* (1980) and the texts he discusses in it.

It is generally assumed that studying the history of linguistics is not only different from studying linguistics, but does not even acquaint one with the methods and problems which are current in linguistics proper. This distinction becomes crucial when talking about twentieth-century linguistics. Does one consider Saussure, Trubetzkoy, Jakobson, and so on, as authors to be studied in a course on the history of linguistics, or in a course on linguistics? My reaction would be that a rigid distinction is not helpful. I cannot, of course, speak with any degree of confidence for the sciences, but it does not seem obvious to me that a scientist has nothing to gain from familiarity with the works of Galileo, Newton, or Einstein. If one considers the history of philosophy one will find it even more difficult to accept that by obtaining a better understanding of Aristotle, Kant, or Peirce one is not practising philosophy. In the field of general history too, the study of what previous historians have written about a given problem can help us to understand better the problem itself. Momigliano, introducing one of his collections of essays (1984: viii) wrote recently of the 'constant need to know how and when a given historical problem with which I was concerned had been tackled by my predecessors', observing that different national cultural traditions behave differently in this respect: 'That history of historiography helps to define, face and solve individual historical problems was one of the basic lessons of Benedetto Croce which I hope I have gratefully followed.' This belief, he adds, seems to be a guiding principle for historians and philologists with an Italian cultural background, but not with an English, American, or French one. Perhaps something similar can be said about linguistics. For an Italian linguist like De Mauro it is natural to write an introduction to semantics (1970) in which the history of the discipline and its

200   GIULIO LEPSCHY

theoretical problems are thoroughly integrated. Even though the two aspects are usually kept separate in Anglo-American studies, it seems to me worth observing that they are clearly connected in many of Chomsky's works. I am convinced that one can learn interesting things about language by studying Aristotle, Leibniz, and Saussure, that one should not keep linguistics and the history of linguistics strictly separate, since their contact and cross-fertilization is productive for both.

REFERENCES

Note: A fuller bibliography is found in Lepschy 1982.

Benveniste, E. 1935. *Origines de la formation des noms en indo-européen*. Paris: Adrien-Maisonneuve.

De Mauro, T. 1970. *Introduzione alla semantica*. Bari: Laterza (1st edn. 1965).

Godel, R. 1957. *Les Sources manuscrites du Cours de linguistique générale de F. de Saussure*. Geneva: Droz; Paris: Minard.

(ed.) 1969. *A Geneva School reader in linguistics*. Bloomington & London: Indiana University Press.

Hjelmslev, L. 1959. *Essais linguistiques*. Copenhagen: Nordisk Sprog- og Kulturforlag (Travaux du Cercle linguistique de Copenhague, 12).

1961. *Prolegomena to a theory of language*. Translated by F.J. Whitfield. Madison: The University of Wisconsin Press (original edn. 1943).

1973. *Essais linguistiques II*. Copenhagen: Nordisk Sprog- og Kulturforlag (Travaux du Cercle linguistique de Copenhague, 14).

Jakobson, R. 1962–85. *Selected writings I–VII*. The Hague: Mouton.

1975a. *Coup d'oeil sur le développement de la sémiotique*. Bloomington: Indiana University Press.

(ed.) 1975b. *N.S. Trubetzkoy's letters and notes*. The Hague: Mouton.

Koerner, E.F.K. 1972. *Bibliographia Saussureana 1870–1970*. Metuchen, N.J.: The Scarecrow Press.

1973. *Ferdinand de Saussure. Origin and development of his linguistic thought in western studies of language*. Braunschweig: Vieweg.

Kuryłowicz, J. 1935. *Etudes indoeuropéennes*, I. Kraków: PAU.

Lepschy, G. 1982. *A survey of structural linguistics*. New edition. London: André Deutsch (original edn. 1966).

1984. Linguistica. In *Enciclopedia Europea* XII. Milan: Garzanti.

Malkiel, Y. & Langdon, M. 1969. History and histories of linguistics. *Romance Philology* 22: 530–74.

Martinet, A. 1962. *A functional view of language*. Oxford: Clarendon Press.

1964. *Elements of general linguistics*. London: Faber & Faber (original edn. 1960).

Momigliano, A. 1984. *Sui fondamenti della storia antica*. Turin: Einaudi.

Rijlaarsdam, J.C. 1978. *Platon über die Sprache. Ein Kommentar zum Kratylos. Mit einem Anhang über die Quelle der Zeichentheorie Ferdinand de Saussures*. Utrecht: Bohn, Scheltema & Holkema.

Robins, R.H. 1979. *A short history of linguistics*. London: Longman (1st edn. 1967).
1980. *General linguistics. An introductory survey*. London: Longman (1st edn. 1964).
Saussure, F. de. 1967–74. *Cours de linguistique générale*. Critical edition by R. Engler. Wiesbaden: Harrassowitz.
1972. *Cours de linguistique générale*. Critical edition by T. De Mauro. Paris: Payot. (1st edn. of the *Cours*, 1916; original edn. of De Mauro's commentary in Italian, 1967.)
1983. *Course in general linguistics*. Translated and annotated by R. Harris. London: Duckworth.
Timpanaro, S. 1963. A proposito del parallelismo tra lingua e diritto. *Belfagor* 18: 1–14.
Trubetzkoy, N.S. 1958. *Grundzüge der Phonologie*. Göttingen: Vandenhoeck & Ruprecht (1st edn. 1939; English translation by C.A.M. Baltaxe, 1969. *Principles of phonology*. Berkeley & Los Angeles: University of California Press).
Vendryes, J. 1921. *Le Langage. Introduction linguistique à l'histoire*. Paris: La Renaissance du livre.

13

EDWARD SAPIR'S SIX-UNIT CLASSIFICATION OF AMERICAN INDIAN LANGUAGES: THE SEARCH FOR TIME PERSPECTIVE

REGNA DARNELL AND DELL HYMES

Introduction

The classification of American Indian languages has been a persistently burning issue in the North American disciplines of both linguistics and anthropology, which have remained closely tied in the study of Indian languages. This is one of the rare cases in the history of linguistics where a linguistic problem is of interest to a wider audience than specialists. Shortly after the centennial year of the birth of Edward Sapir, the greatest of Amerindian linguists, 1984, it is appropriate to turn again to his contributions to the classification. It is even more appropriate to do so in honour of R.H. Robins, in light of his own research in the 1950s on Yurok, the subject of one of Sapir's important classificatory suggestions. The history and practice of linguistics, as so often, come together herein.

The folk histories of both anthropology and linguistics have enshrined, through oral narratives which are an essential part of professional socialization, a view of American Indian language classification juxtaposing the fifty-eight stocks proposed by John Wesley Powell of the Bureau of American Ethnology in 1891 and the six-unit classification of Edward Sapir, best known in its 1929 formulation for the Encyclopaedia Britannica. Both classifications represented an attempt to fill in the gaps in the map of native America, to sort out the enormous cultural diversity of the continent in terms of linguistic affiliation. Because the two classifications pose such clearly polar versions of American linguistic history, later practitioners have found themselves compelled to choose either a 'lumping' or a 'splitting' stance, without serious attention to the variable quality of the evidence for particular connections proposed by Sapir and his colleagues to reduce the number of linguistic families.

Both authors of this paper have long been intrigued by the history of Sapir's six-unit classification, from the dual standpoint of practitioner and historian of science. Hymes (1983 [1962]) stressed the importance of Sapir's intermediate classification in 1929, of his recognition that the six-unit classification was preliminary and that many colleagues would prefer a more conservative consensus of the fieldwork which had changed the linguistic map of North America in the years since the presentation of the Powell classification. Although Sapir's own hypothesis went further than those of his collaborators, he also saw his own classification as resting upon a collective effort which he codified. Implicitly, then, he offered an alternative, moderate, classification: 'The following [twelve] reductions of linguistic stocks which have been proposed may be looked upon as either probable or very plausible' (1949 [1929] 171–2). Hymes further noted that the polarization of linguistics and anthropology over issues of classification could have been largely avoided had the reality of Sapir's intermediate classification not been lost from historical view.

Darnell (1969, 1971a, b) treated the Sapir six-unit classification as part of the general question of time perspective in Boasian anthropology during the first two decades of the century, arguing that both the Powell and Sapir classifications drew on a prior period of intensive field research and summarized its results, providing a set baseline for further work. Darnell stressed that a linguistic classification is by definition a theoretical statement and that there can be no abstract answer to the question of how many linguistic stocks there are in native North America. Rather, it is necessary to return to the relationship between data and theoretical assumptions, to the details of Sapir's intentions in particular cases, within the context of the disciplines as practised at the time.

There are several motivations for a reassessment of the historical bases of the Sapir classification at the present time. The 1984 centenary of Edward Sapir's birth has given rise to a great deal of relevant research. Darnell is currently engaged in writing an intellectual biography of Sapir which stresses the integration or interaction of his thought across subject areas. Sapir's work on linguistic classification was not clearly separable from his descriptive work on particular American Indian languages. His attention to issues of time perspective within a Boasian diffusional model was not, in his own view, incompatible with the effort to attain reduction of the number of linguistic stocks in native America. The decision to present an overall classification of Indian languages was at least partially related to the effort to articulate an argument about linguistic typology for Sapir's book *Language*, which appeared in 1921, the same year as the first formulation of the six-unit classification. Sapir was alone among Boasian anthropologists in his Indo-European training and attempted to extend these models of linguistic process to the study of unwritten languages. Indeed, the whole question of classification, for Sapir, is framed in a larger context, encompassing virtually the full scope of anthropology and linguistics as he practised them. It is Sapir's latter-day intellectual heirs who have narrowed the focus.

Moreover, additional documents have become available as a result of centenary research, most particularly the detailed outline of Sapir's 1920 paper read to the American Association for the Advancement of Science in which the six-unit classification was first set forth.[1] Sapir's correspondence with various colleagues just prior to this momentous announcement is also available and provides invaluable supplement to the simple one-page note which appeared in *Science* in October 1921. These documents allow reconstruction of Sapir's immediate intentions in a way not accessible previously.[2]

Finally, there has been considerable change in recent years in the climate of thought regarding classification in American Indian linguistics. For many years, the six-unit classification was widely utilized as a framework for the ethnological study of native America. Sapir's reputation for linguistic 'genius' contributed to a reification of his tentative superstocks and there was little further research on classificatory problems. Although Sapir saw himself as applying the comparative method of Indo-European to his data, later scholars have restricted the scope of this method far beyond the limits of the data at Sapir's disposal. As early as 1942, C.F. Voegelin, himself a former student of Sapir's, paid homage to 'all the flair and ingenuity and insight' of the six-unit classification, with the qualifying judgement that: 'All Sapir's work bringing together the distantly related languages falls under the general category of "other comparisons", and not of the comparative method' (1942: 322–3). The most recent summary of the state of American Indian language classification, Campbell and Mithun (1979) is more consistently conservative than even the Powell classification of 1891. Standards for establishment of relationship stress the existence of a well-defined reconstruction of the sound system of the proto-language. As a result, numerous connections which Sapir considered to have been demonstrated are now rejected. In line with traditional Boasian arguments, there is considerable scepticism about the possibility of distinguishing areal and genetic causes of similarity at great time depth. As Campbell and Mithun (1979: 22) summarize their position:

American Indian linguistics has been haunted by Sapir's dual legacy of distrust for the diffusion of structural elements of language and of emphasis on genetic reduction. As the role of diffusion in the explanation of cross-family similarities is recognized, it becomes clear that the level of proof for remoter relationships must be much higher than thought by many of Sapir's followers.

Sapir himself, of course, acknowledged the problem but avoided invalidation of his results by describing the six great stocks as 'presumably genetic' (1921a: 408). That is, it was more important to Sapir that the similarities, lexical and morphological, existed and reflected common history than it was to see genetic and areal processes as totally different.[3] In any case, the new classificatory conservatism makes it imperative to return to what Sapir was actually doing and how this relates to current understandings of North American Indian linguistics.

Neither anthropology nor linguistics has been noted for the historicism of its view of the disciplinary past. Those who reject Sapir's particular conclusions on classification have certainly acknowledged his 'genius' and insight into many of the languages so classified, but generally without attention to the context of his work. To dismiss previous classifications as 'the result of accidents of history and the influence of powerful personalities' (Campbell and Mithun 1979: 46) is to ignore the actual complexity of Sapir's intentions, their realization and their later interpretation. Sapir's personality was powerful precisely because of his ability to synthesize the descriptive work of his generation, thereby uncovering larger vistas of native American prehistory. The six-unit classification is still compelling in its glimpses of the migration and contact of large groups of American Indians.

This paper will proceed by examining the genesis of each part of the classification in Sapir's own research and that of other linguists of the period immediately preceding the 1920 formulation of the six-unit scheme. Emphasis will be placed on how the principals viewed their efforts. Sapir's 1920 and 1929 versions of the classification will, then, fall into place as part of the ongoing process of American Indian linguistics, rather than as bizarre and radical generalizations based on limited evidence.

The mania for classification: language families of California

Kroeber, Boas' first Ph.D. from Columbia, went to the University of California, Berkeley in 1901 to begin the task of classifying the cultural diversity of the state. Like Powell, he settled on linguistic affiliation as the only practical classificatory feature. By 1908 he had worked personally on seven languages chosen for their typological diversity and had obtained sketches on most of the others (Golla 1984).[4] In 1907–8 he obtained the services of Edward Sapir, already a veteran of two seasons of fieldwork on the northwest coast, including his dissertation research on Takelma. Sapir devoted his California year to the study of Yana, failing to produce the phonological and morphological sketch and extensive vocabulary necessary to Kroeber for his classificatory schemes, but instead completing a set of Yana texts. Sapir was still operating within the Boasian descriptivism in linguistics and his goals were internal to the Yana language itself. Lowie recalls (1956 introduction to Sapir 1965) that Sapir had changed from Germanic philology to anthropology after realizing that Boas had a counter-example to every generalization he produced about language. Sapir accepted Boas' emphasis on the need to describe each language in terms of its own unique categories.

Campbell and Mithun (1979: 26) suggest that it was during this year in California that Sapir 'was caught up in the reductionist zeal of Kroeber and Dixon which prevailed at the time'. Certainly, this was where the process of reduction began, but Sapir's allegiance to the task came after his departure from California. Yet enthusiasm there surely was: Kroeber wrote to Sapir (30 June 1913: A L K): 'We seem at last to have got Powell's old fifty-five families on the run, and the farther we can drive them into a heap, the more fun and profit.' Sapir commented to Kroeber (28 January 1914: A L K): 'I have, like you, lost my love for an unlimited number of stocks.' To Lowie, Sapir noted (12 August 1916: R H L): 'The isolated chaps are gradually coming around.' Kroeber was convinced that the new results changed the framework of American anthropology dramatically (to Goldenweiser, 8 September 1914: A L K): 'I feel very enthusiastic about the revelations that are now pouring in, in spite of their obviousness, for it means an entirely new basis for classification both for our ethnography and linguistics.' In the 1921 presentation of the six-unit classification, Sapir himself referred to the Powell classification as 'tantamount to a historical absurdity' (1921a: 408).

Kroeber retrospectively dated the shared commitment to seeking reductions in the number of linguistic stocks to a considerably later period (1940: 7):

About 1915, however, there began to be some stirrings of dissatisfaction, and more or less simultaneously, and mainly independently, Dixon and I in the West, Sapir in the north and elsewhere, began to indicate evidences, however preliminary, of similarities between particular languages suggestive of a common origin.

There is a good deal of territoriality involved here. Kroeber considered California his private domain and was eager to assign to Sapir the extension of California families into the northwest coast. Sapir had his own domain in Ottawa by this time and could be seen as an equal collaborator.

It is, in fact, quite correct that Sapir had little direct input into the classification of the languages of California. The first efforts by Dixon and Kroeber (1903: 2–3) were wholly within the Boasian model of diffusion and typological comparison:

It must be clearly understood, however, that the classification that has been attempted deals only with structural resemblances, not with definite genetic relationships; that we are establishing not families, but types of families. . . . The classification here proposed is really one of another order from that used by Powell, for structure and not lexical content is made the basis on which all comparisons are made.

Already, however, Kroeber was attempting to break the news to Boas that the explanation of these types of languages was possibly genetic (24 April 1903):

You may be interested to hear that on comparing vocabularies recently I found an unexpectedly large number of words common to two or more languages. . . I do not know quite what to make of the case. I think there has been extensive borrowing, but it is by no means impossible that many of the languages will turn out to be related.

By 1913, Dixon and Kroeber explicitly claimed a genetic basis for the stocks (1913a: 225):

. . . it became apparent that the only satisfactory explanation of the resemblances between certain languages was genetic relationship. On the basis of these indications the grammatical information extant on the same languages was reexamined, and in every instance was found strongly confirmatory. Lexical and structural similarities coinciding and being found relatively abundant, true relationships have been accepted as established.

California Penutian, Hokan and Ritwan were considered conservative categories (1913b: 649):

This relationship would have been recognized previously, were it not that attention has been directed chiefly toward phrases of structure that, while conspicuous, were not typical of the group in question; and especially because comparisons have been instituted between single languages instead of the whole five [Penutian languages].

The correspondence between Kroeber and Sapir at this time confirms the startling nature of the genetic conclusion to Kroeber.[5] He wrote to Sapir (3 January 1913: ALK):

I could, however, get no intelligible result from our data until finally in desperation I dropped the assumption, under which we had all along been working, that all resemblances were due to accident or borrowing, and assumed genetic relationship between those languages that had the greatest number of similarities. From this time on the skein unwound itself and when I turned to grammatical structure for confirmation it was lying ready made in every instance. My wonder now is that we have overlooked the obvious so long, and my only explanation is that we missed the clue and, comparing each language sometimes with the related and sometimes with unrelated ones, confounded genetic with induced similarities until we were in such a state of demoralization that we gave up the problem.

Kroeber was further convinced that Sapir's own California language, Yana, was part of the Hokan stock. Sapir's response was reticent, though superficially encouraging (to Kroeber, 5 January 1913); The results were 'extremely interesting' and 'rather exciting' with 'no theoretical reason' they could not be true, although judgement would have to await the presentation of specific evidence. Sapir soon found himself in need of protesting that he was not opposed to the reductions (to Kroeber, 11 February 1913: ALK): 'I hope you do not have the idea that I am personally opposed to such syntheses. In fact, I feel strongly that there will be more of them made as our knowledge progresses.' He cites Indo-Germanic examples of grammatical change within a linguistic stock and insists that 'I should be delighted if the total number of linguistic stocks in California should turn out to be very few in number after all.'

Sapir's greatest objection to the hypotheses, however, rests on methodological grounds, particularly the phonetic quality of the basic data (to Kroeber, 27 February 1913: NMM):

> You must realize, sooner or later, that exact phonetic material is indispensable for any solid comparative work. Once definite phonetic relationships have been worked out, other examples, that at first sight would have seemed far-fetched, fall right into one's hands. To be sure, some examples which, at first sight, seem plausible enough have later to be discarded.

Sapir is especially distressed by Dixon's 'amateurish' recording and poor ear for sound. Kroeber (6 March 1913: NMM) responds optimistically that Sapir has acknowledged the making of a case for the California stocks and asserts that others can prove or disprove the claims.

By 1915, Kroeber has decided that at least some of the evidence should be published and is asking Sapir not to object (30 March 1915: ALK): 'Will you promise to commend instead of belaboring us if we make some fraction of the evidence available?' Clearly, Sapir is not yet considered entirely an ally, in spite of the frequent contact between Kroeber and Sapir at this time. Sapir is still complaining about Dixon, and Kroeber notes: 'He does the best he can, and about as well as I – certainly as well as I used to. We can't all have your ear, or Goddard's eighteen years of experience with one group [Hupa].' Sapir is, however, eager to have Dixon and Kroeber publish their results, 'even if most of the sound relationships have not yet been worked out' (to Kroeber, 7 April 1915: ALK). Sapir in fact asserts that sound correspondences in the Indo-European sense probably *cannot* be worked out given the phonetic quality of the evidence available. This obviously does not invalidate the hypotheses, for Sapir.

By the time the evidence actually appeared in print (Dixon and Kroeber 1919), Sapir had already joined their Hokan and Penutian stocks to even larger units. Even in this final statement of their no-longer revolutionary hypothesis, Dixon and Kroeber continue to assert that they turned to a genetic model only after geographical contiguity failed to explain observed similarities (1919: 30). In any case, Kroeber had essentially succeeded in classifying the languages of California. Although he continued to follow Sapir's work in reducing the number of linguistic stocks, Kroeber himself turned to non-linguistic problems after this time (Hymes 1983 [1961]).

There was a deep and undeniable ambivalence in the relations between Sapir and Kroeber. Sapir had wanted a permanent position at California and thought Kroeber had opposed that possibility. Kroeber was a self-appointed gadfly to Sapir's more daring linguistic hypotheses, consistently avoiding competition with Sapir's greater linguistic ability and training. Sapir, for his part, was generally ready to criticize the details of Kroeber's work, and certainly of his intuitions in correspondence. Kroeber noted (to Sapir, 4 February 1913: NMM): 'While I see that I must be more careful with you than with most people in citing analogies, I will take a chance with another in this connection.' He then proceeded to cite an Indo-European example, apparently assuming that his willingness to be apologetic would substitute for Indo-European training. Kroeber was, however, generous in applauding Sapir's own work, responding to the connection of Ritwan to Algonkin (21 June 1913: NMM):

I can only congratulate you on your critical ability and capacity for work. Much of what you have accomplished I am scarcely equipped to do, but now that you have covered the ground, I feel that there are some points which I should certainly have worked out some years ago if I had given it my attention. . . . If anyone can still doubt the general proposition of relationship he is obviously prejudiced. I am glad, however, that you have brought the situation to the point where the question is no longer one of fact as to relationship, but one of working out its circumstances and tracing the history of the individual languages.

Kroeber appears to be grateful if Sapir takes on the demonstration of detailed relationship, thereby sparing him the task, for instance (to Sapir 13 December 1916: ALK): 'Every nail of proof you drive in absolves me from so much that I haven't got around to doing.' He is, in general, willing to accept Sapir's results before having seen the evidence, such is his faith in Sapir's abilities. It is unquestionable that this positive feedback for his classificatory work was important to Sapir, particularly in light of the objections which consistently appeared from other quarters. Sapir was often unsure of his abilities or of the likely response to his work and Kroeber pushed him to publish (21 August 1917: NMM):

If I said 'duty', I was wrong. I'll change it to 'opportunity'. You can make the whole damn bunch of philologists, – and there are thousands of them and they hold an assured repute in the world's eyes – either stand on their heads or get up and toe the mark. If that isn't worth while there's absolutely nothing in the whole linguistic game, and it's only irresolution that holds you from chucking it. I'm not arguing for the thing the way it's done but as it might be done. . . . I don't say you have no sense of duty. I've never thought about it. I certainly hope you haven't very much. I do doubt whether you have determination – in plain English, courage – enough to win the whole stakes that fortune has laid out before your 'individuality'.

(This is the year of the 'superorganic debate' in which Sapir defended individuality as a more useful analytic construct than the more traditional notion of culture argued by Kroeber.)

Late in 1917, Sapir was discouraged that no one was interested in American Indian linguistics. Kroeber (4 November 1917: NMM) responded that it was up to Sapir to create such interest: 'The decadence of linguistics is largely your own fault. You're an individualist and haven't built up a school. Do something general in character.' In fact, over the next few years, Sapir did exactly that – with his six-unit classification and his general book *Language*.

In spite of the great influence of the collaboration with Kroeber, however, Sapir's forays into reduction of linguistic stocks came largely earlier and in areas where he worked alone. His work on Kroeber's hypotheses was done only intermittently and in terms of Sapir's own timing. He chose to proceed largely independently, stressing areas of his own fieldwork, to which we now turn.

Defining Uto-Aztekan philology

Sapir's 1909 fieldwork with Ute and 1910 work on Southern Paiute with Tony Tillohash of Carlisle School turned him to the study of comparative Uto-Aztekan. Newman (1954) has emphasized that Sapir was the first to apply classical philological methods to American data, in reconstructing the phonemic system of Proto-Uto-Aztekan. In addition to his own field data, Sapir was able to draw on the work of two students from his teaching at the University of Pennsylvania between 1908 and 1910, J. Alden Mason and William Mechling, both of whom did Uto-Aztekan fieldwork in Mexico under Boas. Sapir wrote to Mechling (8 February 1912: NMM):

I have had some correspondence with Boas about Uto-Aztekan and find that he is not at all favorably disposed towards the hypothesis. However I believe he goes somewhat too far with his caution and personally I am as convinced as ever of the soundness of the theory. . . . It is strange that all three of us [including Mason] should have attacked the Uto-Aztekan pie at such far distant points.

Mason wrote to Sapir from the field (n.d. 1912):

Your observations on Uto-Aztekan are most interesting. We are all agreed, I think, that Shoshonean and Pima are related; there are so many resemblances, lexical, morphological and phonetic, that I think a little intensive work will settle that matter conclusively. The relation of Shoshonean-Pima to Nahua will be more difficult. Undoubtedly the two belong to a morphologically similar linguistic group, but as yet we haven't run across enough lexical similarities to prove the point.

Sapir was, of course, at that time completing his manuscript on Southern Paiute and Nahuatl which appeared in 1913. In fact, Mason became somewhat discouraged about his own abilities and training when he compared his ethnology to Boas or his linguistics to Sapir (22 September 1922: NMM): 'I should not be attempting serious linguistic work on the same scale as you or Harrington with the little training that you gave me and knowing nothing of Indo-European, nor should I be doing ethnological work with the few ideas that Gordon and Speck were able to impart to me.' Sapir's Uto-Aztekan work was, indeed, setting new standards for the linguist within Amerindian anthropology.

In any case, by the end of 1912 Sapir believed that he had 'enough phonetic, morphological and lexical evidence' to demonstrate the unity of the Uto-Aztekan stock 'beyond cavil' (to Kroeber 23 December 1912: NMM): 'I have even unearthed some morphological resemblances of detail which are so peculiar as to defy all interpretation on any assumption but that of genetic relationship.' Sapir was justifiably smug, given that Kroeber had dealt briefly with Uto-Aztekan during his early California years but had been unable to present detailed evidence. He wrote to Mason (n.d. 1913: NMM) regarding the clear demonstration of Uto-Aztekan and Boas' currently less sceptical attitude, then noting Kroeber's postulation of Hokan and Penutian in California: 'Going some isn't it? As usual, however, I imagine that Kroeber will guess what is right or almost right and leave it to others to so demonstrate.'

Kroeber continued, albeit unsuccessfully, to believe that Uto-Aztekan was the linguistic stock which would enable Sapir to demonstrate the applicability of Indo-European methods to Amerindian languages (to Sapir, 24 July 1917: NMM):

I think it's up to you to write a paper that will drive the significance of mora and glottal stop and other traits of the Uto-Aztekan soul home to a larger group – something à la Huxley – the real goods, but even the finest inessentials suppressed, so that fools included must take notice. At least, some of us would make enough noise to drive it into the fools that there was something doing. Now they shrug their shoulders and say 'technical'. By Jove, old man, if I had your knowledge and power of assimilation and skill in handling the damn brute material, I'd have cut you out in reputation as a linguist long ago. At least I'm not afraid to try. You had no business to leave that little incorporation thing [1911] to lie undone until I jolted you into it. Since then you've probably slept on half a dozen like it. If I had half your philological wits I'd have five times your place and influence in the philological world.

One can only speculate that Sapir had demonstrated what he considered to be interesting about Uto-Aztekan, because his later priorities were in other major stocks.

Extending the boundaries of Algonkin

Early in his career, Sapir staked a claim to general interest in all of the native language families of North America. Soon after his appointment as Chief of the Anthropological Division of the Canadian Government, Sapir wrote to Truman Michelson, the foremost American Algonkinist, noting his intention to do brief fieldwork (20 July 1911: NMM):

I hope that I will be able to get first hand acquaintances with several Algonkin dialects

– Delaware, Abenaki, Montagnais, and possibly Malecite and Micmac. Of course, you understand that I have not the remotest intention in the world to work at these thoroughly. All that I mean to do is to get some sort of bird's eye view in order to help me in better appreciating your own and others' work on Algonkin dialects.

This is, of course, an explicit effort not to antagonize a senior colleague. The following year when Michelson sends an advance copy of his map of Algonkin dialects, Sapir has abundant criticism, after his ritual denial of competence in Algonkin (21 March 1912: NMM): 'You ask me to criticize your map but you must remember that my knowledge of Algonkin is too much on the surface to make it worth while for me to suggest any criticisms. However, there are a few points that puzzle me.' The letter goes on at some length. Sapir is particularly eager to know if the main criteria are phonological or morphological. He pursues the same argument in a letter to Frank Speck, his close friend and an Algonkin ethnologist although with little interest in linguistics (21 March 1912: NMM):

Radin [then working for the Bureau of American Ethnology] tells me that Michelson's groupings are based almost entirely upon pronominal schemes. These are important, of course, but I should think that any dialectic mapping would proceed primarily on phonetic considerations. I presume, though, that Michelson has thought the thing out pretty carefully.

Sapir soon found himself in direct conflict with Michelson's Algonkin territory. His exposure to data from Dixon and Kroeber's efforts to unite California stocks stimulated his interest in their Ritwan (Wiyot and Yurok). He wrote on the same day to two close friends, Speck and Paul Radin, about his theory that these languages were distantly related to Algonkin (to Speck, 18 July 1913: NMM):

I have been rummaging around of late in one or two problems of linguistic relationships. . . . Far more exciting than all this [the California stocks] is a trail that I am on in regard to Wishosk and Yurok. I have found some astonishing points of contact, lexically and morphologically, between these, particularly Wishosk, and another well known linguistic stock, which I shall not mention at present because I am certain to be laughed at for my pains. When you get back here we may have an opportunity to say a word about it, provided, of course, you will let me have a chance to put in a word once in a while. Suffice it to say that I am either on the wildest goose chase I have ever indulged in, or else about to land something decidedly revolutionary.

And to Radin (18 July 1913: NMM):

The process of slaughter of linguistic families, upon which several of us seem to have embarked of late, is going on apace. . . . Worse than that, I now seriously believe that Wishosk and Yurok are related to Algonkin. I have been more frank with you in regard to this than with others to whom I have only given dark hints. Please treat this information as strictly confidential, as, should it turn out that I have been hasty, I will present a rather sorry picture. There really are some astonishing points of contact both morphologically and lexically. . . . The consequences of this latest theory are so great that I am hesitating very considerably, even in my own mind, about committing myself, and want to get more and more evidence before I confess to myself that I am convinced. Had Wishosk and Yurok been, let us say, Eskimo or Siouan, I would not have hesitated for a moment, but when you have that vast expanse of country separating the Californian stocks from even the westernmost Algonkin tribes, one may well hesitate.

That is, Sapir's perspective was that of Boasian anthropology. Linguistic data was not to be interpreted in isolation from geographical provenience and likely paths of diffusional contact. Far more purely linguistic evidence was necessary for such an intrinsically implausible connection.

In any case, when Radin read Sapir's paper, there was no question in his mind that Sapir had demonstrated the genetic relationship. He failed to understand the motives or imaginations of those who quibbled (to Sapir, n.d. late 1913: NMM):

. . . it seems to me ridiculous that we should be called upon to defend an attempt to relate languages genetically when those who divided them into different groups were never challenged to do the same for their assumption. Instead of starting out from the fact that we don't know anything about certain languages, we are told that because we don't know anything about certain languages, therefore they are genetically distinct and it is up to us to show that they are related. What a peculiar critical attitude this is! It seems to me that even if a few attempts to show genetic relationship between certain languages were to fail, we would still not be justified in assuming that they are distinct. I feel therefore that if through some chance you should be wrong, your proceeding is more justifiable than that of those who assume that lack of knowledge is a proof of a distinct stock.

Although there were certainly occasions on which Sapir lectured Radin on the need for careful methodology, both were committed in principle to using linguistic classification to elucidate the culture history of native North America. Among his friends, who could be counted on to share his enthusiasm, Sapir was confident of his work. Regarding Wiyot and Yurok, he wrote to Kroeber (6 August 1913: ALK): 'This, of course, was one of my strong pieces. It is laughably obvious.' Kroeber apparently agreed, since his response (14 August 1913: ALK) urged Sapir to publish his results and represent the faithful who wanted to reduce the number of linguistic stocks:

We are going to have a flood of similar cases in the next few years, and the prestige of American anthropology will be better maintained if at least some of the claims come with the backing of your critical faculty than if they are all made by people in whom the rank and file of us have less confidence. I think this is an important reason, in addition to the purely personal one of securing for yourself what you have found.

However, not everyone shared the enthusiasm of Kroeber and Radin.

Michelson had long been unable to formulate sound correspondences within the traditional boundaries of Algonkin (Michelson to Kroeber, 2 February 1911: ALK), and was merely incensed by Sapir's effort to add even more distantly related languages. His published critique (1914: 362–3) dismissed Sapir's resemblances as accidental, arguing that morphology was so divergent that the wrong elements were being compared, that Kroeber was competent and could not have missed a relationship if one existed, that the morphological evidence was too slight for such use, and that similarities to non-Algonkin languages also existed.

Sapir (to Kroeber, 9 September 1914: NMM) objected to Michelson's 'narrowness of outlook' and 'purely negative evidence'. Sapir went on to complain that Michelson

. . . has not himself had to approach a language with complete ignorance of its structure and set before himself the task of working out from the bottom up its fundamental grammatical and phonetic traits. He has never done anything outside of Algonkin and there he found the main structure already completed. . . . He does not realize how long it often takes to get wind of even elementary points of structure in a new language.

Sapir urged Kroeber to clarify the slowness with which realizations of genetic relationship dawn in a fieldwork situation – telling evidence of Sapir's own gradual movement toward larger genetic units. Kroeber agreed that the review was 'puritanical' but urged Sapir to ignore it because 'a technical discussion . . . will be regarded as a quarrel between experts of whom one is as likely to be right as the other' (15 September 1914: NMM).

The argument meandered on, with no change of opinion on either side. Michelson complained to Boas (26 April 1917: APS) that Sapir had 'fallen another victim to the deplorable tendency to consolidate linguistic stocks without adequate proof'. Sapir (to Lowie, 15 February 1921: RHL) generalized with some justification that Indo-Europeanists tended toward conservatism and 'that their perspective is strictly limited, and that differences of morphology that seem somewhat minor to us are of staggering importance to them'. Sapir continued to believe the methods were applicable.

An interesting sidelight to this debate comes in some brief correspondence many years later between Sapir and Leonard Bloomfield, whose reconstruction of Proto-Algonquian first demonstrated to many Indo-Europeanists that their methods could in fact be applied to unwritten languages. When Bloomfield was reconstructing 'Primitive Central Algonquian' he wrote to Sapir noting that the sound pattern 'has quite a northwestern look', a fact which would certainly have been of interest to Sapir in his efforts to trace North American culture history (26 April 1925: NMM). On the subject of Wiyot and Yurok, Bloomfield commented (27 May 1925: NMM):

I see no reason why Wiyot and Yurok may not be Alg., but the proof will be possible only when older Alg. forms are accessible, i.e. when PCA has been determined far better than I can do it and when Eastern and the divergent groups have been joined with it to make comparisons. Until this is done the dispute will not be settled, because the *proof* of relationship is in details, however much the general feel of things is needed for the first indication.

It is perhaps predictable that Bloomfield concentrated on the phonology of the relatively regular central Algonkin dialects, whereas Sapir was intrigued by the California outliers and by the phonologically divergent branches of Algonkin proper.

Kroeber had done his dissertation research on Arapaho and Sapir therefore had access to his data on that language. Sapir failed to find the 'great mysteries' lauded by Michelson (to Lowie, 12 August 1916: RHL) and immediately generalized to culture history of the large linguistic stock: 'I now incline strongly to a single group of Algonkin, as they (the dialects) have certain important traits in common. This may mean that their cultural affiliation is far older than we may have been willing to admit on a priori grounds.' These new generalizations came from his reading of Kroeber's paper on Arapaho (Sapir to Kroeber, 28 August 1916: NMM):

What impressed itself upon me was that once the phonetic laws which differentiate Arapaho are worked out, the divergence of Arapaho from other Algonkin dialects will be seen to be very much less than generally believed. I believe that there are quite a number of points of comparative interest that have escaped you. As a matter of fact, I have been flirting with the idea of writing a more or less formal study of Arapaho comparative phonology. One impression which I have gained is that Arapaho and Cheyenne do belong, after all, to a single subdivision of Algonkin.

Although Sapir gives no examples, Kroeber (5 September 1916: NMM) responds that he is delighted to have his Arapaho obligation absolved and that it is 'absurd' for him to pursue Algonkin studies 'with Michelson and you in the field'. He continues, in habitual style, to urge Sapir to further efforts:

. . . this job will have to be done by you. Michelson has the know, but is either afraid to go to the heart of the issue or incapable of doing so, and Uhlenbeck promises even less. It is extremely unfortunate with all our detailed knowledge we should be, from a broad point of view, so thoroughly in the dark as to the nature of a group of languages that are perhaps the most characteristic in North America.

There is one more Sapirian contribution to the expansion of the Algonkin stock. In his 1920 classification, one of the six superstocks was labelled Algonkin-Wakashan. Into this unit, Sapir included Algonkin-Wiyot-Yurok, the isolate Kootenay, and Wakashan (Nootka and Kwakiutl)-Salish. Sapir himself did extensive fieldwork on Nootka during his years in Ottawa and had access to Boas' data on Kwakiutl. This connection was originally suggested by Boas, and accepted by Powell in 1891. Sapir demonstrated the existence of the connection in 1911, providing a basic statement of sound correspondences and structural similarities. As an offshoot of his Nootka work, Sapir worked briefly with a Comox Salish speaking informant, allowing him greater insight into phonetically limited data collected by Boas and James Teit. The relationship of all of these languages was not entirely opaque to Sapir. He wrote to Kroeber (27 June 1913: NMM) that his parallels between Yurok and Salish were not a serious claim of genetic relationship. He was concerned about Salish comparisons because there were so many different dialects that 'it would require a great deal of specifically Salish work to determine what was really most fundamental in that stock and comparable with other stocks'. Sapir recalled that Boas had noted morphological resemblances of Kwakiutl, Nootka and Salish and that he 'could not help feeling that they may turn out to be genetically related'. Sapir did no further work on these languages before combining them in his six-unit classification, with its explicit effort to fill in all the gaps on the map of native North America.

Hokan-Siouan: the basic American type

The Hokan-Siouan stock was built up gradually from a series of connections by different researchers, beginning in California. In 1905, Dixon combined Shasta and Palaihnihan into Shastan. In 1920, he added Chimariko. Dixon and Kroeber in 1913 labelled the Hokan stock and included as well Karok, Pomo, Esselen, and Yana. In 1915, Kroeber added Brinton's connection of Yuman, Seri and Tequistlatec of Mexico. Harrington combined Chumash and Salinan into Iskoman in 1913 and Sapir included all of these in his 1917 definition of the Hokan stock (in relation to Yana). Harrington and Sapir independently linked Washo to Hokan in the same year. After considerable debate, Kroeber agreed that he and Dixon would treat Washo in their general description of the Hokan stock. Sapir was apparently pleased not to have to do this himself (Kroeber, 17 October 1917: NMM), but was unable to give them his completed analysis:

The morphological resemblances, which are perhaps even important, I have never written down: they are mostly in my head or could be easily verified by a little looking up of source material. There are also a lot of phonetic laws that I have worked out that are implicit in the material.

In any case, when Sapir returned again to Hokan, it was to link this stock with Swanton's 1915 joining of Tonkawa, Coahuiltecan and Karankawa. Swanton had already combined Natchez and Muskogean in 1907 and Tunican (Tunica, Chitimacha and Atakapa) in 1919. Sapir read Swanton's manuscript with enthusiasm, noting that 'I think I shall probably be able to use some of the material for my own Hokan comparisons' (to Swanton, 12 April 1918: NMM). He accepted all of Swanton's connections and went on to generalize about North American prehistory:

If the Hokan languages (including Seri and Chontal) and the Gulf languages are genetically related, we get the impression of a stock formerly occupying perhaps the greater part of Northern Mexico and the southern half of the United States west of Mississippi. This compact mass of probably primitive tribes must have been disturbed at various times by pressures exerted by such important groups as Uto-Aztekan, Caddoan, Tanoan, and possibly others. To a large extent this pressure seems to have brought about a disruption of tribes originally contiguous, further a crowding in the southeastern part of the area, also in the far western. Of course, this does not mean that some of the actual distributions may not represent a secondary spread. This would seem to be particularly true of the Yuman tribes who were doubtless confined to a much smaller area to begin with.

Swanton was basically concerned with the linguistic classification of the tribes of the southeast and was perceived at the time as conservative in spite of his limited linguistic training or experience. The parts of the extended Hokan stock which came from his work were not, therefore, subjected to serious examination.

In his six-unit classification, Sapir added Yuchi as a Siouan outlier and tied all of Siouan, plus Iroquois-Caddoan, to Hokan. For the connection of Iroquois and Caddoan, Boas had presented evidence of grammatical similarity in the 1911 *Handbook of American Indian languages*. Sapir took this to be genetic, without having worked extensively on any of these languages (he did work briefly with Iroquoian).

Somewhat after the first formulation of the six-unit classification, Sapir became aware, through Dixon (Dixon to Sapir, 18 March 1924: NMM) of Lehmann's work linking Subtiaba of Nicaragua to Hokan (as well as various Mexican languages to Penutian). Sapir picked up on this connection, using Subtiaba (1925: 492) to argue that the 'submerged features' of a language were of limited interest to a descriptive grammar but crucial to historical perspective. He wrote to Speck (11 January 1924):

What emerges pretty clearly now in my mind is that Hokan-Coahuiltecan is the linguistic group correlated with the earliest and culturally most primitive people in California, northern Mexico and the Gulf region. This people was quickly scattered by later 'Penutian', Uto-Aztekan, and Athabascan movements. It is not accidental that we get such primitive folk as Seri, Tonkawa, and Shasta in marginal areas. But preceding this 'Hokan-Coahuiltecan' group . . . seems to have been an Otomi-Chintanec, Mixtec-Zapotec-Chiapanec-Mangue group, which was scattered in Mexico and Central America by various incoming movements. (These were Hokan-Siouan, Hokan-Coahuiltecan, Uto-Aztekan; the Athabascan stock was most recent.)

When Sapir revised his six-unit classification for the Encyclopaedia

218 REGNA DARNELL AND DELL HYMES

Britannica in 1929, he discussed the languages of Central and North America in the same article and drew upon all of these new connections, extending the 1920 six super-stocks of North America.

Battling with the conservatives over Penutian

Although Sapir is associated most closely with the extension of the Penutian stock outside California, the first evidence for Penutian was published by Kroeber and the first outside California by Leo Frachtenberg, a conservative student of Boas. Sapir's own fieldwork on Takelma was available before Frachtenberg's on Coos and Siuslaw; but Sapir did not publish on Oregon Penutian until after Frachtenberg had done so. Sapir was delighted when Frachtenberg independently added Chinook (to Kroeber, 14 June 1917: ALK), given his own hesitation over its morphological specialization. Over Tsimshian, Sapir was also hesitant, writing to Lowie (6 July 1918: RHL):

It is technical work of course but quite interesting, as many lines of historical research are opened up. *Yes, my boy. Tsimshian. Not a bit isolated.* Very specialized in development, but showing clear threads, in my humble and heterodox opinion, binding it to Oregonian 'stocks'.

The methodological debate between Sapir and Frachtenberg, particularly in the early years of the Penutian extensions, clarifies the increasing gulf between Boas' concern with diffusion as a cultural process and Sapir's with the feasibility of identifying genetic change. When Boas reported Sapir's connection of Coos and Takelma resulting from Frachtenberg's grammar of the former, Frachtenberg (to Sapir, 29 June 1914: NMM) objected that 'you are pursuing a very wrong method in dealing with accidental phonetic resemblances among two or more Indian languages'. Sapir's response (2 July 1914: NMM) was quite explicit about the nature of his own methodology:

I did say that I thought there was enough evidence to lead one to believe that Coos and Takelma might be genetically related. The case is not as strong for Coos and Takelma as in some others, but there are certainly many surprising points of contact, both lexical and grammatical, also, to be sure, many important points of dissimilarity. You will, of course, understand that I try not to deal with what you call 'accidental phonetic resemblances' but try as much as possible to reduce these resemblances to definite phonetic laws, as I have done for Uto-Aztekan and am now doing for Haida, Tlingit and Athabascan. . . . I hope that you have enough feeling for linguistic history to feel as strongly as I do that our present classification of Indian languages into an immense number of distinct stocks has little inherent probability, and must sooner or later give way to tremendous simplification.

Frachtenberg, however, remained sceptical and continued to lecture Sapir about how to carry out linguistic comparisons (20 October 1914: NMM), cogently summarizing the Boasian position:

You must not forget that 'correspondences', no matter how interesting, are far from proving genetic affiliation. . . . We must, therefore, be very careful in applying the methods that have given us such splendid results in the Indo-European, Semitic, and Ural-Altaic fields to the domain of American Indian linguistics. You must not forget, Sapir, that in those fields, we are dealing with languages that had been preserved in some form of literature . . . which has enabled us to trace historically a certain group of languages from almost the very time of its disintegration into different dialects down to the present day. The best we can do at the present time, to my mind, is the simplification of stocks, not in accordance with their seeming points of resemblance, but with their relationship of type. I mean by that, that we ought to tabulate at first such stocks that express identical psychological concepts by similar grammatical devices and see what this will prove. Of course, in such a tabulation, the question of geographical continuity will play a very important part.

The next exchange goes directly to Boas as the source of the conflict (Sapir to Frachtenberg, 8 January 1915: NMM):

I believe, of course, in reasonable caution in assuming larger linguistic stocks than indicated on Powell's map, but I am convinced that the attitude Boas is taking in this matter is much overdone, and is at last analysis due simply to the fact that he has had no personal experience in historic grammar or comparative linguistics. His main linguistic interest is purely psychological and the bias that this interest gives all his linguistic work may as well be recognized once for all. You probably realize as well as I do to what an alarming extent personal training and interest influence one's scientific point of view. I feel most decidedly that the study of American Indian linguistics is these days turning over a new leaf, as it were, and that the purely historic study of languages as based on comparative evidence must more and more be brought to the fore.

Frachtenberg (to Sapir, 27 January 1915: NMM) expresses his loyalty to Boasian doctrine:

I should not for a moment even hesitate in following your method of study if only we had any basis for a historical study of the American Indian languages. And as long as such a basis is wanting, I must perforce adhere to Boas' cautious conservatism.

Frachtenberg even wrote to Boas on the subject (2 March 1915: APS):

I perfectly agree with you in what you say . . . concerning the methods of Sapir. Like you I do not maintain that some of the stocks are not genetically related, but it is my belief that his methods are wrong, and may lead to wrong conclusions. I know very well that Sapir has been influenced by the methods applied in Indo-European linguistics which he now tries to apply to the field of American Indian linguistics.

It was in 1915 that Sapir himself turned seriously to Penutian. He wrote to Kroeber (24 April: NMM) that not long ago 'I did not feel like looking into the matter myself.' Now he wants to know if Kroeber would publish a paper on Coos and Takelma. Kroeber responds (29 May 1915: NMM) that the university cannot publish work on Oregon languages and that he is concerned about names for the new stocks. The terms Hokan and Penutian had 'perfect definiteness' until extended by Sapir but are now ambiguous. Sapir's current hypothesis is a little more than Kroeber had bargained for. He extended California Penutian to include ('though you may wink with incredulity') Chinook and ('don't faint') Tsimshian, producing a panoramic view of west coast culture history (Sapir to Kroeber, 15 April 1915: ALK):

Now I begin seriously to suspect both Coos (perhaps eventually also Siuslaw, Alsea, and Kalapuya) and Takelma are North Penutian, cut loose from Southern Penutian by northern intrusion . . . of Hokan languages, which seem to gravitate south. . . . If you eliminate Athabascan and Shoshonean, which clearly moved in south and northwest respectively, you can almost read California history from linguistic geography.

Or, a somewhat later formulation (9 December 1915: ALK):

. . . we have a continuum from Yokuts to Chinook, broken only by obviously intrusive Athabascan between Takelma and Coos and doubtless also intrusive Shasta between Takelma and Wintun. Clearly Tsimshian would be really much apart geographically. If its inclusion proves OK, the Wakashan-Salish-Chemakuan group form an interesting problem from the point of view of movements of populations.

Kroeber was apparently convinced because he asked Sapir's permission (17 November 1915: NMM) to cite 'the newer enlarged linguistic families as evidencing movements of population' for a general article on the tribes of the Pacific coast. Sapir (25 November 1915: NMM) agrees that Oregon Penutian and Hokan-Coahuiltecan may be noted as 'very probable' in his opinion. He is, in fact, eager for Kroeber to publish his evidence (19 December 1915: ALK) because 'I should be glad not to be alone in this new series of developments.'

However, objections to the Oregon Penutian were less substantial than Sapir had feared. Frachtenberg visited California and was impressed by the Dixon and Kroeber unpublished vocabularies. In spite of continued claims to methodological purism ('I am too much of a neo-grammarian to be swayed by occasional resemblances'), Frachtenberg insisted (to Sapir, 17 December 1916: NMM) that he was not 'conservative' in a dogmatic way. He listed a number of genetic connections on the northwest coast that he expected to be able to demonstrate in the near future. Sapir responded with reasonable graciousness that he welcomed Frachtenberg's support (9 January 1917: NMM):

I am also delighted to gather that you are far less inclined to be conservative about linguistic relationships than you were some time ago. . . . Well, we are evidently all progressing in the same general direction. After all, the logical facts can not long be withstood. It is only a question of whether one prefers to be conservative as long as he respectably can, or has a bit more courage than the crowd and is willing to take a look ahead.

Frachtenberg interprets this to mean that Sapir realizes they have never really been at odds (to Sapir 12 February 1917: NMM) and optimistically predicts: 'Thus after four years of constant dickering we have at last met on common ground, and I trust in the near future you and I will work shoulder by shoulder and show what can be done in American linguistics.' Shortly after this, however, Frachtenberg dropped out of the discipline, leaving the collaboration to lapse.

Further Penutian discussions were carried on with Boas. In response to Sapir's paper on Penutian stem forms (17 July 1918: NMM), Boas noted: 'The fact of the similarity of stem forms is, of course, very interesting, but I should hesitate very much to consider all phenomena of this kind proof of genetic relationship, but rather as a locally developed habit.' He then cited a similar tendency in the Siouan languages. A few days later, he was lecturing Sapir on the need to consider more than one explanation of similarities (22 July 1918: NMM). Both diffusion and independent development were at least as likely as genetic relationship. 'It seems to my mind that, as a matter of course, you ought to consider, in fundamental questions of this kind, the various possibilities of interpretation and follow these out. Judging from your letter, you have only one of these possibilities in mind, on the basis of which you try to account for the whole phenomenon.' Sapir agreed with Boas (26 July 1918: NMM) that Tsimshian and Chinook had had a long independent development but did not see that as contradicting the hypothesis of common genetic origin:

The great psychological differences that you find do not, I am afraid, frighten me quite as much as they seem to yourself. . . . I must confess that I have always had a feeling that you entirely overdo psychological peculiarities in different languages as presenting insuperable obstacles to genetic theories, and that, on the other hand, you are not specially impressed by the reality of the differentiating processes, phonetic and grammatical, that have so greatly operated in linguistic history all over the world.

There is no evidence that Sapir's reassurances had any effect on Boas' certainty that the genetic explanation was being employed for all cases of similarity by many of his former students.

Sapir made further efforts to extend the Penutian stock into Mexico, stimulated to this task by Dixon, who reported Zoque-Mixe connections (20 March 1924: NMM) and noted that 'I've gone "Penutian-mad".' Dixon was hopeful that Sapir would tackle the details of this connection and, indeed, Sapir did include Mexican Penutian in the 1929 version of his six-unit classification.

Na-dene: the key to American linguistic history

The connection between Haida and Tlingit was first suggested by Boas himself, although he later rescinded and argued that the similarities were due to diffusion rather than genetic connection. By 1911, in the Introduction to the *Handbook of American Indian languages* (54), Boas was arguing that caution was necessary in suggesting genetic connections:

> . . . we must confine ourselves to classifying American Indian languages in those linguistic families for which we can give a proof of relationship that cannot possibly be challenged. Beyond this point we can do no more than give certain definite classifications in which the traits common to certain groups of languages are pointed out, while the decision as to the significance of these common traits must be left to later times.

Boas did, in fact, see himself as being engaged in the classification of Indian languages, through his text publication programme at the Bureau of American Ethnology, elucidating psychological and typological differences among the languages (Boas to Sapir, 2 January 1914: APS); Boas noted that he was 'gradually classifying all the various dialects with a fair degree of success'.

Boas' attitude, however, toward linguistic classification became increasingly negative in response to the increasingly radical modifications of the Powell classification posed by Sapir and others. A thread which runs through Sapir's work on classification is one of frustration at his inability to get Boas to understand what he considered to be very simple linguistic arguments. As early as 1913, Sapir was discussing their mutual mentor with Radin. Radin noted (1 June: NMM) with reference to Sapir's demonstration of the relationship of Tlingit, Haida and Athabascan:

> Boas has driven the independent linguistic stock idea too far. He is, I believe, swayed by two motives here: first, his reluctance to accept as proof what any trained philologist is perfectly willing to accept and secondly, by his theory of an original condition of society – characterized by an unlimited number of linguistic stocks. I believe he will live to see the fifty-seven linguistic stocks dwindle down perceptibly.

Sapir's response stressed the possibilities for culture history (10 June 1913: NMM):

> It is one of the cases in which, in my opinion, he [Boas] allows his judgment to be influenced by a preconceived like or dislike. For some mysterious reason he simply does not like to think of an originally small number of linguistic stocks, which have each of them differentiated tremendously, but prefers, with Powell, to conceive of an almost unlimited number of distinct stocks, many of which, in the course of time, become extinct. To me the former alternative seems a historical necessity. . . . I believe that there are many languages that at last analysis are genetically related where we shall never be able to establish such relationship. Language is

conservative, of course, but conservative is only a matter of degree, not an absolute fact.

Kroeber agreed with Sapir that Boas' conservatism had little relation to evidence in particular cases, remarking (to Sapir, 25 November 1915: NMM) that he had had an amiable discussion with Boas in which 'I tried to make him see that no one would quarrel with his stand if he did not feel it necessary to antagonize ours.' Boas, in fact, became increasingly belligerent on the subject of genetic connections. Sapir was concerned not so much about Boas' personality but about his failure adequately to describe the realities of linguistic patterning, or to understand such descriptions from others (to Lowie, 15 February 1921: NMM):

[Boas'] whole approach is so different from mine and from that of the vast majority of linguistic students that the attempt to argue about the theoretical basis can only result in mutual irritation. He bandies far too many semi-philosophical categories to suit me. I do not see for instance how a classification of American Indian vocabularies from the standpoint of basic categories is going to help the humble student very materially. His wholesale use of the idea of diffusion must also strike anyone that has any real experience with the brass tacks of linguistic history as rather absurd. Worst of all, I do not feel at all that Boas has succeeded in getting at the really fundamental features of the languages that he discusses, that is, features that are not of the psychological or philosophical genre that attracts him so – rather those delusive dynamic features that he probably scorns to discuss in any but a perfunctory manner. I refer to such things as accent, pitch, the typical form of the stem, and what I have come to call 'phonetic pattern', by which I mean the fundamental alignment of sounds in a given language.

By 1920 Boas felt it necessary to dissociate himself from the linguistic conclusions of his various students and made his position publicly explicit in the *American Anthropologist*. By this point, it had become clear to Sapir that Boas would not change his stance. He wrote to Speck in a philosophical vein (2 October 1924: APS):

At last analysis these controversies boil down to a recognition of two states of mind. One, conservative intellectualists, like Boas . . . who refuse absolutely to consider far-reaching suggestions unless they can be demonstrated by a mass of evidence. . . . Hence, from an over-anxious desire to be right, they generally succeed in being more hopelessly and fundamentally wrong, in the long run, than many more superficial minds who are not committed to 'principles'. . . . The second type is more intuitive and, even when the evidence is not as full or theoretically unambiguous as it might be, is prepared to throw out tentative suggestions and to test as it goes along. . . . I have no hope whatever of ever getting Boas and Goddard to see through my eyes or to feel with my hunches. I take their opposition like the weather, which might generally be better but which will have to do.

These issues seemed to come to a head in Sapir's Na-dene stock, perhaps because the original data for Haida and Tlingit came from sketches in the

Handbook of American Indian languages, edited by Boas. Athabascan was also included among the sketches, indicating that Boas saw typological parallels and wanted further information. The Haida and Tlingit material was prepared by John Swanton of the Bureau of American Ethnology who believed the two to be related, and possibly to Athabascan as well. Sapir was just becoming interested in comparative Athabascan at this time through his incidental fieldwork on Chasta Costa in Oregon. After a few hours of work with a Tlingit informant, Sapir identified the language as having tone, a fact which 'it seems astonishing that Swanton could ever have missed' (Sapir to Radin 28 November 1912: NMM). Sapir was thereby firmly convinced of the genetic unity of Haida and Tlingit. Two years later, Radin reported to Sapir (25 November 1914: NMM) that Boas was working with the same Tlingit informant and 'has admitted the relationship of Tlingit to Athabascan. He couldn't help it for it hit him in the face.' If this is correct, Boas never acknowledged it publicly.

Swanton did not feel overly confident of his work on Haida and Tlingit, telling Sapir (20 June 1914: NMM): '. . . the relationship between Athabascan and Tlingit seems almost a foregone conclusion but of course it requires the exact demonstration you are now applying. The case for Haida does not appear to me so strong, but perhaps you can put that beyond question also.' He expresses optimism that there will turn out to be a dozen or less stocks in North America, immediately illustrating in terms of the southeast, his own area of mature expertise.

In 1914 Sapir became convinced that he had the evidence to link Haida as well as Tlingit to Athabascan. He wrote to Mason (18 March: NMM): 'Boas, who is not too enthusiastic about far-reaching genetic theories, recently wrote me that he had long known that this was so, though he has never published much of any consequence on this point.' Again, this is at odds with other documentation. In his published treatment of the question (1915: 534) Sapir summarized the evidence:

Important morphological, to a lesser extent also lexical, resemblances between Haida and Tlingit have long been pointed out by Boas and Swanton, resemblances which have led them to assume, though rather hesitantly, genetic relationship between these languages. Boas has also somewhat vaguely hinted at fundamental resemblances between Athabascan and Haida-Tlingit, but no concrete evidence on this point has been given. A full presentation of the comparative lexical, phonological and morphological evidence serves to show, beyond all reasonable doubt, that Athabascan, Haida and Tlingit are indeed but divergent representatives of a common prototype.

In this article, Sapir proposed the name Na-dene for this linguistic stock.

Acceptance of the Na-dene results was mixed. Michelson accepted the connection on the basis of Sapir's detailed sound correspondences, although he had not been willing to accept connections in his own field of

Algonkin. On the other hand, Pliny Goddard, the dean of Athabascan studies, whom Sapir described to Kroeber as 'absolutely without vision as to the older drift of Athabascan' (1 October 1921: ALK), attacked the results, possibly as much on grounds of territoriality as of evidence. Goddard was more willing to see Sapir work on Na-dene than on the narrower field of Athabascan, however, noting to him (4 November 1920: NMM):

As to your plan of a comparative grammar of Na-dene – as long as it remains that, I express no objections and feel none. If, however, you confine your comparative grammar to Athabascan I should probably die with the feeling that you had not treated me fairly but I doubt if I should ever tell you so. You know how the case stands. I have spent twenty years in getting material ready to do that very thing; that is, to make a comparative statement of Athabascan. . . . Nothing would give me greater pleasure than having someone to share my Athabascan interests with. There are a lot of awfully pretty things in Athabascan.

It is typical of Sapir that, although he complained bitterly to other correspondents about Goddard's linguistic abilities and rigidity on issues of classification, he was still reluctant to undercut the field that Goddard felt belonged to him.

Na-dene was the linguistic stock in which Sapir most wanted to concentrate his field research. He wanted to work seriously on both Haida and Tlingit 'if only to get a proper basis and perspective for the big comparative study I am undertaking' (to Lowie, 9 September 1920: NMM). He continued:

I am seeing and understanding new things about Na-dene all the time. Just now I have a certain working hypothesis about it that would make Goddard very angry (or amused), but I shall not speak of it just yet. There are so many things I'd like to do in American linguistics that my head swims. A sadly neglected field, yet destined to open up tremendous perspectives. And poor workers in it. Boas is about the only decent one I can point to.

Sapir is, of course, referring here to his hypothesis of connection between Na-dene and Indo-Chinese. This letter to Lowie is the same one in which he presents his six-unit classification and precedes by a few months the paper in which he made it public.

There is consistent connection in Sapir's work between Na-dene, Indo-Chinese and the six-unit classification itself. For some time before reaching definite conclusions on either issue, Sapir had been in touch with Berthold Laufer, a noted Sinologist at the Chicago Field Columbian Museum, requesting from him information on Asian languages. His first indication of motivation comes at this time (Sapir to Laufer, 28 September 1920: NMM):

You may be somewhat amused at my preoccupation with Indo-Chinese studies, which are in a way out of my line, but the field really interests me very much, and though I fear to hint anything now, it seems to me to vaguely foreshadow certain points of unexpected significance in other fields.

The Anthropological Association meetings were to be held in Chicago in December 1920 in conjunction with Section H of the American Association for the Advancement of Science. At the last moment, however, the anthropologists went to Baltimore, after Sapir had planned a visit to Laufer, who wrote him (14 November 1920: NMM) in the hope 'that you will come here, especially for a discussion with me of Indo-Chinese languages, whether there is a meeting or not'. Sapir wrote to Boas (22 November 1920: NMM) protesting the change of venue and noting his 'personal interest' in 'an extra week to consult with Laufer on some linguistic problems that interest me very much'. Eventually, therefore, the six-unit classification was presented to the AAAS rather than the AAA and Sapir had 'a very delightful visit with Laufer who was as kind and accommodating as he possibly could be. We formed a common interest along certain lines which I hope may continue. He gave me some bibliographical information which is of the greatest assistance to me.'

Sapir shared the news of his latest consolidation with his usual confreres. Radin, forever willing to espouse radical causes in linguistics, and in general, responded (7 November 1920: NMM):

I am not so terribly surprised at your hypothesis of Indo-Chinese relationship to Na-dene. I never tackled it although I have looked at Tibetan and Chinese grammars. However I did look into the possibility of Ural-Altaic relationship to Pan-American and found some suggestive points.

To Lowie (15 February 1921: NMM), Sapir expressed his vision of American prehistory as opened up by Indo-Chinese:

I no longer believe, nor, for that matter, have I ever definitely held that the differentiation of languages in America has taken place entirely on the American continent. On the contrary, I think that the most far-reaching differences of grouping had already taken place on the Asiatic continent, and I believe it goes almost without saying that America was peopled by a number of historically different waves. I am at present of the opinion that the Na-dene wave is the most recent of all, for a variety of reasons, among which not the least interesting is the fact that it contrasts most sharply with the Eskimo and the languages to the south. I should say that the Na-dene languages are by all means the most 'un-American' of all the languages spoken on the northern continent. My ideas on these fascinating languages are becoming gradually clearer and I am anticipating the most fascinating task in the unravelling of the history of the group.

To Kroeber, Sapir wrote (1 October 1921: NMM), sending a copy to Laufer, presenting detailed similarities between Indo-Chinese and Na-dene, as well as expressing his enthusiasm for time perspective:

It is all so powerfully cumulative and integrated that when you tumble to one point a lot of others fall in line. I am now so thoroughly accustomed to the idea that it no longer startles me. For a while I resisted the notion. Now I can no longer do so. I do *not* feel that Na-dene belongs to the other American languages. I feel it as a great intrusive band that has perhaps ruptured an old Eskimo-Wakashan-Algonkin continuity. And I decidedly feel the old quasi-isolating base. Then there is tone, which feels old. . . . I am all but certain that Athabascan and Haida are like Tlingit as to tone. In short, do not think me an ass if I am seriously entertaining the notion of an old Indo-Chinese offshoot into Northwest America. . . . Am I dreaming?

Laufer responded enthusiastically to the report of Sapir's Indo-Chinese investigations (to Sapir, 1 November 1921: NMM): 'I . . . am amazed at the wonderful progress you have made in the comparative study of Na-dene and Indo-Chinese.' Sapir retaliated with further reassurance of the mass of data at his disposal and the rapidity with which new examples are now coming to light. Nonetheless, Sapir does not consider it appropriate 'to divulge my material to the public at present'. In fact, he never did publish evidence for this claim, although he continued to focus on Na-dene, particularly in terms of his own fieldwork, for the rest of his life. It is, of course, quite likely that he became discouraged as a result of the reception in many quarters of the six-unit classification as radically unsound.

The search for time perspective

In theoretical terms, the six-unit classification had its genesis in 1916 with the publication of Sapir's essay on time perspective in aboriginal American culture. In this essay (1949 [1916]: 452) he suggested that language would permit genuine reconstruction of culture history:

. . . linguistic changes proceed more slowly and what is more important, at a generally more even rate than cultural ones. This means that, particularly where there is abundant comparative linguistic material available, we are enabled to penetrate farther back into the past and to obtain a more reliable feeling of relative durations of such linguistic time sequences as are available.

At the time this essay was written, of course, there was little in the way of time sequence from sources other than linguistics (Hymes 1983 [1962]: 37):[6]

Sapir's truly epoch-making comparative studies in Uto-Aztekan, Na-Dene, Ritwan-Algonquian, and Hokan coincide in time with Kroeber's discovery of surface seriation as a technique of relative chronology for potsherds at Zuni, with the development of stratigraphy in archaeology by others, and with the onset of the heyday of reconstruction from ethnographic distributions, as exemplified in the work of Wissler, Spier, and others.

In fact, Sapir's work was so perceived by his colleagues. Clark Wissler wrote to him (15 October 1915: NMM) regarding the new perspectives on genetic relationship that were emerging:

Although, as you know, I am not much of a linguist, I am very much interested in the work you and Kroeber are doing. While a good many of the examples of similarity you cite do not appeal to me as good evidence, I nevertheless assure you that my sympathies are with the progressives in this movement.

Specifically in reference to the time perspective paper, Wissler stressed (to Sapir, 9 February 1916: NMM) that he liked the linguistic portion of the argument because it showed the potential relevance of linguistic inference for non-specialists.

What Sapir's use of the basic methods of comparative philology permitted him to do was, in essence, to inject chronology into descriptive cultural data. Reduction in the number of linguistic stocks was not, in fact, a simplification only. Newly postulated connections added a previous time level to the data which had to be analyzed (Hymes 1983 [1962]). What did, however, become simpler was the interpretation of linguistic relationship in terms of historical ethnology. And this was the function that Sapir wanted his linguistic classification to serve. He was an anthropologist as well as a linguist and took his questions from the Boasian paradigm, regardless of Boas' difficulties with his actual procedures and results.

The perceived need for a new linguistic classification

Sapir's six-unit classification appeared in his lecture of December 1920. Approximately a year previously, there had been a number of indications that colleagues saw a need for some new consensus in the genetic classification of American Indian languages. Kroeber wrote to Sapir (25 November 1919: NMM) stressing that there were areas of agreement. This position was probably a response to Radin's recent effort (unsupported by either evidence or linguistic reputation) to unite *all* the linguistic stocks of the continent:

We have got so far in this work that it seems desirable that we sit down to take stock and find out what we are in substantial agreement about. There will always be and should be differences, but we have surely got to certain results in which all of us can concur. It seems to me that we have overlooked this common element and are accentuating minor differences so much that our private as well as our public discussions are over-disputatious.

In that same winter, Sapir considered reading a paper on 'The status of linguistic classification in North America' at the Anthropology Association meetings (to Radin, 5 December 1919: NMM). Sapir went on to assure Radin that he was fully aware of various 'Proto-American' elements and quite open to 'much more far-reaching syntheses' than most previous ones.

The implicit rebuke to Radin for his own less than careful recent effort is clear. Radin, however, was pleased at Sapir's position (16 December 1919: NMM) and strongly urged him to 'organize' the existing group of linguistic workers so that the classification might be settled once and for all. Radin was apparently willing to take on such a role himself but first offered it to Sapir. Sapir, however, preferred to work alone, on the basis of work done by colleagues as well as his personal research – and, ultimately to take full responsibility for his own classification.

Radin was, however, not the only one who wanted to see some baseline for further research. Kroeber prepared a memo for the Bureau of American Ethnology (Appendix 1) in which he suggested that the Bureau ought to take on a mediating role between classificatory extremes (represented by Sapir and Radin versus Michelson and Boas). He noted various connections that had not been challenged and proposed that Christmas 1920 would be a good time to seek such consensus (Kroeber to Fewkes, 20 December 1919: BAE). The document is particularly interesting for its conservatism, presumably palatable to the Bureau, but in some contradiction to Kroeber's own consolidation of linguistic stocks with Dixon at this time. He attempts, of course, to define himself as mediating and middle-of-the-road. In any case, Sapir did not go to the 1920 anthropology meeting because he was in Chicago discussing Indo-Chinese with Laufer and presenting his six-unit classification, which was hardly the conservative consensus Kroeber had urged.

Previews of the six-unit classification

Sapir's classification was not presented in a vacuum. It is clear that his thinking about the need for classification was related to the thinking involved in his book, *Language*, which was written at the same time as the six-unit classification. In the book, however, Sapir avoided the subject of linguistic classification, even in Indo-European, as 'disputed ground' and 'hardly fit subject for a purely general study of speech' (1921b: 163 n.5). In the same book, Sapir stressed that the establishment of a linguistic stock of genetically related languages was an arbitrary category, subject to continued revision with more data or more sophisticated methods (1921b: 163). *Language* focused heavily on linguistic typology and Sapir seems to have re-examined some of the typological similarities of native American languages while working out his argument. He then found himself prepared to claim, without further work on the languages, that these similarities were 'presumably genetic'. He then turned to the question of a complete classification into a few large stocks.

The first indication that Sapir was incubating a new synthesis came in a letter to Frank Speck (1 August 1918: APS) in which Sapir was concerned about extensions of Hokan which would show how linguistics might shed light on culture history:

It is becoming fairly clear that *the* great stock of North America is Hokan-Yuchi-Siouan-Muskhogean-Tunican-Coahuiltecan, probably wtih further affiliations southward. Na-dene, Penutian (as extended by me), Algonquian-Yurok-Wiyot, Wakashan-Salish-Chemakuan stand apparently apart but even now there are some suggestive connections visible here and there. Getting down to brass tacks, how in the Hell are you going to explain general American *n-* 'l' except genetically? It's disturbing I know but (more) non-committal conservatism is only dodging after all, isn't it? Great simplifications are in store for us, but we must be critical and not force our evidence. Besides we must try to work out genealogically degrees of relationship. Only so will fascinating perspectives appear. It seems to me that only now is American linguistics becoming really interesting, at least in its ethnological bearings.

Over the following year, Sapir worked out the details to support this enthusiastic vision. His first effort to present the finished classification (although still with a different and more awkward order of presentation) was to Boas, whose approval continued to be extremely important to him. Along with an elaborate explanation of his position (3 September 1920: NMM), Sapir pleaded:

This is my present *feel* about the whole huge problem. . . . Admitting that you do not care to travel in forbidden fields, do you not, after all, feel certain perspectives? . . . But I know you really do feel these things better than anyone else, only you dislike interpreting them in terms of historical perspective. There are some tantalizing Proto-American features too. . . . After all, these are fundamental *facts*. What can you do with them?

Boas did, in fact, respond very gently, with a statement of his own views (18 September 1920: APS):

I do not think our opinions are really as different as they might appear to an outsider. . . . I quite agree with you in regard to the point of view that far-reaching similarities, particularly between neighboring languages must be due to historical causes. I think, however, that we are not sufficiently familiar with the phenomena of mutual influences of languages in primitive life to decide whether we are dealing with a gradual development of divergence or whether the whole linguistic phenomena ought not to be considered from the same point of view as any ethnic phenomena. . . . If there is disagreement, it seems to my mind certain that the linguistic phenomena must be looked at in the same way as the cultural phenomena.

Sapir's whole argument, of course, was based on the principle that it was possible to distinguish the effects of borrowing from common history precisely because language was different from the rest of culture, particularly in its unconscious character and the presence of sound correspondences.

As Sapir's argument reached its final form, he wrote again to Speck (9 October 1920: NMM):

As a matter of fact I have far reaching ideas these days in regard to North American Indian linguistics, some of which will set our friends, the conservatives, by the ears. I have again been greatly interested in Athabaskan and expect to continue one of these days an elaborate work I had begun on Na-Dene relations. I feel now that all the linguistic groups in America from the Maya and Aztec north and including the Eskimo may be classified into six large divisions, each of which I feel to be a genetic unity. Even these six may not prove to be entirely unrelated. The most extensive of these groups is the one I tentatively know as Hokan-Siouan. This extends right across the continent in a great southern bend from the Karok in California to the Iroquois and Muskogi in the East. Let this be enough for the present!

Interestingly, it is often to Speck, who is not an expert in matters linguistic, that Sapir is most relaxed in expressing his newest ideas.

To Kroeber, Sapir presented his six stocks as representing his 'present feeling' (2 October 1920: NMM), but went on to speak of studying the distribution of syntactic features among American languages. Sapir seemed to feel that genetic units would emerge from such structural comparison. Kroeber responded by, as usual, urging Sapir to carry out this task and protesting his own inability to do so. His response to the six units is quite detailed but basically concurs with Sapir's judgement (17 December 1920: NMM): Sapir seems to Kroeber to be 'wholly on the right track' with most of his findings 'probably true'. Some connections, however, are 'hopelessly beyond my depth'. Kroeber further urges Sapir to put his findings on record 'without waiting until you are able to substantiate them in detail, which will be many years. The majority of us won't know what you're talking about, and Boas will think you have turned prophet instead of Philologist, but a pronouncement would at least show which way we were tending and emphasize the nature of the problem that lies ahead.'

The actual presentation consisted of a one-paragraph abstract entitled 'The problems of linguistic relationship in America', a text headed 'A bird's eye view of American languages north of Mexico' and an accompanying map (*Appendix 2*). The outline stressed that a more 'historical and inclusive' classification was called for. Sapir dealt with his objections to the Boasian approach both regarding borrowing and psychological typologizing. He presented a structural description of the six stocks, though noting that not all languages corresponded, at least on the surface. He then noted four possible Proto-American features and a possible regrouping of the six stocks into only three. The final sentence of the prose text notes that 'Movements of population [are] to be revealed through linguistic research.' The word 'revealed' has been written in over 'created'. Presumably the original sentence referred to new perspectives which emerge when linguistic evidence is properly used.

Only three linguistic stocks were omitted from the classification. Beothuk was so poorly recorded that Sapir felt unable to attach it to a larger unit. Kroeber had, for years, been urging him to take a brief time and dispose of this leftover fragment. By 1929, determined to fill all gaps in the map, Sapir put Beothuk with Algonkin. Waiilatpuan, Lutuamian and Sahaptian were left out in 1920; in the 1929 revision, they are lumped together as Plateau Penutian (presumably on the basis of long-available evidence from Frachtenberg). Finally, Sapir was unable to categorize Zuni. When Kroeber worked at Zuni in 1915, Sapir had asked him for an opinion and Kroeber had proposed Siouan, stating with considerable *naïveté* (25 November 1915: NMM): 'I know it is something, but have neglected my American linguistics too much of late years to be able to trust an instinct too far.' Because Sapir was unwilling to accept the possibility of isolates, he linked Zuni, somewhat tentatively, to Uto-Aztekan, a connection for which no evidence was ever presented. The changes in the 1929 version, then, may be seen as aesthetically motivated rather than linguistically. The image predominates of a map with no blank spaces.

In any case, Sapir's paper was 'decidedly well received' (to Wallis, 8 January 1921). Sapir was still unsure whether to publish 'my map and findings just at present', hoping to work further, especially on Na-dene and its possible Asiatic affiliations 'for the next few years'. Predictably, Kroeber (20 January 1921: ALK) urged Sapir to publish immediately. His advice is presumably designed to allay Sapir's fears over the radical and unsupported nature of his claims, but the final response of shock is hardly comforting given that Kroeber was presumably an unusually loyal ally:

I know how you feel about exposed flanks. Neverthe less [sic] if there is any danger you have already incurred it in making your stand public at Chicago. I consider the wisest course therefore to be to put yourself on record and save yourself from misrepresentation. There may not be any great amount of talk about your Chicago presentation, but there is no telling how far it may travel and it is almost certain to be distorted. You can count on the people who are interested in the subject picking up some sort of gossip about it. You will be better protected if their knowledge of your attitude is authoritative. I do not see how publication would lay you open to attack. Since you present no evidence you cannot be charged with misusing it or employing it hastily. . . . To make a confession, I gasped a bit when I realized that you had really presented this outline at Chicago. I was astounded not because your stand seems to me essentially an exposed one, but because I have always been strongly impressed by your cautiousness. I conclude that you must have a lot of ammunition salted away . . .

Sapir decided to take Kroeber's advice and publish the tentative findings, which he did in a one-page note in *Science* in October of 1921, after considerable delay devoted to making this decision. This version constitutes Appendix 3.

The 1929 codification of the six-unit classification

It is the 1929 version of the six-unit classification which has been cited by later scholars. It does in fact give somewhat more information characterizing each of the major stocks, and includes the languages of Central America. This version has the disadvantage that it is further removed from the intensive period of research which it summarized. It does, however, make Sapir's intentions clearer in that the expanded text allows him to note degrees of certainty for groupings and subgroupings within the six major stocks. Sapir states that (1949 [1929]: 171–2):

It is impossible to say at present what is the irreducible number of linguistic stocks that should be recognized for America north of Mexico, as scientific comparative work on these difficult languages is still in its infancy. The following reductions of linguistic stocks which have been proposed may be looked upon as either probable or very possible.

There are twelve such reductions (Appendix 4) which Sapir believes to be a generally accepted consensus among his colleagues. Taking these units, a total classification of twenty-three stocks is obtained – one which is intermediate between the Powell classification and the six-unit classification. Because of Sapir's prestige in the discipline and the intrinsic appeal of the six-unit classification with its facile adaptation to culture historical inference, this intermediate classification has been ignored. It is, if nothing else, a cogent reminder that Sapir saw the classification to which his name has been firmly attached as tentative and unfinished. He himself turned to other kinds of work in later years and the six-unit classification has been taken as a thing to be accepted or rejected *in toto*. The ongoing usefulness of the classification can only be understood in terms of its historical context, both in terms of Sapir and the period.

APPENDIX 1
A.L. KROEBER TO J.W. FEWKES – 20 DECEMBER 1919

While the relationship of American languages is a problem that must be worked out by philological specialists, the solution of this problem is of even greater importance to the ethnologist than to the linguist, because the ethnologist has found by long experience that the only feasible method of broad classifications that will serve him is that made on a linguistic basis. Ethnologists, and anthropologists in general, therefore have a right to demand of the linguists that the latter arrive at definite conclusions as quickly as possible; and while complete agreement on every last point is no doubt impossible and perhaps undesirable, that any common meeting ground of conclusions which may already have been won, be defined by unanimous acceptance at once, instead of continuing to remain obscured by contentions over doubtful territory.

The present situation is this. At one extreme stand workers like Sapir, who reduces nearly half the accepted stocks of the continent to a very few; and Radin, who does not hesitate to assert the ultimate unity of all on a much slenderer basis of adduced evidence. At the other extreme are Michelson, who disclaims theoretical hostility to reductions, but whenever one is made that touches his field, exacts a standard of completeness that would be difficult to attain under the most favorable conditions; and Boas, who instead of rejecting alleged specific proofs, substantially holds any further reductions of stocks to be unprovable, or the attempt at proof to be unprofitable. Between these extremes are to be found students like Swanton, Dixon, Kroeber, and Harrington.

Now in this welter certain facts stand out. The affinity of Shoshonean, Piman and Nahuatl, in other words their reduction into a single larger stock, the Uto-Aztecan, was broached several generations ago by Buschmann, considered without definite rejection by Powell, affirmed by Brinton, accepted by Chamberlain and Kroeber, and exhaustively discussed with affirmative conclusion by Sapir. It has not been challenged by any authority in twenty-five years. A refusal to accept this reduction would therefore not be caution or conservatism, but inertia or prejudice.

Many years ago certain similarities of form between Tlingit, Haida, and Athabascan were pointed out by Boas. Then Swanton produced evidence suggesting a positive connection between Tlingit and Haida. Later, Sapir included them with Athabascan in the single new Na-dene family. The recognized specialist on Athabascan is Goddard. An acceptance by him of the Sapir findings would probably quiet all antagonisms. His declaration that the case for reduction was plausible but required further evidence, would probably lead to the early production of evidence, and so perhaps settle the issue. His unqualified rejection of Na-dene, in print or public conference, would very likely suffice to induce most non-Athabascan specialists to put the proposed reduction into the class of uncertainties, and thus free the ethnologists, archaeologists, and historians from the necessity of considering it until the case had been reopened with fresh evidence.

Swanton's inclusion of Natchez with Muskhogean has never been challenged and therefore deserves to be endorsed and authorized.

Dixon and Kroeber some years ago united about ten Pacific Coast stocks as Hokan. Sapir, in a paper on the position of the Yana language in Hokan, not only accepted the reduction, but adduced hundreds of examples in support. His paper has never been attacked, rejected, or even reviewed. In the interest of progress, and to clarify the situation for non-linguists, it seems that his evidence should either be contradicted, or his findings accepted.

More recently, Dixon and Kroeber attempted in some detail to demonstrate the reduction of five other Californian languages into a so-called Penutian group. While this paper is recent, it seems only fair that within a year or two the alleged findings should either be controverted, pronounced insufficient, or be tentatively or positively accepted.

These instances show that in many cases an agreement is clearly in sight, and that much aid will be afforded to non-linguistic students if linguists, without trying to settle everything at once, will announce those cases of reduction, be they few or many, on which they are unanimously agreed. Extremists of either wing will never be wholly satisfied; but there is no reason why they should be. The needs of the outsider, of the non-contending 'public' of science, come first. Sapir and Michelson would perhaps never agree on just how much evidence constituted positive proof. A radical like Radin would no doubt consider that such findings as won the approval of everyone, or even of the majority, were tame and half-hearted; but he would prefer partial acceptance of his attitude to total rejection. Boas, who deplores all work along these lines as less important than other studies, would nevertheless be likely to welcome a segregation of the more valid and probable reductions from the wildly unsound ones, on the basis that the evil would thereby be limited. In short, in spite of all differences, and future differences, enough work has now been done to find a residuum of common opinion, if only the workers in the subjects can be brought to meet on a basis of tolerance, mutual concessions, and desire to cooperate instead of scoring or refusing to register points off one another. We in this subject have all been guilty of some hastiness of conclusion and disrespect of each other's opinion. Let us try to see what result we can reach by according divergent opinions the fullest weight.

I therefore recommend that Dr Fewkes, as head of the Bureau, the institution most intimately concerned in the matter as the promulgator of the original and forever fundamental Powell map of North American languages, call a meeting in Washington, perhaps for the Christmas week of 1920, of all students who have concerned themselves with the genetic relationships of the American languages; this meeting not to attempt to harmonize all opinions or to bind participants in advance to acceptance of any findings, but to try merely to determine what common element can be arrived at. In preparation, it might be well to appoint a small committee, say of three, to facilitate preliminary exchange of opinions and assemblage of material for discussion.

[note of approval attached by Swanton and Michelson]

APPENDIX 2
THE PROBLEMS OF LINGUISTIC RELATIONSHIP IN AMERICA

Abstract

E. SAPIR

The widespread feeling that Powell's linguistic map has served its purpose and that it needs to be superseded by a classification indicating wider historical perspectives. The difficulties in the way of a revision: difficulties of material; of method. The role of linguistic borrowing in America. The gradual differentiation of linguistic groups. Criteria for genetic inferences: lexical resemblances controlled by phonetic law; phonetic patterns; fundamental morphological patterns and processes; convergences and borrowings within a linguistic framework. An attempt to work back to a provisional classification of American languages: 1. Eskimo-Aleut; 2. Algonkin-Wakashan; 3. Na-dene; 4. Penutian; 5. Hokan-Siouan; 6. Aztec-Tanoan. Suggested extensions of 4 and 5 into Mexico and Central America. Possible significance of wider linguistic classification for inferences as to ancient movements of population. Certain Proto-American possibilities. Peculiar position of Na-dene (group 3).

A bird's eye view of American languages north of Mexico (outline)
General recognition that Powell's linguistic classification has already served its purpose. Something more historical and inclusive required now.
Difficulties in way of serious revision:

1. Not all American languages sufficiently well known yet
2. Persistently descriptive–psychological point of view in spite of all talk of historical method
3. Too much reliance on secondary factors of descriptive order (incorporation, instrumental prefixes, polysynthesis), with no serious attempt to get perspective as to age of different features. Fundamental features never yet isolated for large groups. Importance of subtler features of dynamic order (types of stem, closeness of welding of elements, accent, tone, fundamental phonetic pattern, development of unified form, order); of vestigial *vs.* flourishing features.
4. Disturbing factor of borrowed features

Suggested classification far from permanent:
    merely represents my present feeling in matter and subject to serious revision; not influenced by race or culture factors
Basis: morphological, helped out by lexical evidence
Characteristics of six main groups; generalized for groups, do not always apply to particular languages in descriptive aspect, though survivals sometimes discoverable:

1. Eskimo-Aleut. Polysynthetic and inflective; consistently suffixing; extreme welding of stem and suffixed elements; great elaboration of formal aspect of vb. (mode, person); fundamental importance of trans. *vs.* intr. (subj. intr. and obj. tr.); presence of local cases and two syntactic cases corresponding to verbal classification; noun plural and pronominal elements have formal, not merely material, value. No reduplication, inner stem modification, compounding (no nominal incorporation).

2. Algonkin-Wakashan. Polysynthetic and inflective: primarily suffixing (Algonkin suffixes far older than prefixes, which are only loosely added proclitics) – Wakashan solely so; Algonkin has clearly inflective cast in modal and pronominal verb suffixes and in gender and number and obviative of noun, Wakashan less clearly inflective, but has important stem modifications; fundamental vb. classification into subjective and objective; only obviative in part developed as syntactic case and one local case (also in part). Reduplication well developed, particularly in W.; inner stem changes. No compounding in ordinary sense (partly in Algonkin vb.), incorporation moderately developed in Algonkin. Extreme development of secondary elements, 'suffixes', with concrete significance: local adverbial, concrete verbalizing.

3. Na-dene. Loosely polysynthetic and fundamentally isolating, with quasi-inflective developments. 'Prefixing' in a sense, moderately suffixing (most so in Haida); properly speaking, we have monosyllabic elements in definite order that amalgamate more psychologically than morphologically (cf. Eng. 'he came upon it', where 'came-upon' is not really 'came' and 'upon'); 'word' here actually midway between short sentence and true word (stem and derivative and formal affixes) (See 1 and 2). Inner form is in verb stem and implications of order rather than in explicitly formal elements. No true welding of stem and affixed elements except to form new

stem entities. True stem is monosyllabic of type c + v (probably also c + v + nasal). Secondary phonetic processes bring about appearance of formal verbal development, but coalescence of subj. pronoun with modal 'prefixes' is really independent of verb stem changes. Importance of 'voice' and 'aspect'; tense not so fundamental. Verb classifies into active and static (including object tr. and subj. pas.). Postpositions well developed, mostly nominal in origin. Composition elaborately developed. No reduplication or formal development of gender, case, number; 'relative' forms distinctive, also nominalizing of verb forms by postpositions. Tone developed; intrinsic high-low.

4. Penutian. Not polysynthetic; decidedly inflective (nearest to Indo-European and Semitic of all American languages in general form). Primarily suffixing; prefixes, where found, are clearly secondary in origin. Suffixed elements have almost exclusively formal significance and are closely welded with stem. Pronominal suffixes, case elements, treatment of plurality, tense and aspect and voice in verb give words formal case; also note importance of inner stem changes, including reduplication (sometime final) and vowel insertion (type *haga-*: *ha'g-*). Frequency of stem-type $c + v + c_1 + v$. No incorporation typically developed, in general no concrete complications in verb; composition either absent or very moderately developed. Verb classifies into (subj.) intr. and (subj.) tr., perhaps also tr. obj. as originally distinct 3rd category. Tone systems found (Takelma, Maidu (?), Wintun (?)), apparently rising-falling type; significance not yet clear. Chinook as independent polysynthetic development of Penutian. Adherence to group evident from lexical evidence and from vestigial features. Tsim. profoundly influenced by group 2.

5. Hokan-Siouan. Polysynthetic and agglutinative; inflective tendency practically absent, in spite of formal subtleties and occasional stem modifications. Both prefixing and suffixing, but most characteristically prefixing in more formal elements (particularly pronouns) (Yana has secondary features). Verb: active: static primarily (Chim., Sioux, Iroquois). Incorporation and true compounding best developed in this group. Reduplication not so typical as in groups 2 and 4, sometimes absent; inner stem changes not generally found (Yana exceptional). Great development of concrete affixes, particularly in Hokan (instrumental prefixes – also Siouan; local suffixes and secondary verb stems – based on old compounding). Postpositions well developed. Frequency of stem type $v + c + v_1$ ($+ c_1 + v_2$): *itali, ipali, ama* or *uma*. Tone reported for Achomawi, Mohave, possibly Pomo; said to be significant and high-low; needs further investigation. Group shows rather little stability.

6. Aztec-Tanoan. Moderately polysynthetic and weakly inflective at best. Formally suffixing; prefixes either merely proclitic elements or old compounded stems. Suffixes belong to formal category, as in 4. Possibly polysynthesis formed on basis of 4 *via* simple compounding processes, perhaps due to contact with 5. Verb: subject-object, as in 2, markedly distinct from 1–4, 3–5. Reduplication frequent, also incorporation and compounding. Postpositions common. Noun and verb sharply distinct. Case developed, but rather weakly. All in all, mixed rather than specialized type. Impresses me as old Penutian strongly overlaid by Hokan (same process, but infinitely older, as took place in Maidu). Frequency of stem type $c + v + c_1 + v_1$. Tone in Tanoan-Kiowa; significance not yet made clear.

Proto-American possibilities:

1. Persistence of *n-* 'I' *m-* 'thou'
2. Negative *ka, ku*
3. Continuative – plural – iterative *-l-*
4. Diminutive *-si, -tsi*

Regrouping possible:

1. Eskimo-Aleut
   Algonkin-Wakashan
   Penutian
2. Na-dene
3. Hokan-Siouan

Aztec-Tanoan: transitional between 1 and 3
Valuelessness of polysynthesis as genetic criterion
Na-dene as tremendous wedge in older distribution; 1 and 3 as 2 great foundation groups in America – N and S.
Movements of population to be revealed by linguistic research.

Linguistic groups north of Mexico

E. SAPIR

I.   *Eskimo-Aleut*
II. Algonkin-Wakashan
    1. Algonkian
        (1) *Algonkin*
        (2) Wiyot-Yurok
    2. *Kootenay*
    3. Wakashan-Salish
        (1) *Wakashan (Kwakiutl-Nootka)*
        (2) *Chemakum*
        (3) *Salish*
III. Na-dene
    1. *Haida*
    2. Continental Na-dene   *Tlingit*
                               Athabaskan
IV. Penutian
    1. Californian Penutian   *Miwok*
                               Costanoan
                               Yokuts
                               Maidu
                               Wintun
    2. Oregon Penutian
        (1) *Takelma*
        (2) Coast Penutian
                           Coos
                           Siuslaw
                           Yakonan

(3) *Kalapuya*
(4) *Chinook*
3. *Tsimshian*

V. Hokan-Siouan
  1. *Yuki*
  2. Hokan
   (1) Northern Hokan   *Karok*
                                     Shasta-Achomawi
                                     Chimariko
                                     Pomo
   (2) *Yana*
   (3) *Washo*
   (4) *Salinan*
   (5) *Chumash-Yuman*   *Chumash*
                                     Yuman
   (6) *Esselen*
   (7) *Seri*
   (8) *Tequistlatecan* (Chontal)
  3. Coahuiltecan
   (1) *Coahuilteco*
   (2) *Tonkawa*
   (3) *Karankawa*
  4. *Keres*
  5. *Tunican*
   (1) *Tunica*
   (2) *Chitimacha*
   (3) *Atakapa*
  6. Siouan-Muskogian
   (1) *Siouan*
   (2) *Yuchi*
   (3) *Muskogian* (incl. *Timucua?*)
  7. Iroquois-Caddoan
   (1) *Iroquois*
   (2) *Caddoan*

VI. Aztec-Tanoan
  1. Uto-Aztekan   *Nahuatl*
                                 Piman
                                 Shoshonean
  2. Tanoan-Kiowa   *Tanoan*
                                 Kiowa

As yet unplaced
A. *Waiilatpuan*
 Lutuami
 Sahaptian
B. *Zuni*
C. *Beothuk*

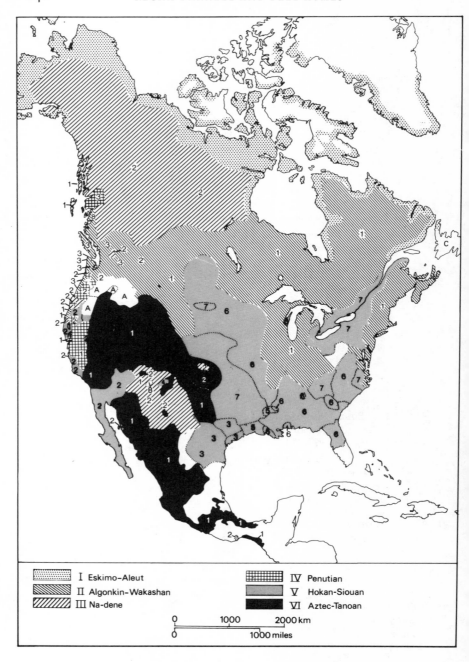

	I Eskimo–Aleut		IV Penutian
	II Algonkin–Wakashan		V Hokan-Siouan
	III Na-dene		VI Aztec-Tanoan

0   1000   2000 km
0   1000 miles

[For key to symbols see classification on pp. 238–9.]

APPENDIX 3
SCIENCE 54: 408 (28 OCTOBER 1921)
DISCUSSION AND CORRESPONDENCE

A bird's eye view of American languages north of Mexico

E. SAPIR

It is clear that the orthodox 'Powell' classification of American languages, useful as it has proved itself to be, needs to be superseded by a more inclusive grouping based on an intensive comparative study of morphological features and lexical elements. The recognition of fifty to sixty genetically independent 'stocks' north of Mexico alone is tantamount to a historical absurdity. Many serious difficulties lie in the way of the task of reduction, among which may be mentioned the fact that our knowledge of many, indeed of most, American languages is still sadly fragmentary; that frequent allowance must be made for linguistic borrowing and for the convergent development of features that are only descriptively, not historically, comparable; and that our persistently, and rather fruitlessly, 'psychological' approach to the study of American languages has tended to dull our sense of underlying drift, of basic linguistic forms, and of lines of historical reconstruction. Any genetic reconstruction that can be offered now is necessarily but an exceedingly rough approximation to the truth at best. It is certain to require the most serious revision as our study progresses. Nevertheless I consider a tentative scheme as possessed of real value. It should act as a stimulus to more profound investigations and as a first attempt to shape the historical problem. On the basis of both morphological and, in part, lexical evidence, the following six great groups, presumably genetic, may be recognized:

1. Eskimo-Aleut
2. Algonkin-Wakashan Algonkin-Wiyot-Yurok
           Kootenay
           Wakashan-Salish
3. Na-dene   Haida
           Tlingit-Athabascan
4. Penutian   Californian Penutian
           Oregon Penutian
           Tsimshian
5. Hokan-Siouan   Yuki
           Hokan
           Coahuiltecan group
           Keres
           Tunica group
           Siouan-Yuchi-Muskogian
           Iroquois-Caddoan
6. Aztec-Tanoan   Uto-Aztekan
           Tanoan-Kiowa

This leaves the Waiilatpuan-Lutuami-Sahaptian group, Zuni, and Beothuk as yet unplaced. The lines of cleavage seem greatest between 4 and 5, and between 3, on the one hand, and 1 and 2, on the other. Group 5 is probably the nearest to the generalized 'typical American' type that is visualized by linguistic students at large.

APPENDIX 4

Sapir 1929 – A	Sapir 1929 – B	Powell 1891
1. Eskimo-Aleut	Eskimo	Eskimo
2. Algonquian-Ritwan	*Algonquian-Ritwan	Algonquian, Beothukan, Wiyot, Yurok
	*Mosan	Wakashan, Chemakuan, Salish
	Kootenay	Kootenay
3. Na-Dene	*Tlingit-Athabascan	Haida, Tlingit, Athabascan
	Haida	
4. Penutian	*California Penutian	Miwok, Costanoan, Yokuts, Maidu, Wintun
	*Oregon Penutian	Takelma, Coos (-Siuslaw), Yakonan, Kalapuya
	*Plateau Penutian	Waiilatpuan, Lutuamian, Sahaptin
	Chinook	Chinook
	Tsimshian	Tsimshian
	(Mexican Penutian)	–
5. Hokan-Siouan	*Hokan	Karok, Chimariko, Salinan, Yana, Pomo, Washo, Esselen, Yuman, Chumash
	*Coahuiltecan	Tonkawa, Karankawa, Coahuiltecan
	*Tunican	Tunica, Atakapa, Chitimacha
	*Iroquois-Caddoan	Iroquois, Caddoan
	Yuki	Yuki
	Keres	Keres
	Timucua	Timucua
	Muskhogean	Muskhogean
	Siouan	Siouan, Yuchi
6. Aztec-Tanoan	*Uto-Aztecan	Nahuatl, Pima, Shoshonean
	*Tanoan-Kiowan	Tanoan, Kiowa
	Zuni ?	Zuni

* Twelve units which Sapir considered as accepted by most of his colleagues. The reduction from twenty-three to six units he felt to be his own work.

1	1	1
2	3	8
3	2	3
4	5	14
5	9	23
6	3	6
—	—	—
6	23	55

NOTES

1 We are grateful to Philip Sapir for making this material available to us. The original of the map which accompanied the 1920 lecture has been presented to the National Museum of Man, Ottawa, by the Sapir family. A sketch based on that map and the text of the abstract and outline form Appendix 2 below.

2 We have cited documents from the Sapir administrative files at the National Museum of Man, Ottawa (NMM), the Franz Boas, J. Alden Mason and Frank Speck papers at the American Philosophical Society, Philadelphia (APS), Bureau of American Ethnology files at the National Anthropological Archives of the Smithsonian Institution, Washington, DC (BAE), and the Alfred Kroeber and Robert Lowie papers at the University of California, Berkeley (ALK) (RHL).
We would also like to thank the following individuals for discussion of various issues about the Sapir classification: William Bright, Raymond Fogelson, Michael Foster, Victor Golla, Mary Haas, and Michael Krauss. We are, of course, responsible for the final interpretations.

3 There is, currently, a trend in American linguistics to consider the mutual interaction of areal and genetic processes, particularly in terms of communicative boundaries of different types of linguistic areas (see especially the work of Joel Sherzer and William Bright). However, this work has tended to proceed quite independently of that on genetic classification which has traditionally had fewer ties to anthropology with its cultural perspective. Sapir, of course, attempted to join every American language to one of his great stocks. It currently seems clear both from linguistic and culture–historical standpoints that there are numerous 'isolates' in native America, in addition to the broadly distributed families characterized by Sapir.

4 Golla (MS) has recently provided a definitive interpretation of the contact between Kroeber and Sapir over classification. We have followed his argument but tried to frame it more widely for Sapir.

5 The tone is one of finding a key that suddenly opens up a whole new perspective on ethnology and linguistics. Essentially the same data are dealt with by Dixon and Kroeber from 1903 to 1919. However, by the final publication the model is firmly and confidently genetic, the issue no longer being seen as problematic.

6 The first North American dating sequence based on archaeology was the Pecos classification of Southwestern pottery in 1926. Linguistic evidence was the only available evidence in 1916.

REFERENCES

Boas, Franz. 1911. *Introduction to the handbook of American Indian languages*. Bureau of American Ethnology Bulletin 40.
1920. The classification of American Indian languages. *American Anthropologist* 22: 367–76.
Campbell, Lyle and Mithun, Marianne. 1979. *The languages of native America*. Austin: University of Texas Press.

Darnell, Regna. 1969. The development of American anthropology 1880–1920: from the Bureau of American Ethnology to Franz Boas. Unpublished Ph.D. dissertation, University of Pennsylvania.

    1971a. The Powell classification of American Indian languages. *Papers in Linguistics* 4 (1).

    1971b. The revision of the Powell classification. *Papers in Linguistics* 4 (2).

Dixon, Roland & Kroeber, A.L. 1903. The native languages of California. *American Anthropologist* 5: 1–26.

    1913a. Relationship of the Indian languages of California. *Science* 37: 225.

    1913b. New linguistic families in California. *American Anthropologist* 15: 647–55.

    1919. Linguistic families of California. *University of California Publications in American Archaeology and Ethnology* 16: 48–118.

Golla, Victor. 1984. Sapir, Kroeber, and North American linguistic classification. Paper read at Sapir Centenary Conference, Ottawa, 1984.

Hymes, Dell. 1983. *Essays in the history of linguistic anthropology.* Amsterdam: John Benjamins.

Kroeber, A.L. 1940. The work of John Swanton. *Smithsonian Miscellaneous Contributions* 100: 1–9.

Michelson, Truman. 1914. Two alleged Algonquian languages of California. *American Anthropologist* 16: 361–7.

Newman, Stanley. 1954. American Indian linguistics in the Southwest. *American Anthropologist* 56: 626–44.

Powell, J.W. 1891. Indian linguistic families north of Mexico. *7th Annual Report, Bureau of American Ethnology for 1885–86* 7–39.

Sapir, Edward, 1915. The Na-dene languages. *American Anthropologist* 17:534–58.

    1916. *Time perspective in aboriginal American culture.* Canadian Department of Mines, Geological Survey, Memoir 90, Anthropological Series 13.

    1921a. A bird's eye view of American languages north of Mexico. *Science* 54: 408.

    1921b. *Language.* New York: Harcourt Brace.

    1925. The Hokan affinity of Subtiaba in Nicaragua. *American Anthropologist* 27: 402–35.

    1929. Central and North American languages. *Encyclopaedia Britannica* 5: 138–41.

    1949. *Selected writings of Edward Sapir.* Berkeley: University of California Press.

    1965. *Letters from Edward Sapir to Robert H. Lowie.* Berkeley.

Voegelin, C.F. 1942. Sapir: insight and rigor. *American Anthropologist* 44: 222–3.

14

DISTRIBUTIONAL SYNTAX

P.H. MATTHEWS

Until the middle of this century few scholars would have denied that syntax is concerned both with form and with meaning. Sweet is perfectly explicit: language has two sides – a 'formal side, . . . concerned with the outer form of words and sentences', and a 'logical side, . . . concerned with their inner meaning'. Grammar deals with neither separately, 'but with the connections between them, these being the real phenomena of language' (1891: 6f). Likewise Jespersen: of the two branches of grammar, syntax proceeds from the inner aspect to the outer, while morphology proceeds from the outer to the inner (1924: 39–46). Hence syntax is said to take the viewpoint of the speaker, who starts from the meaning that he wants to communicate and must then work out how to express it (46). According to Paul, a sentence is the linguistic expression corresponding to an association of concepts or groups of concepts that has arisen in the speaker's mind; formal devices – such as inflections, intonation or word order – are the means by which its expression is achieved (1920 [1880]: 121ff). For Sweet, these are similarly 'ways of indicating the relations between words' (30f). Such views were not confined to the turn of the century. In the heyday of European structural linguistics, de Groot draws a clear distinction between the order of words, which is a perceptible phenomenon, and the 'syntactic structure' of the word group, which is concerned with meaning and is not perceptible (1949: 54). A later chapter on 'syntactic means' refers specifically to Paul (238ff). For Tesnière, the whole of structural syntax rests on the relations between the 'linear order' of words and the 'structural order' represented by dependency and other stemmata (1959: 19).

But by the time these last works had been published a different view had arisen in the United States. In Harris's account, descriptive linguistics 'deals not with the whole of speech activities', but only with certain distributional regularities (1951: 5); meaning is thus eliminated, both from the description itself and as a true criterion for analysis (7, esp. n. 4). The consequence for grammar was particularly striking. Syntax cannot start from semantic relations: they are in principle irrelevant. Instead it is reduced to formal patterning, seen not as a means of realization but as a prior and independent object of study. By the end of the 1950s this view was beginning to pass into textbooks. Thus, for Hockett, the 'grammatical system' comprises no more than 'a stock of morphemes, and the arrangements in which they occur' (1958: 137; compare 128f); although both are meaningful, semantics forms a separate 'peripheral' system (138). According to Hill, 'linguists assume' that form must be described first, and the description of meaning 'put off' until this is complete (1958: 3). By the end of his book, 'the reader cannot have failed to observe that meaning has been little discussed . . . and has never been used as a primary tool of analysis' (409). Yet sentence structure has been examined in exemplary detail (173–405).

The purpose of this essay is to review the history of such notions. It falls into two parts. The first is concerned with their origin, especially in the years leading up to the Second World War; the main point both of interest and of difficulty is the influence of Bloomfield. The second part is concerned with the role of distributional syntax in the development of generative grammar. In both parts I will seek by implication to correct what has been said by some commentators.

1

In Bloomfield's first book the treatment of syntax is not dissimilar to those already cited from European writers. The sentence is 'an utterance analyzing an experience into elements' (1914: 60); this is the view of Wundt (1912 [1900]: 243f), which had been rejected by Paul. The relation between elements is psychological and includes both the 'primary division of an experience' into subject and predicate, and subsidiary divisions into 'subject' (= head) and attribute (61). Both these are called 'logical' or 'discursive' relations. A later discussion adds the 'serial' relation (= coordination); also 'other forces . . . play a part in determining' the form of a sentence, of which the 'most important . . . are perhaps the *emotional relations*' in which one element is 'dominant' (= emphasized) (113f). The chapter headed 'Syntax' is concerned in particular with the 'expression' of these relations, the 'formal means' being divided in its middle sections into 'modulation in the sentence', 'cross-referring constructions', 'congruence', 'government' and 'word-order' (176ff). All this is in keeping with the tenor of the book generally. The word too is a semantic unit (49, 99): 'psychologically a complicative association of those perceptual and emotional elements which we call its meaning or experience content with the auditory and motor elements which constitute the linguistic symbol' (66f). Language is throughout described in terms of 'associative habits'.

Within twelve years Bloomfield's views had changed substantially. The psychology of Wundt was replaced by that of Weiss: in particular, this entailed the theory of science that he later described as 'physicalist' (Bloomfield 1936: Hockett, L[eonard] B[loomfield] A[nthology] 322ff). A language is a set of potential utterances ('the totality of utterances that can be made in a speech-community'), an utterance being simply 'an act of speech' (1926: §II, LBA 129f). A sentence is, in turn, a part of an utterance: 'a maximum form in any utterance' (1931: LBA 235f, n. 6, correcting 1926: LBA 132). This last definition (from Meillet 1934 [1903]: 355) had been approved at least four years earlier (1922: LBA 93). Sentences are neither the analysis of a concept or experience, nor the expression of psychologically defined relations; 'express' itself is a term that Bloomfield tends to use less often. Instead the utterances are studied directly. For the mature Bloomfield, concepts, ideas and so on have no reality independent of the 'noises' that the speaker makes. 'If we are right, the term "idea" is simply a traditional obscure synonym for "speech-form"' (1936: LBA 328).

Yet forms have meanings and Bloomfield never wished to exclude them. This is made quite clear in one of his last general papers: 'in language, forms cannot be separated from meanings' (1943: LBA 401). Even in phonology he sees a knowledge of meanings as essential. For detailed confirmation we can turn either to his 'Set of postulates' (1926) or to Language (1933). A form itself is 'a recurrent vocal feature which has meaning' (LBA 130; equivalently for 'linguistic form', 1935 [1933]: 138). The smallest form, the morpheme, has as its meaning a 'sememe' (LBA 130; 1935: 162). In 1926 constructions have 'constructional meanings', each position in a construction has a 'functional meaning', and each form-class, defined in terms of positions, has a 'class-meaning' (LBA 132–4). In 1933 features of grammatical arrangement combine in 'tactic forms'; a 'grammatical form' is 'a tactic form with its meaning'. The 'smallest meaningful units of grammatical form' are called 'tagmemes' and their meanings 'episememes' (1935: 166). Grammar itself comprises 'the meaningful arrangements of forms in a language' (163); it is part of semantics, whose task is to tell 'what meanings are attached to . . . phonetic forms' (138). 'Glosseme' is proposed as a general term for anything that has meaning, the meaning that it has being a 'noeme' (1926: LBA 136; compare 1935: 264).

Reviewers of Language do not give the impression that any of this was found controversial. Three were unhappy with the use of novel terminology (Edgerton 1933: LBA 258f; Sturtevant 1934: LBA 265f; Debrunner 1936: LBA 279). But the chapters on grammar provoke no criticisms of substance. In general, Edgerton describes the book as 'sound and authoritative', presenting 'the best opinion of linguistic scholars on all important aspects of their science'. Kroesch sees Bloomfield as 'not interested primarily in advocating certain theories concerning language but in presenting as objectively as possible a picture of the present status of the study of linguistics' (1933: LBA 260). According to Sturtevant, his 'statement of the case for the generally accepted axioms of linguistic science is the best we have'. Such reviews confirm Bloomfield's own preface: 'I have tried everywhere to present the accepted views . . .' (1935: viii).

Nevertheless it is on these apparently uncontroversial foundations, the work of a scholar who continued to insist that form and meaning could not be considered separately, that the 'Bloomfieldians' were to build a theory in which their separation was axiomatic. We cannot know what Bloomfield himself would have thought of it: his career ended abruptly and early in 1946, with a stroke which left him unable to work for the remaining three years of his life. But his parentage was scarcely doubted. To the psychologist Carroll, surveying the state of American linguistics in the early 1950s, it appeared that 'since the publication of Bloomfield's work in 1933, theoretical discussions among linguists have been largely on matters of refinement . . .'. In the next sentence Carroll describes Harris's *Methods* (1951) as an 'authoritative treatment of the methodology of linguistic analysis, with numerous expansions and modifications of Bloomfield's techniques' (Carroll 1953: 30). Harris himself says that his work 'owes most . . . to the work and friendship of Edward Sapir and of Leonard Bloomfield, and particularly to the latter's book *Language*' (1951: v).

Why then did this development or modification of Bloomfield's theories take the turn that it did? The usual answer is that, however central meaning may have been, it seemed that there was no scientific way of investigating it. As Bloomfield said, 'the statement of meanings is . . . the weak point in language-study, and will remain so until human knowledge advances very far beyond its present state' (1935: 140). It was also essential that the study of a particular language should start from the forms of that language and not from a priori semantic categories. What was more natural, therefore, than that phonetic forms as such, which must and could be described, should have been isolated and studied independently, and the description of meaning, which, however important, was at the time unattainable, should have been set aside? But this answer is not entirely satisfying. Meaning may have been the 'weak point in language-study'; but it is not clear why one had to take this as a warning to lay off. In itself, it might as reasonably be understood as a challenge. Nor is it clear why, in separating things that Bloomfield said could not be separated, his followers believed that they were developing his ideas. Finally, the Americans were not alone in insisting that each language has its own formally realized categories. This is a general tendency of twentieth-century linguistics, shared by scholars as diverse as, for example, Jespersen and Hjelmslev. But it is not general to conclude that formal categories should be established as categories of form alone. Instead it is peculiar to this one increasingly inward-looking school.

In looking for more direct reasons, this inward-looking tendency is perhaps the first thing one should stress. Bloomfield himself was a catholic scholar, as a brief glance at the notes to *Language* will show. For the chapters on grammar he recommends, among others, Ries (1927 [1894]), Sweet (1899), Blümel's introduction to syntax (1914), de Saussure and, from the previous decade, Sapir's *Language* (1921), Jespersen's *Philosophy of grammar* (1924), Wackernagel's *Vorlesungen* (1926); also Hjelmslev's first book (1928). But the next generation seems to have taken his own work as a fresh starting point. The evidence is partly anecdotal: for example, Hockett says that he took a course with Bolling, in the year that *Language* appeared, entirely devoted to reading and discussing it (*LBA* 258). Other evidence is in Bloch and Trager's *Outline*, published nine years later. Their annotated reading list recommends European works on phonetics; also, among the references for grammar, two by Jespersen (one said to be 'illuminating but rather superficial . . .'). But for grammar Bloomfield's *Language* is 'far more rewarding than any other treatment'. It is also 'the best introduction' to language in general; for their introductory chapter they further recommend *Linguistic aspects of science* (Bloomfield 1939) and a late article (1942), with five other readings which are all American. It is again the 'best introduction' to phonemics; surprisingly, when one compares articles in the 1930s, there is no reference to European work on phonology (Bloch and Trager 1942: 80–2).

For the period which follows it is instructive to count actual references. For phonology Harris's notes (1951) are comprehensive, and there is one impressive list for grammar (197, n. 1). But in the remaining footnotes to his chapters on 'morphology' (chapters 12 and following), Bloomfield is referred to far more frequently than any other author: for *Language* seventeen times, for other works nine times. In contrast, Sapir's *Language* is referred to four times and articles by him another four times. A further sixteen references are to theoretical work – I exclude factual notes on individual languages – by other scholars writing in the Bloomfieldian tradition (Bloch and Trager, Hockett, Harris himself, Wells, Voegelin, Swadesh and Voegelin). Only fourteen are to general contributions by Europeans (three of them to Jespersen). For a sampling of articles we may turn to Joos's 1958 collection, *R[eadings] i[n] L[inguistics]*. This includes twelve important papers on morphology and syntax published between 1942 and 1954. Of these all but one refer to Bloomfield at least once; *Language* is mentioned nine times and articles by him eight times. The other references include over a hundred to the authors themselves and their American contemporaries (Bloch, Trager and Bloch, Hockett, Harris, Wells, Swadesh and Voegelin, Nida, Pike). Six are to Sapir, two to Boas, two to Jespersen; there are none to other general works by European scholars, contemporary or earlier. The bias is continued by textbooks. In his second edition Gleason recommends Bloomfield's *Language* as 'long, and deservedly . . . the standard handbook in American descriptive linguistics', suggests American readings for morphology and syntax, and mentions European work by Firth, Hjelmslev and Uldall, and Martinet at the end of a section in the bibliography headed 'History of Linguistics' (1961 [1955]: 484ff). Hockett tells us that, although he has 'intended no adherence to any single "school" of linguistics, the influence of American linguistics, and especially that of Leonard Bloomfield, will be apparent on every page' (1958: vii). His references are too erratic for serious analysis; but, in contrast, the reader will learn nothing of de Saussure, Hjelmslev, Trubetzkoy, Firth or Daniel Jones.

The isolationist trend is well known and was criticized at the time by Haugen (1951: *RiL* 357). It is also well known that, for a crucial period in the Second World War, the American school was genuinely isolated. But it is essential to bear in mind not just their neglect of their contemporaries, but also how little of the earlier tradition, Bloomfield's work apart, they continued to make use of. A historian is therefore obliged to read Bloomfield's *Language* in two modes: on the one hand, as his reviewers and other colleagues read it, with knowledge of its antecedents and of the problems as a scholar of his generation will have seen them; on the other hand, as if it were virtually a 'course book' to be worked through from scratch.

If we read it in the first mode it is indeed very hard to interpret the treatment of meaning as an incitement to ignore it. In an important endnote Bloomfield distinguishes two senses of the term 'semantics', one as the study of 'speech-forms and their meanings' and the other as that of 'meaning or meanings in the abstract' (1935: 513, to §5.1). In the latter sense, 'one is really trying to study the universe in general', a study (we must understand) belonging to other disciplines. In the former sense, which as a linguist he adopts, semantics is 'equivalent to the study of grammar and lexicon'. The distinction is well illustrated in his chapter on substitutes (chapter 15). These are forms with two elements of meaning; a class meaning and a 'substitution type': for example, the pronoun *I* 'replaces any singular substantive expression' (this gives the class meaning), provided that it 'denotes the speaker . . .' (248). The section which follows takes a look outside linguistics, examining the problems as they 'confront the student of sociology and psychology' (§15.3). Here 'we find at once' that '*I*, *we*, and *you* are based upon the speaker–hearer relation', that '*this*, *here*, *now* and *that*, *there*, *then* represent relations of distance from the speaker or from the speaker and the hearer', and so on. To repeat, these findings lie outside linguistics, being concerned with 'practical circumstances, which the linguist, for his part, cannot accurately define' (end of §15.2). But then, in 'returning to the ground of linguistics' (§15.4), he is able to be 'somewhat bolder' – bolder, that is, than generally in his book – about stating what the meanings are. In fact, he gives a succinct but detailed account (half a page) of the meaning of *he* (251). We may take this as a paradigm of how Bloomfield would have liked the treatment of semantics to be. The reason why other chapters are less bold is that neighbouring sciences had not progressed sufficiently; therefore a linguist has to resort to what are earlier called 'makeshift devices' (140).

Such an approach shows, in particular, a concern to detach linguistics from psychology. In a passage already cited in part, Sweet remarks that 'the study of the logical side of language is based on psychology', just as the study of its formal side is based on phonetics. 'But phonetics and psychology do not constitute the science of language, being only preparations for it: language and grammar are concerned not with form and meaning separately, but with the connections between them . . .' (1891: 6f). For Bloomfield himself, it was essential that linguists should not be involved in psychological disputes. In his preface he refers anonymously to Delbrück, saying that we have now learned, 'what one of our masters suspected thirty years ago, namely, that we can pursue the study of language without reference to any one psychological doctrine'; to do so 'safeguards our results and makes them more significant to workers in related fields' (1935: vii). In his second chapter, he makes clear that the linguist 'is not competent to deal with problems of physiology or psychology'. We must avoid the fault of 'many of the older linguists', who 'vitiated or skimped their reports by trying to state everything in terms of some psychological theory' (32). A linguist has to know something about psychology, and in the paragraphs which follow Bloomfield sketches two alternative theories, the 'mentalistic' and the 'materialistic' or 'mechanistic', a contrast which he returns to in the chapter headed 'meaning' (142ff). But a linguist's theory must be that of his own science. A striking illustration is his adoption of Meillet's theory of the sentence. This had been proposed 'au point de vue linguistique, et abstraction faite de toute considération de logique et de psychologie' (cited Bloomfield 1931: *LBA* 235). What is defined is a semantic unit, since a 'linguistic form', of which a sentence is the largest instance, is again 'a phonetic form which has a meaning' (1935: 138). But the definition is not committed to a psychological theory, unlike, notably, those of Paul and Wundt.

What was needed, therefore, was a framework in which linguists could pursue their own studies, taking results from other sciences when they could. For Bloomfield, this rested on the 'fundamental assumption' that 'in every speech-community some utterances are alike in form and meaning' (78, equivalently 144). We thus assume, on the one hand, that there are recurrent or distinctive features of sound. We also assume, on the other hand, that there are recurrent features of meaning; for each form these are 'the *distinctive*, or *linguistic meaning* (the *semantic* features) which are common to all the situations that call forth' its utterance (141). In the state of our knowledge this could be no more than an assumption. But, having made it, a linguist could describe linguistic meanings provisionally, and did not have to wait until all other branches of science were 'close to perfection' (78) before he could proceed.

So much if we read Bloomfield in the first mode. Linguistics is presented as an independent, higher-order science, concerned with the conventional linkage between sounds and meanings; but the study of meanings as such has its foundations in other disciplines, of which psychology is the most relevant. That was true however one viewed the nature of meaning, whether mechanistically, as Bloomfield in fact did, or mentalistically, as his readers were free, if they so wished, to prefer. But if we read him in the second mode, the passages which strike us first are those which refer to his general model of the speech-event. This begins with a division between the 'act of speech' and the 'practical events' preceding and following it (23); it is the former with which 'we, as students of language, are chiefly concerned' (25). More precisely, the act of speech is a reaction by the speaker to a stimulus: S → r (small 'r' for linguistic reaction). This is in turn a stimulus that provokes a reaction in the hearer: s → R (small 's' for linguistic stimulus) (25f). Such a model had been given to him, as he saw it, by psychology (1926: *LBA* 129, with footnote reference to Weiss). We are then told that our concern, 'as students of language', is with 'the speech-event'; 'we distinguish between language, the subject of our study, and real or practical events. . . '. But in the same paragraph the meaning of a speech-utterance (= speech-act, = speech-event) is defined as 'the important things with which [it] is connected, namely the practical events'. This last sentence makes precise reference to the divisions with which the discussion began (27).

Further down the page Bloomfield makes clear that 'to study language' is to study the 'co-ordination of certain sounds with certain meanings'. However, a reader might be forgiven for concluding that, if meaning consists of practical events, and the study of language is distinct from that of practical events, the study of language cannot be concerned with meaning. Nor is this the last remark of that sort. I have cited the passage which leads into a discussion of mentalism and mechanism (32), but without the initial statement that, 'in the division of scientific labor, the linguist deals only with the speech-signal (r . . . s)'. The chapter on phonemes is the next to make use of this model. Bloomfield says there that, 'in principle, the student of language is concerned only with the actual speech'; the preceding sentence makes clear that this means 'the speech-sound'. The study of 'speakers' situations and hearers' responses' – these are explicitly identified with the 'practical events' of the model – 'is equivalent to the sum total of human knowledge' (74). Later in the paragraph he imagines an 'ideal' state of linguistics, which 'would consist of two main investigations: *phonetics*, in which we studied the speech-event without reference to its meaning, . . . and *semantics*, in which we studied the relation of [phonetic] features to features of meaning . . .'. But that would be possible only if we had 'an accurate knowledge of every speaker's situation and every hearer's response'. Now it is a note to this section, cited earlier, which makes clear that there is another, non-ideal sense of 'semantics'. It is also this chapter which introduces Bloomfield's 'fundamental assumption of linguistics' (78), precisely so that we can proceed with an imperfect knowledge. But the impression has been left that, for the time-being, all the linguist can do is study the speech-signal as such.

It is to this reading, if anywhere in Bloomfield's writings, that we must look for the theoretical authority for distributionalism. But it was nearly fifteen years before any writer tried to separate form and meaning consistently. In his first paper on the morpheme, Harris proposes three procedures, the first of which divides 'each expression in the given language into the smallest sequences of phonemes which have what we consider the same meaning when they occur in other expressions . . .' (1942: *RiL* 110; Harris, *Papers [on Syntax]* (1981) 24f). It is not until *Methods* (preface dated 1947) that the purpose of setting up morphemic segments is simply that of 'stating the limitations of occurrence of [phonemes] over long stretches of speech' (Harris 1951: 156). In a review specifically of this chapter, Fowler argued that without appeal to meaning one could not isolate a morpheme, except from environments that were already described as sequences of other morphemes (Fowler 1952); it is perhaps only in a later article (1955) that Harris proposes a genuinely distributional procedure. By the late 1940s other scholars are also giving or citing distributional definitions: thus Hockett 1949; Trager 1949 (both in Hamp 1957: s.v. 'morpheme'). But two years earlier morphemic analysis is still 'the operation by which the analyst isolates minimum meaningful elements . . .' (Hockett 1947: *RiL* 229). Now in the progress of distributionalism the identification of morphemes was the last and most refractory problem; by 1947 Harris had already published an article on syntax requiring 'no elements other than morphemes and sequences of morphemes, and no operation other than substitution, repeated time and again' (1946: *RiL* 142, *Papers* 45f). But even this was not an immediate development.

That it did follow may be ascribed partly to practice and partly to the detailed working out of models. In a collection on the study of American Indian languages, Voegelin and his wife recall Bloomfield's advice, 'repeated over and over again' at Linguistic Institutes, 'to postpone consideration of unsolved or unresolved semantic problems until the more formal problems of grammar (in phonology and syntax) were better stated'. 'Most Americanists', they say, 'heeded' it (Voegelin and Voegelin 1976: 78, 97, n. 7). This is perhaps put anachronistically: in print at least, Bloomfield had not defined semantics and grammar as opposites. But there is no reason to believe that it is not, in fact, the lesson which many of his hearers carried away. In particular, Voegelin and Voegelin mention work with Ojibwa informants 'in which it was found that very explicit formal structure could be obtained with minimum attention to semantics'. It is easy to exaggerate the influence of field-work on theory: in the next generation, the most thorough-going distributionalist (Harris) did not work directly on undescribed languages, and Pike, who did, was a prominent dissenter. But it is true that, in the early stages of such study, formal methods may seem to make remarkable progress.

In the same footnote, Voegelin and Voegelin say that Bloomfield's units of meaning (they say 'sememe and tagmeme' but I will take them to mean 'sememe and episememe') were 'generally understood at the time (after 1933) to be redundant with formal structure and hence dispensible'. Now that could not be concluded from his own example. The plurals *geese* and *glasses* have, for Bloomfield, different 'grammatical forms': in one the morpheme *goose* undergoes 'phonetic modification'; in the other there is 'selection' of a following morpheme *-es*. But the associated meaning is the same: in plurals like *geese*, 'a grammatical feature, phonetic modification, expresses a meaning (namely, the sememe "*more than one* object") which is normally expressed by a linguistic form (namely, the morpheme [-iz, -z, -s])' (1935: 216). The *-en* of *oxen* is a different morpheme, related suppletively to *-es* (215); the implication is that this too has the same sememe. In morphology at least, the relation of forms to meanings was thus many to one. But in the 1940s Bloomfield's treatment of morphology was abandoned. The term 'morpheme' was then applied to an abstract construct ('morpheme unit' in Harris 1942; later simply 'morpheme') of which *-es, -en* and the modification were all alternants or 'allomorphs'. This was seen as a formal unit, on the analogy of phonemes and 'allophones'. But the criteria for grouping were again in part semantic: 'we take any two or more alternants which have what we consider the same meaning . . .' (Harris 1942: *RiL* 110, *Papers* 25). Morphemes such as 'plural' would then correspond precisely to meanings such as 'more than one object', and there is no need to posit the sememe as an additional grammatical unit. Nida's handbook is, I think, the last treatment of morphology to mention it (1949 [1946]: 155).

This work explicitly changes Bloomfield's theory, for reasons which are discussed retrospectively by Hockett (1961: 29f) and, at the time, at the beginning of Harris's article (1942). But once that change had been made the rest of his grammar was ripe for reinterpretation. It begins, in chapter 10 of *Language*, with a distinction of four types of 'grammatical arrangement', which together build up 'complex forms' (1935: 162ff). Of these, 'phonetic modification' included the change of vowel in *geese*; also, for example, that of [-iz] to [-s] in the regular plural suffix of *ducks* (211f). But in the new theory of the morpheme this is entirely subsumed by the description of allomorphs. 'Modulation' covered features of stress and intonation; for Bloomfield these were 'secondary phonemes, . . . which do not appear in any morpheme, but only in grammatical arrangements of morphemes' (163). But in the new theory these are said to be morphemes in themselves (thus Harris 1945: *Papers* 36). 'Selection' referred to the choice of forms: for example, of the substantive in *John!* or the verb in *Run!* or, in *John runs fast*, of *-s* in agreement with *John* (Bloomfield 1935: 164f). It is interesting that Harris's next step, though not followed by others, is to reduce all cases of agreement to 'discontinuous morphemes' (again Harris, 1945). The remaining features of grammatical arrangement are those of order. For Hockett, looking back some twenty years later, that alone is what 'arrangement' ought to have meant; 'to many of us in the 1940s', he adds, Bloomfield's model 'did not make sense' (1968: 20f). But once Harris's theory of the morpheme has been accepted, all that remains is simply the choice of elements (selection) and what Hockett calls the 'geometrical location of elements relative to one another'. There is also no difference, in principle, between the arrangement of morphemes within the word and that of words and larger units within the sentence. The logical division is between (a) the relation of morphemes to allomorphs and (b) the relation of one morpheme to another; not between morphology and syntax as Bloomfield, let alone most earlier writers, had conceived them.

Bloomfield then explains that features of grammatical arrangement, though individually meaningless, combine to form tagmemes, or units of grammatical form, which do have meaning (166). But if arrangement means effectively order, a more important set of passages, in particular for anyone who tries to develop the theory further, are those dealing with 'positions'. In his chapter headed 'syntax', Bloomfield returns for illustration to the grammatical form that has already been called the 'actor–action construction' (184f). This is a type of tagmeme (thus again 276) which has two positions: the 'actor' position, filled by *John* in a sentence such as *John ran*, and the 'action' position, filled by *ran*. He then defines 'the positions in which a form can appear' as 'its *functions* or, collectively, its *function*'. Accordingly, the function or functions of *John* would include that of actor in this construction, that of 'goal' in the 'action–goal' construction of *Tell John* (compare 197), and so on. He also uses this framework to make precise the definition of a 'form-class'. When this term first appears, he talks of forms grouped 'by some recognizable phonetic or grammatical feature' (146), and he later gives as one example 'the forms which, when spoken with exclamatory final-pitch, have the meaning of a call' (164). It is now defined as 'all the forms which can fill a given position'. Thus *John, Bill, our horses, . . .* are members of the form-class defined by the actor position; similarly *ran, fell, ran away, . . .* of that defined by the action position. This notion is in turn important, later in the chapter, for defining types of construction. Thus a subordinative or attributive construction is one in which 'the resultant phrase belongs to the same form-class as one of its constituents' (195).

Now in Bloomfield's 'set of postulates' constructions, like morphemes, had been established by a correspondence between form and meaning. He does not illustrate differences; but, for example, we can say that in *drink milk* and *fresh milk*, whose features of selection are distinguished earlier in *Language* (165), the order of constituents corresponds in one case to an 'action–goal' meaning and in the other to a 'character–substance' meaning. Therefore their constructions are different; therefore *drink* and *fresh* fill different positions and belong to different form-classes. As Bloomfield puts it, the initial assumption is that 'different non-minimum forms may be alike or partly alike as to the order of the constituent forms and as to stimulus–reaction features corresponding to this order' (1926: *LBA* 132). These stimulus–reaction features are defined as the constructional meanings. In *Language* again, the character–substance construction is subdivided into 'quality–substance', as in *fresh milk*, and 'limitation–substance', as in *this milk* (1935: 202). The reason, if we put it in terms of the earlier article, is that in *this fresh milk* a difference in the order of modifiers (*this* before *fresh*, not *fresh* before *this*) corresponds to different 'limiting' and 'descriptive' meanings.

When we return to *Language* it seems clear that Bloomfield's basic theory has not changed. Constructions, to repeat, are tagmemes and tagmemes have meanings, called episememes, just as morphemes have meanings, called sememes. But some of his illustrations might easily suggest that meanings are secondary. In the passage just referred to he does not, in fact, begin by distinguishing the constructions (limitation–substance and quality–substance). Instead he starts from the division between form-classes (limiting adjective and descriptive adjective), which is established 'by the circumstance that when adjectives of both these classes occur in a phrase, the limiting adjective precedes and modifies the group of descriptive adjective plus noun'. This might suggest that the distinction is made simply by the feature of order in phrases such as *this fresh milk*. He then says that the difference between form-classes subdivides the construction. This would suggest that the fundamental distinction is between two sequences of form-classes (member of limiting subclass + substantive expression, member of descriptive subclass + substantive expression), and the difference of meaning between constructions (limitation–substance, quality–substance) is the last thing to be characterized. At the beginning of this section Bloomfield says that 'syntax is obscured . . ., in most treatises, by the use of philosophical instead of formal definitions of constructions and form-classes' (1935: 201). He means that we cannot establish a grammatical distinction simply by referring to a philosophical distinction; there must also be a formal distinction corresponding to it. But one might plausibly conclude that, starting from the formal features of selection and order, which in themselves are meaningless, one can establish first form-classes and then constructions on the evidence of form alone.

In this light it is tempting to reconsider Bloomfield's sequence of definitions. In theory, positions are elements in a construction; they in turn define form-classes. But if form-classes can in practice distinguish constructions, and classes are in turn still understood to be defined by positions, positions might seem prior to both. Furthermore, there is no term, in the system as it is presented in this chapter, for the meaning of a position. In the 'set of postulates' this had been called the 'functional meaning': thus 'actor' was the functional meaning of the position in the construction of *John ran* which is occupied by *John*. The functional meanings of a language, with its class-meanings (meanings of form-classes), were said to form its 'categories' (Bloomfield 1926: *LBA* 133f). But in *Language* categories are simply 'large form-classes . . .'; they are thus composed of forms, not meanings (1935: 270f). Class-meanings remain, and it is notable that, in the discussion of the character–substance construction and its subtypes, it is the class-meanings (for adjectives in general 'something like "*character* of specimens of a species of objects"', for descriptive adjectives 'roughly "*qualitative* character of specimens"') that correspond to the names given to positions (character, quality). But the term 'functional meaning' disappears. In a later chapter Bloomfield talks of 'positional meanings', such as 'performer of an action' (267). But the term is not put into italics, is not indexed, and is not used when the system is first explained and illustrated.

A more prominent notion is that of function. Functions are defined, in the passage already cited from the syntax chapter, as 'the positions in which a form can appear' (1935: 185; compare 1926: *LBA* 134). Eighty pages later the definition is reformulated, in terms of what are called 'privileges of occurrence'. After talking of lexical forms in isolation, Bloomfield says that a 'lexical form in any actual utterance, as a concrete linguistic form, is always accompanied by some grammatical form: it appears in some function, and these privileges of occurrence make up, collectively, the grammatical *function* of the lexical form' (265). As it is put succinctly in a later monograph, 'a *function* of a form is its privilege of appearing in a certain position of a certain construction' (Bloomfield 1939: 26; compare Bloch and Trager 1942: 72, first drafted by Bloomfield (4)). This is a purely formal notion. In his late article on 'meaning', Bloomfield remarks that to earlier students function was an aspect of language intermediate between form and meaning. 'Thus, a word like *apple* . . . functioned as a noun, serving as the subject of verbs . . . and so on.' But 'careful study' has shown that these are simply 'formal features which come into being when two or more forms are combined in a larger form'. Thus *apple*, with certain exceptions, always enters into phrases with preceding adjectives (adjective again includes article), and these phrases can 'enter into larger phrases with following finite verb express-ions'. 'A form's privilege of occurring in any one position' is once more 'a *function* of that form' (1943: *LBA* 403). A distributionalist need merely add that, by 'position', one means just 'position preceding or following some other class of forms'.

In fact, distributionalism followed, and within a few years of this last paper. On the account developed here, it followed not for merely philosophical reasons, in that there seemed no way of studying meaning scientifically, but more specifically because, in his detailed treatment of constructions, Bloomfield had in effect provided a model for establishing form-classes solely by reference to formal features of selection and order. The next step was to redefine the term 'construction'. In Harris's 'From morpheme to utterance' it is used of sequences of substitution classes, resulting directly from the procedure by which the classes are established (1946: *Papers* 62, *RiL* 150). In Wells's paper on immediate constituents, a construction is a class of 'occurrences', an occurrence being a token or instance of a sequence of morphemes (1947: *RiL* 194); Wells stresses that this is not Bloomfield's definition. In Harris's *Methods* the procedures establish first morpheme classes (chapter 15), then morpheme sequences and classes of morpheme sequences (chapter 16), then constructions (chapter 18); a construction is a class of sequences of morpheme classes which are treated as similar (1951: 325). In this way the theory is entirely classificatory.

It is, moreover, in syntax that pure distributionalism became most securely entrenched. 'Distribution' itself had been a technical term at least since 1934, when complementary distribution was formulated as a criterion in phonology (Swadesh 1934: *RiL* 35). From there it was introduced into morphemics (Harris 1942: *Papers* 25f, *RiL* 110). But at this time Harris specified semantic criteria as well, and in Hockett's contemporary treatment of phonology contrasting phones are recognized by non-equivalence of 'biosocial stimuli' (1942: *RiL* 98f). Six years later Bloch expounds an approach to phonemics in which 'we shall avoid all semantic and psychological criteria' (1948: 5). But it was hard for phonologists not to retain at least a notion of 'differential meaning'. In the terms of Hockett's textbook, differences of sound 'keep utterances apart' (1958: 15). In setting up both phonemes and morphemes, Harris makes clear a reliance on substitutability 'without obtaining a change in response from native speakers who hear the utterance before and after the substitution'. In that way 'we approach the reliance on "meaning" usually required by linguists'; however, 'something of this order seems inescapable, at least in the present stage of linguistics' (1951: 20). In Hockett's textbook the morpheme is still the 'smallest individually meaningful element' (1958: 123); compare also Gleason's (1961 [1955]: 66f).

In syntax the morphemes could be taken as given and the problem became simply that of classing them, grouping them into sequences, and classing sequences. In 1947 Wells continued to refer to meanings: thus in the second of three conditions for constructions, that all the occurrences 'have a certain meaning in common'. But Harris's article excludes it. The procedure, as we noted earlier, is of substitution only. Hence the formulae resulting from it 'cannot in themselves indicate what meanings may be associated with the various positions and classes'; such information has to be given in 'separate statements' (1946: *Papers* 67, *RiL* 152f). Nevertheless, in the first paragraph, the procedure is said to cover 'an important part of what is usually included under syntax'. In the next decade, Gleason's textbook avoids resting the identification of constituents on meaning, and stresses that sameness in this context 'cannot mean' that constituents are 'identical in form or meaning, or even similar in form and meaning, but only that they are alike in their potentiality for entering into constructions' (1961 [1955]: 135, 137). Hockett's textbook is conservatively 'Bloomfieldian' (1958: chapter 18 especially). But ten years later, in a retrospective passage already referred to, he asks how 'arrangements' can be identified as same or different. How do we know, for instance, that xy has a different arrangement (an A followed by a B) from wz (a B followed by an A)? 'An assertion such as "x is an A" is based', he answers, 'on distributional information' (1968: 21). This implies that it cannot be based on correlations between form and meaning, as in the 1920s, at the beginning of our period, Bloomfield had naturally assumed.

2

The period covered by the first section of this paper lies partly within the careers of people still living. Many others will have read the works referred to, not as documents for the history of linguistic theory, but as part of the current literature of their subject, to which they responded as students or mature scholars. This may cause embarrassment to a historian. On the one hand, his reading of a text may broadly confirm the image of its author that has been formed by subsequent development and criticism. If so, he will seem to have made heavy weather of what everyone knows already. On the other hand, it may not. In particular, it may conflict with the polemics of a younger generation; or with personal memories, even (since not all scholars can recall the changes in their own minds) of the author himself. It must therefore be stressed that such accounts may not be trustworthy. A reading which is not dispassionate will usually be selective. That of a student will be out of context, and later recollections of what as a younger scholar one took older scholars to be saying may be doubly distorted. Finally, an author is not a monolith, whose views can be summed up in a single canonical version.

Such difficulties are much worse in the period which follows, where we are concerned in particular with Chomsky's early debt to his elders. Chomsky was a pupil of Harris in Philadelphia and gave help with the manuscript of his *Methods* (Harris 1951: v); by his own account, he learned linguistics from it (quoted by Newmeyer 1980: 33). But potted histories of the discipline are apt to put teacher and pupil into different historical boxes. Harris is presented as an 'American structuralist' or 'descriptivist' and is broadly lumped with Bloomfield. In particular, there is one view which Bloomfield did not in fact hold, that there can be no 'General Grammar, which will register similarities between languages' (see Bloomfield 1934: *LBA* 285), which structuralists or descriptivists are said to perpetuate. Chomsky is seen as the founder of a new school, committed to new aims. But these are simplifications which obscure the true progress of ideas. Chomsky's *Syntactic structures* is a striking and original book, which forced its readers to look at familiar things from a fresh angle. But in taking this view, he did not destroy his predecessors' basic concept of the structure of language. Rather he gave new life to it.

Let us start with the definition of 'a language'. For some Bloomfieldians, a language is the underlying system: 'a complex system of habits' (Hockett 1958: 137); 'a system of arbitrary vocal symbols by means of which a social group cooperates' (Bloch and Trager 1942: 5). For Joos (1948: 99), it was 'a set of neural patterns in the speech center' (cited with other definitions by Hamp 1957: s.v.). But in 1926 Bloomfield had defined it as a set of utterances: 'The totality of utterances that can be made in a speech-community is the *language* of that speech-community' (*LBA* 130). In 1933 the term is not defined (there is in fact no entry for it in his index); however, it seems plain that in describing a language one is to be thought of as describing not 'la langue' in the sense by then familiar in European structural linguistics, but the properties of observable 'linguistic forms'. This line of definition is followed by Harris. Thus a language or dialect 'comprises the talk which takes place in a language community' (1951: 13). An utterance is 'any stretch of talk, by one person, before and after which there is silence on the part of that person' (14). Utterances are therefore 'samples of the language'. Chomsky's definition is in the same tradition. Had he been taught otherwise he might have defined a language as a system of rules. In that case, he would not have been led to say, some twenty years later, that grammars and not languages are the primary object of study. But in fact he defines it as 'a set . . . of sentences' (Chomsky 1957: 13). 'All natural languages in their spoken or written form are languages in this sense'; a 'grammar of a language' is a characterization of such a set of sentences.

In reading these passages we must be careful not to make an anachronistic distinction between sentences and utterances. In his important review of Harris's *Methods*, Householder remarks that, despite the definition just cited, Harris in general 'uses "utterance" to mean what old-fashioned linguists called a "sentence" or "sentence fragment"' (Householder 1952: 263). His pupil uses both terms interchangeably, and in all relevant collocations. On the next page of *Syntactic structures* he talks of grammatical sentences and observed sentences: '. . . a linguistic theory that attempts to give a general explanation for the notion "grammatical sentence" in terms of "observed sentence"' (Chomsky 1957: 14). The next paragraph talks of observed utterances and grammatical utterances: 'Any grammar of a language will *project* the finite and somewhat accidental corpus of observed utterances to a set (presumably infinite) of grammatical utterances' (15). This refers to a corpus of utterances; but, on the page before, each grammar is said to be related to a 'corpus of sentences' (see also 49 for both collocations). Chomsky talks at least twice of the speaker's ability 'to produce and understand new utterances' (23); however, speakers are also said to produce sentences. Thus, if a finite state conception of language is adopted, 'we can view the speaker as being essentially a machine' of that type; 'in producing a sentence', he 'begins in the initial state, produces the first word of the sentence', and so on (20). Compare Lees's review of *Syntactic structures*, where the linguist is seen as modelling the 'kind of device' a speaker uses in his head 'to generate the sentences of his language' (Lees 1957: 406). At the end of chapter 4, a grammar is said to associate a sentence with a series of representations at various levels (33); when Chomsky returns to the topic in chapter 5, it is said to yield representations of utterances (47; see also 59). At the end of this chapter he argues that a grammar is neutral between speaker and hearer; it is 'simply a description of a certain set of utterances, namely, those which it generates'. A few lines later he says that 'a grammar generates all grammatically "possible" utterances', just as a chemical theory 'might be said to generate all physically possible compounds' (48). Naturally, he also says that grammars 'generate sentences'. But in a paper delivered the following year, he again talks of 'a grammar that generates utterances with structural descriptions' (Chomsky 1962 [1958]: 132; see also 129).

If a language is a set of possible utterances or sentences, a corpus, which is a set of observed utterances or sentences, is a part or subset of it. According to Harris, a descriptive linguist studies distributional regularities in speech (1951: 5). He must therefore obtain a corpus and adopt research methods which will determine what regularities exist. In his book, such methods are set out 'in the form of successive procedures of analysis imposed by the working linguist upon his data' (1). The procedures are 'ways of arranging the data' (3), which provide a method for identifying all the utterances which occur in a language community as 'relatively few stated arrangements of relatively few stated elements' (1). They lead to a 'compact representation' of utterances (198), or 'a compact statement of what utterances occur in the corpus' (361). 'The over-all purpose of work in descriptive linguistics is to obtain a compact one–one representation of the stock of utterances in the corpus' (366).

But, as Harris points out, a corpus is of interest only as a sample of the language. By 'sample' he means an adequate sample: thus the analysis of one corpus 'becomes of interest only if it is virtually identical with the analysis which would be obtained in like manner from any other sufficiently large corpus of material taken in the same dialect' (13). In that case, the linguist's statements are predictive: 'we can predict the relations among elements in any other corpus of the language on the basis of relations found in our analyzed corpus'. Similarly Hockett, in a brief expostulation published three years earlier, stresses that the purpose of classifying data 'is not simply to account for all the utterances' which are in a corpus 'at a given time'. 'Rather, the analysis of the linguistic SCIENTIST' is to be such 'that the linguist can account also for utterances which are NOT in his corpus at a given time'. That is, 'he must be able to predict what OTHER utterances the speakers of the language might produce . . .' (Hockett 1948: RiL 279). In the paragraphs which follow, Hockett compares this 'analytical process' with 'what goes on in the nervous system of a language learner, particularly, perhaps, that of a child learning his first language'. When the child produces an utterance he has not already heard, it is, 'of course, a kind of prediction'. In the beginning, this is 'often ineffective'; similarly, 'when the linguist's corpus is small, his predictions are inaccurate'. But 'in theory, at least, with a large enough corpus there would no longer be any discernible discrepancy between utterances the linguist predicted and those sooner or later observed'.

This concern with prediction has two important consequences. Firstly, by a corpus one cannot simply mean an arbitrary collection of material. In the first chapter of *Methods*, Harris says that, so far as his procedures are concerned, it does not matter how a linguist gets his data. He may take down texts, record conversations or question informants. He may also intervene deliberately: for example, he may alter a conversation to obtain repetitions in different environments (1). But in the last chapter, he talks of the need to bring in 'controlled material'. Thus, given the utterance *What books came?* 'we do not compare it with arbitrary other utterances, but search for utterances which are partly similar, like *What book came? What maps came? What books are you reading?*'. Such comparisons may be elicited 'from an informant, or from oneself, or from some arranged or indexed body of material'; in this way, 'we have an experimental situation in which the linguist tests variations in the utterance stock in respect to a selected utterance'. The reason for these experiments is precisely that 'we are interested in analyzing such a corpus as will serve as a sample of the language' (368).

Secondly, we have to adopt what Harris calls techniques of approximation. In his chapter on morpheme classes, he points out that few morphemes will be found in exactly the same environments. 'In a sufficiently large corpus', *Dick*, for example, might have the same distribution as *Tom*; but not *Jack*, which also appears in *Jack of all trades*. A single morpheme will also have different distributions from one corpus to another. For example, *root* might be found in one corpus in *That's the root of the trouble*; in another it might not, but might, however, appear in *The square root of 5929 is 77* (244, nn. 4 and 5). Thus our corpus is not a satisfactory sample for 'the exact environments of morphemes'. Nor will we 'effect a great reduction in the number' of classes by grouping together morphemes with precisely the same distribution. 'We will have to be satisfied with some approximation to such a grouping.' Accordingly, we 'disregard' specific distributional differences. Some will be accidental: for example, if we happen to have recorded *Dick's twelve minutes late*, but not *Tom's twelve minutes late*. Others will not. For example, we would group together *four* and *seven*, even though *He left at two seventy sharp*, on the model of *He left at two forty sharp*, is unlikely to appear in any corpus (245). In an appendix to this chapter, Harris deals particularly with what he calls a 'culturally determined limitation' (253). It 'may "mean nothing" to say *The box will be murdered*'; therefore 'even the largest corpus' will not contain it. The distribution of *box* would thus be partly different from that of *man*. But 'it would be desirable, in grouping the morphemes into classes, to devise such an approximation as would disregard' restrictions of that sort (254).

The reason for making approximations is that, once again, we want our corpus to 'serve as a predictive sample of the language' (244). In his second chapter, Harris remarks that, when we analyse a limited corpus, the features of an element will be defined extensionally, relative to just the 'bits of talking' that have been observed (17). But when a linguist aims to represent 'the language as a whole, he is predicting that the elements set up for his corpus will satisfy all other bits of talking in that language'. The features of an element will then be defined intensionally, in opposition (if I can so render his wording) to those of other elements. This is the only place where Harris uses these terms. But at the syntactic level we could envisage a series of extensional definitions which would simply list all the environments in which, in a particular body of material, such and such a morpheme has been found. If two morphemes appear in exactly the same environments then, and only then, would they be classed together. But what we want are intensional definitions which will tell us how the elements are distributed 'in the language as a whole'. For this the 'usual linguistic corpus'

(253) is inadequate; we have to make approximations if our statements are to have any generality. In the section on 'culturally determined limitations', Harris also argues that even if we had an 'exact morpheme classification' its 'predictive usefulness . . . need not be greater than that of an approximative one' (254). For cultural factors will change and exact distributions will change with them.

The particular importance of these passages is that, if the methods can succeed, there will be no discrepancy between a predictive account of the language and what Harris calls a compact representation of a corpus. In his final chapter, he points out that, apart from saying that certain sequences of elements do occur in the utterances of a language 'we may also be able to say that certain sequences almost never occur; we may know this from direct testing, or from the fact that the sequence goes counter to the most general regularities of our corpus' (372). The crucial assumption is that we have 'an adequate sample': as Harris puts it in his final chapter on phonology, 'we derive a statement about all the utterances of the language by assuming that our corpus can be taken as a sample of the language' (152). Similarly, for phonology and grammar as a whole, 'the work of analysis leads right up to the statements which enable anyone to synthesize or predict utterances in the language'. 'These statements', he goes on, 'form a deductive system with axiomatically defined initial elements and with theorems concerning the relations among them. The final theorems would indicate the structure of the utterances of the language in terms of the preceding parts of the system.' This constitutes 'the description of the language structure' (372f).

In the light of this reading of Harris's *Methods*, we can begin to appreciate both the debt that Chomsky owed to older American scholars and his true originality. When Chomsky talks of a grammar it is plainly the same thing as Harris's 'description of the language structure'; indeed he said so (Chomsky 1961: 220, n. 5, referring to the passage just cited). In *Methods* Harris had not used the term 'generate'. But in a later article he does: 'a grammar may be viewed as a set of instructions which generates the sentences of the language' (1954a: 260). So does Hockett in an important paper published in the same year. A grammatical description 'must', he says, 'be prescriptive, . . . in the sense that by following the statements one must be able to generate any number of utterances in the language'. These will again include not only the utterances of the corpus, but also 'new utterances most, if not all, of which will pass the test of casual acceptance by the native speaker' (Hockett 1954: *RiL* 398). This too Chomsky cites, adding only that the statements also assign a structure to each sequence (1961: 221). Earlier in his paper Hockett expounds the form of grammatical description common among Bloomfieldians (the 'Item and Arrangement' model). This is said to set forth 'principles by which one can generate any number of utterances in the language' (*RiL* 390). 'In this sense', Hockett adds, 'it is operationally comparable to the structure of that portion of a human being which enables him to produce utterances in a language; i.e., to speak.' I have already cited a remark of Chomsky's in which the speaker is conceived, hypothetically, as a Finite State machine (1957: 20); also Lees on the kind of device the speaker uses to generate sentences (1957: 406). On the next page Lees says that, granted the validity of scientific method as he sees it, 'it is not too much to assume that human beings talk in the same way that our grammar "talks"'. Hockett's more careful wording seems closer to Chomsky's eventual view of linguistic 'competence' (1965: 4 *et passim*). Hockett also compares an Item and Arrangement description to a cookbook; similarly, Lees talks in one place of rules which 'provide a recipe for constructing English sentences' (1960: 2).

By the mid 1950s Harris was beginning to refer to Chomsky in return (1954b: *Papers* 21, n. 3, for the problems of simplicity) and it might perhaps be difficult to decide exactly who was influencing whom. But the essential step had already been taken in Harris's *Methods*. A distributional analysis is meant to determine what combinations of elements occur; hence also, by implication, those that do not occur. This is done, in the first instance, for a corpus. But the corpus is only a sample; for the language as a whole one tries to say, as generally and as succinctly as possible, what combinations 'could occur'. That again implies that other combinations 'could not' occur. Accordingly, the distributional statements separate a set of possible utterances from other arrangements of elements that are not possible; since each utterance will be covered by several successive statements, they also tell us how they are constructed. This is the logical conclusion of Harris's programme, and one which he had himself explicitly formulated.

Chomsky's real contributions lay elsewhere. Firstly, where Harris spoke of 'bits of talking' that occur or do not occur, Chomsky makes clear that the essential property of sentences or utterances is grammaticality. Hockett talks similarly of the grammatical description being 'prescriptive'; it is interesting, in the light of subsequent development of Chomsky's thinking, that he does not require that every utterance so prescribed should meet a test of casual acceptability (Hockett 1954: *loc cit.*, *RiL* 398; compare Chomsky 1965: 11). In Chomsky's initial formulation a grammatical sentence or utterance is simply one that is 'acceptable to a native speaker, etc.' (1957: 13). The statements which make up the grammar are 'rules' (in *Syntactic structures* the term is introduced quite casually at the beginning of the chapter on phrase structure (26)). A language is thus 'the totality of utterances that can be made in a speech-community' (Bloomfield 1926) in the specific sense that members of the community will recognize them as grammatical. It is not the 'talk' that actually 'takes place', as Harris, at the beginning of *Methods*, had tried to define it. It is an abstract construct, to which mathematical properties, such as that of being infinite (Chomsky 1957: 13 *et passim*) can be attributed.

Secondly, he had concluded that the programme of analysis as Harris had conceived it, which was intended to 'lead right up' (Harris 1951: 372) to the grammar or description of the language structure, was not feasible. He had at first shared these aims (Chomsky 1953; referred to in *Syntactic structures*, 52, n. 3). But he now argues that a linguistic theory need not provide what he calls a 'discovery procedure', but merely an 'evaluation procedure', which, 'given a corpus and given two proposed grammars G_1 and G_2', will 'tell us which is the better grammar of the language from which the corpus is drawn' (1957: 51). In this new programme a grammar is no longer a set of statements that will result automatically provided that appropriate procedures of analysis are followed. Nor does it follow, from a prior specification of procedures, how many levels a description has or what the form of its statements should be. The characterization of a grammar becomes the first preoccupation of the theory.

These are vital changes, which at once removed the problems that had earlier been thought central, and made central what had earlier been neglected. But the basic aim is still that of describing the structure of a language ahead of any consideration of meaning. 'Grammar', Chomsky argues, 'is best formulated as a self-contained study independent of semantics' (1957: 106). In chapter 2 he makes clear that 'the notion "grammatical" cannot be identified with "meaningful"' (15). In chapter 9 he argues at length that differences of meaning are not the basis even for phonemic distinctness (94ff). Instead he advocates a 'pairs test', which, he says, 'provides us with a clear operational criterion for phonemic distinctness in completely non-semantic terms' (97; see also n. 5). He argues against defining the morpheme as a 'meaning-bearing element' (100), casts doubts on the validity of 'structural meanings' (100, 104f, 108) and stresses that transformations are not characterized by 'synonymity' (101). Not only can a grammar be constructed without appeal to meaning; the suggestion that it can be constructed '*with* appeal to meaning' is 'totally unsupported' (93). 'Investigation of such proposals . . . invariably seems to lead to the conclusion that only a purely formal basis can provide a firm and productive foundation for the construction of grammatical theory' (100). 'The motivation for this self-imposed formality requirement for grammars is quite simple – there seems to be no other basis that will yield a rigorous, effective, and "revealing" theory of linguistic structure' (103).

Of the chapters which assess alternative grammars, all but one are, again in Chomsky's words, 'completely formal and non-semantic' (93). Thus the initial argument for the passive transformation (42f) is that it avoids restating lexical restrictions which hold equally in both the active and the passive constructions. The argument for a transformational treatment of coordination is that it 'simplifies' description; in particular, 'the grammar is enormously simplified' if constituents are so established that the general rule proposed 'holds even approximately' (37). Throughout chapter 7 ('Some transformations in English'), Chomsky talks of the 'simplest way' to describe constructions (e.g. 61f on negation), of rules so stated that, when new constructions are brought in, 'almost nothing new is required in the grammar' (66), of the grammar becoming 'much more simple and orderly' (68) if transformations are posited. At the end of this longish chapter he again says that 'our sole concern has been to decrease the complexity of the grammar' (83). In chapter 9 he acknowledges that the notion of simplicity has been 'left unanalyzed'; but it will not help, with that or any other outstanding problem, to construct the theory 'on a partially semantic basis' (103). Our eventual goal, explained in chapter 6, is to 'formulate a general theory of linguistic structure in which such notions as "phoneme in L", "phrase in L", "transformation in L" are defined for an arbitrary language L in terms of physical and distributional properties of utterances of L and formal properties of grammars of L' (54). It is in such a theory that simplicity will be defined.

The exception is chapter 8, in which Chomsky proposes, as a separate criterion, that a grammar should 'provide explanations' (85) for certain semantic facts. But the status of this is again made very clear. On the one hand, we retain a purely formal theory of grammar, and purely formal arguments which, for example, may lead a particular grammar to assign two different representations to the same sequence of phonemes. For instance, /əneym/ will have two analyses at the level of morphology (/ə + neym/ or /ən + eym/); this is not because of their meaning, but is 'an automatic consequence of the attempt to set up the morphology in the simplest possible way' (85). Similarly, *the shooting of the hunters* will have two transformational derivations, from the structure either of *The hunters shoot* or *They shoot the hunters*. Again, 'careful analysis of English shows that we can simplify the grammar' (89) if we so treat them. Such sequences are 'constructional homonyms'. By definition (86), a constructional homonym is simply any form to which a particular grammar has assigned more than one structure.

On the other hand, we can envisage a 'more general theory of language' (102) which will have as subparts both 'a theory of linguistic form' – as, for example, the theory of transformational grammar – and 'a theory of the use of language'. Only there can we address the 'real question' (93) about grammar and meaning, which is: 'How are the syntactic devices available in a given language put to work in the actual use of this language?' Now the examples cited are 'understood ambiguously' by native speakers: /əneym/ as either 'a name' or 'an aim' (85); *the shooting of the hunters* 'analogously to' either *the growling of lions* or *the raising of flowers* (88). These, to repeat, are facts about the 'use' and not the form of such sequences. However, they are explained by a grammar in which, quite independently, the forms are set up as constructional homonyms. They can therefore be seen as independent confirmation that the grammar is right; also that the theory of grammar within which these were the simplest analyses – a theory, therefore, which among other things has levels both of morphology and of transformational derivation – is right.

In this way we test the adequacy of grammars and theories of grammar by 'asking whether or not each case of constructional homonymity is a real case of ambiguity and each case of the proper kind of ambiguity is actually a case of constructional homonymity' (86). More generally, 'we should like the syntactic framework of the language that is isolated and exhibited by the grammar to be able to support semantic description, and we shall naturally rate more highly a theory of formal structure that leads to grammars that meet this requirement more fully' (102). But Chomsky is at pains to stress that, by arguing in this way, 'we have not altered the purely formal character of the theory of grammatical structure itself' (102). On the next page he speaks of language as 'an instrument or tool', whose structure should be described 'with no explicit reference' to its use (103). This formal description 'may be expected to provide insight' into its use – 'i.e., into the process of understanding sentences' (103). But 'systematic semantic considerations are apparently not helpful in determining it in the first place' (108).

This approach can be seen as a development of others current in the 1950s. As will be clear from the introduction to this essay, the Bloomfieldians did not in general want to ignore meaning. They merely assumed that its description should be 'put off' – I again cite Hill (1958: 3) – until the formal patterning had been dealt with. Hill stresses that this is not 'a denial of meaning'; it is 'no more than an application of the principle of working from the more knowable to the less knowable'. 'The next few decades', he hopes, 'will see results of real value in semantics.' Towards the end of the book he describes his study of purely formal patterning as an 'attempt . . . to lay some of the foundation on which a study of English meanings might be built' (409). In the next paragraph Hill alludes to a 'familiar . . . map of linguistics', drawn originally by Trager (1949). According to this map, meaning belongs to the level of 'metalinguistics', which in Trager's definition is concerned with relations between the language system and any other cultural systems or patterns of behaviour in the community (Trager 1949: 7). The study of the language system itself is Trager's 'microlinguistics'. At that level only 'differential meaning' is relevant: we simply need to know whether form *a* will be judged by speakers to be the same as or different from form *b*.

Harris's account is in different terms but in spirit very similar. 'Descriptive, or, more exactly, structural, linguistics' deals only with distributional regularities (1951: 1, 5). Again, we need to know whether utterance *a* is or is not a repetition of utterance *b*; but although such data is 'meaning-like' (363, echoing 20), it is the only data other than the recorded utterances themselves that Harris's procedures will make use of. Any reference to meaning as such would be a 'short cut' (7, n. 4), would be to use 'hints' which 'must always be checked' by formal operations (189), would be justified only 'heuristically' (365, n. 6), and would leave certain cases 'indeterminate or open to conflicting opinion' when distributional criteria will resolve them (8, n. 7). It is clear from such passages that Harris's descriptive or structural linguistics does not differ in scope either from Trager's microlinguistics or, in this respect, from Chomsky's linguistic theory or 'theory of grammar'.

But Harris also talks of meaning as an object of further study. Thus it is not a criterion, within descriptive linguistics, for establishing morphemes (chapter 12, 186ff especially). However, 'when the results of descriptive linguistics are used in other linguistic and social investigations, one of the chief desiderata is the correlation of utterances and their morphemic segments on the one hand with social situations and features of them on the other' (173). Such correlations are equivalent to meanings (187, n. 63); their study is 'entirely independent' and uses 'techniques quite different from those of current descriptive linguistics' (189). Morpheme classes, though again 'distributionally determined', may be found to have 'a common class meaning' (252, n. 21); there are also correlations of constructions with meaning (347f), and of some positions in constructions with 'what may be called semantic categories of the grammar' (348, n. 49), such as 'plural' or 'object'. Earlier, in a discussion of 'morphemic long components', he claims that 'distributional methods are able to bring out' the meaning categories which traditionally form paradigms – 'an indication', he says, 'that the old results are not lost in the new methods' (311, n. 21). In his important paper on 'distributional structure', Harris again insists that 'distribution suffices to determine the phonemes and morphemes, and to state a grammar in terms of them' (1954b: *Papers* 12). He asks whether there is a parallel 'meaning structure' (title of §2.1) and stresses that, 'although there is a great interconnection between language and meaning', there is 'no independently known structure of meanings which exactly parallels linguistic structure' (8–9). That is why investigations of distribution and meaning 'cannot be mixed'; compare again Chomsky, 1957: 100f. But he then talks of cases in which meaning can be seen as 'a function of distribution' (§2.3). Once more there are meanings of distributionally established classes (13). The meaning of words and morphemes 'correlates with difference of distribution': thus synonyms have 'almost identical environments' and, where the meanings are different, 'the amount of . . . difference correspond[s] roughly to the amount of difference in their environments' (14). There are further parallels in units larger than the sentence (see earlier Harris 1952); but 'it should be clear that only after we discover what kinds of distributional regularities there are . . . can we attempt any organised semantic interpretation of the successions discovered' (22, n. 19).

Chomsky himself denied that similarities of distribution can explicate synonymy (1955: 44; see also Lees 1957: 394f); and, in the case of syntax, his proposal in chapter 8 of *Syntactic structures* is sharper and in the event more fruitful. But he is addressing a problem that had been on the agenda of other American linguists and he argues, as they had argued, that it can best be solved if the formal structure of the tool is studied first – again the metaphor is Harris's (1954b: *Papers* 13) – and the study of what he calls its use, or what they saw as the relationship of language to other social behaviour, is based on this prior formal description. There is indeed one place in *Methods* where, in advance of his own work on transformations (1952, 1957), Harris discusses the form and meaning of an example very similar to those that Chomsky was later to make famous (1951: 271f, on the differing grammar of *made* in *She made him a good husband because she made him a good wife*).

In the middle 1960s Chomsky's theory of grammar was widened to include Katz's semantics (Katz and Fodor 1963; Katz and Postal 1964), which envisaged rules assigning a semantic representation or 'intrinsic meaning' (Chomsky 1972 [1968]: 71) to each sentence. The distinction between language and the use of language was accordingly redrawn, so that a generative grammar was required to 'relate signals to the semantic interpretation of these signals' (Chomsky 1966: 12) and no longer treat them as if they were meaningless. But how important were these changes for the relationship between the rules of syntax and what now became the 'semantic component'? A detailed answer would extend this essay beyond its natural term. But it is worth pointing out in general the extent to which the ideas of earlier American scholars persisted, and in part, twenty years later, still persist.

One obvious point is that the syntactic component continued to specify which sequences of morphemes were grammatical. It alone, in Chomsky's words, constituted the 'creative' part of the grammar (1965: 136). The rules of semantics, like those of phonology, 'play no part in the recursive generation of sentence structures' (141), but merely assign a 'semantic interpretation' (16) to each sentence generated. They are 'purely interpretive' (e.g. 75, 141), and were to remain so, in fact as in principle, until Chomsky's views began to shift more radically (1973 and subsequently). Nor is this the first scheme in which semantics is admitted as a peripheral component. We may recall that of Hockett's textbook (1958: 138); for Hockett it had been 'a matter of personal taste, and not important', whether this and his other peripheral system, which was concerned with the articulation and perception of phonemes, were or were not included under the definition of 'language'. It is also of interest that Harris, in attempting to define meanings, had proposed that it should be done 'in such a way that the meaning of an utterance as a whole would be the sum of the meanings of the constituent morphemes' (1951: 190; see also n. 70). This is an obvious model if the semantic description is based on a prior statement of distributional syntax. It was correspondingly assumed, at this stage, by Chomsky's associates. According to Katz and Postal, 'the semantic component . . . provides an explanation of the speaker's ability to determine the meaning of any sentence . . . as a compositional function of the antecedently known meanings of the lexical items in it' (1964: 12f). It did so by rules referring specifically to the prior syntactic grouping of smaller constituents into larger constituents.

A more important point concerns the nature of the syntactic representations themselves. In Harris's account of morpheme sequences, the basic form of statement had been a substitution formula. For example, a sequence of a noun root (N) followed by a nominal suffix (Nn) is distributionally equivalent to a noun root on its own: N Nn = N. But this particular substitution is, as Harris puts it, 'non-repeatable': one can substitute *boyhood* (N Nn) for, for instance, *life*, but one cannot then substitute *boyhoodhood*, which would represent N Nn Nn. He therefore introduces a system of superscripts, in which *boy* in *boyhood* represents a lowest order noun (N^1), while the sequence *boyhood* as a whole is a noun of a higher order (N^2). With these superscripts the formula becomes: N^1 Nn = N^2; so that, in the frame *His — was obsessed by many fears*, both the sequence *boyhood* and the single morpheme *life* are now classed as N^2. Similarly, a noun on its own can be replaced, non-repeatably, by a noun plus the plural morpheme (-s); raising the superscript again, this gives the formula: N^2 -s = N^3. Thus, in the frame *Such is the story of their —*, both the sequence *lives* and the single morpheme *life* are now classed as N^3. At a still higher level, both *their life* and *their lives* would be classed as N^4, according to a further formula: T N^3 = N^4 (T standing generally for articles and other determiners). Turning this round, we can then say that in *Such is the story of their boyhoods*, the sequence *their boyhoods* is an N^4, consisting of a T (*their*) followed by an N^3; the N^3 in turn consists of an N^2 (*boyhood*) followed by the plural morpheme; and the N^2 in turn consists of an N^1 followed by an Nn. For the system of formulae and subscripts see Harris, 1951: 265ff (earlier, Harris 1946); in a section headed 'Immediate constituents' he sets out the structure of an utterance as a series of lines in which each constituent is classed and then divided into smaller constituents which are in turn classed (1951: 279).

Such formulae were natural to a distributional syntax, and were as naturally restated, in the form of 'phrase structure rules', in the distributional syntax of *Syntactic structures*. These in turn were retained in the 1960s; so that, through the influence of Chomsky's theories and the textbooks that followed, the received view of syntactic relationship, perhaps for the majority of linguists now living, is still one originally developed by Harris and Wells in the middle 1940s, in which a sequence of constituents of classes $a_1, a_2, \ldots$ merely forms a larger constituent of class b. Notions of function were treated as derivative. For example, the function of a direct object was defined as that of a noun phrase – a term already taken to include distributional equivalents such as clauses – which formed part of Harris's 'V⁴' or Chomsky's 'verb phrase' (Chomsky 1965: 71). Harris's superscripts were for the moment forgotten. But a system reminiscent of them was developed later (Chomsky 1970: 210f; Jackendoff 1972: 60; 1977, the first and last with acknowledgement). On that basis the function of head could also be defined secondarily (Jackendoff 1977: 30). Such strategies are characteristically 'Bloomfieldian'; in the last case the precursor is Bloomfield's own attempt to define 'head' and 'attribute' in terms of equivalence or non-equivalence of form classes (1935 [1933]: 195).

Finally, the belief has persisted that syntactic arguments and evidence are distinct from semantic arguments and evidence. Chomsky himself was later to abandon it, and although at the time of writing he maintains a thesis of the 'autonomy' of syntax, its basis has changed. But the distinction was taken for granted at the end of the 1960s. In the paper just referred to in another connection, Chomsky talks of 'empirical evidence . . . regarding the semantic interpretation' of certain sentences, with 'supporting' syntactic evidence of co-occurrence (1970: 186). In a contribution to the same volume, Lees remarks that 'much recent grammatical research has been directed toward an explanation' of the way 'a native user of a language understands as similar' expressions which are formally different. The method is to justify a common 'underlying grammatical form' from which they are derived by transformations 'each of which is itself of some greater or lesser generality by virtue of independent motivations' (Lees 1970: 135). That is still the explanatory programme of *Syntactic structures*. Lees then argued that, 'as underlying grammatical representations are made more and more abstract', they 'come to resemble more and more a direct picture of the meaning[s]' themselves (136). The same argument was elaborated by Postal (1970: 101f). 'Transformations', he says, 'have usually been wholly or largely justified on assumptions independent of hypotheses about the Semantic Representations of sentences.' But each transformation adds to the remoteness or abstractness of the underlying structure. 'Consequently, to a large extent, the Remote Structures which have been justified have a "directionality of abstractness" which is *defined independently* of assumptions about Semantic Representation.' Nevertheless they turn out not to be 'semantically arbitrary'.

These passages are fragments of a complicated story, and it might be hard to say when it ends. But the mid 1970s saw at least one textbook which is more 'Bloomfieldian' than Bloomfield ever was. Culicover (1976) insists that 'whether a string of words is a grammatical sentence . . . is completely independent' of whether it 'makes a true statement, is logically consistent, or makes much sense at all'. The distinction between form and content 'is a fundamental one and is maintained quite strictly in this book' (4). A few pages later a 'syntactic category' is defined as 'a group of words . . . that can replace one another in any sentence . . . without affecting grammaticality' (9); the definition is then extended, in impeccably distributionalist fashion, to cover both 'words and sequences of words' (13). 'The justification of a syntactic analysis must appeal', the student is told, 'to regularities of form, not function.' 'Syntactic arguments' alone justify syntactic structure; 'semantic correspondences do not suffice as justification, even in those cases where they can be clearly established' (45). In a later chapter Culicover comments on the so-called 'Katz–Postal hypothesis', in accordance with which one sought to establish common underlying structures for sentences that are judged to be 'synonymous' or 'paraphrases'. He cites with approval their insistence that it is 'necessary to find *independent syntactic justification*' (Katz and Postal 1964: 157). But, 'unfortunately, there has been a tendency in linguistics to use the hypothesis as a justification for analyses, rather than as merely a device for finding analyses to investigate'; 'to avoid these consequences', it is not 'a working principle in this book' (116). Behind this there is still the crucial assumption that 'syntactic arguments' and 'semantic arguments' exist separately.

Culicover's text was published exactly half a century after Bloomfield's 'set of postulates', and stands at the end of a tradition, which for more than three-fifths of this period is almost wholly American, that can be traced back to it. But the two halves of our story show an interesting asymmetry. In the 'Bloomfieldian' or 'Post-Bloomfieldian' era the leading scholars insisted on their intellectual allegiance to him, even though, as Robins remarks with studied restraint in his *Short history of linguistics*, 'it cannot be said that every one of its characteristics can be directly traced back to Bloomfield's teaching' (Robins 1967: 209). By contrast, Chomsky's exegetes have tended to insist on his complete originality, even, and sometimes particularly, in matters where he not only followed and developed the ideas of Harris and Hockett, but made quite clear that he was doing so. The history of the period is accordingly presented in two blocks. In the earlier, Bloomfield's theories (ignoring his first book) are said to be worked out with greater and greater precision. In the latter, Bloomfieldian linguistics is overthrown, Chomsky introduces a fresh set of ideas, and they – once more, of course, with many changes and refinements – have been developed since.

The reasons for this might make a revealing study in academic loyalty and rivalry. But this essay has dealt solely with the history of ideas. So far as that of syntax is concerned, the more obvious divisions are between Bloomfield's *Language* and Harris's *Methods*, and again between the Chomsky of *Syntactic structures* and the Chomsky of the 1980s (especially from 1981). The heyday of distributionalism was from the mid 1940s to the early 1960s, and in that Harris and the first Chomsky were linked.[1]

NOTE

1 I have not referred specifically to secondary sources; however, I would be ungenerous if I did not end this essay by acknowledging the inspiration of Hymes and Fought (1981 [1975]), whose scholarship shines amid surrounding propaganda.

REFERENCES

Bloch, B. 1948. A set of postulates for phonemic analysis. *Language* 24: 1–46.
Bloch, B. & Trager, G.L. 1942. *Outline of linguistic analysis*. Baltimore: Linguistic Society of America.
Bloomfield, L. 1914. *An introduction to the study of language*. New York: Holt.
    1922. Review of Sapir, 1921. *The Classical Weekly* 15: 142–3. Cited from Hockett, *LBA* 91–4.
    1926. A set of postulates for the science of language. *Language* 2: 153–64. Cited from Hockett, *LBA* 128–38.
    1931. Review of Ries, *Was ist ein Satz? Language* 7: 204–9. Cited from Hockett, *LBA* 231–6.
    1934. Review of Havers, *Handbuch der erklärenden Syntax. Language* 10: 32–9. Cited from Hockett, *LBA* 281–8.
    1935. *Language*. London: Allen & Unwin. [New York edition, 1933]
    1936. Language or ideas? *Language* 12: 89–95. Cited from Hockett, *LBA* 322–8.
    1939. *Linguistic aspects of science*. Chicago: University of Chicago Press.
    1942. Philosophical aspects of language. In *Studies in the history of culture: the disciplines of the humanities*. Menasha, Wis. Cited from Hockett, *LBA* 396–9.
    1943. Meaning. *Monatshefte für deutschen Unterricht* 35: 101–6. Cited from Hockett, *LBA* 400–5.
Blümel, R. 1914. *Einführung in die Syntax*. Heidelberg: Winter.
Carroll, J.B. 1953. *The study of language: a survey of linguistics and related disciplines in America*. Cambridge, Mass.: Harvard University Press.
Chomsky, N. 1953. Systems of syntactic analysis. *Journal of Symbolic Logic* 18: 242–56.
    1955. Logical syntax and semantics: their linguistic relevance. *Language* 31: 36–45.
    1957. *Syntactic structures*. The Hague: Mouton.
    1961. Some methodological remarks on generative grammar. *Word* 17: 219–39.

1962. A transformational approach to syntax. In Hill, A.A. (ed.), *Third Texas conference on problems of linguistic analysis in English, May 9–12, 1958*. Austin, Tex.: University of Texas. 124–58.

1965. *Aspects of the theory of syntax*. Cambridge, Mass.: MIT Press.

1966. *Topics in the theory of generative grammar*. The Hague: Mouton.

1970. Remarks on nominalization. In Jacobs & Rosenbaum, 1970: 184–221.

1972. *Language and mind*. New York: Harcourt Brace Jovanovich. [First edition, 1968]

1973. Conditions on transformations. In S.R. Anderson & P. Kiparsky (eds.) *A Festschrift for Morris Halle*. New York: Holt, Rinehart & Winston. 232–86.

1981. *Lectures on government and binding*. Dordrecht: Foris.

Culicover, P.W. 1976. *Syntax*. New York: Academic Press.

de Groot, A.W. 1949. *Structurele syntaxis*. The Hague: Servire.

Debrunner, A. 1936. Review of Bloomfield, 1935. *Indogermanische Forschungen* 54: 148–9. Cited from Hockett, *LBA* 278–80.

Edgerton, F. 1933. Review of Bloomfield, 1935. *Journal of the American Oriental Society* 53: 295–7. Cited from Hockett, *LBA* 258–60.

Fowler, M. 1952. Review of Harris, 1951. *Language* 28: 504–9.

Gleason, H.A. 1961. *An introduction to descriptive linguistics*. New York: Holt, Rinehart & Winston. [First edition, 1955]

Hamp, E.P. 1957. *A glossary of American technical linguistic usage 1925–1950*. Utrecht, Antwerp: Spectrum.

Harris, Z.S. 1942. Morpheme alternants in linguistic analysis. *Language* 18: 169–80. Cited from Joos, *RiL* 109–15; Harris, *Papers* 23–35.

1945. Discontinuous morphemes. *Language* 21: 121–7. Cited from Harris, *Papers* 36–44.

1946. From morpheme to utterance. *Language* 22: 161–83. Cited from Joos, *RiL* 142–53; Harris, *Papers* 45–70.

1951. *Methods in structural linguistics*. Chicago: University of Chicago Press.

1952. Discourse analysis. *Language* 28: 1–30. In Harris, *Papers* 107–42.

1954a. Transfer grammar. *International Journal of American Linguistics* 20: 259–70.

1954b. Distributional structure. *Word* 10: 146–62. Cited from Harris, *Papers* 3–22.

1955. From phoneme to morpheme. *Language* 31: 190–222.

1957. Co-occurrence and transformation in linguistic structure. *Language* 33: 283–340. In Harris, *Papers* 143–210.

1981. *Papers on syntax* (ed.) Hiż, H. Dordrecht: Reidel. Abbreviated *Papers*.

Haugen, E. 1951. Directions in modern linguistics. *Language* 27: 211–22. Cited from Joos, *RiL* 357–63.

Hill, A.A. 1958. *Introduction to linguistic structures: from sound to sentence in English*. New York: Harcourt Brace.

Hjelmslev, L. 1928. *Principes de grammaire générale*. Copenhagen: Høst.

Hockett, C.F. 1942. A system of descriptive phonology. *Language* 18: 3–21. Cited from Joos, *RiL* 97–107.

1947. Problems of morphemic analysis. *Language* 23: 321–43. Cited from Joos, *RiL* 229–42.

1948. A note on 'structure'. *International Journal of American Linguistics* 14: 269–71. Cited from Joos, *RiL* 279–80.

1949. Two fundamental problems in phonemics. *Studies in Linguistics* 7: 29–51.

1954. Two models of grammatical description. *Word* 10: 210–31. Cited from Joos, *RiL* 386–99.

1958. *A course in modern linguistics.* New York: Macmillan.

1961. Linguistic elements and their relations. *Language* 37: 29–53.

1968. *The state of the art.* The Hague: Mouton.

(ed.) 1970. *A Leonard Bloomfield anthology.* Bloomington, Ind.: Indiana University Press. Abbreviated *LBA*.

Householder, F.W. 1952. Review of Harris, 1951. *International Journal of American Linguistics* 18: 260–8.

Hymes, D. and Fought, J. 1981. *American structuralism.* The Hague: Mouton. [First version, 1975]

Jackendoff, R.S. 1972. *Semantic interpretation in generative grammar.* Cambridge, Mass.: MIT Press.

1977. *X̄ syntax: a study of phrase structure.* Cambridge, Mass.: MIT Press.

Jacobs, R.A. & Rosenbaum, P.S. (eds.) 1970. *Readings in English transformational grammar.* Waltham, Mass.: Ginn.

Jespersen, O. 1924. *The philosophy of grammar.* London: Allen & Unwin.

Joos, M. 1948. *Acoustic phonetics.* Baltimore: Linguistic Society of America.

(ed.) 1958. *Readings in linguistics: the development of linguistics in America since 1925.* Second edition. New York: American Council of Learned Societies. Abbreviated *RiL.*

Katz, J.J. & Fodor, J.A. 1963. The structure of a semantic theory. *Language* 39: 170–210.

Katz, J.J. & Postal, P.M. 1964. *An integrated theory of linguistic descriptions.* Cambridge, Mass.: MIT Press.

Kroesch, S. 1933. Review of Bloomfield, 1935. *Journal of English and Germanic Philology* 32: 594–7. Cited from Hockett, *LBA* 260–4.

Lees, R.B. 1957. Review of Chomsky, 1957. *Language* 33: 375–408.

1960. *The grammar of English nominalizations.* Bloomington, Ind.: Indiana University Research Center in Anthropology, Folklore, and Linguistics.

1970. On very deep grammatical structure. In Jacobs & Rosenbaum, 1970: 134–42.

Meillet, A. 1934. *Introduction à l'étude comparative des langues indo-européennes.* Seventh edition. Paris: Hachette. [First edition, 1903]

Newmeyer, F.J. 1980. *Linguistic theory in America: the first quarter-century of transformational generative grammar.* New York: Academic Press.

Nida, E.A. 1949. *Morphology.* Second edition. Ann Arbor: University of Michigan Press. [First edition, 1946]

Paul, H. 1920. *Prinzipien der Sprachgeschichte.* Fifth edition. Halle: Niemeyer. [First edition, 1880]

Postal, P.M. 1970. On the surface verb 'remind'. *Linguistic Inquiry* 1: 37–120.

Ries, J. 1927. *Was ist Syntax?* Second edition. Prague. [First edition, 1894]

Robins, R.H. 1967. *A short history of linguistics.* London: Longmans.

Sapir, E. 1921. *Language: an introduction to the study of speech.* New York: Harcourt Brace.

Sturtevant, E.H. 1934. Review of Bloomfield, 1935. *The Classical Weekly* 27: 159–60. Cited from Hockett, *LBA* 265–6.

Swadesh, M. 1934. The phonemic principle. *Language* 10: 117–29. Cited from Joos, *RiL* 32–7.

Sweet, H. 1891. *A new English grammar, logical and historical*. Part 1. Oxford: Clarendon Press.

1899. *The practical study of languages*. London: Dent.

Tesnière, L. 1959. *Élements de syntaxe structurale*. Paris: Klincksieck.

Trager, G.L. 1949. *The field of linguistics*. Norman, Okla.: Battenburg Press.

Voegelin, C.F. & Voegelin, F.M. 1976. Some recent (and not so recent) attempts to interpret semantics of native languages in North America. In Chafe, W.L. (ed.) *American Indian languages and American linguistics*. Lisse: Peter de Ridder Press. 75–98.

Wackernagel, J. 1926. *Vorlesungen über Syntax*. 2 vols. Basle: Birkhäuser.

Wells, R.S. 1947. Immediate constituents. *Language* 23: 81–117. Cited from Joos, *RiL* 186–207.

Wundt, W. 1912. *Völkerpsychologie*. Vol. 2: *Die Sprache*. Part 2. Third edition. Leipzig: Engelmann. [First edition, 1900]

PUBLICATIONS OF R.H. ROBINS

Note: The abbreviation *DB* refers to *Diversions of Bloomsbury* (1970)

1951
Ancient and mediaeval grammatical theory in Europe London: Bell; Japanese translation, Tokyo 1960.

1952
(with Natalie Waterson) Notes on the phonetics of the Georgian word. *Bulletin of the School of Oriental and African Studies* 14: 55–72.
Noun and verb in universal grammar. *Language* 28: 289–98; = *DB* 25–36.
A problem in the statement of meanings. *Lingua* 3: 121–37.

1953
The phonology of the nasalized verbal forms in Sundanese. *Bulletin of the School of Oriental and African Studies* 15, 138–45; = *DB* 227–42.
Formal divisions in Sundanese. *Transactions of the Philological Society* 1953, 109–42.

1956
(with Norma McLeod) Five Yurok songs: a musical and textual analysis. *Bulletin of the School of Oriental and African Studies* 18: 592–609.

1957
(with Norma McLeod) A Yurok song without words. *Bulletin of the School of Oriental and African Studies* 20: 501–6.
Aspects of prosodic analysis. *Proceedings of the University of Durham Philosophical Society (Arts)* 1: 1–11; = *DB* 207–18.
Vowel nasality in Sundanese – a phonological and grammatical study. In *Studies in linguistic analysis* 87–103 (special volume of the Philological Society). Oxford: Blackwell. = *DB* 273–91
Neutralization in grammar and lexicon. *Travaux de l'Institut de Linguistique* 2: 107–13; = *DB* 37–45.

1958
Dionysius Thrax and the Western grammatical tradition. *Transactions of the Philological Society* 1957, 67–106; = *DB* 113–54.
Articles in *Encyclopaedia Britannica*.

The Yurok language: grammar, texts, lexicon. Berkeley and Los Angeles: University of California Press.

The objectives of formal grammar. *Indian Linguistics* (Turner Jubilee volume I), 22–30.

1958–9
Contributions to *Proceedings of the Eighth International Congress of Linguists.* Oslo: Oslo University Press.

1959
Nominal and verbal derivation in Sundanese. *Lingua* 8: 337–69; = *DB* 295–329.

Linguistics and anthropology. *Man* 59, 175–8.

Some considerations on the status of grammar in linguistics. *Archivum Linguisticum* 11: 91–114.

1960
In defence of WP. *Transactions of the Philological Society* 1959, 116–44; = *DB* 47–77.

1961
Syntactic analysis. *Archivum Linguisticum* 13: 78–89.

John Rupert Firth (obit.) *Language* 37: 191–200.

1962
The third person pronominal prefix in Yurok. *International Journal of American Linguistics* 28: 14–18; = *DB* 363–71.

1963
Linguistic comparison. In H.L. Shorto (ed.) *Linguistic comparison in South East Asia and the Pacific,* 7–12 (Collected Papers in Oriental and African Studies, 4) London: School of Oriental and African Studies.

General linguistics in Great Britain, 1930–1960. In C. Mohrmann, F. Norman & A. Sommerfelt (eds.) *Trends in modern linguistics* 11–37; Utrecht & Antwerp: Spectrum.= *DB* 155–83.

1964
Grammar, meaning and the study of language. *Canadian Journal of Linguistics* 9: 98–114; = *DB* 79–97.

Ancient grammarians and modern linguistics. *Didaskalos* 2: 81–9; = *DB* 101–11.

General linguistics: an introductory survey. London: Longman; second edition, 1971; third edition, 1980. American edition, Bloomington: Indiana University Press 1965. Translated into Italian, Bari 1969; Dutch, Utrecht 1969; Spanish, Madrid 1971; French, Paris 1973.

1965
Some typological observations on Sundanese morphology. In G.B. Milner & Eugénie J.A. Henderson (eds.) *Indo-Pacific linguistic studies,* II (Amsterdam: North-Holland), uniform with *Lingua* 15; 435–50.

1966
General linguistics within a liberal education (Inaugural lecture). London: Luzac; = *DB* 3–24

Edited (with C.E. Bazell *et al.*) *In memory of J.R. Firth.* London: Longman.

The development of the word class system of the European grammatical tradition. *Foundations of Language* 2: 3–19; = *DB* 185–203.

Word classes in Yurok. In *Word classes* (Amsterdam: North-Holland), uniform with *Lingua* 17: 210–29; = *DB* 341–62.

1967

A short history of linguistics. London: Longman; second edition 1979. American edition, Bloomington: Indiana University Press 1967. Translated into Italian, Bologna 1971 and Bari 1981; Spanish, Madrid 1974 and 1980; French, Paris 1976; Portuguese, Rio de Janeiro 1979.

Oriental and African languages. In *Caxton Encyclopaedia.*

1968

Morphology and the methods of synchronic linguistics. In *Enzyklopädie der geisteswissenschaftlichen Arbeitsmethoden.* 65–88. Munich: R. Oldenbourg.

Basic sentence structures in Sundanese. *Lingua* 21: 351–8; = *DB* 331–40.

1970

Recent work in linguistics. In R.M. Hutchins, M.J. Adler & O. Bird (eds.) *The great ideas today.* Chicago: Encyclopaedia Britannica, 178–227.

Diversions of Bloomsbury: selected writings on linguistics. Amsterdam: North-Holland; abbreviated here as *DB*.

1971

The structure of language. In N. Minnis (ed.) *Linguistics at large,* 13–33. London: Gollancz.

Malinowski, Firth and the 'context of situation'. In E. Ardener (ed.) *Social anthropology and language,* 33–46. London: Tavistock Publications.

1973

Ideen- und Problemgeschichte der Sprachwissenschaft. Frankfurt on Main: Athenäum.

The current relevance of the Sapir–Whorf hypothesis. *Communication and Cognition* 6: 37–44; also in R. Pinxten (ed.) *Universalism versus relativism in language and thought,* 99–107. The Hague: Mouton 1976.

The history of language classification. In T.A. Sebeok (ed.) *Current trends in linguistics,* vol. 11: *Diachronic, areal and typological linguistics,* 3–41. The Hague: Mouton.

1974

Theory-orientation versus data-orientation: a recurrent theme in linguistics. *Historiographia Linguistica* 1: 11–26.

The case theory of Maximus Planudes. In L. Heilmann (ed.) *Proceedings of the Eleventh International Congress of Linguists,* vol. 1, 107–11. Bologna: Il Mulino.

The elementary text. In *Linguistics: teaching and interdisciplinary relations,* 33–41 (Georgetown University Round Table on Languages and Linguistics, 1974). Washington: Georgetown University Press.

Language. In *Encyclopaedia Britannica* 15th edn., vol. 10, 642–62. Chicago: Benton.

1976

Some continuities and discontinuities in the history of linguistics. In H. Parret (ed.)

History of linguistic thought and contemporary linguistics, 13–31. Berlin: de Gruyter.
Varro and the tactics of analogist grammarians. In A. Morpurgo Davies & W. Meid
(eds.) *Studies in Greek, Italic, and Indo-European linguistics,* 333–6. Innsbruck: Institut
für Sprachwissenschaft.
Linguistics at large. In B.A. Tanner (ed.) *Language and communication in general
practice,* 13–24. London: Hodder & Stoughton.
The teaching of linguistics as a part of a university education today. *Folia Linguistica* 9:
1–15.

1977
Knowledge of natural languages and scientific knowledge. In M. de Mey, R. Pinxten
et al. (eds.) *Colloque international sur le point de vue cognitif,* 83–6. University of Ghent.
Distinctive feature theory. In D. Armstrong & C.H. van Schoonevelt (eds.) *Roman
Jakobson: echoes of his scholarship,* 391–402. Lisse: de Ridder.

1978
The Neogrammarians and their nineteenth-century predecessors. *Transactions of the
Philological Society* 1978, 1–16.
Some essential characteristics of language and their implications. *Revue de phonétique
appliquée,* 46–7, 141–9.
History of linguistics: aims and methods. In W.U. Dressler & W. Meid (eds.)
Proceedings of the Twelfth International Congress of Linguists, 102–7. Innsbruck: Institut
für Sprachwissenschaft.

1979
Functional syntax in medieval Europe. In D.J. Allerton *et al.* (eds.) *Function and context
in linguistic analysis,* 196–205. Cambridge: Cambridge University Press. Also in
Historiographia Linguistica 7: 1980, 231–40.

1980
Grammatical hierarchy and the Yurok bipersonal verb. In G. Brettschneider & C.
Lehmann (eds.) *Wege zur Universalienforschung,* 360–4. Tübingen: Narr.
Rasmus Rask's position in genetic and typological linguistics. *Travaux du Cercle
Linguistique de Copenhague* 20: 29–32.
Postscript. In E.F.K. Koerner (ed.) *Progress in linguistic historiography,* 403–6.
Amsterdam: Benjamins.
Edited (with E.F.K. Koerner & H.-J. Niederehe), and Preface to, *Studies in medieval
linguistic thought.* Amsterdam: Benjamins.

1982
Condillac et l'origine du langage. In J. Sgard (ed.) *Condillac et les problèmes du langage,*
95–101. Geneva & Paris: Editions Slatkine.

1983
J.R. Firth: a reconsideration of his place in twentieth-century linguistics. In W.
Lehfeldt *et al.* (eds.) *Allgemeine Sprachwissenschaft, Sprachtypologie und Textlinguistik:
Festschrift für Peter Hartmann,* 259–67. Tübingen: Narr.
Articles on Jespersen, Pike, and Tesnière. In A. Bullock & R.B. Woodings (eds.)
Fontana biographical companion to modern thought, 365, 599, 752. London: Fontana
Paperbacks.

Sistem dan struktur bahasa sunda. Jakarta: Djambatan.

Presidential addresses. In Shirô Hattori *et al.* (eds.) *Proceedings of the XIIIth International Congress of Linguists*, 5, 13–15. Tokyo.

1984

Ex oriente lux: a contribution of the Byzantine grammarians. In S. Auroux *et al.* (eds.) *Matériaux pour une histoire des théories linguistiques*, 217–25. Lille: Université de Lille III.

The future of linguistics in the light of its past history. *Language Sciences* 6, 203–16.

1985

Linguistics in 1984: retrospect and prospect. In *Linguistics and linguistic evidence: the LAGB Silver Jubilee Lectures 1984*, 1–17. Newcastle upon Tyne: Grevatt & Grevatt.

The young man from Serper: a Yurok folk tale. In G. Heintz & P. Schmitter (eds.) *Collectanea Philologica. Festschrift für Helmut Gipper*, 633–44. Baden-Baden: Koerner.

A linguistic appreciation of a poem by A.E. Housman. In K. R. Jankowski (ed.) *Scientific and humanistic dimensions of language*, Festschrift für Robert Lado, 465–70. Amsterdam: Benjamins.

Numerals as underlying verbs: the case of Yurok. In Ursula Pieper and Gerhard Stickel (eds.) *Studia linguistica, diachronica et synchronica: Werner Winter sexagenario anno MCMLXXXIII*. Berlin: Mouton de Gruyter.

INDEX